Dispatches from Lincoln's White House

The Anonymous Civil War Journalism of
Presidential Secretary William O. Stoddard

Edited by Michael Burlingame

University of Nebraska Press
Lincoln and London

Introduction and notes © 2002 by the University of Nebraska Press
All rights reserved
Manufactured in the United States of America

∞

Library of Congress Cataloging-in-Publication Data

Stoddard, William Osborn, 1835–1925.
Dispatches from Lincoln's White House : the anonymous Civil War journalism
of presidential secretary William O. Stoddard / edited by Michael Burlingame.
p. cm.
"A Bison original"–P. [4] of cover.
Includes bibliographical references (p.) and index.
ISBN 0-8032-9290-2 (pbk.: alk. paper)
1. Lincoln, Abraham, 1809–1865—Anecdotes. 2. United States—Politics and
government—1861–1865—Anecdotes. 3. Presidents—United States—Biography—
Anecdotes. 4. United States—History—Civil War, 1861–1865—Personal narratives.
5. Washington (D.C.)—History—Civil War, 1861–1865—Personal narratives.
I. Burlingame, Michael, 1941–   II. Title.
E457.15.S86 2002
973.7'092–dc21
[B]   2001034670

For Lewis E. Lehrman, the Cosimo di Medici of Lincoln Studies

Contents

Acknowledgments, ix
Editor's Introduction, xi
Chapter One 1861, 1
Chapter Two 1862, 51
Chapter Three 1863, 131
Chapter Four 1864–1865, 198
Notes, 253
Index, 279

Acknowledgments

Thomas F. Schwartz, the Illinois State Historian, has over the years given me the benefit of his vast knowledge of Lincoln and his times and has been a generous host and valued friend.

Another valued friend in Springfield, Wayne C. Temple, deputy director of the Illinois State Archives, has shared with me his many discoveries about Lincoln and has been an inspiration as I seek new information on the sixteenth president.

I am grateful to John Y. Simon, dean of documentary editing in American history, for his encouragement over the years.

Loraqune Grace, director of technical services at the library of Southern Adventist University in Collegedale, Tennessee, obligingly photocopied for me a file of Stoddard's letters at that institution. Other librarians across the country have also provided invaluable assistance, especially at the Detroit Public Library, the Library of Congress, Brown University, the National Archives, the Pierpont Morgan Library, the Huntington Library, the New York Public Library, the New-York Historical Society, the Lincoln Museum in Fort Wayne, Indiana, the Illinois State Historical Library in Springfield, and Connecticut College in New London.

Connecticut College's R. Francis Johnson Faculty Development Fund has helped defray some of the expenses involved in the research and writing of this volume.

My brother, Lloyd, and my sister, Sue, along with her husband, Edwin R. Coover, have been generous hosts who make my research visits to New York and Washington DC, not only enjoyable but affordable.

Sarah Thomas has similarly facilitated extended research binges in Springfield, for which I am most grateful.

As an undergraduate at Princeton University and as a graduate student at Johns Hopkins University, I was fortunate to have the guidance and support of David Herbert Donald.

Lois McDonald has helped more than she knows to make this book and the others possible.

Editor's Introduction

William O. Stoddard (1835–1925) achieved renown as the author of more than seventy children's books, yet is best remembered as Abraham Lincoln's secretary and assistant to presidential aides John G. Nicolay and John Hay.[1] As did Nicolay and Hay, Stoddard published a biography of Lincoln; like them he also wrote anonymously for the press while he served in the White House.[2] Reproduced here are 120 weekly dispatches that Stoddard submitted to the *New York Examiner* under the pseudonym "Illinois." From May 1861 to the summer of 1864 "Illinois" regularly described and commented on events in Washington and on military, diplomatic, economic, and political developments of the nation.

These documents shed both direct and indirect light on Abraham Lincoln. Stoddard occasionally described the president's activities and mood. On 8 July 1861, for example, he reported that "President Lincoln, thus far, bears his load of responsibility wonderfully well. He is a little thinner and paler than on the day of his inauguration, and at times, wears a wearied and harassed look, but is the same kind and cordial man as ever, with now and then a relapse into the humorous pleasantry, which in old times formed so marked a feature in his character."[3] Three months later Stoddard filed a gloomier report: "For a few weeks the President has been looking pale and careworn, as if the perpetual wear-and-tear of the load which presses upon him were becoming too much even for his iron frame and elastic mind."[4]

One source of presidential strain was the torrent of requests from people who regarded Lincoln as an all-powerful sovereign, single-handedly able to solve their every problem. "Not a day passes," Stoddard wrote on 14 October 1861, "but appeals are made to the Executive for action, on his part, that would be all but impossible if he were an absolute monarch, and many honest people doubtless feel themselves aggrieved that the President does not exercise, in their behalf, prerogatives which any crowned head of Europe would hesitate to assume."

Yet, despite his exhausting schedule, Lincoln bore up well. A week later Stoddard had more cheering news to relate: "Our worthy Chief Magistrate is in excellent spirits, and looks much better than he did a fortnight since. He is gathering his strength for the labor and excitement of the coming Congress. I am told that he enters into the plans and arrangements of the campaign in all their varied details with the keenest zest, and that the military chiefs have been indebted to his strong and practical good sense for more than one valuable hint and suggestion."

One of the most painful blows Lincoln suffered during the war was the death of his son Willie, on 20 February 1862. A month after Willie's death Stoddard observed that the president had "recovered much of his old equanimity and cheerfulness; and certainly no one who saw his constant and eager application to his arduous duties, would imagine for a moment that the man carried so large a load of private grief, in addition to the cares of a nation."[5]

Like John Hay, Stoddard believed that Lincoln was the indispensable man without whose guidance the nation would cease to exist.[6] In his dispatch of 21 April 1862 he asked his readers: "Did you ever try to realize the idea of losing our good Chief Magistrate? Perhaps not, but suppose you try, and then look around you in imagination for the man whom you could trust, and whom the people would trust, to take the reins from *his* dead hand. The fact is, that at present the country has entire confidence in no one else, and we might almost say, 'after him the deluge,' in view of our present condition." Six months later Stoddard speculated about Lincoln's place in history: "The President is the same thoughtful, careful, kindly, hard-working man as ever, seeming to labor to make good, by the labors of his own brain and hand, all the shortcomings of his myriad subordinates. What his fame will be when all this confused lava of events, now red and molten in the fire of the Present, shall have been cooled in the rigid mould of time, none can tell; but his history will be false to all that is good and true, if his effigy be not that of a great, wise and patriotic statesman."[7]

On 21 July 1862 Stoddard analyzed what he believed was the source of Lincoln's power:

> The President is almost a mystery. Men no longer query whether such or such a General or statesman directs his actions, but "what will he do with" this statesman or that General. He is the most perfect *representative* of the purely American character now in public life—

perhaps the most perfect that ever has existed. This is why the mutual understanding between him and the people is so perfect. This it is which enables him to exercise powers which would never by any possibility be entrusted to another man, though his equal in other respects. The people know that they can trust their great chief, and so they bid him "see to it that the Republic suffers no detriment," and put in his hands untold treasure and uncounted lives, and the temporary disposal of their time-honored rights. The *habeas corpus* act is suspended—"Lincoln would not do it if it was not needed." The press is muzzled—"Good for him! why don't the old man shut off the *Herald* and the *Tribune*?" Favorite generals are superseded, favorite measures curtailed or disapproved, prejudices rubbed or snubbed, but the President is the stronger for it all.[8]

The president's selflessness, Stoddard maintained, contributed to his popularity and manifest ability to lead: "Among the great civilians of the day, the greatest and the strongest, our good Chief Magistrate, is great and strong chiefly because the people have perfect faith in him that he has no ambition, no selfish lust of power, nor any hope for the future unconnected with the welfare of his country. Destroy this faith, and the power of the President would disappear, or would at best sink to the level of his Cabinet officers."[9]

Stoddard's unfavorable assessment of Wendell Phillips may offer a clue to the identity of the unnamed "well-known abolitionist and orator" whom Lincoln called "a thistle" and about whom he once exclaimed: "I don't see why God lets him live!"[10] On 18 August 1862 Stoddard asked:

> Have you noticed Wendell Phillips's late speeches? He has more fully than ever before defined the true position of himself and friends. He is no longer the apostle of the great reform, even in his own assertion, but seems voluntarily to take his true place once more as a mere vulgar agitator and sensation spouter. The Government was right when he was voted too insignificant for a cell in Fort Warren. Perhaps, however, his present desperate exertions *may* procure for him some sort of cheap and second class martyrdom. Pardon this bit of personality, Mr. Editor, but we who are near the centre of this great and practical fight, see that it is in truth a "good fight of faith," and we are sick and angry with the bleating crowd of fault-finders who help in no one thing, but do their uttermost to clog the chariot wheels of the army which we consider the "host of the Lord." We, as a nation, are just beginning to see and know the true greatness and sublimity

of our strange and mighty war, and we are angry alike with those who scoff and those who hinder."[11]

Stoddard's solicitude for the president's well-being appeared in a report he filed in September 1862:

> A few days since the President's horse ran away with him during a morning ride, scared by the cheering of a marching regiment, and for a short time the Commander-in-Chief was in danger of serious accident. Thanks, however, to his long limbs and strong arms, he succeeded in retaining his place in the saddle, and in calming his furious and plunging Bucephalus, with no other injury than a slightly sprained ankle. However, we were suddenly shocked into an appreciation, momentarily, of how deep an interest we all had in the safety of our wise Chief Magistrate. Strong men turned to each other with an involuntary shudder. "If he *had* been thrown and killed!" After that, indeed, even the most hopeful could discern little beside clouds and thick darkness.[12]

Patronage matters absorbed an undue amount of Lincoln's time and energy, according to Stoddard, who on 6 April 1863 denounced

> the same unceasing throng in the ante-rooms of the President's house, bent on dragging him "for a few minutes only," away from his labors of state to attend to private requests, often selfish, often frivolous, sometimes corrupt or improper, and *not* so often worthy of the precious time and strength thus wasted. The President belongs to the nation—it is seldom that the affairs of any one man cannot be righted, save by bringing to his aid the delegated power of a whole people. No man, however, will see this, when his eyes are veiled by his interest. But who can doubt that our worthy and wise Chief Magistrate would do better, to bring to the grand yet delicate questions which must be finally decided by him alone, a mind unwearied by listening to private griefs or wishes, and unexhausted by pouring out his too ready sympathies upon misfortunes which, powerful as he is, he cannot remedy.[13]

In addition to descriptions and analyses of Lincoln, Stoddard also offers opinions that may reflect the president's thinking. In a discussion of writings by Lincoln's two main secretaries, one scholar has observed: "Hay and Nicolay seem generally to have adopted Lincoln's opinions as their own; and it may be surmised that the observations in their Letters, Diary, and

Notes, were not far out of line with what Lincoln thought at the time, even when they do not quote him directly."[14] The same might well be said of Stoddard, who, like Nicolay and Hay, was a young man who revered his boss extravagantly.

Stoddard's best-known reminiscence of Lincoln is a description of the president's reaction to the crushing Union defeat at Fredericksburg:

> If the same battle were to be fought over again, every day, through a week of days, with the same relative results, the army under Lee would be wiped out to its last man, the Army of the Potomac would still be a mighty host, the war would be over, the Confederacy gone, and peace would be won at a smaller cost of life than it will be if the week of lost battles must be dragged out through yet another year of camps and marches, and of deaths in hospitals rather than upon the field. No general yet found can face the arithmetic, but the end of the war will be at hand when he shall be discovered.[15]

Some historians regard Stoddard's account of the battle and its outcome skeptically.[16] His dispatch of 18 April 1864, however, lends credence to that recollection:

> There are two phases of military doctrine afloat here now-a-days— both of which may be set down as correct, but only one of which can be put into practice. The first, sound enough, with an "if," is that the rebellion is growing rapidly weaker with the very efforts, desperate, exhausting, which it is making to maintain its military establishment. So are we, but we can stand it twenty years longer than they can. So if we did not strike another heavy blow, but acted on the defensive and Fabian policy, merely consolidating and perfecting our occupation of the regions we now hold, and driving in the smaller armies of the rebels, they must soon go under. All very true, but our people have not faith enough to wait, they *must* go in and finish the business. The other creed, the faith of Lincoln and Grant, is that every great battle, even if it is a drawn one, is a defeat to the rebels in its necessary consequences. A battle in which thirty thousand men a side were put *hors du combat*, killed, wounded and missing, but in which neither party could claim a victory, would, nevertheless, drive Lee back to the Lynchburg line, and place Richmond almost at our mercy. Such a thing is horrible to contemplate, but great and desperate battles must and will come.[17]

Stoddard also provided insight into the president's superior intellect and communication skills. A legendary punster, Lincoln was perhaps the author of the following play on words that Stoddard described in 1861: "This reminds me of the answer made a short time since to the remark that the editor of the now defunct *States and Union* was a 'very penetrating man.' 'That may be,' was the reply, 'but his paper is a *pennytraitor.*'"[18]

Stoddard also vividly depicted conditions in wartime Washington. In September 1861 he reported:

> We live a strange life here, as it were in the very shadow of some great and terrible event, suspended over us by a thread as slender as that which of old upheld the impending danger of Damocles. We go about our accustomed duties with a cool, business-like manner, impossible to any other people in such circumstances, but ever and anon, as some signal gun, or the sound of artillery-practice, or the muffled roar of some distant skirmish, breaks in upon the sounds of peaceful life, the workman stays his hammer and the clerk his pen, the sharp bargain is for a moment suspended, and every man's face asks of his neighbor's—"Has it come, at last?"[19]

In October 1862 Stoddard commented on the moral climate in the capital: "The city is in many of the worst features a perpetual camp, with all the vice and corruption of many camps concentrated at one centre. Here is all the plundering, gambling, lust, profanity, obscenity, and the swift growth of corruption, which traditionally follows in the footsteps of a great, long-continued and extravagantly managed war. I cannot paint the picture; it would be unfit to hang in any room of the sober and Christian homes to which THE EXAMINER might carry it."[20]

Stoddard paid special attention to blacks in Washington and in the army. Shortly after Congress emancipated the slaves of the capital he declared:

> It is the firm belief of your correspondent, from what he has seen and heard among the blacks, that this seemingly small seed, sown here in this District, will yet bear the most important fruit in every one of the border slave States. It seems to me that I can see the gradual entering of a new idea into the darkened minds of the downtrodden race—they begin, the best of them, to feel and cherish the notion of their *nationality*, and the development of the consequent emotions and ideas must follow. I have studied them much for a long time, and, except in isolated instances, have never noticed this before. They have all looked at their condition in a narrow and selfish way, each man

for his own hand. There is no stronger civilizing influence, outside of the Christian religion, than a well-directed national feeling, because it leads men to work in unison for the accomplishment of whatever aims they may propose.... The blacks refuse to regard themselves as *Africans*. This, too, is a new idea, and I cannot help thinking it an advance. They insist that they are Americans, while at the same time they appreciate the disadvantages under which they labor here, and earnestly desire to find a new and undisputed theatre *on this Continent* for the *locus* of their future nationality. No doubt there is some sense in the idea of civilizing and Christianizing Africa by their means, but we must first civilize and Christianize our missionaries, or we shall be sending the blind to lead the blind, with a full knowledge of what and how deep a ditch awaits their fall.[21]

The following Thanksgiving Stoddard described a dinner given to freedmen at a "contrband" camp:

The occasion was duly employed by several gentlemen to urge upon them the advantage of the President's favorite scheme of emigration, and seemingly with a very fair degree of success. It was a strange spectacle, that great crowd of black men, fresh from bondage, now, for the first time, beginning to taste of and comprehend that sweet thing called "Liberty;" men, women, and children, who had all their lives listened to orders only, with force to make obedience certain, gathering around their best and wisest friends, and hearkening to the mild voice of persuasion, urging them to their own good.

According to Stoddard, the "crowd contained a large number of thoughtful and intelligent faces, and not a few that lit up with a sudden gleam when, in reply to a remark by Senator [Samuel C.] Pomeroy, a stalwart negro answered, "*I'd fight!*"[22]

When blacks did start to fight as members of the Union army, they at first suffered discrimination. But, as Stoddard reported in May 1863,

It is surprising to see how rapidly men are losing their silly prejudices against the use of black soldiers. I mean in the army. Of course the demagogues of the North are almost as loud as ever, but among the men in the field, the prevailing sentiment is getting to be, in the rough language of the soldiers, "If the niggers will fight, why, let 'em fight— they're as good as rebels, any day." There is reason to believe, too, that the military feeling is on the increase among the blacks themselves. The resurrection of a manhood buried so long and so deeply must needs be slow, and too many of them have been unable even to hear the call of the trumpet, but the race will yet rise to a newness of life, such as God gives in time to all the nations that are oppressed and cast down.[23]

In July 1863 Stoddard commented on the psychological effect that army service had upon blacks: "This arming the negroes is a great thing in many ways. It is my deliberate opinion, that it will yet solve, in the right way, too, the oft-repeated question—'What shall we do with the South, and with the negroes, after the war is over?' We are educating a new race of freemen, who will take care of the South and of themselves too. Even if they labor under white employers, which is most probable, they will not, and they cannot return to their servile condition, for 'the sword ennobles.' "[24]

In 1864 Stoddard sarcastically commented on the record the black troops had compiled on the field of battle:

> It is found not to be such good fun to fight them as was originally supposed. These "spiritless brutes"—"crushed by long servitude and plantation toil"—"peaceful by nature, and destitute of all the elements of the soldier"—have somehow been waked up to a terribly aggressive military manhood. Can it be possible that the mere idea of liberty for themselves and their children makes these follows so good at the bayonet? Can it be that *they*, the degraded, the downtrodden, the mere "cattle" of so much legislation and of so much commerce— that *they* can feel any generous enthusiasm for a Government and a people who are doing so much for them? Of course not! The white man monopolizes all these finer and better feelings, and the negro I was talking with the other day was only a parrot. I will tell you a part of what he said. It was at Barnum's Hotel, Baltimore. Noticing that I was wonderfully well waited on by several darkie friends, I began a chat with one of them. "Oh, yes, massa, we knows you: we *heerd* you at de contraband camp; we knows who *you* is." In this he was referring to some humble efforts of mine a year or so ago. "Oh, yes, we is all here *now*, but we is going out to help Grant pretty soon. Most all de rest of us has gone. We knows very well what it all means, and *you see if de black man can't fight for dose men as be fighting for him.*" The good fellow's face had been all smiles till this last, which closed the conversation, and then it darkened into an expression of the sternest resolution, and the black face wore an expression that would have added a dignity to the purest Caucasian lineaments.

Stoddard concluded that

> the men who have all their lives carried napkins are not thereby unfitted to carry the bayonet. And herein is a great political secret. Herein lies the ability of the United States to carry on this war indefinitely, and should we *not* succeed in breaking the strength of the rebellion before January next, there is that vitality, that force, in the President's policy of employing the black men, that will at the worst go far to make up all losses, and that must eventually set the seal of success upon his efforts to save the nation. It must be a bitter pill to the proud aristocrats of Virginia and the Carolinas to weigh their lives in the fearful balances of war against those of men who were once their property. There will be a great deal of that weighing done before this year is over.[25]

Stoddard may have written the dispatches published in this volume at the behest of Lincoln, who valued friendly publicity. During the quarter century before his presidency, Lincoln had contributed hundreds of anonymous and pseudonymous pieces to the Springfield *Illinois State Journal*.[26] In 1857 Lincoln drafted an agreement stipulating that he and six others would contribute to a five hundred–dollar fund "to be used in giving circulation, in Southern and Middle Illinois, to the newspaper published at St. Louis, Missouri, and called 'The Missouri Democrat.'"[27] In 1859 Lincoln secretly purchased the Springfield *Illinois Staats-Zeitung*, which was to support the Republican cause.[28] In 1861 he appointed many Republican journalists to important offices.[29] The following year Lincoln urged John W. Forney to establish the *Daily Morning Chronicle* in Washington to support his administration.[30]

Though the president may have encouraged Stoddard to write for the *Examiner*, the idea was originally suggested by the editor of the paper, Edward Bright Jr., who was also the young secretary's uncle. As Stoddard later recalled, "I was glad to do so and the success which I attained led to my subsequent staff connection with the Examiner during many years."[31] The *New York Examiner* was a Baptist weekly founded in Utica in 1826. At first known as the *Baptist Register*, over time it changed its name to the *New York Baptist Register*, then the *New York Recorder and Register*, from 1855 to 1865 it was published in New York City as the *New York Examiner*. Stoddard, who was a devout Baptist who taught Sunday school and led church meetings, also submitted material for publication to the *New York Tribune*.[32]

It is not surprising that Stoddard acted as a journalist during his White House days. Born and raised in upstate New York, the youthful Stoddard composed poems and wrote for newspapers. Because "Syracuse and Rochester seemed too small for my ambition," he moved west seeking adventure. He first settled in Chicago and wrote for the *Daily Ledger*. When the financial panic of 1857 killed that newspaper, he bought a farm in eastern Illinois near Tolono as an investment. A brief and unhappy attempt to farm the land himself soon drove Stoddard to nearby Champaign (then known as West Urbana), where in May 1858 he began working for the *Central Illinois Gazette*. The *Gazette* was "an independent paper, devoted to agriculture, education, politics, temperance, literature, social reform, news and the interests of central Illinois." Stoddard described its eccentric editor, Dr. John Walker Scroggs, as "a man of a million," one "of ability, for without school or academy training he had obtained a good deal of professional skill."[33] When he first met the editor, Stoddard, who admitted that he had not "a drop of humility," told him, "You can't run a newspaper, but I can."[34] Scroggs offered to let the brash young man try his hand at editing an issue, an experiment that turned out well. Soon Stoddard became part owner and co-editor of the *Gazette*, doing virtually all the work.[35] As Stoddard recalled, Scroggs "never wrote a line" but only "read it after it was printed."[36]

In the spring of 1859 Abraham Lincoln visited the Champaign area and called on these journalists. Later Scroggs recalled that "a conversation occurred upon the subject of the probable candidates for the Presidency in 1860. I suggested his name, but he—with characteristic modesty—declined."[37] However, in the issue dated 4 May 1859, the *Gazette* said:

> We had the pleasure of introducing to the hospitalities of our sanctum a few days since the Hon. Abraham Lincoln. Few men can make an hour pass away more agreeably. We do not pretend to know whether Mr. Lincoln will ever condescend to occupy the White House or not, but if he should, it is a comfort to know that he has established for himself a character and reputation of sufficient strength and purity to withstand the disreputable and corrupting influences of even that locality. No man in the west at the present time occupies a more enviable position before the people or stands a better chance of obtaining a high position among those to whose guidance our ship of state is to be entrusted.[38]

Stoddard wrote vividly of that meeting with Lincoln:

> He greeted me cordially as though we had known each other for a long time. There was no strangeness about him. He knew men on the

instant. He wasted no time, but plunged at once into the causes of his coming. In a minute he had me not only interested but somewhat astonished. I had supposed that I knew the people and the politics of that county, and he had been told that I did, but so did he. He could ask about the different precincts and their leading men almost as if he had lived among them. As he was then studying Champaign County, so he was investigating the State of Illinois and other states and was getting into close relations with the current of feeling, North and South. The conversation was a long one.[39]

Lincoln, Stoddard said, "seemed to know my prairie neighbors almost man by man."[40]

Six months later the *Gazette* editorialized, "Who Shall Be President?":

We, in Illinois, know [Lincoln] well, in the best sense of the word a true democrat, a man of the people, whose strongest friends and supporters are the hard-handed and strong-limbed laboring men, who hail him as a brother and who look upon him as one of their real representative men. A true friend of freedom, having already done important service for the cause, and proved his abundant ability for still greater service; yet a staunch conservative, whose enlarged and liberal mind descends to no narrow view, but sees both sides of every question, and of whom we need not fear that fanaticism on the one side, or servility on the other, will lead him to the betrayal of any trust.[41]

(Stoddard's later claim that he was the first editor to endorse Lincoln for president was erroneous, as others had done so as early as the fall of 1858.)[42] After the rangy Springfield attorney won the nomination in May 1860, Stoddard, as he put it, "went into the political canvass, head over heels, heels over head, with all the more enthusiasm because I had nearly all the stumping of Champaign County on my own hands."[43]

Following the election, Stoddard expressed interest in joining the White House staff, and Lincoln asked him to put his request in writing and said he would see to it.[44] By late December 1860 the young journalist, despairing at the silence of the president-elect, told Lincoln's law partner, William H. Herndon:

As nearly two months have passed without my receiving any reply as to my application it is not unnatural that I should become a little nervous and desire to know what the indications are, if any. I am fully aware that the chances were from the first against my success, and am most painfully conscious that my request was bold, even presumptuous. Very likely, also, others with greater ability . . . may apply for the same position. The "President-elect," knowing so little of me, must necessarily, if he has thought of the matter at all, have doubts as to my fitness for a post of so much responsibility, and hesitate about according to me the degree of confidence which a man must place in his "private secretary."[45]

That same day Stoddard urged Illinois senator Lyman Trumbull to help him secure a White House job. He assured Trumbull that he had the support of Herndon, of Lincoln's good friend Leonard Swett, and of New York senator Ira Harris.[46] He later claimed that he won the spot because Senator Harris wrote a strong letter of recommendation.[47] The president-elect was unsure whether to offer the job to Stoddard or to Benjamin F. James, a journalist who had been helpful to Lincoln in his quest for a seat in Congress in the 1840s.[48] In September 1860 James had applied for the job.[49] Lincoln's friend Henry C. Whitney reported that both Stoddard and James "told me that Lincoln entertained with favor the idea of appointing one but not wishing to offend the other, he concluded to keep Nicolay" who had started working as his secretary in May 1860.[50] Stoddard later noted that Nicolay "was much better qualified" for the secretary's job than he, for the Bavarian-born Nicolay "was older, more experienced, harder, had a worse temper, and was decidedly German in his manner of telling men what he thought of them." Stoddard was, by his own admission, "more reticent."[51]

Eventually Lincoln summoned Stoddard to Washington to work as the secretary to the president to sign land patents.[52] On 23 February Stoddard arrived in the capital, finding that "[o]ffice-seekers abound in untold and seedy looking multitudes. They roam the streets, seeking introductions, button-holing unfortunate great men."[53] He began work in the Interior Department, daily affixing Lincoln's name to about nine hundred documents, but soon was transferred to the White House.[54] The day war broke out Stoddard enlisted for three months' service in the National Rifles, a militia unit he described as "a company of select and eminent young gentlemen who regarded themselves as the pink of chivalry." This service did not prevent him from signing land patents in his spare time.[55] Eventually, as Nicolay recalled, land-office business "became very slack so that he [Stoddard] had scarcely any official work to do. He was therefore assigned to duty as one of my clerks at the White House, being able just as well to sign there the few Land Patents which were issued from time to time. Also on one or two occasions when Hay and I were both absent, he carried a message to Congress."[56] His main job was to open and sort through the White House mail, which led him to be known as "the paper-cutter."[57] Stoddard described his duties as "exceedingly hard work" which kept him busy until mid-1864, when "a siege of typhoid fever and a relapse unfitted me for so arduous a position."[58]

In his memoirs Stoddard claimed that soon after Hay became ill in the summer of 1861 with a brief attack of Potomac fever, he "took care of him and when he got out at the end of it I heard him say that he could not have been more assiduously watched if his own mother had been with him."[59] During Hay's illness Stoddard began to assume more important secretarial duties. The "business of Private Secretary, per se, was generally pretty well absorbed by Nicolay and Hay, but there were odd days, first during Hay's illness, when I had to go over and take Nicolay's place in the opposite room."[60] Stoddard derived "great pleasure" in recalling that "my relations with John G. Nicolay and John Hay,—with the latter especially,—were unbroken, to the end. I never had a better or more faithful friend than John Hay, as his many letters testify."[61]

Hay's letters tell a somewhat different story. In 1863 he complained that "Stod[dard] is more & more worthless. I can scarcely rely upon him for anything."[62] That same year Hay said that another assistant secretary, Nathaniel S. Howe, was "better than Stod[dard] as he is never stuffy and always on hand."[63] Later Hay sarcastically observed that Stoddard had "been giving the Northern watering places for the last two months a model of high breeding and unquestionable deportment."[64] He told Nicolay in August 1864, "Stod[dard] has been extensively advertising himself in the Western Press. . . . His asininity which is kept a little dark under your shadow at Washington blooms & burgeons in the free air of the West."[65] Stoddard recorded milder criticisms that Hay made to his face, "angrily telling me that he considered me a kind of miracle of hard work and that I could do more without showing it than any other man he had ever seen. He abused me also for being what he called 'statuesque' and always inclined to strike attitudes and take positions,—but I replied that the latter was just what we were wishing the army would succeed in doing."[66]

Stoddard's relations with Nicolay were, he remembered, "from the start, of an entirely satisfactory character."[67] In 1895 Nicolay called Stoddard "a very good fellow, and a man of considerable talent."[68] Ten years earlier, however, when Stoddard sent John Hay a copy of his Lincoln biography and asked for comments and criticisms, he reported that "Nicolay has not left me at liberty to write to him or to send him a copy."[69] A month later Stoddard told Hay,

I did not suppose I was crossing your track or "taking away your market," and so said in my preface. I have left that unchanged in the edition now going out. Long ago I wrote you and Nicolay that I had a book in my mind and it was my idea, year after year, that yours would come out first. Is it too much to say that that idea died of old age? I hope you will make as full and valuable a work as I have thought of your making and that it will succeed enormously. Mine seems to find its place. So will yours. I have certainly done something in the way of advertising you. Never mind if your note nettled me a little but I certainly have not intentionally stolen a march on anybody.[70]

In the spring of 1863 Stoddard suffered a near-fatal attack of typhoid fever; the following year he endured a relapse.[71] "All my business operations had been more or less interrupted by my long bout with typhoid," he recalled. "The one thing most apparent was my need of out-of-door air for as long as might be. I was no longer fit for close confinement and late hours." When he suggested to the president that he undertake an inspection tour of Union armies in the West, Lincoln approved and, as Stoddard recalled, "provided me with abundant passes and letters of introduction, endorsing me as his secretary, entitled to go everywhere and be well received by everybody."[72]

In July 1864 Stoddard departed for Arkansas. On the eighth of that month he informed the editor of the *New York World*: "I have called to see you on my way to a new field of duty. I am going as heretofore to do my uttermost for Uncle Sam and Abraham Lincoln."[73] A few days later he announced to readers of the *New York Examiner* that he was, after more than three years, ending his days as a Washington correspondent.[74] On 13 August he wrote to Hay from Little Rock: "Affairs here do not look well, and it is not the fault of the loyal citizens. I shall have much to say when I return.... I am down with 'summer complaint' today, but shall be up and on my way home shortly. I have got a big job before me here, but think it can be accomplished."[75]

In September he returned to Washington and briefed Lincoln on the situation in the Southwest.[76] In his memoirs Stoddard reported that because the war was drawing to close, "[m]y imagination burned with the desire to get into, to become a part of, the great new venture, the building of a truly united country. I approached Lincoln with the request that I be appointed Marshal of Arkansas."[77] On 24 September Lincoln nominated Stoddard to be marshal for the eastern district of that state.[78] Stoddard's son reported that "[i]n taking this position, he had in mind running for the Senate on the

Republican ticket, when the war was over."[79] Stoddard ascribed his decision to his "love of adventure," which led him "into about the most dangerous post in the United States. As Marshal I represented the federal government, and my responsibilities were practically those of governor of the state."[80] From Little Rock he sent Lincoln lengthy reports on political and military conditions.[81] He also wrote to Illinois congressman Elihu B. Washburne, urging that Confederate lands be distributed to Union troops: "We want twenty thousand soldiers to settle here. I tell you, my dear Sir, you cannot build up a new and free state with the worn out and demoralized debris which is all that this war will leave of the old population of Arkansas. It always was ignorant and wanting in energy, but now—upon my soul Sir they are trash!"[82]

When word of Lincoln's assassination arrived in Arkansas, Stoddard told Hay: "The terrible news was some time in reaching us. Now that the first stunning effects are over, I feel for the first time how much I loved and venerated Abraham Lincoln. I cannot write about him, even to you. I only wish to say that something of personal sympathy for you and Nicolay weighs tonight with my sorrow for the man who has done more for me than all my other friends. Men who had never seen him wept when the news came. How shall we say our sorrow,—who knew him as he really was. To others, the President is dead. I can only remember my benefactor. God bless you, my dear fellow—God have mercy on us all, for we are sorely tried!"[83]

Ill-health forced Stoddard to abandon his Arkansas post in May 1866.[84] Then, according to his son, "he came north to New York and about this time his hearing was seriously affected, so that certain occupations were closed to him." Between 1871 and 1873 he served as chief clerk of the Bureau of Engineering in the New York Dock Department. Stoddard "made and lost various fortunes in those unstable years after the war and finally settled down to authorship" after the panic of 1873 ruined his business career.[85] In 1869 he had published his first book, a satire of Tammany Hall entitled *The Royal Decrees of Scanderoon*.[86]

Stoddard married Susan E. Cooper of New York City in 1870. Their son, William O. Stoddard Jr., who was born four years later, described his father as a man with

> straight black hair, and black eyes that flashed on occasion, but which were always kindly. He was the most dynamic creature I have ever known, and utterly fearless. He was a crack shot with both hands. I have seen him plug a visiting card right and left at twelve paces. He used a short-barreled Derringer, to me an impossible weapon. . . .

Father was a notable raconteur. When he stepped into a room he immediately became its center. While he was quick on the trigger in repartee, he was never unkindly to an opponent. He was and still is my ideal American gentleman. He maintained poise and self-control under all circumstances.[87]

That would have pleased the elder Stoddard, who in 1898 told Nicolay: "Mine had been a toilsome life, with many changes and vicissitudes, but I have fought it through without flinching—not a hair."[88] Reviewers of his books, he said, "are dealing very kindly with me and I ought to be comfortable. It is not exactly what they call fame, but it will do."[89] Twenty-seven years later Stoddard died in Madison, New Jersey, at the age of ninety.

EDITORIAL METHOD

I have retained Stoddard's spelling and punctuation, except in obvious cases of glaring misprints, without using [sic]. In the microfilm edition of the *Examiner*, occasional passages are rendered illegible by creases and folds in the paper. I have inserted "[words illegible]" at those points.

Now and then Stoddard did not date his dispatches. Since he usually wrote them three or four days before they were published, I have indicated an approximate date, preceded by "ca.," for dispatches lacking a date.

Persons mentioned by Stoddard are identified in endnotes when their name first appears, if information on them has been found. No annotation is made for individuals about whom nothing could be discovered. Sources for annotations derived from manuscript collections, newspapers, and specialized monographs and biographies are identified, but not sources taken from easily available published works.

Dispatches from Lincoln's White House

CHAPTER ONE

1861

WASHINGTON, 4 MAY 1861 (PUBLISHED 9 MAY 1861)
Your correspondent would, perhaps, be nearer the exact truth, if he should date his communication at "*Camp* Washington," for the Federal Capital at the present moment offers the strange anomaly of an American city crowded with soldiers. It is indeed a strange picture—we are yet in the land which has, for half a century, been preeminently the "land of peace," and nevertheless two regiments, the *elite* of New-York and Massachusetts, occupy our beautiful Capitol, another watches over the safety of the General Post Office, Sprague's Rhode Islanders throng the echoing corridors of the Patent Office, and over twelve hundred "Bay men" look out from behind the stately granite columns of the Treasury, while the reveille and tattoo sound in front of every serviceable public building, and many private ones, throughout the city.[1]

THE CITY AND THE TROOPS
The city itself is quiet, very quiet; the streets are safe by night and day; the haunts of vice and infamy are closed for lack of business; the police are almost out of employment; and no disturbances of any sort are feared until Congress reassembles, nor even then, unless sundry gentlemen now serving as rebel volunteers shall secure leave of absence.[2] The truth is, that these "Northern hordes" have brought with them the habits acquired in the order-loving communities from which they come, and will be slow to acquire or practice "the license of camps." Nevertheless, many of our citizens are loud in expressing their fears of what may be our condition when "Billy Wilson's New York Roughs" are added to "Ellsworth's Fire Zouaves."[3] We dread the advent of two regiments of shoulder-hitters and fancy men—those "cankers of a calm world and a long peace," and earnestly hope that military discipline will *more* than supply the place of your efficient "Metropolitans."

One of the most difficult of the many problems which the Administration is just now called on to solve, is the proper arrangement of the vast Commissariat Department required by the sudden assemblage of such an army. The errors unavoidably made for the time being, call forth much grumbling and many murmurs from the unlucky volunteers, nearly all of whom are anxious to fight, but would like a good dinner to fight on.

ITS DEFENCES

There are few great cities, there is certainly hardly any other capital of a great nation, so singularly devoid as this is of natural advantages for defensive purposes, and the history of its growth thus far has not been such as to induce the construction of artificial defences. From an attack from the coast, indeed, it is now rendered tolerably safe, and a repetition of the British exploit of 1814 need not be anticipated in any event, but so far as the present difficulties are concerned, with all Eastern Virginia open to the operations of those who threaten us, the frowning ramparts of Fortress Monroe and its compeers are of no avail.[4] The long range of low hills south of the Potomac, known to your readers as "Arlington Heights," and others nearer Alexandria, and a portion of Georgetown Heights, afford numerous positions from which hostile cannon would hold the city at their mercy, and be able to reduce it to a heap of ruins in a few hours. These positions, however, have been carefully surveyed by our topographical engineers, as well as by Major Ben. McCulloch and his rebel associates, and while part of them are already occupied, arrangements are fully made for the speedy seizure of the remainder at the first approach of anything which looks like real danger.[5] Nor is there any danger of a surprise, for not only are all the important movements of the traitors speedily reported at headquarters, but the federal scouts are scattered far and wide over the south bank of the Potomac. The Alexandria *Gazette* (secessionist) relates with much indignation the "insolence" with which the United States troopers drive in their pickets. The amount of dignity assumed by the smallest small-fry of secessiondom is decidedly amusing.

WHAT GEN. SCOTT SAYS

There can be no doubt that the leaders of the rebellion have in mind a speedy attempt upon Washington, which will only be prevented by the presence here of such a force, as will convince even *their* hairbrained vanity that the city cannot be taken. The two "points of contact" between the Government and its present assailants are the District of Columbia and the mouth of the Ohio, but the field will speedily change to a more Southern locality. I am informed, by good authority, that General Scott has expressed his opinion that the first important collision will be in *Eastern Virginia*.[6] The old hero has given abundant evidence of late, that age has not yet robbed him of skill, genius or energy, and his predictions are entitled to full credit.

WHAT SOUTHERN GENTLEMEN THINK
Intelligent Southern gentlemen with whom I have conversed, speak of the present feeling and attitude of the North in terms of utter amazement. Could the secessionists, say these men, only be made to comprehend the extent and nature of the forces opposed to them, and to appreciate the spirit by which the free States are actuated, a hole would be made in the "Southern Confederacy" balloon, through which half its gas would speedily escape. The thousands of men, the millions of money, the real presence of such forces as, for the rebels, only exist in the fervid brains of insane editors and orators, the boundless resources ready to be poured out like water in the defence of the Union—all this is in striking contrast to that sluggish and pusillanimous North, which too many of the chivalry have been educated to despise. Certain it is, that even in the Southern camp the energy of the Administration and its supporters cannot fail to have a wholesome influence.

THROUGH BALTIMORE
The universal determination of the Federal volunteers seems to be that a road "through Baltimore" must be made and maintained, even if it becomes necessary to construct it *over the spot where the city was*; but no doubt such a way will soon be opened, without bloodshed, by the wise action of the President, and the firm stand of the loyal citizens of Baltimore. A friend of mine, a citizen of that place, has just returned to Washington, and reports the "Union feeling" stronger than ever before. God grant that the beautiful metropolis of Maryland may remain true to its best interests.

WASHINGTON, 12 MAY 1861 (PUBLISHED 16 MAY 1861)
The past week has been one of comparatively little excitement in Washington. Rumors and events which would, a few weeks ago, have roused a fever in the minds of all, barely secure sufficient notice to find their way into the insignificant local papers, which reflect so little credit upon the genius and enterprise of Washington. This reminds me of the answer made a short time since to the remark that the editor of the now defunct *States and Union* was a "very penetrating man."[7] "That may be," was the reply, "but his paper is a *penny-traitor*." The people of Washington have been so

long in a chronic "state of attack," that they are getting used to it, if indeed some of them have not begun to find the excitement almost agreeable.

OUR DEFENSES

Our means of defense have been increased since my last in many ways. We have received several fine regiments of troops, and stores of provisions, arms and ammunition, clothing, specie and other necessaries, have been added to the resources of the Government. Best of all, we may now consider our communications with the North permanently established, beyond any fear of interruption. This, of itself, is worth ten regiments. Isolated from our true and loyal friends at the North, a single severe reverse might bring us to the verge of destruction, but *now* the Administration feels as if its back was against a rock and all its foes in *front* only. All the enthusiasm of this eventful month has not been confined to the brave men and loyal-hearted women of the faithful North—there were many here who stood up fearlessly through the brief, but gloomy period of danger, resolved to do their whole duty, come what would; and you can imagine, far better than I can describe, the thrill of grateful admiration felt by these men when, at last, some stray files of New-York papers reached them, and they read the inspiring records of "the great uprising." "The Union is safe now"—was the universal feeling and expression.

OUR REGIMENTS

All the heights surrounding and commanding the city, are being occupied and fortified, and Sprague's regiment of Rhode Island men are to occupy the very ground offered to Virginia by General Lee, the traitor, for a far different purpose. Nor will the "worshippers of free speech and Roger Williams" [i.e., Rhode Island troops] be at a loss how to protect the handsome hill where the shanties of their camp are rising. The conduct of Ellsworth's Fire Zouaves at the fire near Willard's, has given the citizens a view of their better side, and they are vastly more popular than before.[8] The boys were decidedly in their element, and worked with tremendous energy, only stopping now and then to bestow a few snatches of hot breath on the rotten hose and defective machinery of the Washington Fire Department.

A few melancholy accidents have marred the history of the week, but their small number is almost wonderful, if we consider the circumstances. The greatest activity prevails in all the commands, and our officers, many of them new to such business, are displaying unexpected efficiency in drilling their troops. The army will soon be as efficient in discipline as it is overflowing with courage.

PLANS OF THE REBELS

The news from the South is still to a great extent unreliable, except that which comes through the trusted agents of Government, and most of their communications remain unpublished beyond the charmed circle of the President's *confidantes*. Taking it as a whole, however, the judgment of a candid man, willing to admit the exact strength, no more, no less, of the rebels, will be, in the opinion of your correspondent, that an attack upon Washington is contemplated, and that it will be made as soon as possible. Of course, the rebel leaders do not propose to inform the world of their plan of action, or to publish a map of their campaign, but enough is certainly known to point unmistakably to the movement in question.

It is the fashion for many newspaper editors and correspondents to reiterate the assertion that Jefferson Davis will surely not risk so much upon a *useless undertaking*. Let me state a few considerations which may place the matter in a different light, and which may have the force of argument to the minds of the arch-traitor and his counsellors. Being the Capital of the nation, the time-honored centre of political influence and national life, a certain powerful prestige attaches to those who hold, by whatever means obtained, the spot consecrated by so many memories, the National Capitol, the public archives, buildings, &c. Moreover, the seccessionists regard Maryland as being only in the Union by force of federal occupation, and they cannot consider Virginia fairly theirs, while the stars and stripes float unmolested on at least the northern shore of the Potomac. By the capture of Washington, then, they expect to win an important *prestige*, to secure Eastern Virginia, to make sure of Maryland, and to overawe the rising patriotism of Western Virginia, Kentucky, and Eastern Tennessee. Nor should we forget that this rebellion is the child of excitement, and that if the fever once abates, and sober second-thought is allowed one hour in which to dwell upon an empty treasury, an illegal government, grinding taxation, ruined commerce, wasted fields, probable famine, and the certainty of prolonged war, the edifice so hastily built of such rotten materials would crumble to the earth, want and discontent would scatter the gallant army now assembled, and the days of the Montgomery conspirators would be numbered. An attack upon Washington, even if unsuccessful, would revive the enthusiasm, rekindle fanatical hate against the North, and give to Mr. Davis and his "Cabinet" a brief additional lease of ill-won power.

For the sake, then, of winning four great States, and saving the necks of the secession leaders, it may be that Washington will be assailed. It is not impossible that in his next letter, your correspondent may be able to say what the masses of rebels, now collecting at Richmond, Lynchburg, and other points, were brought there for. I will not pray that the struggle may not be made here and speedily, for how to avoid the shedding of blood in this quarrel, passes my comprehension.

WASHINGTON, 27 MAY 1861 (PUBLISHED 30 MAY 1861)
Your correspondent is sitting in "quarters," somewhat the worse for the week's wear and tear. The three "minute guns," the appointed alarm signal, have just sounded, nobody knows what for, and it may be well to record what has already occurred, before the swiftly passing panorama of these troubled times brings new events before us.

The last four days have indeed been of a deeply exciting character. The "movement" so long prophesied by newspaper correspondents, has at last been made, though we in Washington are still ignorant of all its details, except those which have passed under our immediate notice. On Thursday night last, the Third Battalion D.C. Volunteers, Captain Smead commanding, received orders to cross the Potomac at Long Bridge, disperse or capture the rebel pickets on the Alexandria road, and occupy good positions to keep the way open for the march of the army. All this we learned afterwards, for when we started we were in blissful ignorance of our destination, and were kept for some time busily collecting boats of various sorts and sizes. Your correspondent was with the first company of that Battalion, and consequently saw the whole of the night's work. We met a number of patrols, some of them in squads of a dozen or so, but they all retired from hill to hill and bush to bush, without showing fight, and beyond taking a couple of dragoon horses, we made no captures. At last our task was accomplished, and between three and four A.M., we heard the heavy tread of marching men in the direction of Long Bridge. First came the New-York Twelfth, their arms glittering in the brilliant moonlight, after them the Michigan First, the New-Jersey regiments, the New-York Twenty-Fifth, the latter taking the road towards Four Mile Run, then the Second Cavalry, (regulars) Sherman's Light Artillery, and an engineer corps, while the New-York Seventh took post near the bridge, and another detachment of engineers commenced the construction of an earthwork on a knoll which commands both the road and the bridge. The brave fellows cheered heartily as they passed, and from them we learned that the New-York Seventy-First, the Fire Zouaves, and Sprague's Rhode Islanders, were then crossing in boats at Alexandria.

Thus was Virginia invaded (?), and long after the troops passed by, we listened anxiously for the sounds of the expected conflict down the road. All was silent, however, nor was it until late in the forenoon that we heard of the dastardly assassination of the brave young Colonel Ellsworth.[9] The sad tidings threw the whole city into an indescribable excitement and agitation. It is to be feared that it will do much to inflame the passions of our soldiers, and stifle any merciful and generous feelings towards their enemies which they might otherwise have entertained. The Zouaves in particular swear (literally) eternal vengeance for their leader, to whom, rough as they unquestionably are, they were becoming much attached. One great, Herculean fireman was found blubbering at his post this morning, vowing that he and his comrades "would have a life for every hair on the head of the dear little Colonel." The career of this young man is certainly a remarkable comment upon the opportunities which American manners and modes of thought afford to energy and genius. At twenty-two his fame is national, and his name is not unknown on the other side of the Atlantic. Falling before he has reached his twenty-fourth birthday, he leaves a reputation which will last as long as the history of his country, and his funeral is attended by the President of the United States, the Commander-in-Chief, a host of lesser dignitaries, and the sincere regrets of a whole people follow him to his honored but untimely grave.[10] Republican institutions are not a "failure," when results like this follow as matters-of-course from their legitimate workings.

The "military world" of Washington sleeps upon its arms, startled every few hours by alarms, groundless or otherwise, and the whole population is in a state of feverish anxiety. The week before us has strange events hidden behind that impenetrable veil which we almost dread to see lifted. We think we are ready for anything that may transpire. God grant that your correspondent may not be called upon to fill his next communication with tidings of blood and carnage.

WASHINGTON, 3 JUNE 1861 (PUBLISHED 6 JUNE 1861)
Since writing my last, the plans of the Government have steadily developed themselves, and we can no longer doubt the foresight and wisdom of our rulers. With a thoughtful sincerity, which in these times wears almost the appearance of singularity, President Lincoln is endeavoring to keep the promises contained in his inaugural, "that there need be no bloodshed." It is true that the armies of the Union are steadily advancing Southward, but they move with such an imposing exhibition of strength, that the scattered bands of the rebels retire before them without waiting to try the chances of a collision. On Friday night last, the batteries at Acquia Creek were assailed by the federal forces, but this was unavoidable in carrying out the admirable

strategic combinations of General Scott. The week before us may witness a few brief, sharp conflicts, but the great and bloody battle, in which the "invaders of the sacred soil of Virginia" were to be annihilated, will be looked for in vain.

Additional regiments continue to pour into this city from various free States, and we are almost as fully garrisoned as before the movement into Virginia. The entrenchments and field works are rapidly approaching a state of completion, and present a truly formidable appearance. None of the cuts in the daily papers give a correct representation of either their extent or position, and in some of them "our own correspondent" has drawn the angles, bastions, redoubts, &c., chiefly from his own imagination. The whole line of low hills from Arlington House to the little bay south of Alexandria road, is to be fortified, and at the road on either side, a strong bastion commands the bridges, the road, and a long sweep of the breastwork. These entrenchments are not a mere provision for a possible contingency, they are thrown up because necessarily Washington will soon be left with a comparatively small garrison, and by means of these artificial advantages a few men could hold in check a large attacking force.

GENERAL SCOTT'S STRATEGY
It is a well-known characteristic of General Scott's tactics that his advances are always steady, safe, and well-planned, while he never allows a chance to be left his opponents to cut off his supplies or assail him in the rear. When he has once passed through Virginia, that State will be as thoroughly "pacified," as completely disabled of all power for evil, as Maryland is now, and there will be nothing left for the rebellious portion of her people but to return with the best grace they can, to peace, quiet, comfort and prosperity.

BUSINESS REVIVING
Washington is a lively and prosperous town at present. Large sums of money are unavoidably spent here, the markets are busier than ever before, the hotels are full, and almost every department of trade is beginning to awake from the stagnation which overwhelmed us a few weeks ago. Last Tuesday evening, the President held a levee. The East Room was brilliant with uniforms, silks and laces, and the assemblage was certainly unique and interesting in every point of view. We missed, however, more than we could tell, the bright and handsome face of the lamented Ellsworth. It is hard to realize that he will *not* come back. Senator Harris, of New-York, has been here for several days, and is looking in much better health than during the last session of Congress.[11] A few short weeks only remain before the

assembling of the extra session, and we are looking forward with anxious expectation to the action of that most important conclave.

THE NAVY YARD

The utmost activity prevails at the Navy Yard, in all the departments, and the various munitions of war are being prepared with great rapidity. Among the most prominent items, I may mention a number of beautifully-finished brass field guns, rifled and smooth, of from six to twelve pounds calibre. They are destined for the new flying artillery, and will constitute a most effective addition to that important arm of the service. The repairs on the *Pensacola* are rapidly approaching completion, and she will soon be ready for sea.[12]

INVENTIVE GENIUS AWAKENED

Once more let me call attention to the activity and energy with which the inventive genius of the North is directing its efforts to the improvement of the various appliances of war. No less than *five* patents were granted last week for improvements in fire-arms, and several more are in the hands of the Examiners. This important field has been but just opened, and we may expect as important achievements there, as have marked the labors of our countrymen in every other department of mechanical science. Can there be a question as to which side of this great struggle has enlisted the greater mass of *mental* as well as physical energy? Some of the engines now in process of development will match the best skill yet displayed by the rebels in stealing their supplies. The general tone of feeling at the Capital is in the highest degree cheerful and hopeful.

WASHINGTON, 10 JUNE 1861 (PUBLISHED 13 JUNE 1861)

After another week of seeming inaction, full of false alarms, unimportant skirmishes, quarrels with the thieving quartermasters and the dilatory and half-organized commissariat, we seem at the time of this writing, to be on the eve of an important movement. The greatest secresy has been observed, the restrictions on "passes" have been doubled, not a regiment or a battalion knows in what direction it is to march, we only know that to many of us the command to "march" has been given. A gentleman, a Baptist clergyman of high standing, reports that he saw and conversed with Jefferson Davis at Manassas Gap less than three days since, and from his further observation it would appear that we have somewhat underestimated the strength of the force which now lies so near to us. It will be with a feeling of relief that our troops find themselves actually marching

South, and the prospect of a speedy collision with the rebels will dissipate a host of bitter and discontented feelings, engendered by the miseries of an imperfect equipment and an irregular supply of the necessaries of life. Men will endure on a march, or in face of the enemy, many things which would breed a mutiny in a *camp*. This is a truth long familiar to military leaders, and its practical application will be of great value at the present juncture.

The deep feeling momentarily occasioned by the death of Senator Douglas is passing away with a rapidity which is a strong comment on the depth of the general excitement on the absorbing topic.[13] A year ago, the death of such a man would have shaken our political world like the fall of a Samson, and a thousand hands would have reached forth for their share of the party heritage so unexpectedly left for division without a will. Now, the case is different, and few will take suitable cognizance of his departure, until on the return of peace they miss a voice which has long been a power in American politics.

The gunboat fleet, to which several additions have been made, is now lying at the Navy Yard, taking in supplies and stores of all kinds. A huge ten-inch Dahlgren gun has been mounted on the Freeborn.[14] It is a pivot gun, and will vastly increase the efficiency of her armament. The quantity of ten-inch shells shipped with it is such as to induce a surmise that there is an immediate purpose to be served.

Your correspondent has just returned from the camp of the New-York Thirteenth. The location of the camp is, to say the least, peculiar, and has been condemned by competent military men, but it is high, well-drained, and healthy, with a very pleasant prospect northward. Colonel Quinby and his command seem to be in good health, though they have endured an unnecessary amount of vexations and privations.[15] They are a fine, soldierly looking set, and will, no doubt, acquit themselves admirably, if the Fabian policy of the Administration shall ever bring them within striking-distance of an enemy. One of the new features of the fieldworks on the heights near this camp—a portion of Arlington Heights—is the erection of strong "stockades." Others are arising by the quarters of the New-York Sixty-Ninth, the New-Jersey Regiments, &c. The intrenchments have progressed very rapidly, and, if they are ever needed, will be a terrible obstacle in the way of the fiercest onslaught of the rebels. They cannot come into use, however, until either our soldiers are defeated, or our Commander-in-Chief out-generaled, neither of which events are looked for just now. Speaking of the position of our army, reminds me of the absurdly inaccurate maps published by some of your daily contemporaries. It is now almost necessary to say, in the face of some of the said "maps," that the Long Bridge does *not* connect the Capitol with Arlington House, and that our regimental camps do not cover quite a fourth-part of Northern Virginia.

The unexpected stand taken by the leaders of English public opinion, much as it is to be regretted, arouses in army-circles, and among the prominent men at this place, little other feeling than contempt for the misconception and ignorance which can alone account for such presumption. Every steamer which crosses the ocean, from this time forth, will carry some news to open the blinded eyes of our transatlantic cousins.

Every train that arrives brings some noted politicians to swell the throng of those who are already on hand, busily preparing and digesting the business of the Extra Session [of Congress]—a by no means unimportant process, at this crisis in the national affairs.

WASHINGTON, 24 JUNE 1861 (PUBLISHED 27 JUNE 1861)
Two weeks of camp life, including a number of forced marches in the hot sun, has given your correspondent a still further insight into the *modus operandi* of this campaign. He has been enabled to acquire a tolerably thorough experimental knowledge of the region of country on the Maryland side of the Potomac, between Washington and Harper's Ferry. The newspaper croakings about a possible approach from that direction of a strong attacking force, are unmitigated *bosh*.

THE DANGER
The Southern Confederacy does not possess the fourth part of the wagon trains and other equipages necessary to move a large army through one of the roughest of all rough and hilly regions. Not only are all the good roads well and strongly guarded, but the people are mainly loyal, and the number of strong defensive positions is by no means small. It is true that at many points the Potomac is fordable, but nevertheless *that* approach is not one of the weak points of Washington. Our only danger lies in front, and, if we may judge by the rapid increase of our forces here, and the energy with which all the means of defence are urged toward completion, the War Department is inclined to believe that a serious collision between Arlington Heights and Fairfax Court House, may occur at any hour. The rebel chiefs cannot much longer hold together the large force now within their lines. Action of some kind has become an absolute necessity. If the truth were known, we should find that an exhausted exchequer and subsiding enthusiasm are the most prominent incitements to the advance which they now threaten.

We are all, troops and people, once more in just such a condition of excited and painful suspense as preceded the arrival of our first reinforcements from the North. Will the genius of General Scott once more avert the threatened bloodshed, and compel our foes to an inglorious and ruinous retreat? To us who are so near to the great chess-board, such a forced mate seems utterly impossible.

GUERRILLA WARFARE
The "guerrilla" warfare of which the rebels have said so much, seems fairly to have begun, and hardly a night passes that some of our pickets are not fired upon by some skulking traitor. There must, indeed, be a remarkably large allowance of "Indian blood" in the veins of some of our F.F.V. antagonists.[16] Would not "*gorilla*" be a better rendering of the term by which this species of murder is designated?

WHAT IS FEARED
A vast amount of anxious speculation is devoted to the probable action of the extra session of Congress. The well-known characteristics and tendencies of the several members are discussed with eager solicitude, and their probable action on the several points to be laid before them debated with an energy born of a deep-seated conviction that the fate of the country will soon be at the mercy of a little human breath. The great fear seems to be that some false prophet of peace, with a craven heart and a slippery tongue, will bring in specious proposals of some sort to distract our National Council, and impair the unity and energy of its actions. Nor shall we be in anywise at ease until the key-note of the session has been loudly and distinctly struck, and we recognize nothing but trumpet tones. A few brief days will decide the matter.

SPIES IN WASHINGTON
One of our most constant vexations is the consciousness that our city teems with spies, and that by no means in our power can we prevent every important change in our military status from being promptly reported to our enemies. We comfort ourselves with the reflection that these male and female traitors have, thus far, had very little news to carry of a nature to encourage the hearts of the subjects of Jefferson Davis. Let them tell him, if they please, that every hour a new cannon is moulded, that every day a new "sail" is added to our navy, that every train brings some tall regiment of loyal hearts to swell our numbers, and that, for every regiment that comes, five more stand ready, weapons in hand, to step forward in defense of the flag. So let them warm the chilled courage of their rebel leaders. The very air is full of rumors, as usual, but I will not report them.

WASHINGTON, 8 JULY 1861 (PUBLISHED 11 JULY 1861)
Your correspondent has just returned from "looking around" among the camps and military men. Several Regiments, and all the light artillery, have gone over the Long Bridge today. Others, including Colonel Burnside's splendid Brigade of Rhode Island and Massachusetts men, are under marching orders, and may move at any moment.[17] Surely, all this is not for nothing, and there seems to be good reason for the belief entertained by all the officers, and others with whom I have conversed, that *this* is the final and long expected "advance on Richmond."

THE THREE MONTHS' VOLUNTEERS
The troops are in high spirits at the prospect of active service, and the three months' volunteers, especially, are all burning with impatience to, as they express it, "*do* something before they go home." Within two or three weeks the Government will lose the services of some of the finest Regiments now under arms, though large numbers of the men will, no doubt, enlist for the war. The Rhode Islanders, in particular, have already commenced the organization of a new Regiment of picked men, to be armed with the Burnside carbine.[18] This will be a crack corps, adapted to service that will be required constantly during the whole Southern campaign.

ASSAULTS ON GEN. SCOTT
The *Republican*, of this city, and a few of your own newspapers, still carry on their feeble and pusillanimous assaults upon the Commander-in-Chief—discussing the military plans and combinations of one of the best of living soldiers, with the proverbial freedom and confidence of ignorance and conceit.[19] They can do nothing, however, to shake the unbounded confidence reposed in General Scott by the people and the army.

THE MESSAGE
A unanimous outburst of approbation greeted the President's Message, men of all ranks and persuasions joining to express their admiration of the firmness, wisdom, and patriotic moderation of our excellent Chief Magistrate.[20] The Message "reaches the whole case," and will of itself tell with powerful effect among our enemies.

As to the action of Congress, that body cannot fail to sustain the Executive in all that he has done, as well as in all that he proposes to do for the salvation of the country. So far as I can learn, the various leaders, both in the House and Senate, breathe but one will and one purpose, and that will and purpose point to a united and pacified country as their polar star. A few there will be who will raise feeble voices of discontent and disapprobation, but they will hardly make themselves heard among the concordant shouts for the Union.

The appropriations of men and money recommended are, it is true, much larger than we have been accustomed to, but the determination evinced to secure the solid permanence of the "security," will encourage capitalists to invest in the proposed loan, while the number of men can easily be filled, only by accepting those who have so long been begging for an opportunity to fight under the Stars and Stripes. We may wonder how that portion of the Message will sound in the astonished ears of the rebels. How many prospective crops of cotton must be mortgaged before the treasury of the Confederacy will run over with the proceeds of a four hundred million loan? How about that "very desirable investment" which has so long been advertised in the organs of the oligarchy?

Not that this whole loan will be called for at once, or soon, or that so large a portion of the movable capital of the country will be destroyed or permanently absorbed by the necessities of the war. In reality, all that is asked, is that so much money should rapidly pass through the hands of the General Government, speedily to return to its old place as the medium of exchange in the ordinary channels of trade. We shall see soon how this matter will be looked upon by our money-kings. They may be well assured, however, that with them or without them, the *loan will be taken.*

THE FIRST LEVEE

President Lincoln, thus far, bears his load of responsibility wonderfully well. He is a little thinner and paler than on the day of his inauguration, and at times, wears a wearied and harassed look, but is the same kind and cordial man as ever, with now and then a relapse into the humorous pleasantry, which in old times formed so marked a feature in his character. Next Tuesday evening there is to be a grand levee at the White House, and without doubt, the jam will be something fearful. Being the first of the session, it will be "full dress," and the two Houses will be there in a body. The assemblage will glitter with uniforms and blaze with epaulets. The diplomatic corps, in all the glory of gold lace and ugly court dresses will be there, and though we are just now poorly supplied with ladies, as to numbers, there will be a full display of crinoline.

THE TABLES TURNED

Everybody wonders where Mr. Breckinridge mustered the amount of "face" he has shown in presenting his own physiognomy in Washington.[21] He may have come as a spy, or perhaps to sow the seeds of discord; no one imagines that he is here for any good. He will soon find, however, that the old order of things has passed away, and that all things have become new. And for himself, he will find that his consequence is gone, and that he is now an object of contempt where he was once the observed of all observers.

The congratulations which welcomed the venerable Crittenden, were numerous and sincere.[22] He may have erred, but no one can doubt the genuineness of the old man's patriotism. Johnson, of Tennessee, Etheridge, and their brave associates, are the heroes of the day, and well have they won their laurels.[23] Many an eye moistens with sympathy and admiration as it turns upon them, the "faithful found among the faithless."

UNIQUE OFFICE-SEEKERS

We are now afflicted with a new and unique swarm of office-seekers. Young men whom a three-months' drill would hardly prepare for efficient service *in the ranks*, are here in scores asking to be placed in responsible and lucrative *commands*. Some of them succeed, some don't.

WASHINGTON, 29 JULY 1861 (PUBLISHED 1 AUGUST 1861)

When last I wrote you, we were on the eve of a great battle. Even then the vanguard was busy with the work of death. The citizens and others in this now crowded Capital walked the streets in breathless anxiety, wishing, yet almost dreading, to hear the news from the field. Well, the battle was fought, and the news of its decision came to us at first clothed with all the enormous exaggerations it could receive from the heated imaginations of cowards and runaways. *Now*, however, we know the truth. The "twelve thousand left upon the field of battle" has diminished to a few hundreds. The "utter rout" is discovered to have been the almost excusable misconduct of a few weary and ill-disciplined regiments, cursed with cowardly and incompetent officers, and dismayed by the continuous appearance of fresh myriads of enemies. We now know against what terrible odds of numbers and position our gallant soldiery contended, and how nearly they achieved a victory in spite of all. It is true that the panic was unaccountable and disgraceful, but *defeat* there was *none*.

All that happened was but the natural and legitimate consequence of the peculiar manner and circumstances under which our army has been organized, and our officers selected. No fear that the same thing will ever occur again, and we may be sure that many of the regiments who were engaged at Bull Run came out from among that maze of masked batteries no longer raw levies, inexperienced volunteers, but ready to show themselves *veterans* on all subsequent occasions. But enough of the great battle.

General McClellan has arrived upon his new field of action, and his very presence seems to inspire all with new courage and energy.[24] Great expectations are entertained of the wonders he will accomplish. Certainly, never in the history of this country did any officers have grander interests or more important responsibilities committed to his charge. The new commander spent last Saturday afternoon in close and earnest conference with President Lincoln. Whether it is because McClellan is here, it is hard to tell, but the crowds of drunken and uncontrollable soldiers who thronged our streets two days ago, have disappeared as if by magic, and the scarcely less numerous troops of new-fledged officers have withdrawn their dashing uniforms and military swagger from the halls and bar-rooms of Willard's, Brown's, and the National. Enough are left, however, in all conscience. Nothing is more imperatively demanded by the best interests of the army and the people, than the presence of a strong controlling hand in every one of our widely-scattered camps.

In the city and vicinity of Alexandria, more especially, our troops have been guilty of shameful outrages, calculated to arouse to the utmost the fanatical tendencies of all whose prejudices are in any way against the Administration. It should be at once made clearly understood by our soldiers, that in this war *no* license will be permitted.

Your correspondent has just spent a day in making a thorough examination of the new defences on the south side of the Potomac. Suffice it to say that they have been greatly strengthened, and when the remainder of the guns are mounted, they will be as nearly impregnable as such works well can be. The work is carried on continuously and energetically.

WASHINGTON, 5 AUGUST 1861 (PUBLISHED 8 AUGUST 1861)
The weather here during most of the past week has been intensely warm, many of our most capable thermometers having given up in despair all attempt at keeping the record; but neither the heat, nor unpleasant thoughts of our repulse, nor anything else, seems to check the business tendencies of "the great war Congress," or interfere with the development of the "Army of the Potomac." With all due allowances for the inevitable amount of useless talk, where so many professional talking men are brought together, Congress has indeed done well. The Administration is fully endorsed, the army provided for, and the representatives of the people can, most of them, return to their constituents with a pleasant consciousness of having done

their duty, and placed the country in a good state of defense against enemies without and within.

A WEEK OF MCCLELLAN

As to the army, it is hardly the same body of men who returned with disordered ranks and broken spirits from before the masked batteries of "Bloody Run." Better one week of McClellan, than a whole year of the red-tape officials who preceded him. The rapidity with which he has restored good order, strict discipline, and confidence, is almost miraculous. We are almost willing to look upon our repulse as a blessing in disguise, while considering this portion of its consequences. Never was the army in better spirits, or so anxious to be brought once more face to face with its rebel opponents. When or where that opportunity will be given, we can only conjecture. We in Washington are as much in the dark as are you in New-York, as to what may be occurring on the southern bank of the Potomac. No more strolling crowds of new-fledged lieutenants retail the orders of the day, "in strict confidence," to admiring and loose-tongued intimates. For all we know, there may be at this moment another battle going on.

OUR NEW REGIMENTS

The forces here have been increased during the week by the arrival of several splendid regiments, and every day brings its additions. How many are over the river it is impossible to say, but thirty regiments lie encamped in the suburbs of Washington city. The military sages who talk of the danger of the Capital being taken by a smart dash of the secessionists through our "back gate," would do well to make a note of the location of these same thirty regiments, and remember that *they* can fight as well as if they were further South.

CLEANING OUT THE DEPARTMENTS

The work of purging the Departments of secession employees, has gone on merrily the past week, and a number of valuable sources of information to the rebel leaders have been mercilessly dried up. The axe will soon be laid to the roots of sundry other shrubbery of the kind, much to the advantage of the Government.

PRINCE NAPOLEON

On Saturday, Prince Napoleon and his suite arrived in Washington, and became the guests of our worthy chief magistrate.[25] They could hardly have recognized, in the orderly and busy city, with its crowds of buyers and sellers, and its Congress in full session, the besieged and panic-stricken town described by sundry sensation writers for the transatlantic press. In the evening they dined at the Executive Mansion, and the dinner was a brilliant affair. Our "Palais Democratique," however, is hardly the place for the reception of scions of European royalty, except for the purpose of teaching them, in a quiet way, how much of substantial power may exist without the appearance of its outside show and tinsel. But one of these days we shall take one more step towards the abandonment of our republican institutions, when we build some future President a new and splendid hotel "on the European plan."

LOSSES AT BULL RUN

I have learned, from reliable sources, that among the slain at Manassas, were representatives of quite a number of the most prominent families of Washington. A great many youths who figured as *elegantes* on Pennsylvania Avenue, and in the social assemblies of the West End, under the *ancien regime*, are now carrying muskets or hold commissions in the army whose success would involve the ruin of their old home. Poor fellows—one can hardly help pitying their fate, even while condemning most bitterly their insane and criminal folly. In the destruction of the Black Horse Cavalry, some of the most violent families of traitors on either side of the Potomac were thrown into grief and mourning. Indeed, there is very little music in the bells which the rebels have rung over their "great victory;" they cannot disguise from themselves, any more than from us, the fact that their loss was enormous. They, in fact, *confess* to a loss in killed and wounded much larger than our own has been ascertained to be. Let no rumors of "changes in the Cabinet," deceive you—they are not being made, though perhaps they *should* be.

WASHINGTON, 12 AUGUST 1861 (PUBLISHED 15 AUGUST 1861)

We have had a week of intensely hot weather, even for this season and this latitude, and our military chiefs have shown a praiseworthy regard for the health of their troops, by refusing to impose severe exertions upon them under such a burning sun, and in such an exhaustingly close atmosphere. The business of "preparation," however, goes on as briskly as ever, and our army is rapidly becoming, in all respects, the best appointed array that ever moved upon this continent. Hardly any regiments now remain in the field but those enlisted for a term of years or for the war, and we shall not soon witness such a wholesale weakening of important corps as took place just after our repulse at Manassas. The good effects of the present active process of drill and discipline will, therefore, continue to be felt during the continuation of hostilities.

PREPARATIONS FOR THE CAMPAIGN

Time flies with wonderful rapidity in these excited times, and already the summer, which was looked forward to with so much of anticipation and apprehension, has half slipped away from us. A few brief weeks must bring us to the opening of that much discussed "fall campaign" which is to decide forever the destinies of the nation. It needs but a glance at the advertisements of the Quarter-Master and Commissary-Generals, to see that the preparations for that campaign are on a scale of grandeur worthy of remark even by European observers. Horses, wagons, accoutrements, arms, provisions, naval stores, &c., are called for in fabulous numbers and quantity. And for all this the people will be called upon for corresponding millions of hard-earned gold. They will freely give it, but we may almost hold them excused if, with every dollar, they give a bitter execration for the traitors whose insane ambition has rendered such sacrifices necessary.

THE TREASURY

Great activity prevails at present in the Treasury Department, the centre of action being the newly-instituted and not yet completely organized "Loan Bureau." And here let me mention a quaint and unostentatious individual, seldom heard of, unknown to the country at large, but whose cool business brain and almost miraculous memory is of untold value to the nation at the present crisis. I refer to George Harrington, First Assistant Secretary of the Treasury, Governor Chase's right hand man.[26] The best services rendered in this hour of our country's peril are not *all* upon the battle-field. In some of the other departments a constant reduction of the clerical force is going on, made necessary by the falling off of general business, and the reduction of sundry branches to a more perfect and economical system.

THE CHARGES OF CORRUPTION

The "great War Congress" separated quietly and with dignity, and most of the members have returned to their homes. A very few still linger to attend to various business for their constituents, but the absence of all scarcely makes a difference in the crowded condition of our city. The number of harpies and buzzards attracted by the pleasant odor of the loan and the "fat contracts" is immense; but here your correspondent desires to say a few words upon a much discussed topic and in contradiction to the commonly received opinion. Of course the number of contracts given out is large, and among those to whom they are awarded are many men unworthy of trust or responsibility; but a long and careful investigation enables me to say that the prevailing notions concerning "corruption" are for the most part utterly destitute of any foundation in fact. *Never*, in the history of the War Department, were arms, accoutrements, wagons, harness, clothing and provisions purchased at such low prices, or with such a scrupulous regard for goodness of material or workmanship. The provisions, of which so much complaint has been made, were mostly purchased by former Administrations, and not under any contract entered into by the present.

There has been more corruption and favoritism in some individual States, than around the offices of the Central Government. "I speak that I do know, and testify that I have seen." Thus much should be borne in mind, that for every contract there will be many applicants, and but one can be successful, and that all the soured and disappointed expectants of a share in public plunder will straightway raise an outcry about "favoritism and corruption." Let us be reasonably generous to the men whom we have placed in such perplexing and perilous positions, and expect that those who charge them with infamous crimes and scoundrelism will at least bring forward some better proof than their own bald and bitter accusations, before we put our faith in their assertions. I repeat it, this Administration is *not* corrupt, the people are *not* being plundered, except so far as a remnant of *old* abuses still clings to the machinery with which the new men are compelled to labor. It may be true that Smith and Brown did not get the big contracts they bid so skillfully upon, but it does not follow that Jones and Robinson, who were successful, bribed the Government.

I have dwelt on this matter, because it is by no other means so easy to destroy our people's confidence in the Administration, at a time when the safety of the nation demands it, as by these oft-reiterated and puerile charges with which our press is teeming. If anybody has a "true bill" to bring, let him bring it, otherwise let him hold his peace—for the sake of the Union and the nation.

PERSONAL

Several members of the Cabinet are allowing themselves brief vacations, and in a few days, by time this epistle is before your readers, Mrs. Lincoln will be at Long Branch, with a small and select party of friends.[27] The President himself does not leave his post for a day, but remains the same patient and watchful worker, performing the severest labors that ever fell upon the shoulders of one man, with an eye single to the welfare of the people.

One little item more may be of interest to some of your readers, though the fulfillment of the prophecy depends, to a great extent, upon the course of public events. The political and social magnates of the present dynasty, somewhat piqued, perhaps, by the sneers which secession sympathizers have, from time to time, thrown out, have made up their minds that the "season" in Washington, next winter, shall be unsurpassed in brilliancy of social enjoyment by any preceding one. No doubt great preparations will be made, and those who are fortunate enough to have the *entrée* look forward to great times.

WASHINGTON, 19 AUGUST 1861 (PUBLISHED 22 AUGUST 1861)
The weather here for the past week has been dull, heavy, rainy and foggy. Only a few times and for a few hours at a time, have we seen anything like blue sky. This morning is as gloomy as can be, and it takes a tolerably stout heart to keep up good spirits. The only real cause for gloom, however, is the fear that the heat and wet together may generate disease among our overflowing camps. It is true that this may be as bad for one side as for the other, but at best such reflection affords only an imperfect sort of satisfaction. Thus far, if we can credit the reports brought by returning prisoners and deserters, the balance of good health has been decidedly in our favor, and it would seem that the rebels do not derive the benefit they anticipated from their "thorough acclimation." All possible care is being taken to promote the health and comfort of the soldiers, and many changes for the better have been made within the past fortnight.

INSUBORDINATION—GEN. MCCLELLAN
As might have been anticipated, the more effervescent enthusiasm which brought some of our volunteers into service, is dying out, and in the inevitable reaction, we have witnessed some scenes of insubordination like the disgraceful mutiny of a portion of the Seventy-Ninth.[28] Experienced army men, however, are well aware that this passing episode of discontent is a portion of the private history of *every* soldier; and it is worthy of remark, that in an army constituted as ours is, we have seen so few open manifestations of its existence. Under the firm, yet not unkindly, discipline enforced by our noble young General, these things will soon become an undreamed-of impossibility.

Speaking of General McClellan, it is wonderful how rapidly he is securing the confidence and esteem of the army and the people. If *he* cannot manage the volunteers, and make good and efficient soldiers of them, we almost feel as if it were useless for any other man to make the attempt. He is almost a Cabinet officer, so constantly is his judgment appealed to in all matters appertaining to the prosecution of the war.

THE CRY OF "BEAUREGARD IS COMING"

This morning, thanks to the Baltimore *Sun* and the resident secessionists, the city is on the *qui-vive* with rumors of the speedy approach of the rebel army. The oft-repeated cry of "Beauregard is coming," has not yet lost its power to excite the minds of our citizens, and as your correspondent came down the Avenue, he could see in every direction little knots of quidnuncs and idlers of all ranks earnestly discussing the probabilities of the case, and passing sage opinions upon the probable result.[29] One notion, however, appears to be almost universal, and that is, that McClellan would give his epaulettes to learn that the rebels *had* really sent any force, worth crushing, over the river.

The calm of the past four days has had something portentous in it. We do not now know, as of old, the wherefrom and whereto of every movement of the troops; they do not parade down Pennsylvania Avenue with drums beating and colors flying, but the well-disciplined regiments come and go under the direction of their master-hand quietly and soberly, attracting no attention, and scattering no reports of their destination. Can it be possible that these two vast armies will face each other for another week with no more important result than the unmanly murder of a few Federal sentries and pickets? It does not seem possible.

THE PURGING COMMITTEE

Congressman Potter, Chairman of the "Purging Committee," is still in town, actively engaged in ferreting out the traitors who still cling with leech-like tenacity to the public crib at which they so long have fed, and whose interests they are so systematically betraying.[30] Hardly a day passes without some rebel "source of information" being brought to light, and quenched forever. May he make close work and thorough! This is no time for squeamishness or leniency, and none but sound Union men should be left within ear-shot of anything that may concern the workings of the Central Government.

NEW INVENTIONS

The activity of our inventive genius, now for the first time turned into that channel, is exhibiting itself in a remarkable manner in the development of new engines of destruction. New guns and projectiles are the order of the day, and an infinite variety of rifled and breach-loading cannon seems to be the mania. Our patriotic Yankees seem determined that their Government shall be the best armed as well as the best manned in this life struggle.

WASHINGTON, 3 SEPTEMBER 1861 (PUBLISHED 5 SEPTEMBER 1861)
All Washington was on the *qui vive* on Saturday morning, with the glorious news from the Hatteras naval expedition.[31] It was a beautiful day, but the sunlight was brighter, and the floating flags seemed to dance with a gladder grace for the good tidings. God grant that this may be the turning of the tide.

THE STRAITS OF THE REPORTERS
The past week has been one of continuous excitement and suspense, owing to the remarkable and almost unaccountable movements of the enemy. What will be the result, and what is the purpose of all this advancing and retreating, all this backing and filling, is a speculation for the curious. We presume, however, that we shall know the whole before many days. Troops continue to arrive, but, thanks to the timely warning given by the War Department, the whole country, enemies and friends alike, can no longer be instantly informed of the extent, nature and disposition of our reinforcements. This clear and decided action of the Government has been a terrible blow to the legion of daily newspaper reporters and correspondents, who have heretofore infested every avenue of information. Cut off from their accustomed supplies, they roam the streets and camps, "seeking rest, and finding none," and pouncing, with hawk-like avidity, upon every poor little stray item which, in their palmier days, they would have scorned to notice. Hence the Jenkins-like accuracy with which they have chronicled every movement of the various members of the President's household, and touched up every additional coat of paint which has been applied to the White House.[32] Poor fellows, one more such blow, and "Othello's occupation's gone."

OFFERS OF EUROPEAN HELP
Offers of service from distinguished European military men continue to pour in at the War Office, and many of them will doubtless be accepted. Your correspondent has had the pleasure of reading some of these generous and timely communications, and they are replete with the noblest appreciation of our position and our cause. Writes one distinguished soldier of France, whose services added to the glory of some of the best fields of the new empire, "Your cause is the cause of a pure civilization and of enlightened government—I desire to fight for such a cause." The brave

Gaul is right—would that some of our own "white feather" politicians saw as clearly the tremendous interests staked upon the result of this strange, eventful struggle.

NEW-YORK POLITICS

Speaking of politicians, a strong and growing interest is felt here as to the shape to be assumed by the fall campaign in the Empire State. No one can think with indifference of such a battle, even though the weapons are to be ballots, instead of bullets. New-York has a new plume to add to her already glorious crest, nor could the enemy win a more important victory, than by securing a large vote against the Administration at the November polls.

A BLUE DAY

There was one blue day last week—the word passed from mouth to mouth, "McClellan is sick," "malaria," "over-worked," "can't mount his horse," &c., and every countenance fell, and every mind was filled with dark forebodings, so completely has our young and heroic commander concentrated on himself the confidence and affection of the people. The cloud passed away, however, as the next morning found him once more, as usual, in the saddle. I only wish, Mr. EXAMINER, that I could tell you all your correspondent happens to know of the programme of the next few days. However, the people are sufficiently "on tiptoe" already.

THE CLEANING-OUT COMMITTEE

The "Potter Committee" has done and is doing a most important work, and have made themselves a terror to the swarming spies of Washington. Hundreds of sources of information to the enemy have been summarily cut off, and more are every day detected.

WASHINGTON, 9 SEPTEMBER 1861 (PUBLISHED 12 SEPTEMBER 1861)

The past has been emphatically a week of rumors and false alarms. Nor have good reasons been wanting for the excited state of the public mind. Never before, since the beginning of the war, has the enemy been so near to us, or perplexed us with so many audacious and menacing movements. We need no longer explain to visitors the geography of Virginia, in order to tell them the whereabouts of our assailants; we need only ascend to the Capitol, and point across the Potomac. "There they are. That is the flag of the Confederate States now insulting the air of Munson's Hill, and under it the unoffending red clay is fast piling into intrenchments, or making way for ditches." Long familiarity with this state of things has bred a species of apathetic indifference among even the women, and the constant presence of danger has robbed it of its terrors. Still, so close has the possibility of a death-struggle now approached, that we start at the sound of signal guns and artillery practice, and ask one another, "*Has* the fight begun?" We shall never know "the day or the hour," however, until the booming cannon tell us.

DAVIS'S CANNON
The reported death of Jeff. Davis (is he dead?) was a brief variation of our anxiety, and led us off into countless speculations as to the probable effect of such an occurrence. Dead or not dead, his cannon still guard the road to Richmond.

THE SUNDAY PROCLAMATION
General McClellan's proclamation with reference to the better observance of the Sabbath, occasions general satisfaction, and will be welcomed with pleasure by thousands of "the good folks at home." A more humane and considerate order, not to speak of its religious bearings, could hardly have been given. How will it sound to those in the South, who have been in the habit of describing our armies as a "horde of infidels?"

THE LOAN BUREAU
Now that the New-York papers are filled with various items with reference to the new loan, it may not be uninteresting to your readers to know that the arrangements for its management at "this end of the line" are fast approaching completion. The newly-established "Loan Bureau" is under the immediate care and supervision of Assistant Secretary Harrington, the hardest worker I ever knew. The new rooms in the south front of the Treasury Building have been devoted to the new work, and often the weary clerks bend over their labor far into the night, some of them not resting until "daylight doth appear."

It is a curious and suggestive sight, those piles of millions of paper money, the tangible evidences of the pledged faith of a great people for the support of its rightful rulers. Certainly, we have not lost confidence in ourselves, nor do we, as a people, yet "despair of the Republic." We believe our cause to be just, our resources sound and undestroyed, and we believe we are honest, and will keep our "promise to pay," or those bits of paper would be worse than useless. Let foreign capitalists take what course they will, so long as we are true to ourselves, and trust each other, we can furnish our Government with all the funds it will require. Far be the time when the free people of this Republic shall be reduced to the same degrading vassalage to a few over-rich Jew bankers, to which so many European potentates have stooped their crowned but dishonored heads.

THE ARMY ENCLOSURES

The *corrals* of the army are a prominent object of interest to all who visit Washington. The long lines of splendid horses, carefully tethered before their abundant provender; the long-eared mules, with their sonorous "questionings and replies," as each one seeks, with singular earnestness and unerring certainty, for his particular wagon; and the wagons themselves, strong, well-built, and serviceable, with their white coverings, as if all the world had turned emigrants—all these make up a picture long to be remembered by all who have an eye for the picturesque.

OUR FORTIFICATIONS

Occasionally, of late, our countless military critics are heard to express their wonder that Government allows its connection with the fortifications across the river to depend upon so frail an instrumentality as the Long Bridge, "so liable to be destroyed by any bold enterprise of the enemy." To this it might be answered—first, the Long Bridge could hardly be damaged materially by any sudden "enterprise," as every approach to it is well watched, and terribly well defended; and second, if it was annihilated this morning, the transit of all manner of war munitions would hardly be interrupted for an hour, so abundant are other methods of easy transportation. There is no danger, however, that any man, or set of men, will be found, however possessed with the demon of secession, so eager for martyrdom as to attempt the assault in question.

THE SYRACUSE ENIGMA

Does anybody in New-York pretend to explain the resolutions of the late *quasi* Democratic Convention in Syracuse?[33] We in Washington regard them as an inexplicable enigma. Certainly this is the most hopeless attempt on record, to sustain a party organization among a people who think and feel with such wonderful unity. Let us hope that when the *people* come together to organize, no man will be found in the assembly unwise enough to remember that the old dead issues ever created a party for him.

WASHINGTON, 16 SEPTEMBER 1861 (PUBLISHED 19 SEPTEMBER 1861)
The weather is beautifully bright to-day, and the long trains of army wagons raise clouds of dust as they pass noisily under my window. By the way, the streets and avenues of Washington are the worst paved, where they *are*

paved, of any city I was ever in—except only Georgetown, over yonder, where every other cobble-stone weighs a ton.

THE LIFE WE LIVE

We live a strange life here, as it were in the very shadow of some great and terrible event, suspended over us by a thread as slender as that which of old upheld the impending danger of Damocles. We go about our accustomed duties with a cool, business-like manner, impossible to any other people in such circumstances, but ever and anon, as some signal gun, or the sound of artillery-practice, or the muffled roar of some distant skirmish, breaks in upon the sounds of peaceful life, the workman stays his hammer and the clerk his pen, the sharp bargain is for a moment suspended, and every man's face asks of his neighbor's—"Has it come, at last?"

Some of your readers may weary of the numerous "Washington correspondents," that they are always prophesying and speculating concerning the great struggle to come; but if they were only *here*, they would appreciate the intense interest with which we discuss the use of every new fortification, the discipline of the troops, the energy and genius of the leaders, and watch for every indication of active movements in either army.

OUR YOUNG GENERAL

Will you think your correspondent an enthusiast, if he says anything more of the knowledge of human nature, the profound and kindly sympathy with the common soldiers, by which our young General is endearing himself to the brave men whom he is to lead to battle? A friend of mine was with him the other day, during a portion of his tour of inspection; everywhere he was greeted with shouts of hearty welcome and recognition, and as "the boys" crowded around him whenever the restraints of discipline permitted it, he had words of encouragement and good-will for all. He asked about their rations, their quarters, their officers, their treatment, their various comforts and discomforts, with such a genuine interest as won the very hearts of his men. How the gallant fellows will fight in such a cause, and under such a leader.

THE PRESIDENT AND GEN. FRÉMONT

We are listening now for the newspaper comments upon the President's letter to General Frémont, and expect an unmeasured amount of misrepresentation and abuse.[34] No one, however, who will honestly accept Mr. Lincoln's true and obvious meaning, need discover any cause for complaint. In the border States, the effect will be admirable.

THE NEWSPAPERS AND THE CABINET

It is too bad that some of the leading newspapers of the North, pretending the utmost friendship for the cause and the Government, will still weaken the hands of the Administration by the utterance of groundless sensation charges against various members of the Cabinet. According to these worthies, Secretary Seward is a drunkard, thereby incapacitated for the discharge of his duties; and this, while that able and industrious public servant, his pleasant but *old* looking face clouded with care, is adding to its furrows daily as he toils at his never-ending task, and our country, by a seeming miracle of diplomacy and tact, has thus far added no foreign complications to her terrible difficulties.[35] In short, the charge is false.

Again, Secretary Cameron "is a thief," and a thousand ignorant, unthinking tongues, repeat a charge which a host of bitter personal enemies are anxiously but *vainly* seeking to substantiate.[36] "He lacks efficiency," and the same pack take up the strain, while the Herculean task of preparing and keeping in the field a dozen large armies, is performed with rare success under their very noses.

Secretary Welles, forsooth, has long locks of venerable white hair that fall upon his shoulders—he is, therefore, "an old fogy, and should be replaced by some younger and more energetic man;"[37] and in the face of the yelping assailants, all the while, one of the wonders of modern history becomes a present reality—a new navy is created and manned, and day after day, under steam or sail, some gallant bark puts out to bear the flag and vengeance of the Government among the pirates, on the sea or in their lurking places. The Southern coast is blockaded, the Hatteras forts are taken, the Potomac is kept open, distant forts are supplied, and the whole South, from Old Point Comfort to the bluffs behind Galveston, trembles in fearful expectation of the next blow; yet "Welles is an old fogy."

Now and then some incorrigible grumbler lifts up his tongue against the stalwart financier, by whose wise provisions the people who stay at home are enabled to take care of their brethren in the field, without imitating the degrading servitude to money-kings, Jew or Gentile, by which the potentates of another Continent have dishonored their crowned heads. They may make the most they can of Salmon P. Chase.[38]

As for the President—God bless him!—he is so strong in the hearts of the people, that the tongue of detraction cannot reach him.

THE GERMAN ELEMENT

The German element in the army is delighted with the attention shown them, more especially with the honorable notice bestowed upon their favorite leader, General Blenker, and his associate officers.[39] They have all deserved well of their adopted country.

THE MARCHING AND COUNTER-MARCHING
I cannot help being of the opinion that our military chiefs have missed their calculations the past week. It is doubtless better for us that it is so, but there was probably little doubt at headquarters that Beauregard would force a general action. That he must soon do so, all seem to agree, though he naturally shrinks from the responsibility of a step which must involve such tremendous consequences in case of defeat, or even of a drawn battle. What may be the meaning of all the endless marching and counter-marching, and changing of position along the rebel lines, is beyond the comprehension of a civilian; but no one can doubt that, like the eye of a vicious horse, "it means mischief."

WASHINGTON, 22 SEPTEMBER 1861 (PUBLISHED 26 SEPTEMBER 1861)
It is a lowering, dark, and chilly day. At last we have reached that "cool fall weather," believed by newspaper correspondents to be so admirably adapted to army operations in the South. We shall doubtless know erelong how far the deep mud roads of the Old Dominion will counterbalance the favoring report of the thermometer.

PALMETTODOM
Yesterday I was permitted to see a long letter directly from Charleston, by the "underground mail route," written by a planter's wife to a sympathizing friend at the North. The tone of the epistle was boastful in the extreme, and described "South Carolina as it is," in colors that aimed to make it out a little black and white Paradise, in spite of bare feet and homespun habiliments. Already the stock on hand of many comforts, and some necessaries, appears to have run extremely low, and the letter contained a lamentable, though unintentional, confession of the real weakness and paucity of resources of the vaunting aristocracy of Palmettodom. No doubt, however, but the people of South Carolina are far more unanimous and determined in rebellion than any of their co-traitors.

THE SELF-MADE DETECTIVES
Your correspondent has a word or two to say this week upon an intensely disgusting subject: It appears that under the old *regime*, a regular system of toadyism and consequent espionage grew up around the seat of government, whose ramifications extended through every branch of Washington society. The peculiar and unfortunate circumstances of the present Administration

afforded these well trained and observing "lookers-on in Venice" an excellent opportunity for the exercise of their vocation. I doubt if this continent contains a more contemptible set of leeches, than may be found among the office-seeking Republicans (self-styled) of the District of Columbia. I add with pleasure, however, that these persons for the most part, took their degrees in meanness, and "graduated with honor," under the fostering care of the peculiar institutions that are passing away.

To the best of my knowledge and belief, there is not an employé or attaché of the Government, in any civil office, whose loyalty has not been questioned by these people, and against the large majority written complaints have been entered, not sparing the General-in-Chief or the President's confidential friends. If any man has an office which another man wants, that is enough, and the office-holder is at once, in the eyes of these gentry, tainted with "secesh," and must be removed. Fortunately, there is an atmosphere of honesty and frankness around the present "powers that be," which is not encouraging to such a self-constituted corps of detectives. Still, mistakes will occur, and the most execrable meanness will at times meet with undeserved success.

It is to be feared that the most bitter fruits of this rebellion will not be found in the widening sum-totals of the national debt, nor in the barren and blood-stained fields of ruined States. There are worse evils than the ravages of war, and since the fire is kindled, let us hope it may burn, until it has consumed all these "cankers of a long peace," nor leave any putrid sores behind it.

ONE RESULT OF THE WAR

One thing is certain, this war will leave us the *best-armed* people on the globe. Every day, almost literally, brings out some new and terrible contrivance for offensive or defensive warfare. The ingenuity of the most inventive people on the globe is taxed to the uttermost. Repeating rifles, breach-loading, swift-firing cannon, projectiles of every form and object, strange-looking things for cavalry use, new applications of death-dealing chemicals, in short, the material world is being ransacked, and all the "enemies of human life" are being pressed into the regular service. Very few of these contrivances, of course, will ever be brought into actual and general use, but enough of them will prove successful to effect great changes in the management of future campaigns, and it is safe to say that if this war continues three years, the missile weapons with which we entered it will be as obsolete as "old brown Bess" itself.

THE "FRÉMONT QUESTION"
Much agitation has been produced by the "Frémont question," and the discussion is carried on with rancorous bitterness by hundreds who do not comprehend the scope and intent of either the law, the proclamation, or the President's letter. It is believed by many of the best military authorities that General Frémont has made a successful *coup* as a Presidential candidate, but a lamentable failure as a Major-General.[40] Your correspondent only believes *half* of all this, and if asked *which* half, would say, with the urbane and accommodating showman, "You pays your money, and you takes your choice."

THE NOTE-SIGNERS
The Treasury is as busy as ever, all its powers being taxed to the uttermost in the management of the great loan. Night and day, the weary clerks bend over their desks, and the "note signers," with crippled fingers and bandaged wrists, tug away at their strange alchemy, changing paper into money. Tell me, Mr. Editor, has not the old question of a National Bank and a national currency been practically solved by the unexpected exigencies of this Administration? Has not the Gordian knot, which so perplexed and divided the statesmen of the last generation, been cut by the sharp sword of this civil war?

THE RELIGIOUS CONVICTION OF THE NORTH
Your correspondent takes great pleasure in calling attention to the manner in which many of the great religious bodies of the North have made their record, and defined their position upon this war question. That great mass of religious, conscientious, God-fearing, thoughtful men and women, whose sterling worth and solid strength have made this country what it is, have arisen as one man to sustain the Government in its hour of peril. They who fear God honor the king, and these are the men, who, believing that they serve their Master in saving the country, will not fear to meet Him, though they go into his presence fresh from the strife of a just battle.

WASHINGTON, 7 OCTOBER 1861 (PUBLISHED 10 OCTOBER 1861)
Another of the long weeks of this strange war has slowly dragged itself away. Opening with the sad news of the disaster at Lexington, it closes amid such a whirlwind of contradictory reports as might puzzle the most hardened editor.[41]

THE ADVANCE

Our army has slowly but steadily advanced along the track of the retreat from Bull Run, fortifying each fresh position, carefully feeling its way, leaving no possible opening for trap, surprise, or entangling maneuvers, and now holds its own within easy march of the old battleground. Would there not be something to remind one of what is called "practical justice," if the Federal army should open the winter campaign by a victory on the very spot made famous by their disaster a few months since?

THE BREATHLESS SUSPENSE

The one great feature of the week is the inauguration of civil war in Kentucky. The wise men of that State have done their best to save it, but it was not fated that "the dark and bloody ground" should fail in its share in the carnage of this great conflict. The present is a moment of almost breathless suspense:—one hardly knows which way to turn. In the West, Frémont is preparing to retrieve by glorious achievements in the field the tarnished laurels of his Major Generalship. God grant he may do well for his country! and, if he does, he may cease to be anxious for his name or fame. In the centre the plot thickens rapidly, and a few days will do much towards deciding whether or not the Ohio is to be the dividing line between the opposing forces. Opposite Washington the face of affairs changes too slowly to cause much excitement, but the long fuse of preparations has nearly burned to the terrible magazine whose explosion must shake the country from end to end. A net of mystery seems to cover the operations of the fleet, but no one can doubt that ere long a blow will fall somewhere— and oh, how the rebel chiefs wish they knew *where!*

DEFECTS REMOVED

In all the varied and gigantic machinery of Government, the movements are daily acquiring greater steadiness and smoothness. The jar of the rebellion deranged things terribly for a time, but the patient and deep-thinking brains of the "master workmen" are fast remedying all defects, and the beauties of our marvellous and much slandered "system" never shone forth more conspicuously.

THE OVER-WORKED PRESIDENT

For a few weeks the President has been looking pale and careworn, as if the perpetual wear-and-tear of the load which presses upon him were becoming too much even for his iron frame and elastic mind. We hope that ere long he and all of us may have such cheering news as shall "do good like a medicine," and smooth away a few of the deep wrinkles of this long suspense.

OUR NORTHERN SNOBS

The secessionist portion of our population is more quiet than formerly, with less of gasconade, and a shade of gathering doubt as to the result of the struggle they are so deeply responsible for. It may not be proper to mention it here, but I am sorry to say that there still remain among the "upper-tendom" of the North a few of those choice young men who regret that, even for the sake of the Union, the "*gentlemen* of the South" must throw away their valuable lives in combat with the offscourings of Northern cities. I have known a young man go so far as to express a preference to the rebel army, as being "composed of gentlemen." It is almost beyond belief, but such fellows as these *do* disgrace some circles at the North. Your correspondent is oppressed with an appreciation of the sense of utter *loneliness* which must overwhelm one of these insufferable snobs, if by any accident he found himself in a society where all the rest *were* "gentlemen." As if a man with the black crime of treason on his soul, could be the equal in any sense of the roughest yeoman who draws sword for his country in her hour of need.

THE CITY FILLING UP

Washington is rapidly filling up. In spite of the nearness of the enemy, in spite of the increased expense of living, in spite of all the possible chances of the war, it is more difficult to find an untenanted house than it was a year ago, and it is feared that rents will soon go up to their old exorbitant figures. Never was there a more animated and thriving appearance, to all things in the city, at this season of the year. The amount of all the munitions of war now in store at this point is truly enormous, nor can we wonder at the hungry cupidity with which the rebel chiefs hover around the priceless trophy so completely beyond their grasp.

THE COMING SESSION OF CONGRESS

For a few weeks after the close of the special session, we were all busily canvassing the work of that body; now we no longer look backward, but wait with deep anxiety for the action of the Congress which is so soon to assemble. I think I can see the threatening portents of more than one stormy discussion, when the deep questions to which the crisis has given rise, are presented to the conflicting prejudices and jarring views of the earnest men who will be brought together.

If Frémont has done nothing else, he has divided the North, as by a sabre cut, *permanently*, into the new shape of "conservatives" and "radicals," and the two factions, seeking for the most part the same ends but by different means, will be developed into regular form before the adjourning of this Congress. For the present, however, if not for all time, the more conservative men will have it all their own way. Though, mind you, it is only by comparison with their hot-headed antagonists that they will merit any ascription of "conservatism," for with them will be the vast bulk of the very men who placed the President in the chair, and at their head will be the President, with his Cabinet, most of his Generals, and the strong men in both Houses. We may count, however, with unwavering faith, on the unanimity with which all men will turn their attention to the great work of carrying on the war. There will be no divisions when the army or its maintenance is concerned, and the half million bayonets will be rolled steadily forward, and such bold words go forth as shall warn the world of our real intentions, and cause the North to bristle more thickly than ever before with the sharp points that must now decide the fate of the Great Republic.

WASHINGTON, 14 OCTOBER 1861 (PUBLISHED 17 OCTOBER 1861)
Your correspondent feels little like writing you this morning, fearing that by the time his letter reaches you its interest will have been swallowed up by more exciting news. Never, since that fatal Sunday morning when we sat and listened to the far-off thunder of "Bull Run," has a battle been more imminent than at this moment. All the available troops on this side [of] the Potomac have received marching orders, and I rode for hours among their deserted camps this morning. Still, even *this* cloud may blow over without discharging its fatal electricity. All the week long fresh bodies of troops have poured in from the North, in various stages of discipline and equipment, but the stream is all too slow for the grand necessities of the hour. The Eastern States do not yet realize—not so fully as the West—the stern realities of this fearful crisis.

THE COMING DAY
Not a day passes, Mr. Editor, but some new tale of suffering comes to our ears, to embitter us against the evil men who have perpetrated this fearful crime against their country and their race. The cup of vengeance, full to running over, must erelong be forced to their lips—but that will be a sad and terrible day. Judging from the appeals which reach the Executive from every corner of the country, one would think that all the merciful and forbearing spirit with which our people entered the contest had been dissipated by a growing appreciation of the treason and its consequences. God grant the war may be brought to a close before the breach has widened beyond all reach of the healing influence of time.

AN INEXPLICABLE MYSTERY

Things in Washington remain about as usual, though the city is filling up faster than ever, and dwellings of a good quality can hardly be obtained for love or money. At the Treasury, the "demand notes" continue to pour out side by side with the tremendous drain of gold absorbed by the daily expenses of the Grand Army. The unexplained and inexplicable mystery to all inquiring minds is, how our opponents keep *their* forces in the field without such resources, and without such unlimited credit. When we ever arrive at a solution of the enigma, we shall doubtless listen to a tale of violence, oppression and extortion unparalleled in modern history.

FRÉMONT'S CAREER

General Frémont and his strange career still concentrate upon the army in Missouri a large share of the attention of the War Department. That some one has been fearfully culpable in this matter seems certain, but most men are contented to await the result of the careful investigation now in progress.[42]

TREASURY NOTE INCIDENTS

Speaking of the Treasury, a few amusing incidents now and then enliven the weary labors of the slaves in *that* mine. A few days since, one of the rather fresh individuals, whose duty it is to sign for the Treasurer the evidences of Uncle Sam's indebtedness, came to an officer of the Department, and gravely asked "if, in case the Government failed to meet its obligations, the signers became individually liable?" The reply was jocosely grave, that "to be sure they did, and Congress had very inadequately protected them by a contingent fund of forty thousand dollars each!" The young man returned to his notes and coupons, satisfied, but far from comforted. Speaking of coupons, that was a droll but not unnatural mistake of a young lady in the note-room the other day. "Ella, my dear," said the anxious parent, who was explaining the sights, "that is a *coupon*." The direction of the paternal finger was not absolutely accurate, and the young lady turned her mild and wondering blue eyes, with an expression of gentle commisseration, upon the good-looking face of the signer, while his "next door neighbor" asked him, with a malicious grin, "when he was payable?"

"SPOILING FOR A FIGHT"

The weather for the week has been rough and variable, giving our crowded camps a taste of what they may expect during their winter campaign in the South. The troops, however, are in excellent spirits, and "spoiling for a fight." McClellan is full of confidence, and eager, when the right time comes, to wipe out forever the disgrace of our one great battle. We go forward this time, moreover, with the advantage of a thorough knowledge of the ground.

THE BREAKING-UP PROCESS
The exodus of secession sympathizers to the South, and the return of Union people to the North, has not even yet entirely ceased, and every now and then, the red flag of the auctioneer before some respectable looking tenement, indicates the breaking up of some old family locality, or the appearance of worn and battered family-groups in our streets or hotels, hints at a history of patriotic devotion. Verily we have fallen upon strange times.

THE LESSONS WE ARE LEARNING
One effect of current events will necessarily be to make our people better acquainted with the various powers and duties of the Central Government. The degree of ignorance previously existing, was almost beyond belief. Not a day passes but appeals are made to the Executive for action, on his part, that would be all but impossible if he were an absolute monarch, and many honest people doubtless feel themselves aggrieved that the President does not exercise, in their behalf, prerogatives which any crowned head of Europe would hesitate to assume. In truth, it is more than likely that we sorely needed this fearful awakening, that the best part of our political system should not become irretrievably paralyzed and corrupted. It appears that, at last, the "Sage of Wheatland" has come out for the Government:—*qui bono?*—Is Saul also among the prophets?[43]

OUR UPPER TEN
The remainder of the Washington Upper Ten is hurrying back from its summer resorts and watering-places, to make ready for the coming of the political flood in December. And then we shall see if the war has conquered the *milliners*.

WASHINGTON, 21 OCTOBER 1861 (PUBLISHED 24 OCTOBER 1861)
The past week has been varied with a succession of heavy rains which have interfered materially with military operations, and caused much discomfort to the soldiers. It is, however, well worthy of remark, and has been made the subject of warm commendation by experienced military men, that the world has rarely, if ever, seen any army so large as ours so well sheltered and provided for. The comforts of home cannot, of course, accompany

our brave volunteers to their tents and bivouacs, but our commanders are doing very much to promote the well-being of the army. Much, of course, remains to be done, but those in power are fully impressed with their duty in the premises, and propose doing all that circumstances render possible. The bill of health of the army, at the present time, is a striking commentary upon the practical value of all this in a military point of view. The annals of war will hardly furnish a parallel, the number of men, the climate, and the season, being duly taken into consideration. What may be the consequences of a movement southward during the trying changes of a winter in such a latitude, can as yet be only surmised.

MCCLELLAN'S MOVEMENT

The daily papers have, as usual, kept you well advised of the position of the army. Let your readers make a note of the changes of the past week. They will see that Gen. McClellan's slow and cautious advance, up the river, and nearly parallel with it, is in fact turning the enemy's right flank, and threatening their Western railway communications, and must, in due time, compel them to give him battle on ground of his own choosing, or abandon Manassas without fighting. It is becoming a question in the minds of military men which horn of their dilemma they will take. It is hard for a civilian to decide which course our gallant General would prefer. In any event, we all believe that he will give an excellent account of them.

PET NAMES

It is one of the "humors of the campaign" to hear the rank and file discuss the probabilities of their position. With characteristic license they have given pet names to many of their more popular leaders, and their comments upon Gen. McClellan's plans generally end with the confident assertion that "George will fetch 'em." And "George" *will* fetch them, when the time comes. Speaking of "pet names," the De Kalb regiment have christened the miserable fortifications thrown up so pompously by the rebels on Munson's Hill, "Fort Skidaddle."[44]

THE POTOMAC BATTERIES

The closing of the Potomac is one of the temporary complications of the day, which will give an opportunity very soon for some brisk operations in that direction, though thus far the enemy's batteries have only been vexatious and annoying, without inflicting serious injury.

THE GREAT NAVAL EXPEDITION

The departure of the naval expedition, thus far managed so quietly, will leave us all for some days in a state of unpleasant suspense.[45] May He who rules the winds and the waves so order it, that the stormy Atlantic may aid and not oppose the course of the defenders of our Government. What would not the rebels give to know in season just where the blow will fall. Alas, for them! this time they shall not be "forewarned, forearmed."

THE FRÉMONT QUESTION

The Frémont excitement has wearied itself nearly out. His removal now would be a far different affair from the same action three weeks ago. Some little commotion would be made, no doubt, but it would soon subside. Not all the efforts of the *Tribune* and its compeers could make the excitement a national one.[46]

THE PRESIDENT

As nothing which relates to him is without its interest, your correspondent is glad to be able to say that our worthy Chief Magistrate is in excellent spirits, and looks much better than he did a fortnight since. He is gathering his strength for the labor and excitement of the coming Congress. I am told that he enters into the plans and arrangements of the campaign in all their varied details with the keenest zest, and that the military chiefs have been indebted to his strong and practical good sense for more than one valuable hint and suggestion.

THE EAST ROOM

The famous East Room of the White House is in a state of temporary dilapidation, unfurnished, uncarpeted, all that staring and stunning old paper scraped from the walls, and everything in readiness for its new and becoming winter dress. The number of distinguished visitors is already beginning to increase, and soon the tide will fairly set in.

ARTILLERY PRACTICE

As I sit quietly in my room writing to you, my ears are saluted this morning by the almost continuous roar of artillery-practice. The greatest possible attention has been paid to this arm of the service, and the number of admirably armed and appointed light batteries, now ready to take the field, is beyond all precedent on this Continent. It cannot be otherwise than that we enjoy, in this respect, a tremendous advantage over the rebels. The greater proportion of the guns, stolen by them for the purposes of this rebellion, are utterly useless for field purposes, however formidable when mounted in permanent batteries. The work of turning out such guns as are needed by "flying artillery," is one for which few of the foundries of the South are qualified.

When the artillery first began to exercise their pieces to any extent, it was amusing to see how their harmless thunder excited the imaginations of their numerous listeners. Those were the days of numberless skirmishes of which no official report ever came in. They have passed, however, and we sit in sublime calmness, well aware that no cannon roar "means mischief," so long as the concussion is near enough to rattle our windows.

WASHINGTON, 28 OCTOBER 1861 (PUBLISHED 31 OCTOBER 1861)
It is a beautiful autumn day, of the thoroughbred American stamp, cool, hazy and healthful, with a fine breeze to shake the red and yellow leaves from their summer perches, and to carry away the lurking malaria from among the tents of the soldiery.

THE QUIET OF THE CITY
Washington is quiet to-day, undisturbed by any excitement, and with little other noise than the rattle of the army trains. It is quiet as compared with New-York, for instance, but a remarkable scene of life as compared to its ancient and very humdrum self. We call it quiet, because we no longer turn more than a passing glance at the uniforms that go by us, unless indeed some unwonted stripe or color informs us that another transatlantic notability has endorsed the world's estimate of the justice of our cause, by drawing his sword in its behalf.

BADGES OF HONOR
One thing, speaking of our foreign-born officers, seems to your correspondent worthy of the attention of our Government: they are, many, if not most of them, *decoré*, wearing always on their brave bosoms the tokens of gallant and meritorious conduct in past struggles. Why is not this inexpensive method of recognizing merit an eminently appropriate and republican institution? It creates no rank, no order of nobility, involves Government in no expense, while it ministers to the noblest pride of the soldier-citizen.

LEARNING LESSONS
The events of the past week have given us a foretaste of the desperate combats yet to come. We have learned one or two good lessons from the battle of Leesburg.[47] One is for our officers, to keep them mindful of their orders—that no deaths on the field, however glorious, can atone to a soldier's fame for such an error as that of the gallant and noble-hearted

Baker.[48] Alas, for us all, that such and so valuable a life was so needlessly thrown away by its owner. A ripe orator, a soldier without fear, a man without reproach—another of our best and bravest has been laid upon the altar of his country. Another lesson is, that the soldiers in the Army of the Potomac have profited by their months of drill and preparation, and are now ready for the battle-field.

Strange as it may seem at first thought, the battle of Leesburg has done the whole army a good service. The coolness of our men under fire, their desperate courage under the most disheartening circumstances, and in face of overwhelming numbers, has furnished our camp-fires with a theme for conversation, which is having a decided effect upon the *morale* of the army. General Blenker, who came so near breaking his sword at Bull Run, is enthusiastic over what he now sees of American pluck, discipline, and soldierly bearing. He declares that when McClellan is ready to move forward, he will find himself at the head of an army of which every man is ready to prove himself a hero.

THE ELLSWORTH AVENGERS

Your correspondent has seen nearly all the regiments composing this army, as they made their successive entrance, but not one has excelled, in any respect, the "Ellsworth Avengers," Col. Stryker, which came in last week.[49] They are already very well drilled, and the *personelle* of the regiment is beyond praise. Their uniform is sensible and serviceable, and their other appointments perfect. With anything like good management, they cannot fail to become one of the most valuable bodies of men in the service.

WASHINGTON, 4 NOVEMBER 1861 (PUBLISHED 7 NOVEMBER 1861)

The great storm is over, and though the long and dangerous swell still rocks the fleets of the Republic, along our Atlantic seaboard, the movements of the army of the Potomac were resumed almost instantaneously on the cessation of the rain. In spite of the deep and cumbering mud, a number of well-appointed regiments have crossed the river within the last twenty-four hours, many of their camps being at once occupied by fresh arrivals.

ANXIETY FOR THE FLEET

We have passed a week of more than usual anxiety and excitement, and nothing has transpired at this writing to afford any relief to our suspense. We must soon, however, be fully informed of the best or the worst. Speculation as to the fate of the brave men who have had the winds and waves for enemies, in addition to their human foes, is therefore worse than useless.

THE NOBLE OLD SOLDIER

The great event of the week is, perhaps, the retirement of our venerable Commander-in-Chief.⁵⁰ Your correspondent will leave to other pens the privilege of accumulating eloquent periods upon the life and services of the noble old soldier, who now lays aside forever the sword which he has worn so worthily. At another time our attention might possibly be concentrated upon the *man*: in this hour of darkness and danger we only care to consider what effect his retirement will have upon the fortunes of his country. After careful examination of all the points of the case, after listening to all the varying comments of the political and military circles of Washington, your correspondent can report but one prevailing sentiment *here*, to wit: Glorious as has been his past career, great as are his military talents, unstained as is his honor, and unimpeached as is his patriotism, it is well for his country that the worn-out and broken-down commander resigns the conduct of this campaign into younger and more vigorous hands. What this war requires is activity, energy, Napoleonic rapidity of movement, blow following blow with lightning quickness and destructiveness; and this we could not expect from a Commander-in-Chief who could hardly turn in his easy chair. All honor to the grand old chieftain, may his sun set in peace and glory! but we must think of nothing now but the terrible struggle for the life of the nation.

OUR YOUNG GENERAL

The demeanor of the young General whom the swift events of this war have called to so high a position, and so vast a responsibility, is singularly modest, unassuming, and therefore admirable. Seldom, indeed, have shoulders so youthful been called upon to assume a load so weighty. Can it be that this man, with the bloom of early manhood fresh on his cheek, realizes that the eyes of half the world are on him, and that his action will have a lasting influence on the fate of the greatest political experiment the ages have yet seen? If he does realize his position, and if he thus can sleep, and wake again to his labor like other men, it can only be because he feels within himself the strength necessary for the work before him. And more than this, you and your readers, Mr. Editor, will agree with me in the firm belief that the hand of Him who has called himself the God of Battles, will be with our young Commander-in-Chief.

OF WHAT OUR ARMY IS MADE

Surely nothing could be more interesting to one who really desires to understand our people, and to comprehend this issue, than a careful study of the various and remarkable elements of which our army is made up. I would call your attention at present only to the European portion. The Irish have long been a portion of the great empire in which the Saxon is the dominant race, and have entered too largely into the substance of our own composite nationality, for us easily to regard them as in any large sense *foreigners*. Here, however, are Frenchmen, Germans, Hungarians, Italians, Swiss, Poles, Russians, representatives from every one of the many nationalities of Europe. We have no better soldiers, for we have here the graduates of the best military schools of Europe, and among others, hundreds, thousands of the men of 1848 and 1849, men who understand far better than do the masses of our own people for what and how important a stake this war is waged.

THE GRAND ISSUE

Your correspondent was conversing, a few days since, with a man whose achievements with pen and sword have given him a transatlantic reputation surpassed by very few. Said he, "We have long been accustomed to look to the United States as the stronghold of constitutional liberty. Her position and prosperity have been one of the most important elements in our strength, while she has been a thorn in the side of our enemies and oppressors. In our misfortunes her open arms have been our refuge. Her fall would set back the progress of the good cause in Europe at least a century. The despots of Europe, with the unerring instincts of kingcraft, have bestowed all their sympathies, and would, if they dared, lend their aid, to the rebellious aristocracy of the South. It therefore becomes the patriots of Europe to come to the assistance of their friend. In fighting the battles of your Government we well know that we are serving in our own great cause."

PROVING OURSELVES WORTHY

This is a brief synopsis of a long conversation; indeed, a fair representation of many such. The scholars, the students, poets, philosophers, historians, of Germany, are in the ranks of the Republic, and their own well-known leaders command them. I know of men with white hair, but with still vigorous and enthusiastic hearts, serving in comparatively humble positions under Blenker and Siegel, who have shaken thrones in Europe in the stormy days gone by.[51] It will be well for them and well for the world if the children of the soil, the men whose birthright is assailed, are as true to the good cause as these battle-scarred heroes from another hemisphere. Disasters may come—indeed, we may reasonably expect that many will come, before our nation has fairly passed its fiery trial—but come what may, let us not be unworthy [of] the brotherhood of the men who in defeat, misfortune, prison, exile, are still true, still faithful to the cause of freedom.

WASHINGTON, 11 NOVEMBER 1861 (PUBLISHED 14 NOVEMBER 1861)
The members of both Houses of Congress are already beginning to assemble, one by one, and will soon be gathering in little *impromptu* caucuses, to discuss the probabilities of the session before them.

Additional regiments are almost daily increasing the strength of our army here, and never have the soldiers been in better spirits, in spite of the discomforts of the season. Our men are rapidly acquiring that steady and patient endurance, which is one of the most valuable characteristics of the trained soldier.

A "FALSE POINT"
Here let me refer briefly to a "false point" frequently made by newspaper men, at home and abroad, with respect to the peculiar characteristics of our Northern soldiers and the Southern rebels. While they are willing to admit the steady courage of Northern blood, they are prone to ascribe to our opponents an overwhelming proportion of fire, dash, and impetuosity. I may be wrong, Mr. Editor, but "I can't see it" in the record of this war. Thus far the desperate daring and the fiery charges have been made from our side. Have the enemy done anything like the cavalry dash of Fairfax Court House, Zagonyi's charge at Springfield, the "cutting out" affair at Pensacola?[52] or have any of their vaunted chiefs died at the head of their advancing columns, as did Lyon and Baker?[53] Verily, our troops have been only too prone to rush upon superior numbers, and have faced altogether too many well-placed batteries. History tells us that the world has seen no more rash and fiery warriors than the Norsemen *par excellence*, and this war will show that the snow and the frost do not settle upon Northern courage.

WHAT MCCLELLAN IS DOING
The foreign officers in our service declare themselves perfectly satisfied with the present achievements of Gen. McClellan. I asked one of them what the new Commander-in-Chief was doing, and received this significant answer:—"The General is *making soldiers* out of the volunteers." The strong bands of army discipline are daily drawing more tightly, and the last vestiges of militia license and volunteer recklessness are rapidly disappearing. The

General is well aware that this campaign will be no child's-play, and he is preparing to meet all its emergencies with the care and foresight which mark him as a great leader.

NO MORE BRIGADIERS
The Cabinet has determined to create no more Brigadier Generals at present, though it is said that a long list of well-known names have been presented for its consideration. The chances and achievements of the field will ere long, indeed already, begin to have their influences upon the changes in the appointment and promotion list. Our long peace has not been well adapted for the development of military genius, but one of the natural results of our present condition must be that wherever that valuable commodity exists it will be brought out, noticed, and assigned to its appropriate rank and power. Such fame begins around the camp fire, and there are already more than a few towards whom the eyes of their fellow-soldiers are turning.

CARNAGE OF OFFICERS
This has been, and will be a terrible war for officers. The loss of the brave unfortunates whose uniforms single them out as targets for riflemen, must be out of all proportion to the numbers engaged. Speaking of losses, a number of tables have been published in the New York papers, professing to give approximate estimates of the slaughter thus far. Now, I have been so placed as to enable me to make many very fair "guesses," and it is a *fact*, that these tables underrate the loss on both sides in almost every case. The real figures can never be known, unless conjectured from the huge aggregate of "missing" on the army rolls, and as for our enemies, whether beaten or victorious, none of them *ever* get killed, if we may trust their lying "reports." All this is folly. Why should we not know the truth in every instance, at least in a proper time? And as for our enemies, we well know that the hearts of an army keep a record of its losses, no matter how the bulletins may falsify. Let us, therefore, know the whole truth, be it triumphant, or be it sad.

WASHINGTON, 2 DECEMBER 1861 (PUBLISHED 5 DECEMBER 1861)
To-day is an important and busy one. The members of both Houses are "gathering themselves" for the commencement of their labors. Willard's, the grand central point until Congress *does* open, is in a terrible state of ferment. Congressmen, Senators, reporters, jobbers, &c., rush to and fro, evidently with very vague ideas of their proper destination for the moment.

The weather is cool, cloudy, and a trifle wintry, and so admirably adapted to "wholesome exercise in the open air," that it of itself suggests the propriety of a military movement.

THE WHITE HOUSE

The city is busy, prosperous, flourishing, given up to the great business of money-making, and being comfortable, attending to its varied selfish interests with the coolest nonchalance. At the White House things are nearly ready for the "season." The new carpets are down, the new curtains are up, the new furniture is in, and sorely were they all needed, that the nation might not look "seedy and out at the elbows" in the house of its Chief Magistrate.

THE BLENKER TROUBLE

Among the events of the week, a prominent one is the trouble with General Blenker, and while it is to be hoped that that efficient and able officer will continue his career of usefulness, it is pleasant to know that his brother German officers are almost unanimous in declaring that their friend and leader is, this time, in the wrong, and that Gen. McClellan has acted well and wisely.[54] This, I am informed, is the view which Gen. Blenker himself begins to take of the matter. If this is true, we may hope that his magnanimous but irritable mind will soon return to its old round of duties.

THE UNOCCUPIED CHAIRS

The last time that I was anything of a regular attendant upon the Congressional debates, was during the closing scenes of the last memorable winter session, when each returning day found me in the Senate gallery. The changes since then are numerous and important. Douglas was then in his place, a great party in himself, and uttering his short and stirring sentences with a consciousness that he was a power in the nation, and that what he said would have its due influence outside, even though he stood alone upon that floor. He has gone forever, nor can the most enthusiastic constituency bid him return to his long-accustomed chair and desk. Will he be there in the spirit? Breckinridge, too, is gone, as Judas did, "to his own place." I heard his last grand effort, before he passed away to hide himself in the outer darkness of treason and rebellion. He should have had the better sense and dignity to go in silence. Mason, the pompous old aristocrat, who won the hearty anathemas of all lookers-on, by the persistence with which he called for the clearing of the galleries, whenever the utterance of some patriotic sentiment drew from our oppressed and aching hearts the slightest token of approval.[55] Crittenden, whose last appeal, during that stormy night session, was so vain an attempt to assuage an angry ocean with a little oil—the good old man, grander now than in the best days of his prime, will still be among us, but not in his old seat in the Senate.

I will not go through the catalogue of changes, but must not leave unmentioned one more vacant chair—the seat of him whose star went down behind the clouds and smoke of that disastrous battle on the banks of the Potomac. The flashing eye, the silver hair, the clear cut and determined mouth of Senator Baker—that remarkable face and voice, all gone; and the laborer for his country's good, the soldier of her best war, has become a martyr to her holiest cause. Johnson, of Tennessee, will be at his post, and I would sit out the debates for a month to hear him give to some other white-feathered traitor such another pulling as that weak old sinner, Joe Lane, received at his hands, at a time when few dared speak out so plainly.[56] On our side, indeed, the changes have not been very numerous, and we shall hear the old familiar voices. It will seem strange, however, to look down and see so many unoccupied chairs, and to think where and why their former occupants have gone.

Washington, 8 December 1861 (published 11 December 1861)
Such is the irregularity of our mails, in the present overworked condition of the Washington Post Office, that I have little faith or hope that this epistle will reach you in time. The mail facilities which would have abundantly sufficed for the "large country village," described by Prince Jerome, are altogether too meagre for a letter-writing population, in town and camp, of near three hundred thousand. Seldom, we may well imagine, was there an army collected, which made such free and constant use of the post. The plainest common soldier seems to think that his friends at home have a right to complain of him if he does not oftener than once a week inform them that he has not yet fallen a victim to the war.

It will be from these letters, if he can get a sufficient number of them, that the future historian of these campaigns will derive his most valuable materials—more piquant, more full of incident, and to the full as "reliable" as the labored official reports on either side.

ROMANCING
Those official reports, by the way, what miracles of perversion and untruth have they thus far proved themselves to be! The mind of the ordinary romance-writer must shrink back bewildered, to find how terribly he is beaten at his own trade by these epauletted novelists North and South. I, however, am not romancing, when I say, that the weather in Washington for

a few days has rendered overcoats a superfluity, and that I sit now at my desk in perfect comfort with the wide grate beside me empty and fireless. All this is a blessing of no small value to the thousands who pass these December nights and mornings on those desolate-looking hills beyond the Potomac. I have been on an exploring expedition "over there," and wandered for a portion of the day among scenes which in former days were tolerably familiar to me. When I first explored that vicinity, while as yet it was a stranger to any sights and sounds but those of peace, I was charmed at the rustic beauty, albeit somewhat out at the elbows, which made the Virginians so fond of the southern shore of the Potomac. To-day, all is changed. The country is bare, stripped, and desolate, and the Virginians know what war means, when they look around them upon the omnipresent traces of his destroying feet.

FLAG PRESENTATION

I wound up my day's work by witnessing the presentation of a handsome flag to the "Harris Light Cavalry," by the distinguished Senator whose name the corps has adopted. The speech of Senator Harris was brief, dignified and earnest, worthy of him, and the reply of Colonel Davies was preeminently soldierly and manly.[57] A second banner was then presented by Judge Davies, of the New-York Supreme Court, with a neat and forcible harangue, replied to by the Lieutenant-Colonel of the regiment.[58] The President, Secretary of War, and a large number of military and civil notables were in attendance. Reviews, parades, inspections, etc., are the order of the day, and with each successive occasion, we hail with delight the evidences of the progress our brave men are making in their study of the great art of war.

REBEL UNEASINESS

Reports from beyond our lines are significant, if reliable, for they all agree in indicating a very much disturbed state of things in the camp of our enemies. The soldiers from the other States of the Confederacy are trembling for the safety of their own homes, and display great uneasiness at being compelled to remain in their present position. These blows on the sea-coast are surely doing their appointed work.

CONGRESSIONAL DISCUSSIONS

Congress has begun its business, but already we can see the indications of trouble to come. All seem to be anxious that the war should go forward with the utmost possible energy, but some have peculiar notions as to the best manner of accomplishing the great end in view. Let us hope that all these conflicting views will be wisely made subservient to that unity of counsel and of action which is so necessary to the best good of the country. So shall the sunlight brighten continually through the clouds that now overshadow us.

Washington, 15 December 1861 (published 19 December 1861)
We have had another week of unparalleled good weather. Glorious winter days, cold without being disagreeable, bright, clear, healthful, with nights of almost unclouded beauty.

how the knowing ones look
Still the troops pour in, still our lines slowly encroach upon positions previously occupied by the enemy. During the whole week, no discouraging return has been made from any division of our vast and widely-scattered army. The President and the Commander-in-Chief look forward to the ripening movements of this somewhat tedious campaign, with bright hope and high expectation. It is said by the knowing ones, that in the last Cabinet meeting opinions of the most encouraging character were freely expressed. It is pleasant to know that those who do comprehend this mysterious and complicated "position," wear bright faces and cheerful hearts, even if we, to whom all is dark and incomprehensible, are unable to see from what quarter of the heavens the sunshine is to come. In spite of all efforts of pretended friends or of open enemies, the confidence of the masses remains unshaken as to the ability and patriotism of those whom they have placed in power.

sustaining the administration
One point has been established beyond controversy, by the action of Congress since my last epistle, to wit:—this Congress sustains the Administration, and there is in it no faction, nor the constituent parts of a faction, with sufficient numbers and power to seriously embarrass the action of the Executive. As to the President, he is firm as a rock in the course indicated by his Message, and as he expected, the people over the whole country have already sent forward their cordial approval and "God speed you!"

our foreign relations
Your readers would give themselves no manner of uneasiness as to our foreign relations, could they see with what philosophical ease every apparent cloud is examined, and its portents interpreted for the best, by our clear-headed and far-sighted Secretary of State. Still, no man can deny that it will require admirable management to prevent the untoward occurrences of the last fortnight from leaving behind them much of that irritation and vindic-

tiveness of feeling, out of which future difficulties and misunderstandings are so prone to grow.

MRS. LINCOLN'S RECEPTIONS

Mrs. Lincoln has commenced holding her Saturday afternoon "receptions," and they are well and largely attended by the brilliant crowds drawn here by the joint attractions of the army and the Congress. The "season" has hardly opened, nor will it until after the holidays, though a good deal of social gaiety begins to make itself manifest in our suddenly created "circles." There are those who grimly condemn anything that looks like systematic and premeditated enjoyment, in view of the sad condition of our public affairs, and the perpetual danger of so many of our best and best beloved. They are bad philosophers:—we will not say, "Let us eat and drink, for to-morrow we die;" but "Sufficient unto the day is the evil thereof," and our mental and bodily health will be best served by throwing off, at times, some portion of our load of anxiety and care.

CONGRESS AND THE ICONOCLASTS

The debates of Congress are well attended, but thus far, have not been marked by any display of more than good business ability, and a good deal of right-down pluck and determination when treating of war matters. Some of the members seem laboring to "talk themselves clear" on the question of immediate emancipation, striving to convince themselves and others that they are beginning to comprehend the great facts of our condition. Your paper is not the proper medium for personal animadversion, or it would be pleasant to trace out a few of the contradictory "Will-o'-the-Wisp" directions, in which sundry of our talking men are trying to reach the same profitless end—their own personal aggrandizement.

There are men, Mr. Editor, who are *constitutionally* in the opposition, and whose only normal condition is that of an assailant: Iconoclasts by nature, bound to break the image before them, even if their own hands have helped to raise it to its place. Such men are useful, and fill an important place in the political economy of our institutions; but the Congressional market is at present a trifle overstocked with them. Still, it may be that their work is not yet complete. I steadfastly believe that nothing was created in vain, and am waiting, with a faith a little edged with curiosity, to see to what good purpose such men as ———, and ———, and their associate agitators, can be turned.

OUR YOUNG GENERAL

It is perhaps unfortunate for General McClellan, that his plan of the campaign—we presume that of course he *has* a plan—does not, in its development, bring him now and then brilliantly out before the people. The President and Secretary Cameron, his constant advisers, as they are his superiors in rank, share the credit of the war as a whole, and his subordinate generals will absorb the stray bits of glory in the minor operations. The "great General" must do something himself soon, or people will begin to say—"how? and if so, *why?*"

CHAPTER TWO

1862

WASHINGTON, 13 JANUARY 1862 (PUBLISHED 16 JANUARY 1862)
Now that the latest advices received by the State Department from England have relieved us from all anxiety on the subject of a foreign war, we as a people may take a long breath, and look around upon the very peculiar facts of our position.

At home we seem to be hesitating upon the perilous edge of great events. Some may smile, and tell us that the condition of things has become chronic, and that they despair of any advance *beyond* the edge; but those who read the signs of the times aright see differently. We must soon hear of the success or failure of the greatest naval expeditions we have yet sent out, and we are told that upon that success or failure hang momentous results of strategy in the further prosecution of the war.

We are assured, by all those in the confidence of the Executive, that these expeditions are but parts of the great flank movements called for by the plan of the campaign, whose completion is essential to the safety of any large demonstrations in front. Should they be successful, other heavy blows must follow, with reasonable speed, or the nation will indeed have ground to accuse our military magnates of trifling with the wishes and expectations of a whole people, and falsifying their own repeated declarations.

Still, deep as must be our anxiety for some days, it cannot be denied that the position, condition and evident power of our army, are in a high degree inspiriting and cheering. The severe fight at Dranesville has proved the superior discipline and soldiership of our troops;[1] the news from the West tells us of the completion of the effectiveness of the army of the Mississippi; and along the whole length of our tremendous line of battle all things seem nearly in readiness for the giant contraction which is to "crush the rebellion."

The people, as a general thing, have become nervous and feverish with long watching and waiting. They have strained their eyes so long in vain for the light and smoke of a great battle, and are angry only to see the motionless white tents of the army of the Potomac. The long suspense must now speedily be broken. The roads of Virginia must soon be proved *not* impassable by the armies of the Union.

In the meantime Congress, that inexplicable conglomerate, seems slowly awakening to the financial necessities of the position, and spurred on by the stern common sense of the moneyed community, promises to forget its hereditary dread of taxation, and come forward to the assistance of the exhausted Treasury.

Our advices from Europe, too, would seem to indicate such a reaction in our favor as must, for a time at least, relieve us from all fear of further foreign complications. Both in England and on the Continent, there seems a growing disposition to do us justice—a popular movement in behalf of our cause, which is of the last importance to us at this stage of our great national tragedy.

Looking then upon things as they really are, acknowledging all the sad difficulties of our position, who shall yet dare to despair of the Republic? An hour of trial has come, to be sure, one of the dark hours that are inevitable in every life, personal or national, but have we not seen darker ones? I watched the return from Manassas, on that dark and gloomy day, when "all, even honor" seemed to have been thrown away in the mad panic of the hour. Shall we who remember the setting of *that* gloomy day, see any cause for desponding in the present proud and strong position of the nation? Rather let us wait patiently until we see the white tents of the army of the Potomac fall before the word of command, when the flood-gates are opened before the torrent which must soon pass over Eastern Virginia. "The night is far spent and the day is at hand."

WASHINGTON, 19 JANUARY 1862 (PUBLISHED 23 JANUARY 1862)
The last week has been like the others, the cruel hoax of the Mississippi Expedition scarcely constituting a noticeable feature. Now, however, we *know* that our patient waiting is not to endure much longer. The news *must* speedily reach us of the success or failure of important military movements. Not less important must be the action of the Legislature. Wise provisions for the future supply of the Treasury would be worth a battle at this juncture. The Committee assure their friends that they have almost completed their momentous task, and that the system they have framed will be speedily laid before Congress for its approval. Should the common sense of the nation decide that they have been equal to the emergency, the wheels of the national finances, so nearly blocked, will again run smoothly and rapidly as before.

OUR CONGRESS

Of this Congress, as a whole, and its daily treatment of the subjects brought before it, there is very little to be said. It seems impossible for some men—even when the part assigned them by circumstances is that of the patriot—to forget their natural character of politician and demagogue. The pressure of public and private sorrow may yet do, for this portion of our public men, what no thought of our present necessities has yet accomplished. It may be that in the fiery furnace, through which we are passing, much of the national and personal dross will be burned away, and the body politic relieved of the devouring "cankers of a calm world and a long peace."

CORRUPTION

Speaking of corruption, Mr. Editor, if your readers will bear with me, I would like to say a few words on a subject to which I have given some attention, with good opportunities of observation. The universal opinion of the corruptions in Washington, at the beginning of this Administration, was not in any respect an exaggeration. The tone of morals, public and private, was lamentably low. The swarms of gamblers, lurking around their gilded and but half-hidden dens, were all here as described, and are *still here*. I have visited more than one of their "banks" to see if it could be true that men, whom I had been taught to reverence, passed their time over the red checks and the green baize. The other provocatives and incentives to vice have been provided with terrible profusion. Why should anything be concealed from the people? Should they not know to what a place they send men of like passions and weaknesses with themselves? This was the condition of things twelve months ago;—to a certain extent all is the same yet, outside of the Government itself, though a large share of the worst of our population has been drained off by the Secession exodus.

As to the Government and its functionaries, a great change is manifest. In proportion to the amount of money handled, the bribery and corruption is as nothing compared to the past. Government employees are generally of a better moral character—partially dormant patriotism has been aroused in men who, under other circumstances, might have been no better than their predecessors—and it is the deliberate opinion of those who are best informed, that most departments of the Government are administered with a degree of correctness and honesty, if not wisdom, which forms an encouraging contrast to the old order of things. The present generation of politicians must pass away, however, before the arrival of that era, so dearly longed for by all true friends of their country, when money will be of no use in urging an important measure through Congress. It will long be necessary for public opinion to apply its roughest surgery of knife and caustic, before we can hope for that purity in whose presence alone there is safety for the life of such a nationality as our own.

HEALTH OF THE CITY

To return once more to local matters. The gravest apprehensions are entertained for the health of camp and city during the remainder of winter and the spring months. Already we have sufficient cause for alarm, in the number of dangerous and contagious diseases which are making their appearance. The "camp measles" has, in several cases, assumed a malignant type, and if it should begin to spread in that form, woe to the army and the town. Small-pox, though not uncommon, especially in its milder form, is checked by the general care taken to secure thorough vaccination. The triumph of science over the once dreaded scourge seems to be very nearly complete. Not so, however, with the long list of fevers and other complaints so easily developed by this damp, warm atmosphere. We can but look forward with anxiety, and many are making their preparations for a trip North immediately on the return of warm weather, or sooner, if the condition of things here demands it. So far, the health of the army, owing to the care exercised by the health officers, for good food, clothing and quarters, has been unparalleled in history, but who shall say how long this state of things can be made to continue?

THE CITY OVERCROWDED

Our city is overcrowded; never before was rent or board so high, or room so scarce. The proposed reduction by Congress of the salaries of all Government employees, will be a terrible blow to hundreds, in view of the present cost of living. A salary of $1,200 is no more now than $800 was a year ago, and if a further reduction is made, it will go very hard with many a struggling family. The cool barbarity with which Congressmen thus attempt to replace the sums they have wasted in many extravagances, by a paltry pittance wrung from helpless employees, is worthy of men who have sat for six weeks during a period like this, with a stricken nation begging them to *act*, and can as yet point to no one achievement worthy [of] their station or their trust.

OTHER MATTERS

The abolition of the franking privilege is a step in a better direction, unless all the virtue of it is taken away by the cash compensation proposed by

Senator Sherman.[2] This and other hoary abuses must be allowed to fall, if the country is really to have faith in the unselfish patriotism of its representatives.

The President seems to retain his usual health and spirits, and labors on as indefatigably as ever. Socially, Washington is doing its best to make itself merry, and seems almost to succeed, in spite of its external and internal fogs.

WASHINGTON, CA. 3 FEBRUARY 1862 (PUBLISHED 6 FEBRUARY 1862)
Will your readers think me an optimist if I give as my deliberate conclusion, from all that I see and hear in Washington, that "all is well," or at least, that all is tending in the best possible direction? "All this I do most steadfastly believe"—believe that the army is doing just what, under the circumstances, it had best be doing, and that the plans which army and navy are serving are the best, most comprehensive, most certain of desirable results, which our strange position admits of. No doubt the patience of the people is sorely tried; no doubt they are weary with long watching, and some are beginning to think this night of ours an eternal one; but if they will imagine for a moment that they do not know all, that they do not from the outside see all that is accomplished in the mysterious interior of this complicated machine of government, they may perhaps be convinced that more is done, and that more can and *will* be done, than appears to their surveying.

SIGNS OF GOOD
There are many signs which breathe encouragement, but they cannot and must not be put in the papers. One thing seems to be from time to time brought out more and more clearly by the changing events of the day: those to whom we have confided our destinies are faithful to their trust, and labor on earnestly and untiringly in their respective spheres, with as much unselfish integrity as is possible for human nature—a thousand times more than we have been accustomed to expect from our public men, for many a long day.

UNJUST DENUNCIATION
Speaking of the faithfulness of many of our leading men, do we not often forget, in our hot haste to denounce corruption, what a terrible thing is the injustice which deprives a man causelessly of that honor and reputation which is dearer than life? I have known cases, of men sent home in disgrace and ruin after long, severe and self-sacrificing public service, on the strength of accusations brought against them by personal and political

enemies. There can be [no] doubt that every such fall weakens the republic dangerously. We should be careful of the honor of those in power, chary of believing aught to their discredit, even if we add to this a more vengeful bitterness in punishing the undeniably guilty.

OUR VISITORS

The city is still crowded with visitors, and many, ladies as well as gentlemen, brave all the horrors of rainstorms and Virginia mud, to take a fleeting glance through the fog at the white tents which they hope will so soon be struck. We are sometimes surprised at the strength of the conviction among our Northern visitors that an advance is to be made at an early day, and wonder if the impression continues as vivid after they have gone the rounds of the fortifications through the mud.

A SIGHT TO SEE

A parade of cavalry or artillery now-a-days is a sight to see; the poor jaded horses, literally covered and crusted with mud, the damp, splashed, uncomfortable looking riders, the "caked" wheels, furnish an idea of the least attractive side of soldier life. There is no romance, no glitter, nothing but the sad and suggestive *brown* of the winter campaign in the Old Dominion.

SUMMARY JUSTICE

Still, we do not hear of any serious augmentation of disease in the camps, and the various sanitary regulations are enforced with far more efficiency than formerly. Speaking of these, reminds me of a case in point. It is the custom to destroy the stock in trade of any man found guilty of selling liquor to soldiers, and yesterday I was witness to a most rigorous enforcement of this just and necessary regulation at a dingy looking corner grocery on F street. The gaily painted and gilded pipes, with their humbler fellows, the common casks, tumbled together in the gutter, discharging their odoriferous contents through their battered heads. The forlorn-looking owner stood with his hands in his pocket, surveying the devastation, and evidently thinking it rather a wholesale penalty for a retail offence.

WASHINGTON, 9 FEBRUARY 1862 (PUBLISHED 13 FEBRUARY 1862)

The week has been one of much animation, and has added several highly important points to our teeming record.

WESTERN VICTORIES

The fighting in the West has placed us in a very advantageous position, as regards the future operations of that campaign, while our success has carried dismay to the hearts of the rebel leaders. They find themselves forced to assume the offensive, and to do it successfully, or surrender Kentucky and East Tennessee, and with them the "keys of success." From the coast we have, it is true, little besides large promises, whose fulfilment, though strongly probable, is not yet made certain.

RELIEF OF MCCLELLAN

One of the most important acts of the Administration has been the highly sensible and really necessary course of the President, in relieving General McClellan of a portion of his too cumbrous responsibilities.[3] The brave young commander will doubtless find full scope for all his powers in the proper management of the great department confided to him, and must feel a very pleasant sensation of relief at being no longer in any way responsible for the errors of men a thousand miles removed from his guidance and direction. We are reforming the palpable errors and absurdities of our old military establishment, if we are doing nothing more.

OUR FINANCES

The action of Congress on the "legal tender" business, whatever the friends or enemies of the measure may say, has assuredly launched us on a sea of indefinite expansion, which has no other shore than financial ruin, unless a better one be speedily found for it by the success of our armies. This is a point which few men care to argue or contradict. Now must come, in speedy and efficient succession, those other measures which are required to sustain the credit of the Republic.

CLOUDS

Across the water there are clouds larger than any man's hand, and, to tell the truth, they have occasioned more than a little uneasiness in the minds of our rulers; and those who have hitherto seemed to see the farthest seem to fear the most. Again and again do we hear such expressions as this, "To be sure, an European war must come, it *will* come, sooner or later, but if they will only give us time, *time!*" A little more time, well used, and there will be no further danger that the expected strife can come in the shape of transatlantic recognition of the Confederacy, for there will be none worth the recognizing.

THE GRAND PARTY

Among the social events of the past week has been the grand party at the President's House.[4] It was not a "ball," for there was no dancing, but in the eyes of your correspondent, it was an exceedingly brilliant and distinguished assembly. Seldom, indeed, on this Continent, have so many men of mark been gathered at one time under one roof. The daily papers have given tolerably full accounts of it, omitting, as usual, the finest toilettes among the ladies. It was almost strictly "official," few, indeed, obtaining admission, who had no official claim to an invitation. Whatever some may think of such festivities at this crisis, more would have murmured if the President and his lady allowed the winter to pass without contributing their share to the social life of the National Capital.

THE VIRGINIA ROADS

The weather has been decidedly better, for a few days, and we are looking forward with high hopes for the coming of [illegible words] shall repave the roads of Virginia for the feet of our advancing army. It has been a gloomy time in camp of late, and the soldiers will hail with exultation these few brief hours of fleeting sunshine.

THE INDIANA SENATOR

The expulsion of Senator Bright has hardly left a ripple of sensation.[5] We are too busy with weightier matters to pause long over the disgrace of one man, right or wrong. The course of Senator Harris, of your State, has occasioned some remark. Few men would have ventured to take such a stand, even if sure that they were in the right; and no man can question the upright motives of the Senator from New-York.

WASHINGTON, 17 FEBRUARY 1862 (PUBLISHED 20 FEBRUARY 1862)

A host of great events has crowded the few brief days since my last. The victories achieved by the Union forces, by land and water, are of value, not only for their direct bearing upon the military success of this prolonged campaign, but also because they set the Government and its war policy in the true light before the people. The long delay, the careful preparation, the patient waiting for "the inevitable hour," are all at last vindicated; and the dullest can see that the President and his advisers have been right, and those who assailed them *wrong*. No man now asks, "Why was not all this done before?" for all feel that it could not; and those who look into the future begin to prophesy a time when thoughtful men will look back with wonder at the great achievements of this strange, eventful year.

THE REBELLION PASSED ITS CLIMAX

The President is right in saying, through the proclamation of Secretary Stanton, that the great rebellion has passed the climax of its energy and power, and is visibly on the wane.[6] And well for us is it that it is true, and that it is true *now*. This is the important fact which will stand between us and further transatlantic complications, when no other consideration could have much longer restrained the greed and jealousy of the grim despotisms who desire the downfall of the Republic.

OUR GRAND SUCCESSES

It may not be out of place to review our military successes, and to see what is their real sum. Their importance is not to be measured by the numbers of the opposing forces, by the dead, the wounded, or the prisoners. In a military point of view, we have done far more than appears to the superficial observer.

On the North Carolina coast, Gen. Burnside has turned the right flank of the enemy's central column at Manassas, while their left flank is menaced by the movements in the West.[7] So far as that position is concerned, they are reduced to a point where only a great, and now almost impossible victory, can save them from destruction. The day is at hand when the record of our disgrace at Bull Run will be overspread by the glory of our success at Manassas.

As to the West, we must bear in mind that Price, at Springfield, or wherever else his will-o'-wisp array may next be heard from, is not contending for Missouri, now hopelessly and irredeemably our own, but for the staunchly rebellious State of Arkansas; and that in his precipitate retreat, he acknowledges his want of power to keep the seat of war north of the Missouri line a day longer than the development of our own plans will allow.[8] At Bowling Green, Fort Donelson and Columbus, the prize at stake has not been Kentucky, but Tennessee;[9] and the reduction of those positions involves the rescue of a State largely loyal from the withering grip of the conspiracy. There may yet be some hard fighting in Middle and West Tennessee, but the fate of the Mississippi valley, as far down as middle Alabama, is sealed so soon as Buell crosses the Tennessee river with his central column.[10]

The gallant dash of our gunboat fleet up the Tennessee and into Alabama, has struck a panic to the very heart of the rebellion, and the Stars and Stripes have been spread in a region where many men feared they would never shine again. Even while I write, we may hope that news is on the way of further successes, adding to the completeness of this portion of our plan of operations.

HAVE WE "A PLAN"?

And does any sane man now doubt that the War Department "has a plan"— a scientific, comprehensive, masterly combination, equal to its objects, and in its completion sure of the utter demolition of the frail temple of the Confederacy? Sketched in outline long ago by the trained and experienced genius of Scott; completed in its details by the President, and the wise men who have been his councillors; and carried into triumphant effect by the skill, daring and perseverance of our generals and our citizen soldiery. Let no one hereafter vaunt the superior generalship of the rebels; not only have they been outnumbered and outfought by our soldiers; they have been *outgeneralled.* The science and skill, as well as the preponderance of physical force, is on the side of the Government, and the delusive halo of undeserved reputation has faded from the brows of many whom we were once disposed to praise and fear unduly.

GENERAL MCCLELLAN AGAIN

I regret to see that many are disposed to regard the late change in the nature of General McClellan's responsibilities in the light of a *quasi* disgrace of that able and meritorious officer, and to speak as if the confidence of the President in his ability and energy had deteriorated. Nothing could be further from the truth; the war office has issued no general order upon this point, and we are, therefore, left somewhat in the dark; but your correspondent is persuaded that the good of the whole service, and especially the efficiency of the vitally important Department of the Potomac, were alone consulted in making whatever changes have been thought advisable. General McClellan has occupied an anomalous and most trying position, without any opportunity for the display of those more dashing and brilliant qualities which he unquestionably possesses, and which, more than any profundity of military science, endear the name of a successful soldier to the hearts of his countrymen. He has been compelled to confine himself to the intense and overwearying labors of his station at the centre of power, while other men, of less capacity, win undying honor in carrying out his well judged and carefully matured orders. Sooner or later his own time will come, and we shall see if in active field operations he does not regain, and far surpass, the enthusiasm of popular confidence which hailed his first assumption of supreme command. At all events, let no one imagine, from any newspaper canard, that he has been "superseded" or disgraced, or that he is anything else than the senior Major General of the Army, commanding its central and most important department, and the constant military advisor of the constitutional Commander-in-Chief.

SECRETARY STANTON

The new Secretary of War continues to win golden opinions by his energy, efficiency, and conscientiousness. He has won, to a most remarkable degree, the confidence of the whole people. They believe him to be in earnest, *terribly* in earnest, and that he will be the strong right hand of the President. God grant that he be spared to the end of the mighty task to which he has put his nervous and patriotic hand.

CONGRESS AND ITS WORK

Congress does not change for the better, nor much for the worse, and we may hope to see, in some time, if not in due time, the result of its long cogitation upon the national finances. Perhaps, however, we are wrong to be impatient with our representatives, for they too have a doubtful and serious campaign before them, in the proper care and management of the National credit and resources. They do well to beware of haste, for they are now laying the broad foundation of a system of taxation hitherto unknown to them or their constituents, and upon the justice and equity of which will depend much of its success in creating a revenue, and restoring the damaged credit of the nation. The "legal tender" bill but furnishes a bridge upon which the Treasury can cross the gulf of bankruptcy to the firm ground of just and general taxation.

WASHINGTON, CA. 3 MARCH 1862 (PUBLISHED 6 MARCH 1862)

We have had a week of strong excitements. The storms, the movements of the army, and the endless series of sensation reports, have kept us on the *qui vive*. The closing, for the time being, of the accustomed avenues of information, has given tenfold activity to the tongue of Madam Rumor.

MOVEMENTS OF THE ARMY

While it would not be well for me to write, or for you to publish, any definite information as to the position or proposed movements of the army, you may rest assured that up to *this date* all is going on well—that the reports of battles in Missouri and at Nashville are false. Buell is not cut up, Banks has had no "desperate engagement on the Upper Potomac," Sickles still lives, and as a rule, you may deny all the other flying reports.[11] The public thirst for war news from Washington will be unsatiated for several days, as the injunctions of prudent silence are imperative. The soldiers are in high spirits, and impatient for action, the roads are steadily improving, the weather for several days has been excellent, and we look forward to the future with bright hopes.

PERSONAL

The President is looking somewhat better, the all-absorbing interest of this hour of action serving to draw his thoughts away from his bereavement.[12] I have heard it said that the loss of a little of his usual good nature has rendered his subordinates more than ever anxious to succeed in promptly fulfilling his orders. If so, it is not a bad idea.

Gen. Cameron is still in the city, and numerous surmises are made as to the causes of his delay. He is not staying here for nothing, of course, and his known ability in prosecuting any plans he may conceive, renders him the centre of much curious interest.

Please deny, emphatically, the reports of the failing health of Secretary Stanton. It is wicked to mock the sympathies of a whole people by spreading these rumors of his sufferings. In conversation with a friend, night before last, the Secretary himself referred to this matter, asserting that he never was in better health in his life, his late attack of vertigo being directly traceable to a close room, the gas from a hot coal-stove, and a too long strain at his work. Every other man you meet knows how soon the Cabinet is to be changed, and who are to go out and in. Your correspondent has failed to see so much as yet, though we know not what a day may bring forth.

The strife for the vacant places on the Supreme Bench still goes forward, but the knowing ones are beginning to fix upon a favorite. General Hunter is now here, but will shortly set out to resume command of his expeditionary army, now at Fort Scott.[13]

A LOOK AT FORT DONELSON PRISONERS

While in Illinois, a few days since, your correspondent had a good look at several trains full of rebel prisoners from Fort Donelson. Clothed in butternut-colored homespun, of every imaginable cut and style, and not over-particular in their care of their persons, they certainly presented a forlorn appearance, though evidently very good material for soldiers. The result of many conversations with them is the conviction that their utter and almost incredible ignorance, and their lifelong prejudices, form an all-sufficient excuse for the part these deluded men have taken. They appeared utterly bewildered by the good treatment they received, and by the evidences all around them of a civilization, comfort, and wealth, far superior to their own. Many were still angry and defiant, the Mississippians especially; but the major part, including the greater number of Kentuckians and Tennesseeans, appeared almost satisfied with the turn affairs have taken. These men, after a few months at the North, will go back to their former homes as a sort of political missionaries, carrying with them a large stock of new ideas and enlarged views. For the officers, little can be said; some of them were but a few removes above their rank and file in point of intelligence and information, while others have no such excuse for their treason.

Generally, affairs in the West are looking pretty well, though there, as elsewhere, there is a strong feeling in favor of a general bankrupt law, that old scores may be wiped out, and all men set free to turn their unfettered strength to the work of restoring the nation to its lost prosperity. I hope that, in my next, I may have more stirring events to record.

WASHINGTON, 17 MARCH 1862 (PUBLISHED 20 MARCH 1862)
A week ago to-day a panic reigned in this Capital, only surpassed by that which followed the reverse at Bull Run. The best military authorities, the soundest and most far-seeing judges of the position, felt most keenly the extent of our disaster, and the real danger of the moment. The danger is over, passed like the shadow of a driving cloud; but let your readers, for a moment, try and grasp the fact that the ruin of our fleet came upon us like lightning out of a clear sky, that by that one blow, *if completed*, a dozen proposed movements became impossible, and that we could offer no important impediment to the advance of a destroyer which seemed of itself powerful enough to turn the left flank of the Army of the Potomac, and hold Washington at its mercy.[14] We knew, too, that the opposing hosts were in motion—how could we know why or where? It required no very vivid fancy to draw a dark, and by no means improbable, picture of swift-coming disaster. Rumor, for the moment, held her tongue, though only to loose it with tenfold activity the next morning.

A REAL SCARE
People try now to deny the scare, but it really was a scare, and a very bad one, with good cause. Strange stories floated about the streets, of the monster mass of iron, like the roof of a house, impenetrable, as safe as Achilles, and as terrible, before which our proudest frigates sank, fled, or surrendered, and upon which the iron balls of our columbiads crumbled like clay, or from which they glanced like peas. Then came another dispatch from Fortress Monroe, "The *Ericsson* is here;"[15] and people wondered if the little, queer looking thing described by those who had seen her, could make any decent opposition to her giant opponent. After that came the intensely exciting details of that few hours' desperate struggle, with its triumphant termination, and then, in quick succession, the news of the taking of the Potomac batteries, the victory in Arkansas, the evacuation of Manassas,

the successes on the Mississippi, and the discovery that the "shell" of the rebellion was forever broken, leaving a meagre show of kernel to be pounced upon by our advancing armies.[16]

A NEW ERA IN WARFARE

Pardon me if I dwell too long on what has been to many, the most exciting and interesting week of the war. Let us, moreover, take a note of this, that the fight between the *Ericsson* (her *best* name) and the *Merrimac*, has opened for the whole world a new era in the annals of naval warfare. The cumbrous and costly three-deckers, with their hundred guns, and their swarms of fighting men, are as useless as would be the triremes of Marc Anthony, for a few dwarf-like *Ericssons* would destroy an armada of them between sunrise and sunset, with little loss to themselves, beside the waste of powder and ball. Even land-fortifications, wherever intended to guard a coast, must partake in the changes brought about by that four hours' contest.

Nor will the lessons of Fort Henry and Fort Donelson be lost on our future Vaubans and Todlebens.[17] As the creation of American inventive skill and genius, though infamously misdirected, we may even point to the *Merrimac*, and tell the Old World to read another of the many lessons the New has taught it. Alas for us, if our enemies have another *Merrimac* in the Gulf of Mexico, for we have no *Ericsson* there.

THE NAME TO BE USED

You see that I persist in giving our iron-clad deliverer the name it is best known by, for its inventor deserves that to all time the history of that fight should preserve the memory of him to whom our great relief is due. Was there not something providential in that whole affair? First we were allowed to learn, by bitter and costly experience—the only way our people ever will acquire wisdom—that our old navy, with all its swiftness and beauty, was to avail us nothing in the great contest before us, and then, the lesson being well impressed upon the national mind, it is further enforced, with a wonderful explanation, by the opportune arrival of the only relief which could have come!

THE DESOLATED DISTRICT

The other day I took advantage of a few hours' sunshine, to try a swift drive through a portion of the Virginia shore which was, from its extreme beauty, a favorite haunt of mine before the beginning of the war. The army had already moved and no long rows of white tents relieved the brown barrenness of the deserted and devastated hillsides. On every commanding elevation frowned the guns of the batteries, but they looked down on a ruined and desolate land. Fences, trees, the signs of cultivation, the cheerful sights and sounds of rural life, had disappeared, and everywhere, stamped deep into the very soil, were the traces of the iron feet of War. In fact, a space of country as large as several New-York counties has been wholly or partially ruined. Between the Potomac and Manassas, through all the widely extended lines, and probably for many miles beyond the latter point, the ruin is complete, and the land is deserted, and the evil effects, with more or less rigor, are felt "through all the regions round about."

The people of the Cotton States may well praise the selfish and perfidious wisdom of their leaders, in making the border States the theatre of a war for which *they* are responsible. Their cunning has been of little avail, however, for the hour is rapidly drawing near, when the dregs of the cup of which Virginia and Missouri have drunk, will be drained by the dark conspirators and fierce, fanatical traitors, of the erring commonwealths where Cotton is King, and men forget all other fealty and duty.

WASHINGTON, 24 MARCH 1862 (PUBLISHED 27 MARCH 1862)
The past week has been one of excited expectation. We have been waiting and listening for reports of army action at every point of the great field, and those who should know most about the matter, assure us that, in a few days, a portion of the cloud of secresy will be lifted from around the operations of our troops.

GENERAL MCCLELLAN'S POSITION
Perhaps the history of this country does not afford us a parallel picture to the one now presented by the General commanding the Army of the Potomac. He has been a popular idol, and a numerous and enthusiastic band of admirers still cling to him, avowing their unshaken faith in his ability, courage, and patriotism. It is true that the patience of the people has been sorely tried, and many of General McClellan's assailants seem to make out a tolerably strong case, but it is at least possible that, after all, the General may be right, and the civilians wrong. At all events, he has now put himself on his trial before the military world. With the largest, best equipped, and most thoroughly disciplined army ever commanded by any General on this side of the Atlantic; with abundant artillery, pontoon trains, flotilla, and all the most valued appliances of modern warfare, he is entering a campaign in a country the best adapted for successful defence of any on the continent, and which will be defended by all the power which the remaining strength of the Confederacy can possibly bring to bear. He will meet Generals who have learned the science of war in the same schools

and from the same masters as himself—leading soldiers of the same race and lineage with his own, and who will oppose to his superior equipment the advantages of position, of fortifications, and a thorough knowledge of the country they are fighting in.

Those who imagine that all the military advantages are on our own side, and that the victory will necessarily be an easy one, have made an error which could not fail to be fatal, were it shared in by our generals. Moreover, the enemy are now making a stand which will, if unsuccessful, be *their last*, and they know it, and will be very likely to cling to their positions with the tenacity of despair. Therefore, I say, that a full and fair test awaits the movement of General McClellan, and if he victoriously surmounts the obstacles before him, he can afford to laugh to scorn the malice of his detractors. Should he fail, by his own fault, or otherwise, it would not be easy to build again the fallen fabric of his military fame.

PERSONAL LIFE IN WASHINGTON

The Secretary of War still stands at his difficult post, as full of energy as ever, though his friends are fond of saying, with ominous shakes of the head, "he works too hard—he *works* too hard." It is to be hoped that this patriotic and popular Cabinet officer will not forget the value of that life, whose continuance adds so much to the strength of the Administration.

The President has recovered much of his old equanimity and cheerfulness; and certainly no one who saw his constant and eager application to his arduous duties, would imagine for a moment that the man carried so large a load of private grief, in addition to the cares of a nation. His youngest boy is beginning to run around the house again, but, no doubt, sadly misses his former playfellow.[18]

The visitors come and go in a still undiminished stream, and by their ever-changing influence keep up a certain round of gayeties, though the uniforms are no longer so brilliantly numerous at our social gatherings. The shoulder straps have met with great success here this winter, and the number of weddings has been beyond parallel. Strange, that the queens of the social world should be so easily dazzled by a little glitter.

THE NEW VITALITY

The Southern element in Washington opens its eyes in undisguised amazement at the palpable evidences everywhere of the presence of a new vitality—Northern enterprise. The city is revolutionized—socially, financially, politically. There is more of life, more bustle, more activity. The last thing I saw, as I came up the street this morning, was a freshly-posted placard, announcing a newly-established line of regular stages for *Manassas*. If this sort of thing follows the path of the Union armies, it will be the best sort of a blessing to the South if they are speedily and utterly beaten. The secessionists in Washington are a blue set of people. They cannot read the papers, for the double-leaded lines of small-caps tell only of the successes of the National arms. They cannot go about the streets without passing and repassing under the Stars and Stripes, hearing regimental bands play national airs, and seeing all around them the proofs of Northern triumph. If they go to church, they hear earnest prayers for the country to which their hearts tell them they are traitors; and hearty thanksgivings for the glorious victories which the God of Battles has given to his servants the soldiers of the Union. And even in the stillness of the night their dreams are disturbed by the heavy tramp of marching men, and the rumbling wheels of cannon, whose lips will open not to comfort *them*. "Well, let them *grind* over it!"

WASHINGTON, 31 MARCH 1862 (PUBLISHED 3 APRIL 1862)
It is merely expressing a truism to say that the only real vitality of our Government, now or at any other period of our history, consists in the confidence and goodwill of the people. Our armies, at present, are only an expression of the will of the people that the rebellion shall be put down, and our Treasury, sustaining successfully a drain unprecedented in the history of this new world, is a constantly varying measure of the popular confidence in the permanence of the Government. No patriot can, therefore, look with indifference upon a course of events which has placed one important department, the Navy, in a most disadvantageous light before the people. Some of the most brilliant achievements of the war have been made by our gallant tars, or with their indispensable assistance, but we have received our latest and severest reverses on the water, and nowhere else are we now menaced with such terrible dangers at this moment. The merchants and underwriters of New-York, Boston and Philadelphia tremble in their counting-rooms, as they think of the havoc which might, with impunity, be made upon our commerce by a few mail-clad pirates, while every breeze that blows from the South brings rumors of iron monsters now nearly ready to follow the fearful example of the *Merrimac*.

THE "ISLAND NO. TENS"
Those who declared that the "back of the rebellion was broken" by the fall of Fort Donelson forgot, or failed to foresee, that there might be "Island No. Tens" between our armies and complete success, and that we, as well

as our opponents, might be called to eat the bitter bread of reverse and defeat.[19] Rumors to the contrary not withstanding, it may be that we shall march onward to the Gulf in an unbroken career of triumph, but it would be unwise to accustom our minds to any such extravagant and improbable expectations. The army of the Potomac, for instance, is advancing to a struggle of unknown bitterness and duration, and every battle may not be like the fight near Winchester.[20] Your correspondent, as you may see, has been made gloomy by watching the departure of our gallant men, and shaking hands with scores of friends who go to leave their bones, it may be, on the treason-polluted soil of the Old Dominion.

LOOKING WELL ON PARADE

As I sit here writing, a fine-looking regiment of lancers are passing under my window, "bound over the river." These are the fellows whom one of our enlightened Congressmen described in debate as "fellows who go ridin' round the streets, carryin' a red rag on the end of a stick." The opinions of military men are divided as to their practical utility, and they are by no means popular in the army. They certainly *look well on parade*.

A QUEER RULE

A curious rule has been made in the Treasury, in the redemption of its demand notes—any note from which a portion has been torn, though all the signatures and numbers should be perfect, is paid for *pro rata*, the supposed fraction being deducted, and the note then destroyed—the reason being an insane fear that out of many torn patches some indefatigable Jew may make and present a *whole one*. The day of funny things is evidently still with us. The new notes, legal tender, will begin to make their appearance this week, much to the joy of our long-deferred and patient creditors.[21] They will present a similar appearance to the old notes, with the exception of being sealed, and bearing a small inscription on their backs to the intent that they are receivable for all dues to Government except duties on imports.

THE WEATHER

The weather for the past week has been excellent, well adapted to facilitate military movements of any kind, but last night we had a smart little snowstorm, and to-day it is raining. This must be the last effort of winter, and with the opening month spring will be here in earnest.

WASHINGTON, 7 APRIL 1862 (PUBLISHED 10 APRIL 1862)
It is a most lovely morning, "bright will all the full-rayed promise of the spring," but Washington cannot enjoy it. In fact, it is difficult to turn our

minds to anything but "the situation." We know that fighting is now going on at or near Yorktown, between the advancing columns of Gen. McClellan and the entrenched masses of the traitor army.[22] We cannot hear the guns, but we know that our brave friends are doing their best to clear this long, and difficult, and bloody road to Richmond. By the time this reaches you the result may be announced. We have all faith in our army, and we do not doubt that it will be well and bravely led. From the West, too, we must soon have stirring news, and it can hardly happen that the week before us shall be like the past.

THE MILITARY CRISIS

The most absorbing reflection of all is that this bids fair to be the military crisis of this war. The largest armies which either side has raised or at present *can* raise, are meeting each other upon fields so located that, in the opinion of military men, a decisive defeat for either is almost irretrievable ruin. So then, if we win at all the contested points of this hour of fierce struggle, *the day is ours*, for our enemies cannot rally again to meet us on fresh fields with renewed strength, as they have thus far been able to do.

THE SORROWS TO COME

Pardon me, Mr. Editor, but it seems so strange, so beyond all power of realization, to be sitting here this quiet morning, with the warm sun looking in at my window and the April wind upon my face, while bloody battle-fields are being lost and won. Not a brigade will charge in this week's fighting, but will leave in its path the wrecks of many household circles, and the shadows of sorrow are already settling, as it were in prophecy, over thousands of the fond hearts left at home. There will be mourning among the tall old forests of Maine, the scattered villages of New-York, in the lonely cabins of the settlers on the prairies, and in the miners' cottages along the mountain sides of Pennsylvania. There will be sorrow too, in stately city houses, from whose elegance and luxury the young heirs have gone to fight for what they had been taught to believe a more valuable inheritance.

THE PASS SYSTEM

But I am forgetting the proper business of a letter-writer. One of the best things of the week has been the relaxation of the pass system across the Potomac. The lines of the army are now so far beyond it, that the old rigor became unnecessary, and we are now free to come and go. We are not allowed entirely to forget that the city is still under military occupation, but the pressure of the strong hand is made to fall as lightly as possible.

THE YEAR OF FEDERAL SUPREMACY

Washington is another city from the gloomy, panic-stricken, semi-rebellious town of a year ago. A year of Federal supremacy and strong government has done wonders, even for the secession portion of our inhabitants, and from this change some have drawn an argument as to the future condition of some of the States now in rebellion. Let them once be put under the control of the Government, and a judicious course of treatment will accomplish elsewhere all that has been done here, or in Maryland. And those who incline to accept this hope are beginning to point to Missouri, Kentucky and Tennessee, as already giving proof of the working of the system. At all events, it is the only course left us, and time will tell whether the noxious weeds of rebellion and treason have taken such root in our land that neither time nor the sword can repel them.

NO MORE RECRUITING

The order closing the recruiting stations is another indication. It means that the army is large enough to carry to full completion all the plans and purposes of the Government. It means, too, that no more vacancies will be filled from the people, but that the trained warriors now in the field are expected to end the war.

THE SNOB SNUBBED

Another of the good things of the week was the expulsion of Russell, the "hired man of the London *Times*," from the steamer in which he had embarked himself and luggage. The campaign in Virginia is not to be caricatured by a paid slanderer, while Secretary Stanton has prevented any ill effects of his action by permitting three British officers of high rank to accompany the army. It was a cool way of saying to Dr. Russell, "These men are *gentlemen*, I believe that they will tell the truth about what they may see. We have endured *you* long enough." Russell came back in high dudgeon and appealed to the President, but Mr. Lincoln declined interfering, and the discomfited scribbler threatens to return to England.[23]

DISGRACEFUL FACTS

Would it help your readers, as to certain mooted points, if your correspondent should say that he has settled, to his entire satisfaction, the fact that there *were* wooden guns at Centreville, in considerable numbers; the fact that the rebels did dig up and insult the bones of those of our brave men who fell at Bull Run; and the fact that the rebel cavalry *did* murder in cold blood many of our wounded, after that disastrous day? If any one has any doubt of these things, the truth can be well established.

WASHINGTON, 14 APRIL 1862 (PUBLISHED 17 APRIL 1862)
Was there ever anything so tantalizing as the history of this war? A few days since, we were told that if the army under Gen. A. Sidney Johnston was defeated, the rebellion would be at an end in the Southwest.[24] Well, we have won a great victory over that army, but the promised result still looms up beyond us like the mirage in the desert.[25] Fort Pillow still frowns down on the muddy Mississippi, the gunners still watch behind the endless mounds at Memphis, and a large army still opposes its bristling front to the now united hosts of Buell and Grant.[26]

THE PITTSBURGH BATTLE

The truth is, that in defeating the enemy at Pittsburgh Landing, we did *not* win the precise victory the military men wanted. Beauregard, in imitation of Napoleon, attempted to destroy the comparatively small force of General Grant before its junction with that of Buell could be accomplished. The attack was well planned, well managed, and the battle was fought by the Confederates and their leaders with consummate skill and courage. They came near, very near, a complete success. Had they been twenty-four hours earlier, their second day's fighting, aided as they were by fresh troops, must have given them a fearful advantage over the inferior force of Grant, wearied by a long fight, and weakened by the loss of guns and men. Perhaps, too, the enemy had not counted on the stubborn pluck of the prairie men, which kept him at bay until the hour for success had gone by. The *Herald's* awful estimate of the casualties on either side will, of course, dwindle, and with it some portion of the importance of the advantage gained; but nothing can take from our brave men the glory they have won, or wipe from the annals of this war the splendor of that last grand charge across the field, with General Grant waving his sword in front of his shouting soldiers. There will be more fighting there before many days, but the whole country feels that we have, at least at *that* point, the right men in the right place.

THE PATHFINDER

Frémont seems to be buried among his mountains for the moment, but no one doubts that we shall hear from him before long. The Pathfinder has a curious way of his own, of doing something extraordinary whenever he finds himself among the mountains, and we wonder that it will be this time.[27]

MCCLELLAN AND YORKTOWN

The war in Virginia is at a curious pass, and a cloud of mystery seems to cover the movements of both armies. Those are not wanting who wonder why Gen. McClellan seems always to find himself stuck in such wonderfully deep *mud*. They say they cannot remember a time when the mire in front of his army was not deeper by several feet than at any other point on the Continent. The fact is, that no one of the sundry objects of popular criticism since these troubles begun, has ever been assailed with such bitter and persevering animosity, as is now the commander of the Army of the Potomac. Right or wrong, the storm pelts away, and it is possible that even the light of a great victory would fail to dissipate the cloud which envelopes the former idol of army and people. As in time past, however, we have nothing to do but to "wait," trusting more to that God in whom we have put our last confidence, than in the skill or foresight of any, or all of our generals. With *His* assistance, our armies will "blunder" into more great triumphs than Caesar could lead them to.

THE HOWL OF THE SLAVE-OWNERS
In the Capital itself there is little stirring, except the howl of resident slave-owners on the action of Congress.[28] The law may be a trifle severe, but no man need waste any sympathy on the losers, whatever may be his views on the slavery question, for the said slaveholders of the District have been from the first, with a few exceptions, the most arrant and outrageous traitors in the land. It is no hardship that the young sprigs, who left this place to join the armies that menaced it, should, if they ever return, miss the attentive and obedient "property" which they thought so secure a patrimony. As to the effect of the ordinance upon Maryland and Virginia, though generally overrated, we may make the same wholesome reflections. A State which was only compelled to be safe and happy by the presence of myriads of bayonets, and which dyed the streets of its chief city with the blood of the soldiers of the Union, has little claims to sympathy from the loyal and the true.

WASHINGTON DRIFTING NORTH
During the last week, a severe snow-storm added strong conviction to my surmise, in a former letter, that the Federal City was visibly drifting further North. If this sort of progress will only give our armies in Alabama and Louisiana a cool summer to fight in, what a comment it will be upon the universal and undeniable fitness of things!

THE CONFISCATION QUESTION
This afternoon, if nothing prevents, Senator Harris is to give his long-expected speech on the confiscation question, and the galleries will be crowded, for the course of the honorable Senator, thus far, has been such

as to give an unusual weight to his counsel upon the great questions of the day. This confiscation business involves so many important considerations of law, justice, and policy, that it may be taken as a fair test of the wisdom of our legislators. The quacks, of whom we have too many, both in House and Senate, will be ready with their nostrums, and we shall hear from the vindictive, the visionary, and the rebel-sympathizers; but there is strong ground for hoping that none of these will be allowed to control the measures which must form the basis of the great work of reconstruction.[29]

A DISCRIMINATING POLICE

The Washington police, unable any longer to entirely close their eyes to all the evils around them, have actually closed several gambling hells during the past week, taking care, of course, not to disturb any of the larger institutions, whose wealth, splendor and antiquity entitled them to continue to receive and fleece their distinguished guests from the civil and military service. It would look so bad, you know, to mix up the names of M.C.s, Brigadiers and Colonels with such low things as "a full assortment of all the implements belonging to the profession, including," &c.

WASHINGTON, 21 APRIL 1862 (PUBLISHED 24 APRIL 1862)

The cloud of secresy and mystery has settled once more over the operations of the army. To be sure, we know that glorious old Foote, the praying Commodore, is pitching his shells among the rebels away down the Mississippi, and we have a tolerably settled idea of McClellan's whereabouts;[30] but who knows where Frémont will emerge from among his mountains, or where Banks is pushing his columns, or at what point McDowell is to strike, or what is the truth about the army in Tennessee?[31] Does any one know how the war is going in Arkansas, or along the shores of the Gulf? We may be willing to trust the Atlantic coast with Burnside and Hunter and Dupont, but who shall say what they are doing? Verily the newspaper world has had a genuine scare for once, if it will permit these things to be. A reaction in favor of Gen. McClellan seems to have taken place during the past week; too many other fates are now bound up with his, to allow anything but the strongest and most earnest aspirations in his behalf. Men may dislike him never so much, but they pray for him now.

A WASHINGTON PANIC

We have our full share of panics and rumors at present, and the sudden marching of a regiment will set a thousand tongues busily at work. For instance, on Saturday last the President went down the river a short distance, accompanied by Secretary Chase.³² Night came, and he did not return, while a messenger came riding in in haste, from no-one-knows-where, to say that Gen. McCall had been defeated and killed, and that our troops had retreated to Centreville. "Can it be possible!" "In what force are the enemy?" "How many men have we here?" "The army is all gone." Such was the staple of hotel conversation for several hours, receiving in some cases an extra shade of apprehensive horror from a knowledge of the President's prolonged absence.

OUR NOBLE PRESIDENT

Did you ever try to realize the idea of losing our good Chief Magistrate? Perhaps not, but suppose you try, and then look around you in imagination for the man whom you could trust, and whom the people would trust, to take the reins from *his* dead hand. The fact is, that at present the country has entire confidence in no one else, and we might almost say, "after him the deluge," in view of our present condition.

THE WEATHER, AND THE HOSPITALS

The weather has been very warm and summer-like for the past week, winding up in a tremendous storm of wind and dust and rain, which still continues to pour. From this time forward we may look for heat and its consequences.

We have now enormous hospital arrangements, but with all their appliances for ventilation, comfort and care, they would be frightful retreats in which to spend the June, July and August afternoons of this latitude. There should be some system by which our soldier invalids may be transported, as fast as possible, to cool retreats in the North. By this means we can prevent crowding here, and offer to the sufferers every possible chance for recovery.

BRIGADIER-MAKING

The business of making Brigadiers still goes forward with considerable activity, and although many promotions have been made for meritorious conduct in the field, we have put far too many stars on shoulders which have borne, and are fit to bear, no other military responsibility. European commanders do well to sneer at Brigadier-Generals who have never seen a gun fired in anger, and who have the merest smattering of military science. In the present war, we may comfort ourselves with the reflection that our enemies are in the same boat, so far as this error is concerned, but in some future struggle we may learn, to our cost, a truth *sufficiently* evident in the returns from the Sunday fight at Pittsburgh Landing. The mere *number* of our generals cannot, however, be objected to, as far too many of our brigades are in charge of Colonels, and too many divisions are under the orders of Brigadiers;—let the stars multiply as fast as the service requires, but let those who are to wear them win them fairly.

A SIGNIFICANT SIGHT

The various public buildings present a curious spectacle. The danger of the nation seems hardly to impede their growth, as if the solid masonry had faith in the solidity of the institutions it was to serve, and so the dome of the Capitol rises, and one by one the granite pillars of the Treasury west front are lifted into their places. This calm, confident self-assertion on the part of the Government, is not without its effect. Men see that the Administration is strong in the faith, and somehow they become inoculated with a similar feeling. Even in the smallest things we may see the steady, unflinching, unwavering mind of a great people, upholding great institutions with a strength of will the world has never known before.

WASHINGTON, 28 APRIL 1862 (PUBLISHED 1 MAY 1862)

After a week of stormy and disagreeable weather, the sun has once more gladdened us with a promise of better things to come. The mid-day heats may be unpleasant until a little use has made them once more second nature, but they will be of great value in a military point of view. They will prepare the roads and dry up the marshes before McClellan, and surely and rapidly construct the causeways whereon his heavy siege guns must move, as they draw nearer and nearer the bristling lines of Yorktown.

THE YOUNG COMMANDER

In my last, I believe I spoke of a reaction in favor of McClellan. The whole country is fully aware how pertinaciously he has been assailed, but it can hardly appreciate the vehemence with which his personal friends defend him. If the power of securing the enthusiastic attachment of subordinates is any real evidence of greatness, we must make a large confession in favor of McClellan. It is more than possible that no victory the young commander can win at Yorktown, will restore to him the prestige and position he has lost in these months of seeming inaction, but it is yet in his power to confirm a large and powerful body of friends in their devotion and admiration.

DOLEFUL FOREBODINGS

In a late number of a leading New-York daily we were treated to a doleful foreboding of the wonderful things which *might* happen, should Davis or Lee be seized with a Napoleonic idea and leave troops enough at Yorktown to defeat McClellan, while the remainder went and destroyed McDowell. The only things in the way of the speedy fulfillment of such a prophecy are the armies on the Rappahannock and the peninsula, the distance to be travelled, the condition of the rebel forces, and the proximity of reinforcements to either wing of our army which might be menaced. These obstacles overcome, and the destruction of McDowell, Banks and Frémont, would be merely a question of a few days.

The fact is, that there is nothing in this campaign which bears the ghost of a resemblance to any one of Napoleon's. The very vastness of the armies prevent such a similitude from being created, were the "Little Corporal" here in person, except in actual battle, and not often even then.

SUNDAY BATTLES

It can hardly be possible that yesterday (Sunday) passed without a fight somewhere. It would seem that the bad fashion set at Bull Run had been followed through the whole war. Who shall say why it is so many of our contending armies should find it necessary to begin their bloody work on the first day of the week?

CITY DISPLAYS AND AMUSEMENTS

In the Capital City, affairs seem to be getting on swimmingly. Military displays are not so every-day an occurrence as formerly, but we have enough to keep up our interest in such matters, and to keep the war forever before our eyes as a present reality.

The city is overrun with theatres of all sorts and sizes, brought in, perhaps, to supply the morbid appetite for excitement created by the events of the past year among our inhabitants. Of course every grade of taste and habit has its special caterers, from the crowd of self-complaisant and criticizing fashionables, who wish to see the performances of the "Great American Tragedian," to the sailors and soldiers who throng the class of haunts with whose New-York prototypes the Legislature and the police have lately been dealing. Such indications are not beneath the notice of the men who are to write the chronicles of this era in our national existence.

WORDY WORK

In Congress they have been enjoying a spicy time for the past week, both in Senate and House, and some of the passages have hardly been of a character to aid much in the promised "restoration" of either. At present our worthy legislators are wasting their time upon that unrighteous absurdity, the "Van Wyck Committee," which has made itself and its members so unpleasantly conspicuous.[33] Schuyler Colfax and others paid their respects on Friday, and Thad. Stevens is to do his share to-day.[34] There will be a crowd to hear him, for while he is one of the most unpopular men in either House, he has a singular faculty for saying sharp and bitter things. People are not so much afraid of seeing edge tools used as they once were.

CABINET RECONSTRUCTING

The Cabinet continues to go through its multiform newspaper reconstructions, without any visible changes in its external semblance. Would it not be a trifle funny, if *all* the many predictions should fail? Or has any one rendered that impossible, by prophesying that the President will retain his present advisers?

INAUGURATING SUMMER

Next Saturday afternoon, the Washington summer season is to be fairly inaugurated by the appearance of the Marine Band at its usual post in the President's grounds. This pleasant and genial custom is one of the most attractive of all our summer arrangements, and affords the general public a delightful promenade at least as often as once a week, or rather twice a week, as the same band performs on Wednesday evenings in the handsome grounds of the Capitol.[35]

Measures are at last promised which will, it is hoped, have a tendency to preserve the health of the city during the warm weather. The diminished number of troops, and their attendant circumstances, also encourage us to hope for the best.

WASHINGTON, CA. 5 MAY 1862 (PUBLISHED 8 MAY 1862)

A lovely May morning this, with a sunshine that is swiftly drawing the green leaves from their winter hiding places. The birds have been here for several days, and are noisy enough. Here at home we are rather quiet than otherwise, the city settling slowly back to its humdrum life, and the country around beginning to make feeble efforts to recover itself from the paralysis produced by its long military occupation. It will take years for it to fully recuperate. The iron heel of Mars sinks deep into the sod it presses, and the diligent hand of the husbandman cannot soon efface the print.

SLAVERY AND THE COLORED RACE

The little band of local slave-owners are still loud in their complaints at being "plundered of their property," and roundly assert their determination to test the Emancipation Act before the Supreme Court, with Reverdy Johnson for their counsel.[36] Whether they do so or not, the die is cast, and the retrograde step cannot be effectually taken. The slaves have already tasted freedom, and they find it very sweet indeed, after ever so mild a bondage.

It is the firm belief of your correspondent, from what he has seen and heard among the blacks, that this seemingly small seed, sown here in this District, will yet bear the most important fruit in every one of the border slave States. It seems to me that I can see the gradual entering of a new idea into the darkened minds of the downtrodden race—they begin, the best of them, to feel and cherish the notion of their *nationality*, and the development of the consequent emotions and ideas must follow. I have studied them much for a long time, and, except in isolated instances, have never noticed this before. They have all looked at their condition in a narrow and selfish way, each man for his own hand. There is no stronger civilizing influence, outside of the Christian religion, than a well-directed national feeling, because it leads men to work in unison for the accomplishment of whatever aims they may propose.

Another marked and remarkable point is that the blacks refuse to regard themselves as *Africans*. This, too, is a new idea, and I cannot help thinking it an advance. They insist that they are Americans, while at the same time they appreciate the disadvantages under which they labor here, and earnestly desire to find a new and undisputed theatre *on this Continent* for the *locus* of their future nationality. No doubt there is some sense in the idea of civilizing and Christianizing Africa by their means, but we must first civilize and Christianize our missionaries, or we shall be sending the blind to lead the blind, with a full knowledge of what and how deep a ditch awaits their fall. But I must leave this subject, deeply interesting as it must be to one who has the great problem of our nation so constantly before him.

THE CAPTURE OF NEW-ORLEANS

The taking of New-Orleans, and the prompt action of the President and Senate in opening so important a port once more to the commerce of the world, has had a most excellent effect upon the representatives of the leading commercial powers.[37] At last they seem to see, what we wonder they could ever have been blind to, that in Federal success is their only hope for renewed access to the great Southern States. The keen-eyed managers of Lyons and Birmingham are now under bonds to follow the armies of the Union with warmest wishes for their swift success. And before long they must hear from us again, and few have any doubt as to the purport of the news. Beat them we must and will.

THE FASHIONABLES

Since "Lent" we have had a number of parties among the higher circles, and a few more are coming, and then the last of the fashionables will take wing for the North. Something in the warm, unnerving atmosphere, this morning, prevents me from touching on one or two points which I will reserve for further examination, and a more vigorous day.

WASHINGTON, CA. 12 MAY 1862 (PUBLISHED 15 MAY 1862)
The capture of Norfolk adds another to the continued series of successes which has made the last week one of the most important of the war. As usual, the good news came Sunday morning. With the destruction of the *Merrimac*, all that corner of Virginia falls into our hands. It is wonderful at what a rapid rate General McClellan has recovered confidence since he moved upon Yorktown.[38]

The President has had a very pleasant little vacation, observing the operations of the army on the Peninsula—a relief of which he stood very much in need.[39] He is, as ever, strong in the faith that this campaign, as at present laid out and organized, must compel the speedy restoration of at least "an armed peace."

The restoration, by the way, is the all-absorbing topic of the day among statesmen and would-be statesmen in every corner of the Capitol. Taking it for granted that the end of the war is near, the minds of all are busy with the complications of the settlement of affairs. The Republican leaders seem to be lying on their oars, waiting their time for movement—whether wisely or not, remains to be seen. The late caucuses of the Democrats and "conservatives" have thus far accomplished nothing, except to draw in a few of the weaker-kneed among their old opponents, who failed to foresee what sort of name a political infant must receive when Sunset Cox and Vallandigham stood as sponsors.[40] There is not a secessionist in the South who would have many conscientious objections to following in *their* wake. A caucus, however, does not always succeed in organizing a party, however respectable may be the names which may appear on its muster-roll. Unless your correspondent is very much mistaken, the people, as such, will have more than usual to say in the organization of the political bodies to which the power of this Government will be entrusted for some time to come.

The disposal of the contrabands affords a prolific source of discussion and proposition.[41] Among other outlets for these unfortunate wanderers, Mexico begins to stand prominent. The managers and contractors of a Mexican railway offer very good terms, including fair pay and steady work, for a large number of able-bodied men with their families, in a climate every way healthful, and suited to the peculiar constitution of the race.

We trust too little to Providence in this age, when we talk of doing any great "right," or undoing any great wrong; we must, with our own mole-eyed wisdom, see to the far results, or we tread timorously, as if the laws of nature and the will of Him who made them were not on our side. This Mexican proposition is a small one, to be sure, but there will be many ways whereby a nation of laborers may earn their bread, on a Continent like this.

Much attention has been attracted by the bold attitude and statesmanlike views of the representatives of the Pacific coast in urging forward the Pacific Railroad Bill. Our empire beyond the mountains is advancing with wonderful strides, in wealth, population, and in all the real elements of power. We do well to forge rapidly the iron bands which are to hold us all together, for without them our very magnitude may produce unwieldiness, and develope those well-known centrifugal forces which have rent in sunder the great empires of history. Nor should we lose sight of the fact that the citizens of the Mexican State of Sonora call loudly to us for protection from our own filibustering traitors, declaring that their interests and sympathies unite them with the American people, and more than hinting a strong desire to become legally entitled to be covered by the shield of our power.

In more ways than one we may soon demonstrate to cavilers on either side the Atlantic, that the vitality and expansive force of the Republic has been strengthened, rather than otherwise, by the fiery ordeal through which it is passing. The history of the Old World teaches us that all periods of revolution—not of mere vulgar conquest—are also periods of great material development, and no doubt our people, their minds stimulated and aroused by constant struggle and as constant success, will find themselves meditating and attempting enterprises which seemed too great for them in the comparatively quiet period that has passed away. That was a period of development, however, upon which the world gazed in wonder and alarm. What, then, will effete despotisms and weary or worn-out races say, when the New World begins its third era of progress? The third, counting our Colonial history as one, our career up to the fall of Fort Sumter, another, and looking to the future for the third. Do not think me enthusiastic, or carried away by the fever of the day, for if all comes true, it will not be the first time that Europe has sat at the feet of America to learn how empires are made.

WASHINGTON, 23 JUNE 1862 (PUBLISHED 26 JUNE 1862)
After a protracted absence, I am again able to send you a report from the capital. Most of the time I have been with the army of Gen. Burnside in North Carolina, and would like to condense for your readers a few remarks on what I saw there. The news, as such, you have already.

GEN. BURNSIDE AND HIS ARMY

Our army in North Carolina is in admirable condition in all respects, as to drill, health, discipline, spirits, equipment, commissariat, and has that precise amount of confidence in and affection for its leader, which is so large an element in all successful military operations. Gen. Burnside has given the most conclusive evidence that he is the right man in the right place.

After a careful analysis of the various positions of the enemy which are now in his hands, having visited the various battle-fields, accompanied by men who had been the most active participators in their dangers and glories, I cannot refrain from recording my astonishment at the complete success of our brave troops. I cannot doubt the declaration of the brave officer who led the last assault at the entrenchments at Newbern, "had *we* been on the other side of such a position, ten times our number could not have driven us out." The men who could carry such defences could surely keep them. The diseases pertaining to a warm climate and a swampy region are making sad havoc among our men, but if we may trust the testimony of the graveyards—safe witnesses in such a case—the mortality among the Southern troops, before the battle, was even greater; owing, no doubt, to their inferior commissariat and medical department.

GOV. STANLEY'S COURSE

The army is bitterly opposed to the course thus far pursued by Gov. Stanley, and there is good reason to believe that his Excellency is slowly yielding to better and wiser counsels.[42] He seems to be an honest man, sincerely desirous of accomplishing all that could be expected of him, but unable to throw off lifelong prejudices sufficiently to read correctly the signs of the times. It is to be feared that after we have finished the war, we shall find that the South, like the Bourbons, has "learned nothing and forgotten nothing."

THE PENDING CRISIS

On returning to my old haunts here, it required a few days of careful canvassing to discover just how matters were situated. Nothing can be stronger than the conviction of the "powers that be" that the crisis has come, and that all the dearly-bought results of many bloody fields are being fought for once more in the lines before Richmond; nor have I much doubt that by the time these pages are before your readers, they will be anxiously examining the returns from another great battle.

The feeling here for McClellan is overwhelming. Men who were his assailants three months since, start up in angry menace if a word is spoken in derogation of the skill or patriotism of the man upon whom so much depends. He *must* be victorious! We dare not look beyond into the state of things that might ensue should we at this last lose the Army of the Potomac. Not that we could not send a million men more in the path which these are carving, but that the National honor is at stake, and with it much of the hard-won prestige of the Administration. Well, we must await the result with what share of patience we may, certain that it is now near, even at the doors.

THE PRESIDENT
The President and his family have removed for the summer to the charming country seat known as the "Soldiers' Home," about three miles from the city.[43] Mr. Lincoln usually rides in on horseback, about nine o'clock in the morning, accompanied by "little Fred" [Tad] on his pony. His health is better this season than last, and he manages to keep up his spirits, in spite of his burden of anxiety.

MAKING HOSPITALS OF CHURCHES
The course of the War Department in occupying the churches of Washington as hospitals, has called forth a deal of comment on both sides, and there are indeed many reasons for doubting both its expediency and its economy, but it may be the best that could be done under the circumstances. It at least affords the indolent pew-holders of some of our ultra-fashionable societies an excellent opportunity to display any *active* and charitable religion they may have imbibed in the edifices now devoted to so good a purpose. A morning visit to an extensive military hospital may possibly afford as much wholesome instruction as the most correct rhetorical rendering of the "lesson of the day."

TOURS AMONG THE SICK AND WOUNDED
Your correspondent has managed to make sundry exploring tours among the various wards now crowded with the wrecks of humanity from the camp and battle-field, and too many of your readers are, or will be there represented, to make his observations uninteresting. The first feeling of an inexperienced person, on finding himself surrounded with so many ghastly proofs of man's inhumanity to man—the empty sleeves, the bloody bandages, the suppressed groans of the wounded, or the flushed faces, sunken eyes, and delirious babblings of the fever wards—is a sinking of the heart, an instinctive recoil towards the sunshine and the outer air; but the

next moment, remembering who are the sufferers before him, where they are from, and in what great cause they have incurred such suffering and such sacrifices, the heart of any visitor fills with pity, admiration, and an earnest desire to be of service. The friends of these poor fellows may comfort themselves as well as they can, with the reflection that never was any army so well provided in this respect as ours. The well-ventilated rooms, the clean and comfortable beds, the low-voiced and soft-stepping attendants, and the little cupboards well supplied with delicacies for those who can use them, assure us that nothing is left undone to give to each his best and speediest chance for life and health. It is to be hoped that arrangements will be made to transfer the convalescents as rapidly as possible to some cooler climate and purer air.

But I have used my allotted space, and must leave many things for my next.

WASHINGTON, 30 JUNE 1862 (PUBLISHED 3 JULY 1862)
The past week has been one of feverish anxiety for the metropolis, as well as for the country at large. Its results, such as they are, are now before us. At home we have had the organization of the Army of Virginia, the appointment of Pope, and the resignation of Frémont, to distract our attention from the slow and cautious advances of McClellan.[44] So far as your correspondent has been able to observe, the expression of satisfaction with the President's action in this matter is general. The ultra-abolitionists, to be sure, are displeased with the elevation of a general of Democratic antecedents, over the heads of Banks and Frémont, but Pope has been too successful in the field against the rebellion to allow of any very loud or violent declamation.

The course of Banks, the representative man of Massachusetts in the field, is placed in strong contrast with Frémont's preference of his personal dignity to the public service, and the strongest supporters of the latter are fain to express their regret at the course he has seen fit to pursue. The general impression seems to be that the creation of the new Department was loudly called for by our late reverses among the independent commands of the three generals, and that the President has fully vindicated his reputation for wisdom and decision.

There is an observation that may as well be made here:—As I have been to and fro through the country, I have been frequently catechised by anxious and patriotic inquirers, as to the present power and standing of this or that political or military favorite. Too much interest seems to be felt in the fitness of generals and Cabinet officers, when, if any one fact stands out more prominently than another upon the record of the times, it is that individual fortunes are losing their value in view of the magnitude of the public interests at stake. The people, as a mass, are forgetting their democratic proneness to idolatry, and I hazard little in saying that no man or set of men will win overshadowing fame or popularity during the present struggle.

The war has thus far developed no general to whom the army looks up as the heroic embodiment of its victories or its glory, and no great party has been formed to sustain the power of any one great leader. It may even be said that the President himself, strong as he is in the confidence and love of the people, is only strong because the unerring popular intuition comprehends that he forgets himself, and mingles no emotion of sordid and mean ambition with his earnest aspirations for the welfare of his country. Certainly there is no other name or fame than his, whose utter disappearance would cause more than a temporary ripple on the stormy waters of this revolution. There are generals whom we might mourn with deep sorrow, and statesmen whose faces would be sadly missed in the councils of the nation, but not one of them holds bound up with his individual life or fortune the welfare of the nation.

Much of the feeling of which I speak, may be well attributed to the strength of the popular faith in our cause, our strength and our final success; and this faith was never stronger than at this very moment, when the European mails assure us that our enemies on the other side of the Atlantic dream that the hour of our weakness and their opportunity is fast drawing near. I suppose no one need assure you of the contemptuous anger with which the idea of intervention or mediation is treated in official and legislative circles. The English, for instance, may gather a fair conception of our present feelings towards *them* from the biting and caustic harangues of George Francis Train, who has already, in their own assemblies, told them so many plain and unpleasant truths.[45]

With France our relations are at present more complicated, and there is no telling to what extremes her persistence in her insane treatment of the Mexican question may lead us. We may not "have a foreign policy," as has so often been sneeringly asserted, but we have a very clearly defined one, so far as European interference in the affairs of this Continent is concerned, as France may yet learn to her cost. Should Mr. Corwin's admirable treaty with Mexico be ratified by the Senate, our relations with our Southern neighbor will be more intimate than ever before, and we shall have acquired an additional right to shield her weakness under the protecting aegis of the Great Republic.[46]

The health of the city does not seem, as yet, to have suffered materially by the continued increase of hospitals and their inmates, and with the proper sanitary precautions we may escape with but little more than the usual diseases of this climate and season. The tone of public sentiment among the residents also seems to be growing more patriotic, and Washington may yet become as thoroughly loyal as New-York.

WASHINGTON, 7 JULY 1862 (PUBLISHED 10 JULY 1862)
Sunday came to us bright and warm, but calm and quiet—a strange seal to a week of such terrible strife and excitement.

The clouds are gradually lifting from the bloodiest battle-field in American history, thus far, and in spite of our horror at the carnage, and our regret that such a struggle should not have been crowned with complete victory, we cannot repress a feeling of gratified pride, that "in all that dark and desperate fight" our brave boys did not waver or fall back, and that to the last the serried columns of rebellion broke in vain upon their rock-like front. We did not, it is true, win an apparent victory, but we did win a real one, in spite of tremendous odds and desperate ferocity.[47]

This is the result of our long course of discipline. Our volunteers are now *soldiers*, veterans, fit to meet the best and bravest troops of the Old World or the New. And now the reinforcements are pouring in steadily:—not the new men, as yet, but detachments of well-trained corps, which have not hitherto joined in this last death-clinch on the peninsula. It cannot be long before those fields are fought over again, and we can have little doubt as to the results.

The President is as cool, as brave, as confident as ever, relying fully on the people and the righteous cause; troubled by the loss of so many valuable lives, but esteeming them all, as their owners did, a worthy sacrifice on the altar of our country's life.

Among the civilians in and about Washington, the old war of words continues. The enemies of McClellan seem to be headed, in bitterness, at least, by old Count Gurowski, of Russian fame, whose remaining eye flashes fire through his tinted glasses, as he denounces the military blunders which his heated fancy creates with wonderful fecundity.[48] Stanton, too, has his coteries of ill-wishers, who attribute to his course all that has happened of ill to our arms. It is not impossible that all the gentry who seek in any one man the ultimate cause of either success or failure, may be in error.

Your correspondent has been as busy as any man among the "wheels within wheels," and after a year and a half of constant study, draws back his aching head, and acknowledges that the mainspring is invisible. Others may cry "Eureka," and say that this enamelled face, or that case of brass, or that polished iron, conceals the responsible and motive power, but they differ one from another, and they are all wrong. Therefore let us be consistent, and if any of our wheels are defective, let us put others in their places quietly, remembering that after all they are only *wheels*.

The weather is fast gathering its usual intense July heat, boding no good to those who must dig trenches, and march, and charge at double quick, under such a sun.

Three marks may be made in our legislative history, where the President signed the Tax bill, the Pacific Railroad bill, and the bill prohibiting Polygamy.[49] They were all of vast importance, the one providing a stable foundation for our revenue, and giving solidity to our Government securities, at the same time that it opens a new era in our social history; the second pledging the young States on the Pacific that no excitement of public peril can make us forget or neglect them, at the same time that it opens a new era in trade; while the third strikes a deathblow at the "twin relic of barbarism," assuring the world that *our* civilization, now that it is in power, is mindful of all things that concern the decent fame of the model Republic.

The newspapers tell us that the panic among moneyed men has been great in New-York. All will be sorry for that, for the national purse has bled as freely in this cause as the national valor; but a few days will bring back the wonted faith, and even Wall street will smile again.

The sick and the wounded continue to pour in, and our hospitals increase in number daily. It is a pitiful sight, the long lines of ambulances, with their ghastly burdens. The poor fellows are generally cheerful and courageous, and foreign surgeons wonder at the uniform fortitude of our sufferers. It is a settled fact that no other nation possesses the same stoical firmness. Whether we take it from the red men, or whether it belongs to soil and climate, I cannot tell, but if you were here, I could prove the *fact* to you in short time. The ladies of Washington are doing their duty at last, and doing it well. Alas, there is room for all who have a heart for the work.

WASHINGTON, 21 JULY 1862 (PUBLISHED 24 JULY 1862)
This long and eventful Congress is at last at an end, and most of the members have departed. Some to watering-places, some to the management of private business neglected for public affairs, some to attend to their political interests, some to reappear at the next assembling of the National Legislature, but many to return to the shades of private life.

THE CONGRESS WHICH HAS GONE HOME

Neither the House of Representatives nor Senate can boast of many shining names. Few rise above the level of good lawyers and business men. The statesmen whose fame is unquestioned may be counted on the fingers, without minding the thumbs; and considering all things, we have rarely had a more unpopular Congress; and yet, Mr. Editor, it is only fair justice to say that no similar assembly, within the memory of this generation, has accomplished so large an amount of genuine hard work, or labored so steadily and conscientiously to discharge its duty to the people.

UNDERTONES

A new and wonderful era has been opened by the action of this body of hard-working, *mediocre* men. The old question of internal improvements is settled forever in favor of the proposed improvements. We shall now have them, one after the other, in rapid succession, and our internal strength and resources cannot fail to expand with a swiftness hitherto unknown. The labors in connection with the public credit and the preservation of the national unity, are recorded too well in all our memories to require reference. Some things there are, however, that escape the notice of the distant observer. There are undertones of thought and feeling, of purpose and hope, which have not as yet been made the property of the press or public. They are only heard in quiet conversational circles, in after-dinner discussions, and in the secret conferences of the committees. It is the belief of your correspondent that our public men are, even in this hour of anxiety and excitement, obtaining glimpses of many things which they have fatally neglected in the mad partisanship of the past few years.

They see that we are contemptuously considered by European commercial powers in the light, not of a great people, but *a market*—only to be considered with reference to our ability to purchase goods, or to furnish material. They see that we have not yet taken our place as the acknowledged controller of affairs in the New World; that we have allowed the commerce of our sister nationalities on this side of the water to be absorbed by nations over whom we had every imaginable material advantage, and that we had almost thrown away the best portion of our commercial birthright. More than ever should they detest the selfish faction which, in seeking its own aggrandisement, has sacrificed all these, and superadded the curse of this civil war to the evils of its long mismanagement. We may now hope that the future will witness a different state of things.

The next session will find the ideas to which I have referred taking life and form in the shape of great and salutary measures. The commerce of the nation must supply the national purse—in one way or another—and we need to deepen every spring that promises to swell the current of the national income.

STOPPING TO TAKE BREATH

You remember the opening lines of Webster's reply to Hayne—let us imitate the Great Expounder's mariner.[50] Presuming that the "ways and means" are provided for the last great effort now making for the suppression of the rebellion, we find ourselves looking upon the entire forces of the Union in the act of resting—stopping to take breath for another blow. East, and West, and centre, with the exception of Pope's gallant column, nobody is moving forward. The military departments are agitated by rumors, seemingly well-founded, of changes in commanders and in plans. The State Department listens with eager ear to threatening murmurs from over the water. The Treasury glances anxiously at the reports from Wall street. The Navy is busy with its newly-created Admirals and Commodores. But the Executive, strong in the confidence of the people, whether retiring from July heats at the "Soldier's Home," or holding long conferences in the old room looking out on the Potomac, or listening to the "click" in the telegraph room at the War Office, wears the same firm yet thoughtful face, and ponders his orders and proclamations with the same sound common sense and coolness, as if McClellan's dispatches came from the other side of Richmond.

SOURCES OF THE PRESIDENT'S POWER

The President is almost a mystery. Men no longer query whether such or such a General or statesman directs his actions, but "what will he do with" this statesman or that General. He is the most perfect *representative* of the purely American character now in public life—perhaps the most perfect that ever has existed. This is why the mutual understanding between him and the people is so perfect. This it is which enables him to exercise powers which would never by any possibility be entrusted to another man, though his equal in other respects.

The people know that they can trust their great chief, and so they bid him "see to it that the Republic suffers no detriment," and put in his hands untold treasure and uncounted lives, and the temporary disposal of their time-honored rights. The *habeas corpus* act is suspended—"Lincoln would not do it if it was not needed." The press is muzzled—"Good for him! why don't the old man shut off the *Herald* and the *Tribune*?" Favorite generals are superseded, favorite measures curtailed or disapproved, prejudices rubbed or snubbed, but the President is the stronger for it all. Pardon me if I dwell on this too much, but it impresses me as one of the most essential elements of all that we retain of steady purpose or united action.

THE RECRUITS WILL COME

The recruits for the new levy do not come in as rapidly as we could wish—the harvest-field keeps many at home; let us hope and believe that few stay from lack of patriotism, or too vivid a mental conception of McClellan's six days' fighting. Still, *one way or another*, the men will come, for the battles must be fought, and the rebellion must be put down.

HOPE FOR THE SOUTH

It is perhaps worth our while to draw a few ideas from the concurrent testimony which we receive, in many ways, of the existing condition of affairs at the South. From refugee Unionists, from returned prisoners, from their own newspapers and public documents, we may gather what has been the consequence of a year and a half of separation. During that time, of course, much has been done to create for the Confederacy that "national" character and feeling for which their leaders have done so much. They certainly have a deeper respect for Northern courage, character, and power. They also are more than ever averse to a return of the old state of things. The Union party, in all the actually seceded States, has steadily decreased, and in equal ratio has the spirit of rebellion gained ground.

So far, then, there would *seem* to be nothing to encourage us, except the actual and tangible success of our arms; but he who supposes this, has been a poor student of history or of human nature, and has failed to notice many important items of Southern news. It is clearly evident, then, that a large and growing party at the South are weary of war, worn out with the terrible sacrifices they have made, sick and disgusted with military despotism, and anxious for peace. These men would be glad of a truce, an armistice, if that were possible—anything for a breathing spell. And here is the largest rift in the clouds above our national fortunes. Through this the sun begins to shine. The oftener we beat them, the worse their defeats and losses, whether in cities, in territory, or in men, the stronger will become the *peace* (not *Union*) men, and the weaker will be our enemy. Let us strike, then, hard and quickly, for the "Ebony Idol" is falling with his temple and his devotees!

WASHINGTON, 28 JULY 1862 (PUBLISHED 31 JULY 1862)

The changes hinted at in my last have, most of them, been made, and the "literature of the war" is enriched with sundry more of those important

Presidential manifestoes which have thus far marked the successive changes of this "strange, eventful history."

A DISAPPOINTED HOPE

In the immediate vicinity of the Capitol, we have heard little else but the most unqualified approbation of the action of the Executive, in the trying circumstances which he found himself compelled to meet and provide for. We who are so attached to the President, and who have such unbounded confidence in the soundness of his judgment, that we can hardly ever believe him to have erred, fondly imagined that for once, at least, there was no party or faction which could show a reason for disagreeing with him, or for criticizing his action. The friends of McClellan were apparently rejoiced that he had now an experienced and successful soldier, instead of a civilian, to attend to the forwarding of his supplies and reinforcements; while no atom of power or dignity had been taken from the "Young Napoleon." The enemies of that leader, on the other hand, were openly jubilant over the selection of another person for the responsible post of military Commander-in-Chief.[51] As for the proclamations, or more correctly, the *orders*, as they obviously contained all that the occasion called for, and no more, we looked to have them hailed with a unanimous expression of approval. Judge, then, of our surprise at the actual result.

THE DAILY PRESS OF NEW-YORK

Allow me to say that the course of certain prominent portions of the New-York press is without parallel in the history of American journalism. The conservatives, falsely so called, seem to be in an agony of fear lest the President is on the eve of launching the country into a war of rapine, pillage and destruction. The fanatical radicals are in a foaming rage because he makes provision for the carrying out of his proposition to the Border States representatives, even in his army orders.

The whole secret is here: so accustomed are these gentlemen to the juggling illusions of party platforms and political manifestoes, that they can neither understand nor appreciate an honest man who is in earnest. They seem unable to conceive that the President actually means to go the insane length of keeping his word, and that Union men in the Border States are to be compensated under any circumstances; for this, and no more, is the meaning of the "compensation" clause in the President's order relative to the employment of slaves. They may rest assured that the policy thus marked out will be religiously observed until the end. On the other hand, do those who, for an opposite reason, condemn the same action of the

Executive, forget that all this has been again and again foreshadowed in previous documents from the same hand? It is time that we all understood the man in whose strong hand we have placed our destinies, and were ready to believe that to all men, and in all circumstances, he will *do what he says*. It will be well for those to whom the Confiscation act is addressed, if they will take the same wholesome unction to their souls.

THE NEXT MILITARY MOVEMENT

As a nation, we move, and always have moved, by impulses and in cycles. Such, especially, has been our financial history in times gone by, and such is now the history of this war. We have, every now and then, to summon fresh energy and enthusiasm, make a new draft on our resources, and take a fresh start. So it was after the fall of Sumter; so it was after the Bull Run defeat; so it was when Halleck was sent to Missouri; and now we have just made another. The last grand movement gave us the Atlantic coast and the Valley of the Mississippi; we shall not have long to wait for the fruits of this one.

The great armies are again moving to new victories, and a fresh impulse seems to have been given to volunteering. The three hundred thousand men will come—are coming now, and they will move at once to battle-fields East and West.

DOOM OF THE GUERRILLA BANDS

One of the greatest evils of the present stage of the war—an evil not by any means unforeseen—is the increasing number and daring of the guerrilla bands—the last resort of a beaten but vindictive people. These collections of renegades, desperadoes, and outlaws, while without power to accomplish any definite military result, are still able to inflict unmeasured calamities upon the unfortunate populations whose territory is made the scene of their brigand-like exploits. There is but one medicine for a disease like this, and there is reason to believe that it will, from this time forth, be freely applied—if all the oaks in Kentucky are made to bear a crop of human acorns. Guerrilla warfare is war gone to seed, and cannot long be maintained in any region.

THE CABINET RUMORS

Do not be deceived by rumors of changes in the Cabinet: they have been incessant from the very commencement of this Administration, and are as well grounded as the others. When such a change comes, it will be "like a thief in the night"—suddenly, and no blanket daily will be allowed to canvass its why and wherefore for days and weeks beforehand. The day has gone by when the reporters could sit in the President's ante-room, and claim a report of the Cabinet meetings as a prescriptive right of their position. *Ives* was the last man who attempted to pierce the penetralia of *this* Administration.[52]

WASHINGTON, 4 AUGUST 1862 (PUBLISHED 7 AUGUST 1862)
The new week opens with a more cheerful feeling. The returns from most of the States, with reference to the new levy, are encouraging; the people seem to be in better heart, and from all portions of our widely-scattered hosts the dispatches indicate a renewal of hope, of energy, and of enterprise. It cannot be long before we have some new title or other to add to the long list of our victories.

The nation is, in truth, taking its lessons in the severe school of experience and adversity, with far more equanimity than was expected by those, at home or abroad, who were only acquainted with its mercurial impatience and hotheaded turbulence. The enduring patience and the inexhaustible pluck, as well as the dash and enterprise of the American character, will at last be duly appreciated by the world. Meanwhile the [illegible word] from our harvest-fields, as well as from the markets, are all encouraging. We shall have plenty to sell, and no end of purchasers, if all the prophecies of the knowing ones do not fail.

Such, then, being our own case, even in this, the darkest hour of our national history, let us look, so far as we are able, at the condition of those with whom we are struggling. The condition of the foreign market is a matter of small concern to them, without a marine or serviceable harbors, and they have been wise enough to resolve to do without the numberless luxuries and comforts of life that continue to cheer and strengthen us, as well in camp and hospital as at home. Their only anxiety, then, is for absolute necessaries, such as will keep their armies in the field, and save from actual suffering those who stay at home.

The testimony of the entire rebel press would go far to prove a crop of less than average bulk through all the food-producing portion of the States still within the power of the rebellion, while the flocks and herds of Kentucky, the wheat and corn of Missouri and Tennessee and Western Virginia, must be left out of their calculations. No more supplies can cross the Mississippi from Arkansas and Louisiana, with any certainty that they do not pass into the Federal commissariat, while Northern Mississippi, Alabama, Eastern Virginia, and long and fertile regions on the coast of Georgia, Florida, and the Carolinas, are either ravaged and stripped by contending armies, or beyond the reach of rebel foraging parties.

These must be fearful facts for the arch-traitors to look in the face, at a time, too, when the North is preparing larger hosts than ever before, so that to meet us, they must keep in the field every platoon of the vast force assembled by the frenzied energy of their efforts for the last four months. It is only too evident that all these things are beginning to make themselves felt and heard in the counsels of Davis and his co-conspirators, and if we may trust what seems to be reliable information, they are studying how they may arrest the impending ruin by "carrying the war into Africa."

The brilliant rush of Stonewall Jackson and the daring raid of Morgan are said to be feelers only, trying and learning the way over which grander invasions may attempt to pass.[53] There is evidence of desperation in the very conception of this invasion of the North, and we may hope and pray that the insane idea will culminate in the still wilder attempt. Should the rebels once abandon their defensive policy, they cast from them every advantage of position, territory, supply, superior information—everything which has thus far enabled them to oppose a steady front to the advancing columns of the Union army. The military probability is, however, that the development of the plans now in process of execution by our Generals will transfer the scene of the fall campaign, with its accompanying desolations, to regions south of the Richmond line, and further east from the Mississippi.

Gen. Halleck is in constant communication and consultation with the President and Secretary of War, and from all the indications, we in Washington believe that, thus far, the three work together in perfect harmony.

The city itself is deserted by all except the *workers*, and indeed many of them are taking their brief vacations. These are hard times for Cabinet officers, however, and little respite will they be able to take, until the return of the peace for which they are laboring.

The semi-traitors who attempted to disturb the unity of the last Congress in its support of the Administration, seem to have gone home to marshal their forces for the fall elections, hoping that *there* at least they may be able to strike home the infamous blows so steadily parried by the men who confronted them on the floor of the House and Senate. But they will fail before the people, as they did in the Capitol, and no amount of Indiana "butternut conventions" will add to the number of Jeff. Davis's bondsmen among the loyal people of the North.

Many prominent gentlemen have paid flying visits to Washington during the past fortnight, in connection with the numerous appointments under the Tax bill, but all things considered, the rush for office is not very great, and the general character of the applicants is decidedly respectable. The fact is, that political hacks and shysters, men without character or position, are dismayed by the tremendous responsibilities and the proportionate "bonds" required by the more remunerative of the new offices. The chances for "plunder," too, are reduced to the minimum by the wise provisions of the bill, and it takes a certain amount of that sort of carrion to call the political buzzards together. Hoping for an active and brilliant military week, I remain.

WASHINGTON, 18 AUGUST 1862 (PUBLISHED 21 AUGUST 1862)
The "heated term" seems at last to have burned itself out, and we no longer roll sleeplessly in our uncomfortable beds, but slumber cool o' nights, lulled by the drowsy hum of Virginia musquitoes.

HOW THEY COME
The new troops are beginning to pour in in considerable numbers, and their *personelle* and bearing is excellent. *This* time, at least, we have drawn on the real bone and sinew of the North, and the average of the new regiments will compare with the best of the old, for the character of the men who compose them. Hosts of men are now coming forward who could not afford to come at first, but whose patriotism now forbids them longer to delay the sacrifice. Honor indeed to the brave men who came at once and without hesitation; but let us not forget that those who are now volunteering do so with a full knowledge of the stern realities of the strife on which they are entering. They know they are marching to battle, probably to death, nor will they do their duty less perfectly that they thus count the cost beforehand. Here at headquarters all is hope and expectation. Disasters, defeats, heartrending losses, must and will come, but "the end is nearer than it was," and the Departments, under the ceaseless urging and spurring of the President, are straining every nerve to achieve speedy and complete success. The armies move more rapidly and secretly, the generals know that more is expected of them than ever before, the army is full of life and electricity, and we have every reason for assuring the good folks at home that our fall campaign will more than equal any series of successes we have yet attained.

THE DOOM OF THE GUERRILLAS
The feature of the war which at present attracts more especial attention, is the strange and alarming increase of guerilla bands in those portions of the Southern States from which all organized and permanent resistance has been swept by our victorious armies. The barbarous murder of the brave and brilliant Gen. Robert L. McCook, first of a whole family of heroes, has

excited a degree of indignation which needed only this to become an active element of vengeance and destruction.[54] Perhaps in no country, and among no people, was there ever so large an amount of the material of which these wolves of war are made. The South furnishes not only the utmost amount of material, but the best possible field for their employment, and the opinion is becoming pretty well settled among military men, that nothing but measures of bloody and unrelenting severity will in any degree mitigate, much less suppress, an evil which threatens to degrade and demoralize both parties to this great struggle.

THE NEUTRAL GROUND DEPOPULATED

Both of the contending powers in this war are fast "crystallizing" into permanent form. We have less difficulty now, than formerly, in discovering at once who are for us and who are against us, and we believe, from sad experience, more fully than we used, that all men are either the one thing or the other. The "neutral ground," which held so large a population at the beginning of the war, is fast being depopulated, and the timorous or time-serving squatters thereon are turning their faces South or North, as fear or interest impels.

A singular feature of the war, the natural outgrowth, possibly, of our previous history and development, is the fact that so many seem unable to connect the idea of *moral* turpitude, of any *sin* against God, man, or a high sense of duty, in the great crime of rebellion. Treason seems to them a sin created by statute law, and one whose commission will leave no stain upon a man's conscience or honor, or for which God will ever hold him accountable. Verily "this people's heart is waxed gross, and their ears dull of hearing." Nor need we wonder that those who thus begin should be found as utterly faithless as foes, as ever they were when the Capitol or the hustings rang with their hollow pretences of patriotism.

WENDELL PHILLIPS

Have you noticed Wendell Phillips's late speeches?[55] He has more fully than ever before defined the true position of himself and friends. He is no longer the apostle of the great reform, even in his own assertion, but seems voluntarily to take his true place once more as a mere vulgar agitator and sensation spouter. The Government was right when he was voted too insignificant for a cell in Fort Warren. Perhaps, however, his present desperate exertions *may* procure for him some sort of cheap and second class martyrdom.

Pardon this bit of personality, Mr. Editor, but we who are near the centre of this great and practical fight, see that it is in truth a "good fight of faith," and we are sick and angry with the bleating crowd of fault-finders who help in no one thing, but do their uttermost to clog the chariot wheels of the army which we consider the "host of the Lord." We, as a nation, are just beginning to see and know the true greatness and sublimity of our strange and mighty war, and we are angry alike with those who scoff and those who hinder.

THE RACE WHICH HAS NO END
I wonder if, during this Administration, the flood of office seekers will ever cease to pour in upon this devoted Government. Swarm after swarm has come and gone, of every stripe and dye; and now our hotels are filled with would-be Assessors and Collectors, with their backers and bottle holders. But this, too, must have an end, and then—what next?

THE DEAR OLD AIRS
The Saturday evening musical promenades are held in the Capitol, instead of the White House grounds, this summer, and the Marine Band discourses sweet music to gay and wandering crowds; but the striking features are changed. The swarm of army officers, brilliant in new uniforms, and heroic with battles yet to be fought and won, has disappeared. The throng is composed mainly of civilians—ladies in a large majority—with here and there a blue coat, too often with its arm in a sling, or resting on its crutches to gaze at the pretty girls and listen to the music. It is almost amusing, were there not a lesson in it, to see the sad faces of these convalescents brighten with a gleam of enthusiasm, when they recognize the opening chords of some well known national air. The music has a deep meaning to them, for they have fought, and toiled, and suffered, that the "Star Spangled Banner" and its brother harmonies might *not* be a forbidden sound under the shadow of the trees by the towering Capitol, and they know the worth of that for which they have paid so dear a price.

MEMORIALS OF GRIEF
The mourning festoons and wreaths still hang from the pillared fronts of the President's house and the public buildings; and all men, as they look at them, seem to have some kindly word to say for the courteous old Knickerbocker who passes from his high dignities to so graceful and honorable retirement.[56] I have looked in vain for some trace or memorial of his former presence or habits in the Presidential mansion; but none remain. Jackson left his favorite chair, and the marks of his boots on the bricks of

the old mantel-piece; but his pupil carried with him all but his pleasant memory.

EVENTS OF THE WEEK

Strange rumors are in circulation as to the probable military events of the week; but all that is true in these prophecies will be history so soon that I refrain from giving any of them. The feeling among the soldiers about the base indignities heaped upon the few prisoners taken in the late battle, is very strong and bitter. In the next fight there will be fewer prisoners taken on *either* side. Unless much care is taken to prevent it, we may yet make truth out of some of the rebel slanders concerning the bloody severity with which we prosecute the war. The fiend of retaliation is abroad, and there is only too much that calls for vengeance and retribution. For one, Mr. Editor, I earnestly hope that just punishment may be sternly meted out, but that our brave soldiers will not allow the bright honor of the Union armies to be tarnished by a single act of uncalled-for cruelty.

WASHINGTON, 24 AUGUST 1862 (PUBLISHED 28 AUGUST 1862)

The weather of this region becomes rapidly more and more autumnal. To-day almost requires a blazing grate for comfort, though, no doubt, warmer days are yet to come.

THE GREAT STRUGGLE

We have passed through a week of intense excitement, though we have had few signs of anything like a panic. Bringers of bad news meet with so poor a reception now-a-days, that few care to assume the unwelcome office gratuitously. We are now looking earnestly forward to the apparently certain result of all these stupendous changes in the plan of the campaign. It would seem inevitable that the banks of the Rappahannock should soon become the arena of the most desperate encounter of the war.[57]

As this struggle draws to its close, whatever that close may be, the scene of the combat narrows, and our attention is allowed to concentrate more and more with the concentration of the opposing forces. The armies, too, on either side, swell to gigantic proportions. It is a war of the Titans. Even supercilious Europe, snobbishly proud of three thousand years of blood and misery, forgets to sneer, and watches with hushed breath these strange developments of the inherent energy of a free people. "Surely," they say among themselves, "it is time we interfered and put a stop to this, but which side shall we interfere with? We sympathize with the South, but who shall lay hands upon the North while the towering rage is strong upon the young giant?" Let them counsel and whisper together across the Channel, and behind the deadened walls of their cabinets, they will undoubtedly see fit to wait and see if the six hundred thousand really come at the call of the President—to see if the iron men-of-war are actually built—and to see what sort of fate hangs over the vast camps on either bank of the Rappahannock.

It is now generally conceded that Gen. Pope's retreat across Culpepper county was a masterly affair, and a bitter disappointment to the enemy, who thought to catch him napping.[58] Nor was the great enterprise of moving the Army of the Potomac managed less discreetly by its commander. They are now—where the Commander-in-Chief would have them—a host of tried and seasoned veterans, with an endless stream of fresh men pouring in to fill up any gaps which war may make in their ranks. Can the enemy say the same? Is there not a confession in Jeff. Davis's Message to his Congress that their young men are gone or going, and that now the *old* men must be called out to stem the tide that is rushing in upon his doomed Confederacy? At this rate they will soon be cursing the policy which renders their "laboring population" useless for the purposes of war, and looking around in vain for any to take the places of the old men who have gone where the young ones went before them—untimely.

MR. LINCOLN'S LETTER

Have you noticed President Lincoln's reply to Horace Greeley?[59] Has this country seen a more thoroughly dignified, self-possessed, powerful *crystallization* of policy or purpose? The President talks as one speaking from a lofty height to a man hopelessly below him. It is an appeal, too, to the American people, which they will thoroughly appreciate. It says to them, "Do you see how an honest man can thus be true to *all* his trusts, nor fail in any of the great matters which his country has required of him?" And in the last clause recurs one of the noblest "confessions of faith political" to be found in this or any other language:

> I have here stated my purpose according to my *official* duty; and I intend no modification of my oft-expressed *personal* wish that all men everywhere could be free.

FRAUDS

The gross and contemptible frauds and errors of the managers of the public building fund are bringing down tardy but certain punishment on the heads of the thieves and imbeciles who have disgraced themselves and those who appointed them. We have still a few unexamined heirlooms of our political predecessors which will pay well for inspection. I sometimes fear that even the river of civil war will hardly cleanse *our* stables from the filth which has been so long in gathering.

THE TAX-GATHERERS

The business of appointing the necessary officers under the new tax bill, will be completed this week, we hope, and the work of filling our exhausted treasury will be pushed forward with all energy. To me this tax is more an experiment than the establishment of a permanent system. There will be many changes and modifications necessary before the gigantic machine will work smoothly and well. We have not been, like the European governments, educated for centuries in the art of getting at as much as possible of the people's money, and it will be no easy task to acquire the necessary skill. We must beware of putting new wine into old bottles.

And now I must close this letter to go down to Willard's and see what new battle—victory or defeat—the hotel loungers are fighting for Pope or Halleck. By this time yesterday the *quid nuncs* had taken two thousand prisoners and destroyed Stonewall Jackson's pontoon train. To-day there may be something still more wonderful.

WASHINGTON, 8 SEPTEMBER 1862 (PUBLISHED 11 SEPTEMBER 1862)

If indeed the darkest hour is just before the dawning, surely we have now a right to look expectingly eastward; for never, in all this long night of our great national trouble, have the clouds hung so heavily as at present.

AT LOW-WATER MARK

The ebb and flow of the tide of events has been tremendous, but we are again at low water mark. We were at flood when our victorious armies held the Mississippi Valley as in a vice, and McClellan was thundering at the gates of Richmond. Then the ebb set in, and day by day ever since, we have receded further and further. Even well-won victories seem to do us no good, for an unkind fate snatches from us all their dearly purchased fruits; and after nine days of successful struggling, the army of General Pope finds it good policy to abandon Centreville and all its bristling lines of fortifications.[60]

A NEW REVELATION

But it is not the defeat on the old ill-omened battle-ground—a defeat as useless and causeless as the panic of a year ago: it is not the beleaguered capital, or even the presence of a rebel *corps d' armee* in Maryland, for the first time in the war, that fills the mind of your correspondent with gloomy forebodings. I have seen, during the past fortnight, more than ever before of the different spirit that actuates the two armies. A year and a half of hard fighting has done very much to elevate the character and the motives of the rebel soldiery, and render them, what they certainly were *not* at first, the moral equals of our own. They actually deem themselves patriots, fighting for their liberties and their homes, and cheer the haggard and squalid starvation of their campfire gatherings with stories of '76, and bright pictures of the nation yet to rise from the ashes of this fearful war. *We* know them to be the deluded tools of an infamous oligarchy; but they consider themselves the worthy representatives in this day of the patriots of Washington's army—and the worst of it is, that they fight according to the delusion, and not according to the truth. Our own troops, on the other hand, have become good soldiers, fight well, endure all suffering courageously, obey the officers, love their flag and their country, but lack the headlong, fanatical desperation of their opponents. Perhaps I shall be censured for admitting thus much—but why not, if it is the truth, and who will deny that it is the truth?

THE "SITUATION"

As to the immediate position of affairs, in a military point of view, little can be said, except that a week or two of hard fighting is before us, in which we shall probably be victorious; and if we *are*, little of this vast array of rebels will ever see the south shore of the Rappahannock—as an army. If, on the other hand, we are beaten, it may be that you will be compelled to dispense with your Washington correspondence.

General McClellan again commands the forces assembled for the defence of the city of Washington.[61] Two others of our best officers, with an adequate force, face the enemy in Maryland; it would seem that the rebels cannot possibly break through the terrible lines of defence upon which they are so confidently casting themselves. We shall soon see, however, and the sword must decide, under God, whether the fortunes of the Great Republic are to sink lower, or whether for us, too, the tide shall turn again.

Other nations have passed through hours of peril as extreme, and lived to enjoy ages of prosperity. There remain, too, strong evidences of our national vitality. The new levies come forward in an endless stream; the public confidence in Government securities seems to be but little shaken; we have hardly touched our tremendous resources as yet; and the people seem to care less for peace, and to be far more determined about the war, than when they began to answer the first call for volunteers.

THE CITY AND THE PRESIDENT

The city is alive with martial sights and sounds, and long lines of wagons, horses and marching men again obstruct our streets. A regiment is passing my window, now, and the band plays, "Hail to the Chief, who in triumph advances!"—who *can* they mean? or is the strain meant as a prophecy?

The President pays little attention to anything but army matters, and is doing all a man can, to ensure our success in the great battle before us. He is giving his personal attention to many matters rarely touched by a President before, and you may see the traces of his hand in summary action hereafter.

WAITING FOR LIGHT

We are indeed looking for the development of some things that seem dark and inexplicable in the events of this short Virginia campaign. We trust that the truth will see the light, and awaiting the proper investigations, we refuse to believe that Franz Sigel is a coward, or McDowell a traitor, or John Pope an imbecile; while we can readily imagine that some subordinate officers may have allowed personal feeling, low jealousy, or that factious spirit which sometimes drives men on to their ruin, to influence their action in the *field* as well as in the *camp*.

Rumor, the crazy fiend, is rampant, and we alternate between hope and panic in a way that would be ludicrous, if [it] were not for our "Hannibal at the gates."

WASHINGTON, CA. 14 SEPTEMBER 1862 (PUBLISHED 18 SEPTEMBER 1862)

McClellan is commander of all the forces assembled for the defence of the Capital. He has a large moiety of these forces with him in the field, sufficient, it is believed, to enable him to carry out that portion of his plans which relates to the rebels in Maryland. If it is *not* sufficient, the fault is his own, for no man hinders him from increasing his army this time, whatever truth there may be in the oft-repeated complaints of his partisans as to War-office interference with his peninsular failure. Gen. Banks, the man true and tried and trusty, found singularly well adapted to every position in which he has been placed, holds the Capital under McClellan, aided by such leaders as Heintzelman beyond the fortifications, and Porter within them.[62] Of the forces at his command, or their disposition, Fort Warren forbids that any correspondent should speak, although swarms of rebel spies pass in and out under the noses of our eagle-eyed officials. The campaign of the defence of Washington promises to be a brief one, and beyond the desolation of Upper Maryland, we may not suffer materially by the daring movement of Lee and Jackson.

BAD USE OF AN OLD WORD

I do not like to see the term "raid"—well used of old when "the blue bonnets were over the border" on a cow-stealing and hay-burning tour—applied to an invasion by a vast and well-led "corps d'armee" which threatens a capital, and sends panic through large cities and populous States. We have made very little by our childish attempts to make ourselves believe that our enemies are contemptible, and the Chinese style of waging war is going out of fashion. Let us rather frankly own that the great danger of our history thunders at the portals of our National life, and, if we have sufficient nobility of soul and patriotism left, forget for a few days to find fault with our rulers and leaders, forbear to throw dirt and stones at each other, desist from our preparations for future political campaigns, and rally for the salvation of the Republic, with as much singleness of heart as those we call *rebels* rally for its *ruin*.

GIVING COMFORT IN THE WRONG QUARTER

It must have been with a smile of grim delight, a chuckle of derision which even his chronic neuralgia could not entirely subdue, that Jefferson Davis perused the records of your late Democratic Conventions, with their resolutions against the Government and in favor of the war. Beauregard must have forgotten his dyspepsia, and Johnson his stray bit of shell in the flesh;[63] on reading in the *Herald* the unrebuked treason which the hired agents of the Confederacy have for ten days poured upon the people through the old, accustomed channel. With consummate tact, the assassins of our national existence have selected the hour when the bruised hearts of the people are sore with defeat and disaster, when the States are mourning over their dead and their dying, when first the bitter cup of taxation is approaching the lips of a Mammon-worshipping crowd, and when a new distribution of political power at the hands of the people is approaching—they have chosen such a time, I say, to send forth through a thousand channels the emissaries of distrust, disorganization and anarchy. They are tempting alike the people at the polls and the General at the head of his army, and they seem to rely, with a faith sublime in the perfection of its brazen impudence, upon a degree of forbearance, on the part of Government, which to your correspondent seems to somewhat step over the narrow line between mercy and imbecility.

Believe me, Mr. Editor, the Republic is fighting other battles than those on the banks of the Potomac, the Ohio, and the Mississippi, and it may be that her best victories will be won, after all, in the inner souls of individual men, under canvass, or under home roof-trees.

MCCLELLAN A GREAT ORGANIZER

Speaking of McClellan, he has vindicated his fame for a remarkable faculty of "organization," by the rapidity and perfection with which he has restored to working order an army demoralized by long marches, much fighting and disaster. Even his worst enemies accord him this meed of praise. We hope for him that the assertions of his admirers are true, and that he has no other ambition than to perform his duty as a soldier. Otherwise we may have one step lower to make in our national degradation, and a name in the history of this great infamy to write below that of Davis, or of Twiggs.[64]

THE NEW TROOPS

The new troops are continually arriving, and fresh from the people, will infuse a new and healthy vigor into the war-worn ranks of the veterans by whom they will be surrounded. They all look well, and are full of life and energy. By the time your readers have this letter before them, they may very likely have heard how the new levies stand fire; unless, indeed, our enemies again prove too much for the slow strategy of our leaders, and find their way back to the dry desert that used to be Virginia.

A STORM YET TO COME

In either case, however, whether we beat them in the open field, or whether they skedaddle deftly under cover of rainy nights, and by favor of blind watchers, the solid advantage of the movement, together with a fair, handsome bill of costs, will remain with us. They, too, have their distractions and troubles, which would burst out in all fury under the pressure of a fruitless expedition, or the chagrin of a great defeat. We fondly hope to afford their discontented spirits both these stimulants, and many more, before a great while.

THE PRESIDENT IN PERIL

A few days since the President's horse ran away with him during a morning ride, scared by the cheering of a marching regiment, and for a short time the Commander-in-Chief was in danger of serious accident. Thanks, however, to his long limbs and strong arms, he succeeded in retaining his place in the saddle, and in calming his furious and plunging Bucephalus, with no other injury than a slightly sprained ankle. However, we were suddenly shocked into an appreciation, momentarily, of how deep an interest we all had in the safety of our wise Chief Magistrate. Strong men turned to each other with an involuntary shudder. "If he *had* been thrown and killed!" After that, indeed, even the most hopeful could discern little beside clouds and thick darkness.

SAFE FROM CAPTURE

In almost any event, Washington seems to be safe from a capture by assault, and as for taking it any other way, with the Potomac full of our gunboats, and all the North behind us, it is hardly to be thought of. Cowardice and treachery, however, have grown to the dignity of "vital forces" of late, and we are compelled to take them systematically into all our calculations. In one of his late works, Victor Hugo says "the pressure of a great hand overshadowed Waterloo"—that is the idea, though my translation may be defective—but who shall deny the presence of some unseen hand, if the armies of the Union fail to play the man on the decisive battle-fields before them. Let us, therefore, believing that *the* Hand is with us in our just strife, look forward with courage and hope to a triumph which shall let the light in through the dark sky of the present.

WASHINGTON, 22 SEPTEMBER 1862 (PUBLISHED 25 SEPTEMBER 1862)

My last letter, I fear, was written in a somewhat sour and gloomy mood, nor has the cloud yet entirely passed away. Thus far, well done; but is it so vast a thing that the enemies of the Republic are once more hurled back into a wilderness of their own making, and that actually we are not now in danger of invasion?[65] I trow *not!* They are still on the south bank of the Potomac—a stream they ought never to have crossed again as an organized army—and they may even now be gathering their ragged and dirty hordes for a desperate effort to place themselves once more where they were two weeks ago. This time, at least, they will hardly feel like marching to the tune of "Maryland, my Maryland;" but they have an unlimited choice of quicksteps, and we seem not to be overstocked with lively music for marching purposes.

THE REBEL EBB TIDE

Looking back, however, on the week gone by, we can say, with some approach to certainty, that the tide of this war has again turned, and that it is once more an *ebb* with the rebellion. They threw away, when they crossed the Potomac, all the hardly-won fruits of many desperate battles, and in the ravines along the Monocacy and the Catocton they have left all the laurels and advantages of the James, the Chickahominy, and *the* "Run." Let us be sparing, hereafter, in our praises of generalship which is ready to make such blunders under the intoxication of a few successes.

The summer campaign fairly ended when, on Friday last, General Pleasanton sat on his horse to look at the dust of the last squadron that descended the river bank, and escaped our "strategy" by the marvellous magic of its unmolested skedaddle.[66]

Honor to the gallant men of all ranks who fought so steadily and bravely through those five September days. We can well mourn over the sleepers whose bones will hallow the soil of Maryland. Martyrs in a great and worthy cause, not fallen in vain—alas, that in this day we should need so many "witnesses" unto the death for the good faith and freedom of our fathers.

THE NEW CAMPAIGN

Now begins a new campaign, East and West. No plan may yet have crystallized in the brain of the General-in-Chief, and it may be many days before we see what new maps we shall need to trace the turnings and changes of the struggle; but the new campaign is before us, to be fought out in cool and pleasant October and November days. This, too, bids fair to be a hard-fought and desperate campaign, for the Southern journals are exclaiming with one voice, that they cannot face another winter in the field or in the camp. To this, perhaps, we owe the late desperate attempt to adopt an invasive policy, and to wind up all in a few short, decisive encounters.

Now, however, that the tables are turned, and every new success of our arms will deprive the rebel armies of more and more of their resources, and hem them in, like the Italian victim, in a forever-contracting prison, no one can doubt that all the dying strength of the Confederacy will be put forth. They will turn at bay like hunted wolves, and we know already, too well, that these men are of the same indomitable race with ourselves, and can meet us on any fair field with as good hope of success as our own. Now, therefore, ought the blockade to be trebly watchful. Every pound of powder chased away from our coasts, or sent into our ports as a prize, might otherwise be breath in the laboring nostrils of rebellion. Now ought their wide frontier to be penetrated wherever they have deemed it worth defending, and column after column, each strong enough in itself to defend itself, should be poured across their devoted territory.

There is a chance now to make the remainder of this war bloody indeed, but short, and therefore merciful. No European mutterings or threats will be so loud that the thunder of the feet of a million of marching men cannot drown them, so that the world shall hear no sound but the tread of that advance. Let us believe that our leaders and rulers, civil and military, will do the Republic the justice to realize such hopes and expectations as these, for on every hand we see armies gathering, ships building, great columns moving. The roar of one battle has hardly died on our ears, before the smoke on some far horizon begins to gather over another.

"NOT FIGHTING ENOUGH"

There are those, Mr. Editor, who accuse this Administration of an aversion to fighting. How just the accusation may be, we can only judge from the record. The men must be hungry for horrors, if the incessant bloodshed of July, August, and September, leaves them still unsatisfied. "But," say they, "we want *results—favorable* results." That's what's the matter. Our armies have been beaten in several bloody battles, led though they were by the best of our generals, so far as we know them, and forsooth the President is to blame, and the Administration is weak and all but imbecile. "Why was not Jones in McClellan's place, and why was not Scrub allowed to dictate to Pope? *I'll* tell you why—Jones would have gone in a minute, and Scrub stood with his mouth ready open, but the Administration would not let them have the power. Go to, now. Let us pitch into this Administration. You curse Stanton, and I'll pass a vote of want of confidence in the President, and we will get a Senator drunk, and make him swear he has urged him to resign, and let Hamlin try it.[67] Who knows how much we can all accomplish?"

THE PULL ALL TOGETHER

Now is such a good time for a patriot to do what he can to make his country weaker than it is—it can so well afford it—that each would-be patriot strikes with his dagger of glass or tin, and thinks himself a very Brutus. No, Mr. Editor, now is the time for us all to gather as one man, with one voice, one hope, one energy, and strengthen the hands of our Government, lest it fail, and go down into the darkness forever. A long pull, a strong pull, though many of us pull no more—let us give it now.

WASHINGTON, 29 SEPTEMBER 1862 (PUBLISHED 2 OCTOBER 1862)

Never was there better weather for military operations than these cool, yet sunny September days have been, yet the whole week has passed over us without any perceptible change in the position of our army. It must be that extended and important movements are on foot, but the outside world cannot see the indications. It is well, in one sense, that they cannot, provided our leaders have kept their secrets from their enemies as completely as from their friends.

THE REBELS AT THEIR OLD TRICKS

The Richmond papers still claim the late battles in Maryland as victories for themselves, and it is very true that they acquitted themselves admirably, saved their armies, and effected a safe retreat from a most dangerous position; but the more we learn of the actual facts, the more clearly does the fact appear that the victory was with us. Their loss was not only vastly greater than our own in killed and wounded, but in *deserters alone* it is supposed that they have lost more than they took from us in the disgrace at Harper's Ferry.[68]

So far, so good; the results of that brief and bloody campaign are with us, but it remains to be seen in what manner and how well we will avail ourselves of advantages so dearly purchased. We have yet before us, in all probability, bloodier contests than any that have yet dyed our plains with blood. Between this and the first of January it will be necessary for us to annihilate our enemies. We can do it. Let us hope that the doing will be equal to the power.

THE EMANCIPATION PROCLAMATION

One victory, a moral one, has been gained by the President during the week that has passed, in sending out to the country and the world his Emancipation Proclamation.[69] It was a bold movement, in face of many probabilities and some disagreeable certainties; and even now it depends upon those at the North who agree with it in principle, to show that its grand announcement of approaching liberation is not all "*brutum fulmen.*"

Of course a large class, even at the North, will condemn the action of the President, will sneer at the Proclamation as useless, pointless, hopeless of all enforcement. Others will assail it upon Constitutional grounds, and in the approaching State elections it will be held up to the mob of the "Home Guard," as a new evidence of the "nigger loving" tendencies of the party in power.

All the old party war-cries will be sounded again, all the old party jealousies will gather around the November polls, and unless the people are true to themselves, we may fear that the first effect of the President's action may be injurious to the good and holy cause in which it was taken. I say the *first* effect, for none who truly believe in the final triumph of the right, can doubt the last result of any blow struck for justice.

The people will only hurry on to deserved disaster, if they now fail to sustain a Government which has planted itself, more firmly than ever, on the broadest and best of foundations. Now, therefore, let the new regiments press forward, for there may soon be great gaps in the ranks for them to fill, and battles of the last importance, where they can show themselves not unworthy of the men who have gone before them.

THE BIRTH OF A VERY SMALL MOUSE

By the way, was there ever such a man of straw as that innocent little pleasure excursion and spouting party of "the Governors?"[70] Was ever so much fuss made over the birth of a mouse of that size? The quid-nuncs of the press wandered through hotel passages, applied their ears to numberless keyholes, peered through aggravating curtained windows, snuffing treason, seeing ghosts of Frémont, and transforming a squad of patriotic gentlemen over their "refreshments" into a gang of Catilines plotting the ruin of—McClellan. Never was anything more cordial and harmonious than the meeting of the President and his gubernatorial guests, and nothing could have been more full of good-will and mutual promises of active cooperation than their parting. So ends a mist that had like to become a cloud.[71]

BUSY AT HIS OLD TRADE

There are the usual rumors afloat of changes in the Cabinet, all from "reliable sources," and the "gentleman confidentially connected with one of the Departments" has been as busy as ever in his old trade of tearing down and building up again. Still, Cabinet meeting after Cabinet meeting is called, and still the accustomed seats are filled by the old familiar forms. That long table in the President's business room could tell tales, no doubt, if it could speak; but as no other witness is in a position to be questioned, we must even take things as they are.

RETURNING HOME

A few families are beginning to return from their summer haunts, and before long our "society" will once more lift its diminished head. Not for much gaiety, however; the thoughts of too many of us are with the dead and the suffering, and the latter are around us in far too great numbers for us to think much of other "hospitalities."

WASHINGTON, 3 OCTOBER 1862 (PUBLISHED 6 OCTOBER 1862)

As time passes onward through this wonderful cycle of our nation's history, the air seems to become thick with the mingling shadows of possible events, through which it is sometimes hard to discern, even with the eye of faith, any light around the goal towards which we hopefully believe that we are steering. There are so many things that *may* happen, which, to the blindest, it is clear would change the whole current of our affairs for the better or the worse.

Among others, we have daily before us the probability of a great struggle in Virginia, to decide the fate of the largest and best appointed armies now in the field for either side, commanded respectively by the first skill and science on this continent. This would in ordinary times be enough of suspense and anxiety; though we have long since ceased to hope that any one victory or defeat, however complete or overwhelming, can have power to stay the tide of war, or force either of the contending powers into an unwished-for peace. More blood must flow, more treasures be expended, and wider areas laid waste, before this fierce spirit of rebellion can be permanently laid. Nevertheless, we may reasonably look for valuable results from this fall campaign, for any important success on our part would drive still further into the future the possibility of those foreign complications which at present constitute our national "skeleton in the closet." Until we can have something more reliable than the declarations and assurances of the ambitious Napoleon and "perfidious Albion," we can hardly rest quietly in confidence of continued neutrality, except in the light of such evidences of our own National vitality and power as shall scare away any European nations from their wished for transatlantic feast.

ENGLISH "NEUTRALITY"

Nor is there anything to encourage us in the precise manner in which England has maintained her boasted "neutrality." Not only have we met on every battle-field of the war, English guns and cannon, rendered effective with English ammunition; at the hands of men clothed with goods of English manufacture—not only have three-fourths of the prizes seized by our blockading squadrons been vessels of English build, but—last and foulest breach of faith—the infamous pirates now preying upon our commerce, and sending terror to the hearts of our whole mercantile marine, are in everything but in name *English privateers*. They were built, armed, equipped, and all but officered, in England; and under other circumstances our Government would be fully justified in granting to our plundered merchants letters of marque and reprisal against the commerce of Great Britain. This, however, the posture of affairs forbids that we should do, and we can only smother our wrath, and wait for the day of reckoning which cannot fail to come. But, judging the future by the past, we need fear at present nothing worse than this from any European power.

THE TIDE OF SUCCESS

To return to our home affairs: the aspect of the war has changed very much for the better within the past thirty days, both in the East and West. The tide of success which turned in our favor at South Mountain, seems to flow with a steady current, if slower than we could wish;[72] and never before did we have in the field, at any one time, such a mass of trained and available strength, both in officers and men. Let us then look upon their gathering thousands hopefully and cheerfully, not doubting that they will yet fulfill the promise of their setting forth.

THE MESSAGE

In other matters, we are entering upon a month of councils involving the gravest interests, and deliberations in which victories are to be won not less important than those of the army in the field. Already, it is said, the President is at work upon his Message [to Congress, due to reconvene in December], and the several Cabinet officers are preparing the reports and exhibits which will teach the nation its actual strength and condition, as well as shape the legislation of the winter session of Congress. From day to day, then, the future policy of this Administration—in war, finance, and foreign intercourse—must be gradually taking form, and the few weeks before its official promulgation will be passed by the people in anxious solicitude.

THE ELECTIONS

There are also the elections of Nov. 4th, all of which are declared, in advance, to be hopelessly against the party now in power. Too much importance should not be attached to these expressions of the feeling of one party, while so much of the opposing strength is in the field. Let the elections result as they will, they can hardly change the policy of the Government in any important result, nor can the Congressmen now elected hamper the President at present, for the short session of THIS Congress will doubtless provide for all the Administration at present needs; and even should the new Congress be against the Government, which I decidedly refuse to believe, the country and the world will wear another face by the time it shall be called together.

WASHINGTON, 6 OCTOBER 1862 (PUBLISHED 9 OCTOBER 1862)

Well might the distracted multitude, whose doom it is to read and to listen, plug their ears with cotton, and sit by with closed eyes, waiting for the end of this fearful war panorama of ours. Certainly, the past week has been surpassingly fertile in rumors. According to the reporters, the Cabinet has been rent and torn like a village debating society; the generals have quarrelled like disappointed schoolboys; the rebels have sent forward proposals for peace, at the same time that they raise the black flag and double the severity of their conscription; and the threatening despotisms of Europe have at last agreed that the turbulent democracy of the New World must no longer monopolize the horror and the ruin of the day. All this, and more; yet the end of our current week finds us where we were at the beginning, except that the tide of battle still turns strongly in our favor.

THOSE FLYING RUMORS

If any one will take the trouble to read the debates in the rebel Congress on the peace resolutions, they will see that the *only* ground for such proposals, was the supposed fact that a long succession of victories had placed the Confederacy in a position to dictate terms to the United States, and that all such ideas must have vanished like a bevy of wild fowl on the announcement of the true position of the armies in the field. No, the end is not yet—and in all the wide field before him, Jeff. Davis has found no olive tree from which to pluck a branch to send northward.

As to the reported bickerings among our more prominent military men, who can doubt that these gentlemen occasionally find themselves taking different views even of vital points, and upholding the same with all the energy of conviction; but let us do these gentlemen the justice to believe that now, as in times past, their discussions as to what is best for the public good will not be allowed to descend to the level of personal altercation. It will be enough for us, in this regard, if we reserve our faith for what may appear, if anything, upon the official and public record. Why need we make gossip of a private heart-burn if the man who endured it faces courageously, all the same, the enemies of the Republic?

As to the complicated diplomacy of self-seeking cabinets in Europe, no man can penetrate their "refuges of lies," but we will do well to pile Corinth on Antietam, and spur on the workmen in our navy-yards, for here only shall we find arguments that Europe can really appreciate. To these more distant foes every additional *Monitor* extends its iron fingers, and says, "I am a warning—there are more of us coming, and the knife which would divide the Republic may have its edge turned by our iron mail before it touches the national life."

PREJUDGING THE ADMINISTRATION

I see that some of your dailies have already written down this Administration as "a failure." "Let no man's epitaph be written until he dies," is a safe rule with governments as well as with people, and there will be time enough yet to decide the question of success, when the President and his advisers surrender their power to those who shall come after them.

THE PRESIDENT'S TRIP

The President's visit to the army was a wise and well-advised action, and Mr. Lincoln has, no doubt, obtained from personal observation and friendly consultation with his favorite general, a far better and clearer idea of the position and capabilities of the army, than he could ever have done from the garbled and unfair reports of either the friends or the enemies of McClellan.[73] The former, by the way, seem to be doing their uttermost to effect the ruin of their idol. They seem to take it for granted that all the world besides themselves are striving to do him harm, and by their frantic charges at every flag of any other color, they are fast transferring to him much ill feeling and distrust that they alone have merited. I do not harbor the idea, for one, that his many tempters will succeed in making McClellan anything else than an honest and loyal man, however wofully they may fail in creating a Napoleon. We need not look to him for anything like the Corsican's Italian Campaign, but at the same time we need fear no burlesque attempt at a *coup d'etat*.

BRIGHTER DAYS

On the whole, then, the national skies are brightening, and might look even brighter, if we had faith to wipe the mist of the Past from the spectacles through which we take our glimpses of the Future. The fall campaign in the West has opened handsomely, and the results to be obtained there are second only, but still *second*, to those we have now a right to expect from the army of the East. The whole Mississippi Valley would not compensate us for a defeat of the forces on the upper Potomac, for the one would neutralize the other. The result, however, seems gradually becoming more and more safe, as our ever cautious and provident general draws steadily around his enemy the forces from which he must escape, or *to* which he must inevitably succumb.

The new levies are wanted now. Oh, that we had two hundred thousand more! They are needed on the Potomac, on the shores of the Gulf, at the mouth of the Mississippi, in all the Great Valley, and at a dozen points along the Atlantic coast. Why do they not hasten on? Now is our time for a brief and glorious campaign, that shall by its grand results insure us alike against domestic treason and foreign jealousy.

HITTING THEM WHERE THEY LIVE

The President's Emancipation Proclamation is having a greater effect at the South than even its friends anticipated. "It is the *hit* bird that flutters." Every report, from every source, would seem to indicate an immense sensation all over the regions now in rebellion. Further to exasperate the traitors is simply impossible; if then they are experiencing any large degree of new emotion, it must be that mixture of rage and fear which puzzles the brain of counsel, and unstrings the nerves of action. At the North little effect can yet be seen, unless an extra spice of bitterness in the stump harangues of the Opposition may be called an "effect." Let us wait and see; the deed was right in itself; well intended; well guarded. *Can* its last results be otherwise than good? I trow not.

WASHINGTON, 13 OCTOBER 1862 (PUBLISHED 16 OCTOBER 1862)
Again the end of the week finds you with good news from the army, to lay before your readers. Up to this writing, the achievements in the West far exceed in practical importance any that have yet been secured east of the Blue Ridge.

CLOSING UP THE WAYS
By a glance at the map, it will be seen that if the success of Rosecrans, near Corinth, shall be well followed up, he will sever, finally and completely, the great thoroughfare by which the rebellion beyond the Mississippi has maintained its connection with its heart and centre, and by which so large a portion of its supplies have come.[74] It is now pretty well established that large quantities of various munitions of war, of the utmost importance to the rebels, instead of running the blockade, have been quietly landed at Matamoras, and a small port in Texas, about forty miles north. From this point they have been conveyed overland through Texas, and, together with vast supplies of Texas beef, have crossed the Mississippi at Vicksburg, after completing the armament of the rebel armies in Arkansas and Missouri. This route will now be closed up, and we may rely on the Navy Department to do much towards drying up the long-concealed fountainhead of so much evil.

A great effect of the active and decisive operations in Kentucky and Tennessee, scarcely less in importance than the safety of those much harassed communities, will be the consequent impossibility of sending reinforcements to Lee from the West, as was so successfully done during McClellan's Peninsular campaign. The rebels on the Upper Potomac must now fight it out alone, and the best they can hope for is that winter will find them in their comfortless camps not *yet* killed or taken.

MOVEMENTS ON FOOT
There are developments of the power of the Government yet to be made in the valley of the Mississippi, of whose progress and extent many are aware,

but of which it would be treason now to speak more definitely. Nor need the people fear that the remainder of this fall weather will be spent idly in camp by the forces on the Potomac.

The enemy are evidently trying to inspirit their troops by brilliant and daring enterprises, like the late wonderful raid by Stewart and his bold riders.[75] A very good plan, by the way, which might be occasionally tried to good advantage by our own leaders, though in truth, as matters stand now, we have no need to run any unnecessary risks, with the game so much in our own hands.

THE SOUTHERN FORCE

Late accounts from the South place their whole force in the field at somewhat over six hundred and fifty thousand men, of whom over half are now in Virginia. Allowing this as true, which is probably allowing about half too much, and granting their ability to furnish such an army with all supplies, we need see nothing in it to alarm us, knowing, as we do, from statistics, that it must be the *last* great army which can be drawn for this war, from the revolted States. Especially, when in the last ten days we have defeated and demoralized at least twenty per cent. of the whole number, at Corinth, Perryville, &c.[76]

OUR FOREIGN RELATIONS

So far as appears from anything yet seen or known on this side of the water, our foreign relations remain without material change, either for the better or the worse. Still I insist upon my old position, that our victories on the land, backed up by our gunboats on the sea, are our only guaranty against the hatred and jealousy of Oligarchy in England and Imperialism in France. They only wait for the hour of our sorest trouble, our most helpless necessity, to prove to us how false have been their many protestations of friendship in times past. Gradually but surely, however, the *people* of Europe, the masses, now more powerful than ever, are gaining correct views of the relative position of the contending forces in this country, and all that is worth having of popular love or sympathy is unquestionably with us.

THE FALL ELECTIONS

Here in Washington, we are awaiting with much anxiety the result of the fall elections in the North, to know if the people have really condemned the Administration. Should the result be generally favorable, nothing could be more strengthening to the Government, for it is well understood here that the truest and staunchest of its friends are in the field, with sharper arguments than ballots in their hands. If of those who remain at home from any cause, there is still a majority who approve the course of the President, under whatever name they may come to his support, a tremendous lesson will have been given to the country and the world.

THE PAY DEPARTMENT

I have good reason for believing that the temporary difficulties in the Treasury Department are *only* temporary, and that simultaneously with their disappearance, there will be inaugurated sundry much-needed reforms in the Pay Department, designed to insure the more prompt and regular satisfaction of the just demands of the army and the contractors. Nothing just now is more loudly called for than such a reform. Not that our brave soldiers are in any sense mercenaries, but that all of them, or nearly all, have left those at home who will look for the periodical visits of the paymaster with anxious interest, when the winter winds are adding to the loneliness of their desolate hearthstones.

OUR NEW HEROES

Nothing is more cheering than the universal report from every battle-field of the admirable conduct of the new levies. These men came *to fight*, well-knowing what and how deadly a strife was before them. They came with minds made up, memories stored with descriptions of brave deeds done by those by whose side they were called to stand, and they have done their duty wonderfully well, adding the fire of fresh troops to the steadiness of veterans.

On the whole, then, we may look forward hopefully, if anxiously, believing that the end is nearer now than when we first began.

WASHINGTON, 20 OCTOBER 1862 (PUBLISHED 23 OCTOBER 1862)

After a brief absence among more peaceful and "old time" looking regions at the North, it takes several days to bring one's self once more into sympathy with the currents of thought and feeling in the immediate vicinity of the battle-field. The people of the North are just beginning to find out that there *is* a rebellion, and that, sadly, by the many vacant seats in the broken circles around their snug evening firesides. From this time forward, the North will really *suffer* until the end of this struggle. Nor can we doubt, in spite of all appearances to the contrary, that the people will be found equal to the hour, however much some of their leaders may fail.

THE SHARKS AND SUCKERS

Washington is crowded to overflowing, more so than even at this time last fall. When Congress and its swarms of followers and retainers shall return, they will find it difficult indeed to secure their accustomed accommodations. It would be odd if the idlers and civilians were also driven to "camp it" for their winter quarters. Far too many of this motley throng are of that class of sharks and suckers who have done so much to add to the financial difficulties of the Government. The town is infested with "claim agents," ready to undertake anything which affords the promise of a dig at the Treasury. They peer around the purlieus of the public offices; in out-of-the-way corners where "committees" hold or *have* held their consultations; in the hotels—each man trying to conceal his dark lantern and his "jimmie," but each one anxious to find some metaphorical padlock to break for some one "on shares."

Well, well, even these men have their use, perhaps. They say that in some countries the buzzard and the jackal are necessaries of life. The city is in many of the worst features a perpetual camp, with all the vice and corruption of many camps concentrated at one centre. Here is all the plundering, gambling, lust, profanity, obscenity, and the swift growth of corruption, which traditionally follows in the footsteps of a great, long-continued and extravagantly managed war. I cannot paint the picture; it would be unfit to hang in any room of the sober and Christian homes to which THE EXAMINER might carry it. Perhaps, however, it is better that so much of all this should stay and rot here, instead of travelling from place to place with our regiments of patriotic soldiers.

THE TIME TO MOVE

The weather here, though clear, sunny and beautiful, begins to give unmistakable signs of the approach of the colder season. It is time for our army to be on the way towards a warmer latitude. And indeed they are moving, but oh, how slowly! It may be all right, it may be the perfection of strategy, but no one seems to believe it, and even the soldiers are getting feverish at the prospect of a repetition of their last winter's experience—and who shall blame them?

By the way, you have seen the much-talked-of "Kearney letter?"[77] Well, whether the dead hero has spoken well or not, the documents are genuine, for I have seen the originals of that, and many more to the same party. The fact is, that even McClellan's best friends begin to tremble lest he should lose this last opportunity for placing his fame and popularity upon a more enduring basis. Let him then, not only if he loves his country, but if he loves his army and *himself,* press this campaign forward with daily increasing vigor. Let him in very truth, for once, drive some hostile army to the wall, and pin them there. Then he can easily prevent too correct a history of any errors he may have committed in the sad and sorrowful times gone by. The air is full of rumors, of every size and wing—strange ephemera, which die as the light strikes them.

THE LATE ELECTIONS

The result of the elections has surprised some, and pained others; but without making any other comment, I would say that it is easy to attribute to them too much importance, as they afford but a dubious indication of the true condition of the country.[78] Nor shall we ever again be able to gauge our real political status, until the war is over, and the army once more mingles with the people, bringing back and disseminating the lessons and the thoughts which have been received and matured in the camp and on the battle-field.

WASHINGTON, 27 OCTOBER 1862 (PUBLISHED 6 NOVEMBER 1862)
The heavy rain for which General McClellan is supposed to have been so anxiously waiting, has come at last. The clouds hang heavy and gloomy over the whole face of the country, the dull mists creep slowly along the banks of the muddy and swelling Potomac, and the ceaseless patter of the chilling drops warns me, sitting by my blazing grate, what bitter discomforts there may be to-day in the tents and on the dismal marches.

A TIMELY RAIN

Such a rain as this takes some days to make deep mud in the sandy soil of this region, and in the mountainous district where the opposing armies lie, it soon drains off through the ravines and gullies, to swell the currents of the larger and slower streams. This is a fact of vast importance in the development and prosecution of military movements, as the several campaigns of the Revolution abundantly testify; and it remains to be seen whether, in the great issue before our troops, the rain will be found to fight for or against them. Of one thing we may rest assured, such weather, on the high and hilly country where they are, is invariably far more severe than here, and attended by a much lower temperature. Our own troops are sufficiently well clad and provided to guard, as well as may be, against both the cold and the wet, but the ragged hordes of the rebels have no such protection, and the consequences cannot fail to do much towards meting out to them a species of natural retribution for their treason and rebellion.

A WEEK OF EVENTS

The week before us, then, bids fair to furnish more stirring material for thought and comment than the dull and anxious one that is past. Both in the East and West, if we may trust the official accounts lately laid before the public, our armies are ready for their work, and have it well cut out for them. If their leaders will only let them, we have little doubt that the brave boys will do it, and do it well.

THE GUERRILLA CAMPS

Have you noticed, Mr. Editor, that for several weeks our side has been steadily and visibly gaining ground in the field? The visible success has been mainly in the West, where, within that time, the rebels have had nothing to report except defeats, retreats, and the breaking up of their most dangerous guerrilla camps.

These guerrilla operations, by the way, have been of great service to the rebels, in a way of which our newspapers have taken little notice: they have formed a most efficient and valuable source of *recruits*; in them many thousands of the very best troops in the rebel armies have been trained and disciplined. If a guerrilla band is effectually scattered, as so many of them lately have been, the majority of its members, afraid to return to their homes in a country in the possession of those from whom they have merited so much severity, find their way as speedily as possible to the nearest organized Confederate force, in whose ranks they sink their character of land-pirates in the somewhat less dangerous one of "recognized traitors." The cavalry service of the Confederacy is especially affected by these hard-riding and daring cut-throats.

RELATIONS ABROAD

In our foreign relations I have been able to notice few changes of any great significance, except *this*: while the great maritime powers of Europe seem to adhere as closely as ever to their declared policy of non-intervention, a policy born of their own mutual distrust and jealousy, and emphatically *not* of any friendship for us, or regard for right and justice—while, I say, they keep their promises to the ear, they are more and more boldly breaking them to the heart. The number of iron-clads, privateers, and transports laden with contraband goods, now preparing in the ports of England, France, and Belgium, is beginning to cause serious alarm among our commercial communities, who receive regular and correct information concerning them from their private European correspondents.

LETTERS OF MARQUE

While it is not probable that our own Government will deem it wise to take any official notice of these things at the present important and perilous juncture, there is no doubt that every means will be taken to ensure the destruction of all these piratical craft as rapidly and certainly as may be. The idea of issuing "letters of marque" to some of our brave and enterprising "merchant admirals," has already been openly and not unfavorably discussed in high, unofficial circles. Cotton, tar, turpentine, &c., has already found its way through our blockading fleets in quantities sufficient to make the fortunes of a swarm of "Yankee privateers." The only fear would be that such dangerous cruisers might now and then remember too well how many of their *bona fide* prizes were of French or English construction, and at the same time forget other important features of international jurisprudence. Let this be as it may, there is an urgent necessity that the seas be cleared of every craft which dares to hoist the "Gridiron," the modern representative of the old-time "skull and bones."

WASHINGTON, 10 NOVEMBER 1862 (PUBLISHED 13 NOVEMBER 1862)
Well, the elections are over, and, as was predicted, the result has been adverse to the Administration.[79] In what respects the people condemn the Government does not clearly appear. It is probable that by far the most powerful feeling among the masses, except in a few populous and demagogue-ridden localities, is one of feverish impatience at the duration and destructiveness of the war, and an undefined conviction that "something must be wrong" at headquarters. Nor is the popular instinct altogether wrong in this respect, though in its blindness it might err widely in attempting to locate the blame it is disposed to bestow so freely.

CHANGE OF COMMANDERS
The Government itself has at last shown clearly that it attributes the delay and the common want of anything like brilliant and decided successes, to grave defects in the military management of its two most prominent generals [McClellan and Buell], and they have in consequence been summarily removed.

Nor can any one doubt, who has been in a position to note carefully the course of events in Washington, that both of the important steps referred to would have been taken long since, had it been an easy matter to determine who, among our crowds of starred and buttoned heroes, was competent to assume the vacated commands, with any reasonable promise of a real improvement.

Pope was tried, and from various causes, not all to be traced to that somewhat unfortunate leader, the experiment was by no means a satisfactory one. It is at last definitely settled, however, that whoever *is* to lead our armies in the important campaign, George B. McClellan is *not*.[80]

MCCLELLAN'S CAREER

It is not the time, nor is this the place, for any extended comments on the somewhat singular and remarkable career so abruptly terminated, nor can the history of McClellan's campaigns be fairly and impartially written until the termination of this war. Then, in the clear light of peace, even justice will acquit or condemn him, and for that, if he be a wise and patriotic man, he will calmly wait.

No doubt that this action of the President will raise a storm of no mean proportions, and there are even rumors of trouble in the army. As to the street talk of New-York, and the hotel gossip of Washington, it is unworthy [of] a moment's consideration. In the army, a few enthusiastic young men may return in high dudgeon to the shades of private life, but we cannot fear that any officer of rank, reputation and standing, will so far disgrace his cloth and his cause. As to the rank and file, if this army is fighting for their general, and not for their country, it is time the fact was known, that the destinies of the nation may be entrusted to men of better principles. A few days, however, will settle all these things, and a few more will tell us if we have gained anything by the change in the leadership of the Army of the Potomac.

WINTER HARBINGERS

A few scattering Senators and Congressmen begin to make their appearance, joint harbingers of winter with our late terrific snow storm. You have doubtless read flourishing accounts of it in our papers, but the truth is, that it would have made a tolerably respectable show in Western New-York, as a good, snowy December day, but for a *storm*, any one-horse New-England community could beat it all the time after Thanksgiving. The weather has cleared up again, and is now pleasant, cold and bracing—just the weather for active operations in the field.

THE NEWS FROM ABROAD

So far as can be known to the outside world, all our late dispatches from across the Atlantic are favorable. It may be that some of them go so far as to threaten that if we do not do the very things we are straining every nerve and muscle to accomplish, we may look for something in the way of remonstrance from Europe; but the general impression is, that we shall, for the present, have the supreme permission of our dear friends and allies to mind our own affairs. No doubt Secretary Seward will give them to understand that the said permission is reciprocal. In the mean time, the preparations go on in European ports for a further extension of the present system of piratical war upon our commerce, and here indeed the sharp-eyed ones discern a cloud larger than any man's hand. We shall soon see whether or not it will grow.

Taken as a whole, then, the past week has been a propitious one, and at its close many things are wearing an improved aspect. The winter campaign is fairly opened, with every prospect of success at all points, and the different expeditions and movements are being pressed forward with all vigor. It will, we may be sure, be no detriment to the activity and efficiency of our various leaders, that they have the fate of Buell and McClellan before them, and can bear in mind that the greatest fault proven against either of them was want of rapidity, and that they each allowed a beaten enemy to escape them.

WASHINGTON, 17 NOVEMBER 1862 (PUBLISHED 20 NOVEMBER 1862)
Still, though day by day the approach of winter is more and more palpable, the weather continues favorable to active operations in the field. The cold nights, and the bracing northeast winds, seem to have promoted the general health of the army, rather than otherwise, and never were our forces in better spirits, or more eager to be led against the enemies of their country. Indeed, the partisans of McClellan seem more than a little disappointed, that so few have allowed their personal feelings to interfere with their sense of duty. They might well, in this matter, take a valuable lesson from the behavior, thus far, of their own peculiar chief and idol. Assuredly they can trust him to move in his own behalf, at the proper time, should that ever come. I have no patience with that evil mind which can look forward complacently, and almost with hope, to those often-predicted disasters which will compel the Administration "once more to call upon McClellan to save the Capital."

But this question is fast becoming a thing of the past, or at least is being put in temporary abeyance, by the absorbing interest with which all eyes are being turned to the armies in the field. Questions of finance, of local politics, of foreign complications, all hang upon this central one, and few of them can be well decided, certainly not *all*, in our favor, until we hear that something decisive has been done by the vast and well-appointed army under Burnside and his Generals.[81]

Vast as have been the previous efforts of both the parties in this desperate war, they all dwindle almost to insignificance beside the display of power now before the country and the world. In the South, almost every man capable of bearing arms is now in the field. The resources of the Confederate States have been proved greater than our most liberal calculations, and they now present to us on every side an unbroken wall of steel and fire. Through that wall we must and will break before the end of this winter campaign;

and the finger of destiny seems to indicate that it will be broken at its strongest point, on the banks of the Rappahannock, or in the rough and dangerous valleys between that river and the mountains.

Terrible indeed will be the disappointment of the nation, if the veterans of so many well-fought fields are compelled to retreat once more in disgrace to the line of the Potomac.

The members of both Houses are beginning to make their appearance in their old haunts, and to gather in knots to discuss the important topics so soon to be brought before them for their official action. The prayers of a whole people will be with them in all their deliberations, and weighty indeed is the responsibility resting upon them.

The late significant memorial of the business men of New-York, may not be without important influence in determining the future financial policy of the Treasury, albeit many of the positions taken therein are strenuously controverted by our ablest and most successful financiers, both here and at the North. The other branches of the Administration are mum as to the future, except that from day to day they seem striving to retrieve the errors of the past, and to do their best in the present. Perhaps the most universally unpopular is the present management of the War Department. Strangely enough, however, almost every one, even in the ranks of their bitterest opponents, acquits Mr. Stanton and his immediate assistants of any taint of dishonesty or corruption. "Red tape may be *honest*, but a nation may nevertheless be strangled therewith," is the sharp retort of those who profess to have suffered by the dilatoriness of the War Office.

The President is the same thoughtful, careful, kindly, hard-working man as ever, seeming to labor to make good, by the labors of his own brain and hand, all the shortcomings of his myriad subordinates. What his fame will be when all this confused lava of events, now red and molten in the fire of the Present, shall have been cooled in the rigid mould of time, none can tell; but his history will be false to all that is good and true, if his effigy be not that of a great, wise and patriotic statesman.

WASHINGTON, 1 DECEMBER 1862 (PUBLISHED 4 DECEMBER 1862)
No one who knows the President imagines that he will do otherwise than sustain and urge his previously declared and settled policy, in all its bearings. The rebellion must be put down; the army and navy must be kept on a first-class footing; we will not listen to any foreign proposals of intervention; the emancipation policy must be carried out, at any cost; and the Administration will still present the same bold and unflinching front to traitors at home and enemies abroad.

Nor is it reasonably to be feared that Congress will not stand by the President, so long as he is thus true to himself and the country. If only the talking men and the quarrelsome men will let the working ones alone, we may look for a swift series of well-digested and important measures, affecting seriously and permanently our whole social and financial *status*.

The army is still at Fredericksburg, and grave and deep have been the surmises of faulty cooperation by subordinate departments of the War Office. We hope that none of them are true, but if it *should* turn out a fact that our pontoon train stood in its place, ready mounted on its trucks, and the horses by it, for *eight days* after the order came to go forward, verily, some man ought to die the death. We look forward, however, hopefully, still believing that our great army will surely accomplish something, before it settles down and allows itself to be surrounded by the mud and misery of a Virginia winter.

One of the interesting occurrences of the past week, was the great Thanksgiving dinner to the "contrabands" at their camp. The occasion was duly employed by several gentlemen to urge upon them the advantage of the President's favorite scheme of emigration, and seemingly with a very fair degree of success. It was a strange spectacle, that great crowd of black men, fresh from bondage, now, for the first time, beginning to taste of and comprehend that sweet thing called "Liberty;" men, women, and children, who had all their lives listened to orders only, with force to make obedience certain, gathering around their best and wisest friends, and hearkening to the mild voice of persuasion, urging them to their own good.

The crowd contained a large number of thoughtful and intelligent faces, and not a few that lit up with a sudden gleam when, in reply to a remark by Senator Pomeroy, a stalwart negro answered, "*I'd fight!*"[82]

It is not all nervousness, on the part of the Southern people, that makes them speak of a slave insurrection with a cold shiver of horror. They know better than we do, that in many of these dusky, and it may be crouching forms, there still lurks the fierce passions and savage instincts of the savage warrior of the Guinea Coast. Late experiments are going far to prove that the negro will make a good soldier, but it needs no experiment to make an observing mind believe that, under the long-worn mask of submission, there slumber possibilities that may well make the blood curdle in the veins of those who may yet have them to deal with. It is to be hoped that the Colonization plan may at least be found a valuable safety-valve, if nothing more.

One by one the military authorities now propose to surrender to their former occupants the church edifices so long used as hospitals. The new erections for this especial purpose are more appropriate, and far more convenient in many ways. Our citizens have borne the deprivation a long time, and with a very fair degree of patience, and have shown a good deal of active benevolence in their attention to the sick and wounded, and it is time that Government relieved them of a burden which cannot be now necessary.

The weather continues to be fine, as much like Indian Summer as anything else, and the roads are all that our armies can ask.

WASHINGTON, 8 DECEMBER 1862 (PUBLISHED 11 DECEMBER 1862)
Winter is at last upon us in bitter earnest, and the northwest wind howls drearily through the half deserted streets of the city, and among the flapping tents of the scattered camps. The ground is frozen almost solid enough to relieve the roads of the effect of the late rains, and the long trains of army wagons lumber along, loaded now more with *wood* than anything else. But for the frost, the storm would have made the roads impassable. What they may become when it thaws again, requires a Virginia-bred imagination to fairly conceive. The suffering in the army must have been great for the past ten days, but this extreme cold weather cannot continue long in this latitude, unless the winters of the North are following southward in the path of its armies and its freedom.

The movements of the army, for the past week, have been shrouded in a kind of mystery, but enough is known to convince us that the army is only seemingly inactive. Nor need we be surprised, if in this, as in the last campaign, the first good news came from the Valley of the Mississippi. If we may trust the facts and figures of the War Department, the people have a good right to build high hopes and expectations upon the army they have placed in the field at so great a sacrifice.

I was in the Senate Chamber at the opening of Congress, and during the reading of the [President's] Message, with the exception of a visit to the House. Your readers will bear in mind that this is the last session of this Congress, and that its *materiel* has not changed much since its adjournment. Accordingly, one looks around him now upon familiar faces, and the voices, as they join in the debates, have a sound of old times that recalls the stirring scenes at the close of the last and the beginning of this Administration. I will not go into particulars or personalities, but must express my satisfaction that, in this peculiar juncture, our National Legislature is filled by men so many of whom are experienced in the important duties before them, and who have all been relieved by the late elections from any considerations that can affect their independent action. This latter is true, both of the defeated and the reelected.

The "Copperheads" have early given evidence of their disposition to make all the trouble in their power, and to embarrass the Government to their utmost, rightly believing that they can thus best aid the evil cause to whose interests they have devoted themselves. Those loud-talking gentlemen who berate our Government as an "irresponsible tyranny," will do well to remark that these men, in their sacred character of Representatives, are allowed to pursue their calling of spy and traitor unmolested, and without the fear of Fort Warren before their eyes.[83]

The great military trials drag their slow length along, and are the fruitful source of acrimonious discussion at "Willard's," and elsewhere.[84] It is certain that some one's reputation, if not now, will be sufficiently blackened before the various revelations are completed. By the way, is it not a singular rule of military courts, which allows a well known infamous character to testify against a Major-General of the United States Army? A man whose testimony would not hang a dog in any other court? It seems odd to me. It would be out of place to remark upon the merits of these investigations, until they are completed, but the general public seems to look on with a grim feeling of satisfaction that some of our blunderers and marplots are in a fair way to be brought to justice—if justice, after all, is in any wise sure to follow conviction. There was a spice of truth in Talleyrand's bitter jest over the execution of Admiral Byng, and it might not have a bad effect if we, too, used a little wholesome severity, *"pour encourager les autres."*[85]

Among the important questions to be brought up at this session, is the renewed application of Western Virginia for admission to the Union as a free State. The late resolutions of the Legislature of this new body politic, approving of Emancipation, and requesting Senator Carlile to resign, are a sufficient indication of what may be expected of these worthy sons of the once venerable, but now fallen Old Dominion.[86] The signs of the times are dubious and hard to read, but whatever clear indications we *have*, assure us that this revolution, in its last results, must be in behalf of freedom. The shadow is not going back upon the dial-plate of the Nineteenth Century.

WASHINGTON 15 DECEMBER 1862 (PUBLISHED 18 DECEMBER 1862)
How I shall be able to sit down calmly to-day, and pen my weekly letter for THE EXAMINER, is more than I can tell. Washington, and I suppose, as much of the country as can know the facts of the case, is suffering all the agony of suspense. For three days we have known that the great battle so long deferred, would be put off no longer, and the time had come. We have sat and waited for dispatches, eagerly devoured by scores before passing into the hands of the Press; and many who have rarely prayed before, have

sent up heart-felt aspirations for the success of the Union armies. By the time this is before your readers, no doubt, the result will be known to the Nation, North and South; but *now* we are still watching the slow unfolding of the bloody page on which is to be written the loss or winning of the battle of Fredericksburg. So far, at least, General Burnside seems to have handled his army with skill, coolness, and prompt courage. We all feel more and more confidence in him. He has at least sent out no premature bulletins of a great victory, to be belied by the slow tortures of the "official returns." The men are behaving nobly—alas, that the list of those who have made this their last blow for their country is already so large! If we are entirely successful now, it will not be hoping too much of the future, to think that a welcome peace cannot be far off. But we can do no more now than to wait, in faith that the best hopes of the Great Republic are not to be buried on the banks of the Rappahannock.[87]

CURRENT SCANDAL

Washington has been more than usually well supplied with current talk and scandal of late. The expected change in the Department of the Interior has been a fruitful topic. The names most prominently mentioned in connection with the "succession," are those of Senator Browning, of Illinois, Judge Holt, and Judge Usher of Indiana, now Assistant Secretary of the Interior.[88] Besides these, there are many others whose chances seem to be thought less of. For some reason or other, Secretary Smith has failed to make himself very popular, and his contemplated withdrawal occasions little or no stir.[89] Other Cabinet changes are talked of by the wise ones, but no one appears able to "speak from the book."

THE NEWLY ADMITTED STATE

The admission of the new State of Kanawha [i.e., West Virginia] has been commented upon by its opponents with all the acerbity of helplessness, the more so as they think they see in it the successful fulfillment of a line of policy steadily followed on the part of the Administration.[90] It is to them the beginning of the end. Other new States, they say, will follow, and thus one by one the Territories will all be made free, and probably *Republican*. A very shrewd process of reasoning, and I would like to add, for their comfort, that not the Territories only will ere long be free, and forever beyond the grasp of the slave power, *even if* it succeeds in establishing its now tottering Confederacy. If I am not mistaken, the close of this session will see this conspiracy hopelessly bereft of all that rich and broad domain which it once haughtily offered to "divide with the North." And this, whatever may be the issue of this war for the Union.

THE MONEY QUESTION

The subject of the national finances, we are told, can hardly be arranged finally with adequate wisdom, until our legislators can form some idea of the result of our current operations in the field, and that the question of "Greenbacks *vs.* Loans" must be decided, partially, at least, by Burnside, Banks, and their fellow-chieftains. So be it, then; we have another pound added to the load of suspense with which we watch our advancing banners.

THE CHRISTMAS DINNER

Great preparations are being made to provide a bountiful Christmas dinner for our sick and convalescent soldiers. So the good ladies in charge do not overfeed the feeble objects of their charity, the notion is a good one. The weather is beautiful—when the fog clears away enough for you to see it at all—a sort of Indian-winter, with a perpetual hint of ice in the wind, and of rain in the horizon. Capital for the movements of the Army, and almost enough to make us feel cheerful in spite of all. But cheerful or not, we must be contented to wait.

WASHINGTON, CA. 22 DECEMBER 1862 (PUBLISHED 25 DECEMBER 1862)

The cloud of uncertainty did at last, indeed, lift from over the banks of the Rappahannock, but we would almost prefer the suspense to the grizzly horror of this reality. Four times as many men as won the fight of Buena Vista have been stricken from the army rolls by this desperate attempt to carry impregnable positions. Doubtful upon whom to wreak its just wrath, the nation is furious, even its grief. Some demand one head, and some another, until it would seem that if all are to be satisfied, the Cabinet and the Army will be like the Roman Emperor's garden. I question, however, if we shall be much better off, even with a glut of resignations and dismissions; for if Carnot had been in the War Office, and Napoleon behind Burnside's field-glass, our troops would have been compelled to recoil from before those terrible walls of fire.[91] The Army, sore, angry, disappointed, calls petulantly for their old leader, whose protracted strategy cost them almost thousands where this one rash push has cost its hundreds. The *morale*, in one sense, of the Army, is not materially injured. They feel that they fought well, bravely, faithfully; that they deserved success; that no shadow of disgrace can rest upon their banners from a field thus gallantly contested; and no army, whose military conscience approves of its own conduct, can possibly be demoralized. Nor can we doubt that they would enter a fair field to-morrow, with as much determination and as much confidence in their leader, as when they marched over the pontoons to attack Fredericksburg.

The winter campaign is not over in the field, and it is fairly begun in the Capitol.

The Cabinet changes now taking place or threatening, defy prophecy or prevent explanation. The long ferment in the popular mind is now complete, and the course of political events unconsciously, and almost unwillingly, shapes itself accordingly, as you will, before many days, see. A public servant may have been faithful, to the best of his ability, but in this day and hour the people are madly clamoring for *"Success!"* and they will *not* be denied. How far the Cabinet will be remodelled, and above all, how far it will be improved, does not yet very clearly appear. The amount of "timber" for first-class positions does not seem to be over-abundant—it never is, in any nation or time—but we have certainly men enough who can take the vacant posts with credit to themselves, and advantage to the nation. Meantime, the "slates" made out are innumerable, and as various as the party feelings and personal prejudices of their makers.[92]

We in Washington have so little faith in the New-York newspapers, as indices of the real public feeling, that we are at a loss what the people really think of this unexpected juncture of our national affairs, unless we conclude that they *must* agree with us that by some one a great crime, or blunder—which is a crime—has been committed, and that once again justice is in a fair way to be cheated of the real criminal. *We* also agree that both the President and true-hearted General Burnside have done their duty, and we acquit them. The House and Senate look on in a state of semi-bewilderment, having done their whole duty by appointing a "Committee of Investigation," which is said actually to have visited the battle-field, instead of doing all its work in its own snug committee-room.

The galleries of either assembly room at the Capitol are tolerably well-filled, as a general thing, and the debates have on many occasions been decidedly interesting. Among the best of the session, thus far, was Mr. Kelly, (Pa.,) in defence of the President's Emancipation Proclamation, and in reply to the Border State men.[93] It was a fiery little piece of oratory.

The Emigration Scheme, and other expedients of statesmanship to provide for the great change we hope for, are all at present in *quiescence*, driven temporarily to the wall by the pressure of events, but will all revive again ere long, so soon as this Cabinet crisis is over; and with the return of quiet we will begin to see the results, if any, of the President's policy.

Socially, the city is decorously and in good taste *quiet:* not without hospitality, but without unseasonable gaiety in high places. How it will be when the holidays are over, is a question of the future.

WASHINGTON, CA. 28 DECEMBER 1862 (PUBLISHED 1 JANUARY 1863)
The troubled waters seem to have settled somewhat since my last writing. The Cabinet, good or bad, has returned peacefully to its daily routine; the great changes in the minor departments have not been made, though still as loudly called for as ever; the army still lies on the bank of the Rappahannock, warily watching its powerful and dangerous antagonist, anxious to strike, but not seeing its opportunity very clearly.

THE LATE CHECK

We still feel the effects of our severe check at Fredericksburg, but they are steadily wearing off, and are now manifest in the great cities of the North, rather than in the army. The army, in fact, was never in better condition for a battle than now, and it may have an opportunity sooner than some of us think. At all events, New Year's Day is here, and we are apparently but little nearer the end of the war than when we bade good-bye to 1861. I say *apparently*, because it is my belief that under all this disaster, this waste, this delay, the steady current of events has brought us nearer and nearer to the goal of our labors, and that we shall one day reach it, if we faint not. It is all very dark just now, as it often has been before, with other just and holy causes; but if the country is only true to itself, the darkness will one day disappear in the morning light of some new day of prosperity.

THE CONTRAST

This is not optimism. Let any candid man, undismayed by the murmurs of the fickle and grumbling multitude, or the declamations of demagogues, take a careful estimate of the actual relative condition of the two contending powers which confront each other on this New Year's morning, gathering their forces for the last desperate struggle. Go through the deserted and depopulated cities of the South, through the idle plantations, the untravelled highways. All business is at an end, except that which bears directly upon the war, or the preparation of the actual necessaries of life. The able-bodied men are *all* in the army or in their graves, and the "draft" is now being extended to include a fair share of the old men and boys. Property has depreciated, especially that peculiar species of property in which the wealth of the South formerly consisted. The land is shut in from the outside world, and no commerce comes to the supply of its luxuries or its necessities. Its whole seaboard, with a few exceptions soon to disappear, is in the hands of its powerful enemy. Of the States upon whose aid it originally counted, and whose territory it had marked as its own, Maryland, Delaware, Missouri,

Kentucky, and half of Virginia, and Florida, *irretrievably gone*; Tennessee, Arkansas, Louisiana, fast falling under the control of our armies, and the once wealthy and populous counties of Northern and Eastern Virginia reduced by both the contending armies to a wilderness such as Turenne left in the Palatinate.[94] The last great armies which the Confederacy can raise, are now confronting us in the Valley of the Mississippi, and on the banks of the Rappahannock, and wonderful is the zeal and determination with which the Southern people are laboring to maintain them; but if these fail to terminate the war in their favor, well might Lee and his Generals look Northward and utter despairingly, "After *us*, the *Deluge*."

I need not draw the other picture, nor paint the prosperous and powerful condition of the loyal States of the Union. If only we are ready to make a tithe of the sacrifices daily made by our opponents, no man can have a doubt of the grand result. Let us then face the New Year with determined minds, resolved that even the blunders and failures of our own officers and leaders shall not dishearten, or drive us from our work.

BUSINESS READY

The various Committees have been busily at work during the holiday adjournment of Congress, and have prepared a mass of business which will tax the utmost energies of the National Legislature during the few remaining weeks of the session. They must work now, if they would put the Government in good working order for the great year before it.

It is not believed that the financial bill now before the Committee of Ways and Means is a finality, but that important modifications will be made before ever it becomes a law. Congress is also expected to take some action upon the late depredations of Southern pirates, and the failure of the Navy Department thus far to prevent them. In fact we are looking forward to spicy times in House and Senate.

GOVERNOR SEYMOUR

Men in Washington are also waiting anxiously for your new Governor to strike the key-note of his administration of the most powerful state in the Union.[95] There are some indications which give rise to dark forebodings of evil to come, but Mr. Seymour's friends here claim him pertinaciously as a "War Democrat," and assure us that all he wants is "more vigor." We hope that this is true. Should it not be, the friends of the Republic may indeed begin to tremble for the result.

CHAPTER THREE

1863

WASHINGTON, CA. 5 JANUARY 1863 (PUBLISHED 8 JANUARY 1863)
The holidays are over, and the world of Washington is once more girding its loins for the work before it. It will take several days for Congress to get itself once more into working trim, for while the festivities of the season have been moderately indulged in *here*, many members have availed themselves of this brief vacation to pay brief visits to their homes.

THE GRAND EDICT
The New Year begins not unauspiciously. The President has been true to his declared policy, and we are now to see, as speedily as the course of events will permit, whether the eternal justice embodied in his Emancipation Proclamation will or will not add strength to the good cause in behalf of which it was promulgated. The vaticinations of our multitude of political soothsayers are sufficiently various and at variance, but we hope for the best.

It may be borne in mind that the action of the President does not propose to interfere with local laws, and deals only with those now held as bondsmen; but no man can doubt that the emancipation of *this* mass, *this* generation, provides free papers for all the millions yet unborn. Now, let the armies press forward: every rebellious State that is held for thirty days only, is by that occupation forever deprived of all strength to originate new acts of treason. Vast regions which yield supplies to the rebellion would be powerless for that end, had the present state of things been created twelve months earlier. Only through their slaves do the rebels keep their forces in the field—in so far as they are deprived of them, must their ability fail them. Our policy must be to move forward as fast as possible, for even the temporary occupation of rebel territory is victory.

THE GREAT BATTLE
Active operations in the field appear to be, just at present, transferred once more from the East to the West, and we hope that our successes in the valley of the Mississippi may in some measure atone for our reverses on the Rappahannock. By the time this is before your readers, they will know the truth

about the fight at Murfreesboro, whether victory or defeat.[1] If a victory, the advantages to be reaped by the National arms are beyond calculation, and place us in a very advantageous position for future operations. If a defeat, or a repulse, the forces at our disposal in convenient proximity to that point are such as to prevent the disaster from being a final or irremediable one.

OUR FOREIGN RELATIONS
There seems to be no material change in our relations with nations on the other side of the Atlantic, though it is evident that they are daily becoming more and more restive under the continued loss and trial arising from our prolonged war, and the utmost point of their endurance may be reached at any moment.

GEN. BUTLER
Gen. Butler is now here, and while he keeps as quiet as possible, he evidently keeps at least *one eye* on the motions of those who have so long and so bitterly assailed him.[2] The keen sarcasm in his late proclamation will bite deeply in sundry European circles, and for my part I hope it may strike home to the very hearts of the courtly hypocrites who have been our most dangerous enemies in our hour of need.

THE WEATHER AND THE PRICES
The long spell of clear and pleasant weather which we have enjoyed is evidently at an end, or nearly so, and we may now look forward to the fog and rain and mud which make up that most disagreeable of seasons, a Southern winter. Here begin the worst trials to the health and temper of our armies, and there will be but little respite for them before the end of March or the middle of April.

The exorbitantly high prices of all the necessaries of life in Washington, at the present time, cause more than a little distress among that large portion of our population who live from hand to mouth, and nothing but the abundance of well paid labor on all sides, prevents actual want and suffering to a degree unknown before. But I must close this letter, with the fervent hope that I may find more agreeable topics for 1863 than its predecessor could furnish me.

WASHINGTON, 12 JANUARY 1863 (PUBLISHED 15 JANUARY 1863)
The week opens gloomily enough with the news from Galveston.[3] It comes through rebel sources, to be sure, and from that drunken traitor, Magruder, but it bears all the usual external marks of reliability.[4] It is a disgrace rather than a disaster, for no great immediate good can result to the rebels from

the possession of Galveston; but it is a bitter pill to be beaten in such a way, and by such a man.

On the Mississippi, matters look for the moment a trifle cloudy, but cannot long remain so, as we have learned many things by our temporary check.

There can be no great delay in this matter, for the reopening of the Mississippi may be fairly reckoned second to no other of the single attainments whose sum total is the suppression of the rebellion.

CABINET AFFAIRS

The appointment of Mr. Usher, as Secretary of the Interior, seems to meet with pretty general approval, at least among those who know him; but he has never had anything like a *national* reputation, and there are those who blame the President for passing by so many who have. The fact that he has never been a politician, however, ought certainly not to be counted against him. The fact is, by the way, *if* this nation is really dying, it is dying of its politicians, and nothing else. Dying of the consequences of their mismanagement, past and present, and of the sad results of their insane ambition.

There are several minor, but still important posts, in connection with the Cabinet, yet to be filled. The Assistant-Secretary of the Interior, in place of the present incumbent, who is a son of ex-Secretary Smith, will probably be first attended to.[5] This office, though a new creation, is fast growing into one of great importance, and if the proposed policy with reference to our armies is to be carried out, will require a man of talent and industry. Messrs. Potter, of Wisconsin, Judge Edmonds, now Commissioner of the Land Office, and other parties, are already mentioned.[6]

You will, perhaps, remember that the posts of Second and Third Assistant-Secretary of War were created last winter, to endure for one year only, and that time has nearly expired. The Second Assistant-Secretary, Mr. P. M. Watson, declines acting beyond the expiration of his time, and it is said that ill-health will compel the resignation of the First-Assistant.[7] These posts are not lucrative, and are so laborious that no man, properly qualified, would accept either of them, except from patriotic motives. It is to be hoped that men will be found of sufficient business ability to rescue the War-Office from the semi-chaotic state into which its overpress of business and want of proper organization has thrown it. I do not say this in any fault-finding or censorious spirit, because outsiders may not be able to appreciate the difficulties of the position; but the fact is undeniable, that in all the vast machinery of that important Department, there exists a woful amount of confusion, and consequent delay.

We are not yet rid of our old succession of rumors concerning other changes in the Cabinet, but the knowing ones pay little attention to them, considering that the late flurry has settled all the officials in question only the more firmly in their seats.

SOCIAL GOSSIP

The first reception of the season at the President's house was held Saturday afternoon last, and was well attended, in spite of a dismal Washington fog and rain. There will be no evening receptions for the present, much to the disgust of many of the "birds of passage," of whom the flock is large at present.

The city generally is pleasant, but unhealthy to a degree positively alarming to weak nerves. The number of kinds of fever, colds, sore throats, rheumatics, small pox, gun-shot wounds, and delirium tremens, outside as well as inside the numerous hospitals, is enough to convince any man that "there is something wrong about the air of the place."

THE FORMS OF PARTY

In House and Senate there is nothing of importance beyond what you see in the papers. The new forms of party are slowly but visibly crystalizing, and the number of these who still vacillate is daily becoming smaller. You can see this clearly in each additional "test-question" brought before either body. The anti-Administration men are making the best use in their power of the popularity of their favorite General, that being in fact their heaviest gun at present; while their opponents rally around the Proclamation, and declare that "*Now* we have something to fight for."

WASHINGTON, 9 FEBRUARY 1863 (PUBLISHED 12 FEBRUARY 1863)

After a brief absence, I find myself once more a looker-on at the Capital. I find the streets and highways, not to speak of byways and country roads, muddy and miserable beyond description. A good stone pavement is a fine thing, after all, and Government should take the matter in hand, if they finally make up their minds *to stay here.* Not that we can yet persuade ourselves to entertain any very serious doubts of that, for in spite of the many evil features of the "position," we still all hope bravely for the best.

THE ONE DANGER

The truth is, that there is at this present [moment] but one great danger; only one thing which can possibly stand between us and ultimate success and safety, and that is *division among ourselves.* By this only, can our arms be paralyzed, our strength made unavailing, and our glory converted into our shame. In every corner of the great battle-field, there are signs of promise, in spite of the unpropitious season and our previous disasters. At every salient point the armies of the Republic are either attacking or preparing to attack their desperate antagonists, and the Great Rebellion at last stands fairly at bay, not knowing at what place it may best concentrate its wearied and waning powers.

THE CORNERED WOLF

We surely are not wrong, now, in asserting that our enemies show marked signs of exhaustion. There is a limit to human endurance, and they have had much to endure. To this, as much as to the habitual arrogance and boastfulness of the Southern leaders, we may attribute the growing bitterness and bloodthirstiness of the later manifestoes from the chiefs of the rebellion. Despair fights hard, and the cornered wolf is merciless. In the present case, however, we are likely to find the threat far in excess of the performance.

THE INEVITABLE NEGRO

The "negro question in its most offensive form" is tangibly before Congress. Shall the black man fight for his freedom, or shall he not, is the point at issue, and the decision will probably be that the black man must turn warrior, whether he makes a good one or not. The ferocity with which our black soldiers and employees are treated when they fall into the hands of the rebels, is preparing the darkest page of this terrible war; it will be written before long. There is, under all his servility, his good nature, his seeming stolidity, and his semi-civilization, a strong remnant of the fierce Gold-Coast savage still lurking in the bosom of the American black man. I speak that I do know, and testify that I have seen; let these cruel and brutal massacres of our loyal black men go on a little longer, until the negro is fully and at last convinced that he and his race are "at bay," that the dogs are before him and the abyss behind, and you will see him stand to his terrible work of war, as only despair and hate can. It will be a sad day, and a bloody record, but this foolish and hideous cruelty is a kind of seed from which they who sow it reap that which they have sown—an hundred fold.

WORK FOR THE WEEK

This week can hardly pass over without a final revision and passage of the currency and loan bill, including, in all probability, some modified form of Mr. Chases's great banking scheme. The importance of these measures can hardly be over-estimated; upon their wisdom or folly may depend the entire future of the Republic!

A DISGRACE SUBSIDING

I have been, for some time, carefully watching the progress of the "copperhead movement" in the loyal States, and, in common with many abler and closer observers, have come to the conclusion that that disgraceful reaction has reached its limits, and the tide is turning. The free use of McClellan's name and popularity gave it a spurious strength for a time in the East, while in the West it was urged on by all the art and demagoguism of many who should have known better, even *as* demagogues. The people are truer than their would-be leaders, and cannot and will not be seduced into being false to themselves, and false to the cause for which they have already made so many fearful sacrifices. The usual Anglo Saxon privilege of grumbling will be exercised to an unlimited extent, but the very men who grumble will in the end be found standing by the Government. Not that there is no danger, or that our domestic traitors may not succeed in casting many hindrances in the way of the Administration, but that their power will from this time forward become less and less dangerous.

WASHINGTON, 16 FEBRUARY 1863 (PUBLISHED 19 FEBRUARY 1863)

The week just ended has been a busy and exciting one in Congress, and in social circles as well. Congress has nearly perfected the great measures before it; they have been fully and ably discussed, and nothing now remains but action, so that the remaining two weeks of the Session will be full of bills passed and signed. Nor does this way of doing things necessitate an over-amount of haste in the final vote. Already the leaders in the House and Senate know pretty well what will be the fate of the Bank bill, the Finance, Indemnity, and other great bills, and little more remains to be done than to record the official result of all this discussion.

It is the intention of the best men in both Houses to so arrange matters as to have the Administration fully master of the position, furnished with sword and purse and ample power to employ them in the good cause, for many a month to come, that no less loyal body may come to their seats to hamper the Executive, or undo the work which is drawing to so good an end. I do not at all agree with those gentry who think it an evidence of their own political acumen to rail at the doings and the abilities of this Congress. Faulty it undoubtedly is: it contains no Burke, no Cicero, or Demosthenes, and does not claim any of its members for a Clay or a Webster; but the history of parliamentary legislation will be searched in vain for a similar body which has performed within the same time so vast an amount of downright hard work, including so much and so important legislation. It has been preeminently a patriotic and honest Congress, to which, in this respect, for many years past, we have had no parallel; for the first time in many a long day the "lobby" has found itself weak and profitless. Much has been done to ferret out abuses and frauds, and we cannot doubt that many a dishonest soul has stayed its itching fingers from off the public purse, from fear of the ever-present shadow of an "investigating committee." Well will it be for the Republic, if the Thirty-Eighth Congress shall come up to the work before it, inspired with the same energies and upheld by the same high patriotism.

The social world of Washington puts itself piously in mind that "Lent is near," and thereupon is plunging into every species of fashionable dissipation. Balls, parties, dinners, and receptions, are the order of the day, or rather night. The sensations of New-York, including Tom Thumb and lady, hurry on to Washington to finish up their season, and the wearied votaries of fashion rub their sleepy eyes, and long for Wednesday next, when they can return to a reasonable and Christian way of living without being voted unfashionable.[8]

Colorado Jewett has been here, so have your other new celebrities, in swarms too numerous to mention.[9] C. J. does not seem to succeed as well in this atmosphere as in some others, and I question if he will add to his shining laurels.

Speaking of diplomacy, much praise is accorded here to Secretary Seward's reply to the French offer of mediation. Never, they say, was an unwelcome civility more politely declined. Nor is it thought that the consequences can be at all unpleasant.[10]

The news from the Army does not as yet present any very exciting features, except in the forced suspense, which grows more and more painful every day. We know that great movements are going forward, and that at any moment the flash and roar of a great battle, like an explosion, may lift the cloud of secresy that covers them all.

More ominous than anything else at present are the indications of the growth of a discontented spirit in portions of the North itself, though, in the opinion of the best judges, the tide has reached its highest and worst point, and is slowly turning. All we need now is a military success, and in due time that will surely come.

WASHINGTON, 2 MARCH 1863 (PUBLISHED 5 MARCH 1863)
Theoretically, so to speak, we have seen the last of our winter. It disappeared in a driving rain-storm last night, and the spring opens upon us this morning, cloudy, indeed, and muddy, but calm, and full of faint flashes from above, which promise future sunshine. In a military point of view the

winter is still on us, for the spring winds have much work before them, before the sacred soil of Virginia will carry the heavily laden wheels of our lightest artillery. The said winds, however, will soon be at it, and we will not have long to wait before "fighting Joe" [Joseph Hooker] will be able to make a strike somewhere.

THE IMPENDING BATTLES

How ominously bare of interest has the military bulletin been for some days! rumors enough, but not a fact larger than a man's hand. Is it the calm before the storm, the lull before the hurricane, the hushed breath of all at the thought of the earthquake to come? It is likely. Nearer and nearer come the great victories or defeats at Vicksburg, Charleston and Tullahoma. They can neither of them be now avoided. The Republic is sure of *results* of some kind—glory or shame—profit greater than we can estimate, or loss whose consequences no prophet among us can foretell. We have had many unexpected events in this war, many startling surprises. In almost every instance, the hand of our destiny has been extended from the cloud, and it may be that this time also something new and wonderful will turn the tide for us or against us.

SOLDIERS AT HOME

The condition of the army, here and in the West, is excellent, considering that a tedious winter has been wearing upon them so long with its unavoidable discomforts and hardships. They are, however, eager for action, and anxious, if possible, to bring the war to a speedy end. Many of them look forward longingly to the coming termination of their term of service, and to the firesides that will then be ready for their returning footsteps; but the Government has only to conduct the matter with a moderate amount of worldly wisdom and knowledge of human nature, to make every one of these returning veterans an invaluable recruiting officer, and an apostle of the Union to whom all men will listen. Nor will these brave fellows be of less use in opposing, with the energy learned on the battle-field, the demagoguism and treason now rampant in many portions of the North, and which threaten to injure the country more than even the now waning power of the rebellion itself. How they will speak, we may gather from the published appeals of the soldiers of Illinois, Ohio and Indiana, and we may well believe that the men of other States will not be far behind their Western brethren.

CONGRESSIONAL WORK AND TALK

In Congress the past few days have been a busy time, and in spite of the skirmishing and fillibustering of the opposition, a considerable amount of work has been done. The Conscription bill, the Indemnity bill, the Finance bill, and others, have been discussed and acted on with a great deal of common sense and business tact, though a few men, like Voorhees, of Indiana, have thought it a good time to make long spread-eagle speeches.[11] There has been a splendid chance, lately, for members to call each other and the Administration hard names; and careful observation for many days compels me to accord them this encomium, that they have improved their opportunities to the full extent allowed by good breeding and parliamentary rule. When, however, we compare the decency and moderation of the present with the "plantation scenes" of the not very remote past, we may well congratulate ourselves of the improvement. It should, however, be made a record of, that the Conscription bill passed the Senate as it did only because the leader of the Copperheads in that body had "prepared himself" for his speech one glass too completely, and his satellites dared not move without him.

COOLNESS OF A REPORTER

There are many things a man sees here that perhaps had better not be told, for the credit of the nation, were it not that we have so many foreigners among us taking notes for European circulation, that it matters little what we say of ourselves. Apropos of this, that insufferable slanderer, Charles Mackay, rhymer and *Times* reporter, is in town, and many of our public men receive him. He went to the White House at the Saturday's reception, seemingly forgetting all he had said and written for the English public concerning the lady of that house. I doubt if he will make many more calls *there*.[12]

WINDING UP OF CONGRESS

The last reception of the season comes off to-morrow evening, and will be [a] brilliant affair. Otherwise Washington society is quiescent. Provided Congress works successfully for the next three days, we shall all be glad that the long excitement of the session is at an end. It will be some time before we are again to see the flags rise on the wings of the Capitol; may they never float above a less patriotic set of men! is the prayer of [your correspondent] Illinois.

WASHINGTON, 9 MARCH 1863 (PUBLISHED 12 MARCH 1863)

The people of the Capital, and the armies in and around it, are still struggling ruefully through the rivers of yellow mud, which, in this benighted region, go by the names of streets, avenues and roads. The street-crossing boys are the only business men who really thrive, unless it is the umbrella venders.

No matter how clear and sunny the morning, or how crisp and starry the early evening, neither day nor night can pass without the return of the flood. At present, it has "cleared up cloudy," and promises to remain so for a few hours. But I only care to refer to the weather in its military point of view, that your readers may understand this most important feature of our "position." The spring winds, however, will soon be at work, and then for a move.

IMPATIENT TO BE AT THEM

The late returns from Gen. Hooker's army are of the most encouraging nature.[13] The troops, so often reported demoralized, discontented, almost mutinous, seem to take most kindly to their commanding general, long one of the most prominent of their own favorite officers, and uniformly express their confidence in his generalship and ability. They are, however, in a state of feverish impatience to be getting out of winter quarters, and once more face[d] with their old enemies on the other side of the Rappahannock.

THE CITY JUST NOW

Washington is slowly gathering its summer dullness, beginning thus early, because this has been the short session. Many Congressmen remain behind, busy winding up the business of their several committees, or attending to little affairs with the Departments for some far-off constituents. The Senate is at work with its Executive Session, and daily overhauls the long lists of names, more or less "shining," from the War, Navy, Treasury, State, Judiciary, and Interior. As the pressure upon them becomes less constant, you may see the various high officials draw long mental breaths, and come out of their reserve like bears in the spring. Even Stanton forgets his *brusquerie*, and looks mildly at his visitors through his dreadful spectacles—so that the said visitor have no Congressman at his elbow to apply the leeches of heavy persuasion for fat offices that cannot [be] given.

Most of our floating society, the gay butterflies who come only for the season, have gone, or are going fast. It is actually possible to obtain rooms at Willard's and "rooms to let" is the flag of distress on the doors of many a Washington boarding-house. I would that many should be empty, for if there is a class of people equal to your Jew gold speculators in Wall street, it is the class who dispose of the "furnished lodgings of Washington." Many a shady and dilapidated old family mansion has this past year earned enough to rebuild its battered aristocracy—if not that of its owner.

FRIGHTENED TOO SOON

A droll thing happens now and then:—a seceder seceded southward, leaving a fine house finely furnished. He feared confiscation. He made the casual acquaintance of a Philadelphia lawyer, to whom he offered his house "*sine die*," free of rent, so that confiscation be evaded. Philadelphia accepts, says good-bye to Secesh, rents the house for an enormous rent, and has been hunting ever since for *another* alarmed rebel. But the seceder finds the road to happiness through the C.S.A. very hard to travel, and in due time returns. He hunts up his Philadelphia friend, and asks about his house. "Leased for a term of years." "And the rent?" "Is mine by the terms of our bargain." Such is life—especially in Washington.

PUTTING DOWN THE GOLD

The success of Secretary Chase's financial policy in restoring public confidence, and putting down the price of gold, has caused the keenest satisfaction in Government circles. The Shylocks of the "Second Board," whose greedy and unscrupulous speculations did the mischief in the first place, seem at last to have paid rather dearly for their want of patriotism. For one, I am rejoiced—in the dry slang of the *Tribune* reporter—that "Moses has got it."

BETTER DAYS

We enter upon our spring campaign, as a country, with far higher hopes and under better auspices than many had feared. We have more confidence in ourselves, others, and the Government. All will go well.

WASHINGTON, 30 MARCH 1863 (PUBLISHED 2 APRIL 1863)

The seeming termination of the series of storms which have made March so intensely disagreeable, and the opening of the Southern spring, suggest that we look around us, and see in what sort of condition we enter this desperate campaign, which may so easily be made the last and decisive one. The dangers before us are manifold and beyond human scrutiny, and we can better employ ourselves in looking at our own resources, and at such encouraging circumstances as may appear. First, then, our armies were never in better spirits, or better physical and *military* condition. Never were they more anxious to be led once more against the enemies of the Government, or better able to give a good account of themselves upon the field. I say this, after a very careful collation of evidence from almost all our scattered camps. It is now some time since we have sustained any considerable reverse, and all the while our forces have been slowly but steadily "overshadowing" large sections of rebel territory; and now it only requires a few victories, or, in rebel phrase, such "drawn battles" as Antietam and Murfreesboro, to put us permanently in possession. The battles draw nearer daily, and we believe they will be the victories required.

LAST EFFORT OF THE REBELS

If anything were needed to induce us to strain every nerve in the operations of the next ninety days, it would be given us by the knowledge we have of the almost desperate condition of our opponents. With gold in Richmond at nearly *five hundred per cent.*, with all the necessaries of life in proportion, and the difficulty of keeping large armies in the field consequently increased, it follows with mathematical certainty that the chiefs of the rebellion will waste no time in completing their preparations, but will gather every atom of their strength for the efforts of this campaign. This is the view taken of it in the highest military circles of the country, and more than a little anxiety is expressed lest some despairing rush of the armies of treason should inflict serious damages upon us at some unexpected point.

A MORE HOPEFUL FUELING

It is singular, when we remember how men talked three months ago, to see the almost universal conviction, in the minds of the people, that the time of doubt and uncertainty has passed, and that now the end is sure. Men feel more as they did at the commencement of the war—that the suppression of the rebellion is a question of time only, and they are only disposed to ask, with painful earnestness, "Lord, how long?" Nor are proofs wanting to show that a similar frame of mind exists, to no small extent, in the heart of the tottering "Confederacy."

THE BLACK REGIMENTS

A point worth noticing is the marked diminution in the prejudice against our black regiments. Let them win a fight or so, and the most narrow-minded "Copperhead" will see, as clearly as Colonel Higginson himself, the sound common sense of arming and employing them.[14] Already they are attracting attention by their proficiency in drill, and their usefulness as scouts and skirmishers; and though few are yet convinced that they will be found equal to white troops in the shock of a pitched battle, the majority of our military men are ready to admit that, in one way or another, every thousand of enlisted blacks can be made to supply the places of an equal number of white men.

PUBLIC BUILDINGS GOING UP

To return to our local affairs, it may be said that by nothing is the faith of both Government and people more clearly shown, than in the steady growth of this city, the rise in real estate, and the unchecked work upon our magnificent public buildings. Only a small patch remains to be finished, and the great west wing of the new Treasury Building will be at last covered, and ready for the hands of the carpenters, plasterers, and decorators. The additional stories have been completed on the solid, but old-fashioned War and Navy offices, and the different bureaus are moving into them. The Capitol, the Interior, the General Post Office, all steadily grow towards completion, nor does any tremor of hesitation betray a doubt that these shall be for the uses of our Government for centuries yet to come. There is a touch of the sublime in the faith and self-sacrificing energy of our people, nor has all that they have yet done or suffered by any means sounded the depths of their patriotism or their endurance.

KEEPING AN EYE ON ENGLAND
Strange tales continue to reach us, often through official sources, of the armaments building for rebel uses in the *neutral* ports of Great Britain. *Perfide Albion!* were it not for the honesty and enlightened philanthropy of her *better* classes (the peerage not included), what a fund of bitterness, aye, and of future vengeance, America would have laid up for her. There is, however, an unpleasant thought in all this privateer business of England's— Congress has made ample provision for retaliation, and if this new batch of pirates comes forth, no man can doubt that the power will be promptly and terribly exercised. Our people are not in a very long-suffering mood at present, and we have already borne a great deal for a people already upon the war-path. Beyond this, however, which may yet be averted, there do not seem to be many threatening indications in the European horizon.

BRITISH TESTIMONY
A British orator has forcibly called the attention of his countrymen to the important fact that, with one or two trifling exceptions, we hold, with grim and unyielding strength of grasp, every acre of soil upon which we effect a lodgment, and that at this ratio, if in no other way, the Confederacy must eventually die of "strangulation."

THE NEED OF CAUTION
I am almost sorry, however, to see the Northern newspapers once more speaking in tones of such dangerous confidence about the speedy termination of the war. We shall face our difficulties all the more earnestly when we take a fair, truthful, and comprehensive view of them. We should never have seen the tremendous revulsions in popular feeling, so frequent during the past two years, had we, from the first, taken a wiser view of the two contending powers in this war. Our old danger is upon us again. We see clearly that there is no longer any serious danger of European intervention;

we see that our enemies are grievously straitened for the common necessaries of life, and that their finances have fallen into hopeless and ruinous confusion; we are proud of our numerous, well-tried, well-provided, and well-disciplined armies; we have beaten our domestic traitors in their last effort on behalf of their Southern brethren, and we, all too soon, begin to count the days between us and peace; and should, for any reason, the number of those days be drawn out beyond our calculations, there is danger that we may again be weakened, as before, by that sickness of the heart that arises from hope deferred. Let us, then, bear in mind the desperate courage and undeniable ability of the men who are now gathering every energy for the last despairing death-struggle of the great conspiracy. Their armies in the field are as numerous as ever, and their short supplies will be made a double incentive to success in their projected raids upon the fertile and populous regions which have not as yet felt the desolating tread of armed rebellion. Richmond, Charleston, Savannah, Vicksburgh, Tullahoma, Chattanooga, Mobile, the present great military points of the enemy, are still in their possession, and a defeat for our arms, at either one of them, would be a serious check upon our advancing armies. Such defeats *may* be in store for us; such checks may come; it may be that we have not yet paid the full price, in blood and treasure, which must be told down for the purchase of our inestimable national life to come. In any event, let us bear in mind that checks to our arms can now, at the worst, be but temporary drawbacks, while every effort of our opponents deprives them, even in victory, of strength which their waning energies ill can spare. The *end is sure*.

THE DRAFT

The War Office is busy with the countless applications for appointments under the new Conscription Act, and before long the vast machinery will be in working order.[15] The Southern leaders cannot longer comfort themselves with any delusive hope that *we* are getting weary or exhausted, or that the army before them is the only one they may have to fight with. As they look Northward, the very air must be dark with the shadows of the mighty hosts yet to come forward to put down the foes of the Great republic.

WASHINGTON, 6 APRIL 1863 (PUBLISHED 9 APRIL 1863)

I am compelled, almost, to open this letter with a word about the weather. The past week was generally clear, and so windy that the roads dried with amazing rapidity, and by Saturday the dust was flying in suffocating clouds. Saturday night, however, the north wind, which had prevailed all day, brought us a driving snow storm, and by morning about ten inches of *snow* had fallen, to the intense disgust of all wayfaring men and "such as live in tents." This, at this late season and in this latitude, is something remarkable. It is worth noting, moreover, how all men take account of this and all other changes, almost solely with reference to their bearing upon the well-being and efficiency of the army. "What will Hooker say to this snow?" "I wonder if this will interfere with Rosecrans?" and a thousand similar remarks may be heard at every turn. And well we may note the skies and speculate upon the weather; for has not the weather, thus far, been one of the most important elements in all the great events of this war? We cannot yet tell what effect upon the fate of Charleston was produced by the storm which overwhelmed the *Monitor*, or whether the floods have done us good or harm before Vicksburg; but we do know that in all the history of the war in Virginia, our generals have attributed the greater number of their failures to the rain, and the mud which comes with it in this tenacious and thirsty soil.

PRIVATE WANTS

Other matters go on as usual. The same unceasing throng in the ante-rooms of the President's house, bent on dragging him "for a few minutes only," away from his labors of state to attend to private requests, often selfish, often frivolous, sometimes corrupt or improper, and *not* so often worthy of the precious time and strength thus wasted. The President belongs to the nation—it is seldom that the affairs of any one man cannot be righted, save by bringing to his aid the delegated power of a whole people. No man, however, will see this, when his eyes are veiled by his interest. But who can doubt that our worthy and wise Chief Magistrate would do better, to bring to the grand yet delicate questions which must be finally decided by him alone, a mind unwearied by listening to private griefs or wishes, and unexhausted by pouring out his too ready sympathies upon misfortunes which, powerful as he is, he cannot remedy.

SUFFERING AND NOISE

From the beginning of the war until now, I have been so situated as to see and hear a great deal of its inevitable consequences of sorrow and desolation. It has been my fortune to pass over several of the districts which have been devastated by armed occupancy, and to know much of that devastation which has been scattered, but not thereby lessened, among the homes and firesides of the free North. Is there, can there be, anything else so full of sorrow as a civil war like this? It is of no use to dilate upon such a topic, but there is one point too striking to go unmentioned: Have you, have we any of us fully appreciated the heroic and patriotic fortitude with which this glorious people has borne its bitter bereavements? It is wonderful! Murmurs there have been, and many murmurers are busy now, making the air resound with their complaints, but the murmurs *do not come from the sufferers.*

The men who make all this noise are not the men who have made the sacrifices of this contest—not they, indeed!—they are men whose trade it is to assail the Government, and who weep crocodile tears over the wounds of others, that they may be thought the friends of the people. The real sufferers grieve, weep, but look upward, and march on. The history of the war shows that the men who have lost the most friends in the struggle of to-day, are the men who form the new regiments of to-morrow. There may be this additional good in our new conscript law, that it will force thousands of semi-traitors and cold-hearted sluggards to learn their lesson of patriotism in the camp and on the battle field. Soldiers say that a few hot days under fire will work wonders for even a coward—it seems that the two cases are analogous.

THE ELECTIONS

The result of the late election in Rhode Island has been in a high degree encouraging, and we are looking hopefully towards Connecticut, believing that she will never humble herself to the infamy of practically sueing for peace at this hour of the nation's great struggle for life.[16] The next election to be held is that of Maryland in August, and it will be desperately contested. Who would be left to sing "Maryland, my Maryland," if the old State should once more come out square and strong for the Union, and at the same time for *freedom*? Stranger things than that have happened.

THE OWL OF NEWSPAPERS

Among the queer things of the day is the almost subterranean existence here of a newspaper called the *Constitutional Union*, ostensibly edited and published by Thomas B. Florence, and endorsed by such hearty patriots as Vallandigham, Saulsbury, Richardson, the Woods, and Bayard.[17] It is supposed to be the organ of the Knights of the Golden Circle. It is circulated so quietly that it is hard to obtain a copy. The largest portion of its editions are "for other eyes than ours," and leave town in bundles. It is not seen at the news-agencies, the newsboys call it not aloud in the streets—it is the veritable owl of newspapers, "preferring darkness rather than light." I think I know what would be the probable duration of such an existence in some patriotic town on the prairies of Illinois.

WASHINGTON, CA. 20 APRIL 1863 (PUBLISHED 23 APRIL 1863)
A lovelier spring day than this in which I am writing rarely visits the earth, especially in this region of "many climates." The cavalry horses perspire a little with evident comfort as they trot by, while their riders, glad to be rid of their overcoat and waterproof, sit jauntily in their saddles, listening with lazy pleasure to the jingle of their sabres and spurs. The very sentries on guard seem to glory in the return of sunshine—not yet so warm as to make guard duty a punishment.

THE COMING FAST

I understand that the pastors of the various churches have made a general effort to impress upon their hearers the propriety of their scrupulously observing the coming great National Fast.[18] I hope the same was done throughout the loyal States. To men who have any religion whatever, it is unnecessary to argue such a case, but to those who have *not*, it would be well to repeat the remark of a "free thinker" this morning: "You know I don't believe much in religion, and prayer, and all that sort of thing; but if the President can in this way get the people to sit down soberly for one day, and think of what they are about, and of what future may be before them, why, it will be a wonderful good thing, that's all." And my irreverent friend was right, so far as his darkened eye could see. We need to think, and to think soberly, of the grand, solemn, tremendous responsibility now resting on our feeble shoulders. It may be that as we think, all our hearts will kindle with the fire of our new heroism, and each man go forth like a "resurrected" Cromwellian trooper—

Like a soldier of the Lord,
With his Bible and his sword.

We shall be stronger for action then, and better able to bear such disappointments as yet may be before us.

THE WAR PROPHETS

Speaking of disappointments, I see that many papers of good position at the North are in a hurry to announce that our armies have given up their work [at] both Charleston and Vicksburg, much to the disgust of the people. This is not and cannot be true for at neither place have we suffered anything like a defeat in our late movement.[19] We may have disappointments enough before us, without inventing any.

Almost equally out of the way are the newly-fledged "ninety-day" men of the North, who are already beginning to prophesy before your Union

Leagues and political meetings. The rebellion may be terribly wounded within the ensuing three months—it is more than likely that we shall succeed in striking several terrible "body blows" upon the carcass of this gigantic treason—but the end is not yet. I am very far from being a croaker, yet cannot but see that our great error from the beginning has been that we have under-estimated the mighty task before us, and have been proportionately cast down when things failed to result in accordance with our too sanguine expectations. This is no common war, no mere jarring of angry nations, to be followed by renewed treaties and alliances. We should by this time open our eyes to the fact that we are forced, from our long neutrality in the great strife between the oppressor and the oppressed—a neutrality only not disgraceful because it prepared us for this—and compelled, whether we will or no, to take our appointed place in the very van of those who fight for freedom. Those who cannot yet see this have only to wait.

"God is sifting out the hearts of men
Before his judgment seat."

and if we cannot learn our true mission in any other way, we may yet be taught it by the light of redder flames than have yet been kindled in this, even in *this*, war.

THE PRESIDENT IN THE ARMY

The President's visit to the army is said to have had an excellent effect upon the men.[20] They cheered him vociferously whenever he appeared, and seemed delighted to have him among them. This is the army in whose lines men said, the lives of the President and Cabinet would not be safe for a moment after he had taken away [General McClellan,] their "Idol." All that appears to have been idle talk.

A GRANITE CRITIC

Do you know what gray granite is, Mr. Editor? I thought that all men knew gray granite by heart, but the other day I overheard a white-cravated and pompous kind of a Pickwick lecturing to an admiring circle of spectacled gentry before one of our finest public buildings, and gravely expressing his sorrow that "so fa-ine a structure should have been erected with a kind of *porous sandstone*, that will soon crumble away in this da-amp climate." I only wish I may not begin to crumble until that "sandstone" does. There are men who would be benefitted morally as well as mentally by a good course of lectures on granite—the stone which came out of the terrible fire so clean and so hard and enduring.

A STREAM THAT NEVER DRIES

The everlasting stream of new inventions for warlike purposes continues to swell in volume and in volubility. There are bushels of chaff, of course, whole boat-loads of unutterable humbugs, of no value to man or beast, and dangerous to the inventor only; but every now and then some man strikes out something of real worth. The difficulty is to draw Government attention in the right direction, and convince the authorities that "this is genuine." Of course the great multitude, whose crotchets are not bought and paid for, turn and bitterly assail the "Bureaus" and the Administration; but after all, there is no doubt that all the departments are glad enough to take up anything that really promises to strengthen them, or add to their efficiency. They are too slow at times, but it is *so* easy to be too fast, and that would be ruin, indeed. Of course, the whole country would be glad to recognize an occasional flash of genius, but it would be hard to make genius feel at home amid the dust and red tape of a Government bureau.

WASHINGTON, CA. 4 MAY 1863 (PUBLISHED 7 MAY 1863)

Now that May is here, with a reasonable certainty that we have nothing before us but really warm weather, the fact forces itself upon us that rarely, in this latitude, do we have springs so slow, so cold, so wet, and so ill calculated for military movements, as this has been. Whether in the end this will be found a blessing or the reverse, remains to be seen. At all events, we know that our armies are now moving, and that there seems to be no reason why Hooker should not force the rebels on the Rappahannock to meet him on something like equal terms as to position. It is not believed here that they *can* meet him in equal *force*.

HOOKER'S RESPONSIBILITY

Never did a General march to battle with a heavier weight of personal responsibility upon his shoulders. McClellan failed, and his friends found a thousand excuses for all his blunders, without difficulty. Burnside was foiled, and the people generously forgave his ill success. But it has been General Hooker's bad fortune to be forced forward before the country as the critic of both his former superiors. Right or wrong, he has pointed out what he thought were their errors, and declared what he believed to be a better policy. Now, with the same army, on the same great battle-field, he is called upon to meet the same wily and desperate foe. He must conquer or die—he cannot come back to the people a defeated man. I mention this point, because the history of war shows us that a second-rate commander, doing his very uttermost, is worth more than his superior in genius when crippled by timidity, indolence, or want of heart.

HIS ARMY

The army under General Hooker is, perhaps, the finest on this continent, if not in the world. The return of the two years' volunteers has hardly cost him eight thousand men, and all who remain are veterans, the heroes of many a hard-fought field and daring adventure, under perfect discipline, well led, well equipped, well cared for, and full of fire and hope. Alas, that so many of these gallant fellows will never re-cross the Rappahannock!

The cloud of military secresy covers, for the moment, the whereabouts and intentions of all our moving hosts, and we, the anxious spectators, await in painful suspense until the south wind from over some battle-field shall lift the covering, and reveal the result.

THE DRAFT

The machinery for the enforcement of the Conscript law is nearly perfected, and will soon be everywhere in operation. The ranks must be kept full; the pressure of our armies must at no point fail for lack of numbers, or we may lose by subsequent inaction all we shall win on our battle-fields. Rumors reach us from time to time, of intended resistance here and there to the action of the law, but all that sort of thing will be duly provided for, if by any chance misguided men should so far forget their duty to their country. The President proposes to allow no trifling in this business.

A NEW SOUTH

One of the most encouraging signs of the times is to be found by an examination of those large districts of the territory originally claimed by the "Confederacy," which are already in the possession of our armies. In all these regions, the unwonted enjoyment by all of that freedom of thought, speech and action, which the slave power so sternly and systematically repressed, is already producing good fruit of the most valuable kind. No doubt the number of malignant rebels is still very large, in spite of the very excellent policy of sending such persons south of the lines; but to offset this, we are building up a large party which is not only loyal, true to the Government, but also strongly *anti-slavery* in its views and proposed action. Think of abolitionist clubs of native Tennesseeans in Nashville! The world does move. These men are really the only hope we have for future peace and permanency. It is upon them and their principles, as a foundation, that the future stability and safety of the South must be built. Wherever the sin is found the curse will come, and we shall reap but part of the dearly-bought harvest of all this toil and bloodshed, if the "New South" shall still retain any portion of the fatal cause of our national troubles. We must purge from among us all traces of old world barbarisms, before we can hope to make perfect the new and free civilization which is at present only possible on this continent.

THE HARPIES OF WASHINGTON
The population of Washington is sensibly dwindling as the warm weather approaches, and boarding-house keepers and landlords bate somewhat of their extortionate independence, in view of empty rooms and uncrowded tables. The main excitement just now is the coming charter elections. There is little to choose between the two sets of candidates; each tries to ingratiate himself with the people by bawling for the Union, and the set that makes the most noise about its patriotism will pretty certainly get in. It is pretty much a question of lungs. If, however, either one of them can be persuaded to do anything for the most helpless city in the Union, it would be a good thing.

It seems to me that a good city government might find something worthy of its ambition in putting things to rights here—in correcting abuses, removing intolerable nuisances, diminishing the fearful aggregate of unblushing and open vice, in attending to our superabundant population of sharpers, gamblers and swindlers of every grade. It may be that these Augean stables are never to *be* swept, but I do not think a good Hercules of a city government need fail in a strong, hearty effort towards cleanliness, morality and order. Vice might at least be made to *hide*, instead of being allowed almost to drive shame-faced virtue from the streets.

WASHINGTON, CA. 11 MAY 1863 (PUBLISHED 14 MAY 1863)
After a week of almost continuous northeast storms of wind and rain, the sky is again clear, and the warm May sunshine asserts its dominion over the banks of the Potomac. The clouds have lifted in all directions, and the loyal and true are listening to the bugles and the drums of the marching regiments—horse and foot—with hearts beating higher than ever before, with hope, faith and expectation.

HOOKER NOT DEFEATED
I had thought that it was not in the power of the New-York press to do anything to surprise me, but must confess to astonishment at their treatment of the late movements on the Rappahannock. To dive at once *in medias res*, without discussing this or that editorial, or any of the many

impertinent and childish criticisms of the myriad penny-a-liners who infest the army in the service of Northern dailies, you and your readers may set these down as facts, to wit: It was assuredly not the fault of General Hooker that other armies did not move in concert with his own; it was not his fault that a portion of one Corps broke and ran disgracefully; it was not his fault that the winds of heaven were against him from Monday night to Saturday morning, and that his fords behind him became an impassable torrent, threatening his communications with a power beyond that of any rebel army; it was not his fault that by the usual treachery the enemy was advised of his proposed movement, and was able to concentrate in his front a force double the one he had expected to meet. For these and many other fearful disadvantages under which he labored, his country cannot hold him responsible. On the other hand, only the most malignant and narrow-souled partisanship will deny to him and his brave subordinates the credit of a good plan well executed; a rapidity and precision of movement unattained by any previous commander of the army of the Potomac; for rare courage, coolness, and ability in actual battle, inflicting on his enemy far greater loss than he himself sustained; and, finally, for that prudence which is the better part of valor, which so many had denied him, and which leaves him to-day with his army reinforced—fresh, as strong and as earnest as ever, and ready to strike again, and promptly, upon the shattered and depleted host of treason. Let Copperhead newspapers say what they please, the army under Hooker HAS NOT BEEN DEFEATED, and I do not believe that it will. It is worthy of note, that hardly one-third of his force was even *under fire* in the late battles. Therefore, let no one be disheartened or cast down because we did not accomplish a complete success.[21]

THE NEXT MOVEMENT

As to the movements of the week to come, the city is full of surmises, prophecies, and calculations, backed by more or less of information and good judgement, but the least said of them the better. From the Southwest, every report is encouraging. It cannot be long before the Father of Waters will once more be free from its mouth to its sources, and that will be worth a dozen famine-stricken Richmonds.

OUR TRANSATLANTIC COUSINS

For the last few weeks, our trans-atlantic cousins seem to have had a return of their old difficulty, and to be afflicted with blood on the brain whenever they think or speak of their American betters. However, unless something now unforeseen turns up, we may expect this fit to pass off like so many others, without the necessity of a resort to phlebotomy. Nevertheless, we can but watch with painful anxiety every indication of feeling or intention in the ranks of our European ill-wishers; they could do our struggling national life too much harm, and draw from us far too much of the blood and strength, which should now be concentrated on one great object. The current feeling in official circles here is, that we shall have no difficulty in keeping peace with all the world, unless some one power deliberately resolves to assail us.

THE TREASURY

The condition of the Treasury is a subject of pride and comfort to every loyal man. It is the great national barometer, by which we may measure the exact condition of the national heart. All adjusted accounts are paid, and yet we have a surplus! The people subscribe heavily to the loan, the taxes yield daily more and more, and the credit of the Government is better, at the end of two years' war, than it was at the beginning, and all because the people have an unshaken faith in the result. We *know* what the end will be, and to us all our faith is "the substance of things hoped for, and the evidence of things not seen."

WASHINGTON, CA. 18 MAY 1863 (PUBLISHED 21 MAY 1863)

The morning is magnificent, and the air is alive with the songs of birds. There is hardly a soldier to be seen, except the warm and indolent-looking patrols, who saunter along their posts in the warm sunshine as if they were only "*playing* soldier."

Nevertheless, I cannot help feeling just now as I did before Hooker crossed the Rappahannock, that the week before us is likely to be a stirring one. The strange calm of the past few days is, in this time, too unnatural to last. The silence must speedily be broken by news of victory or defeat.

THE UNION CAUSE ON THE GAIN

If we can afford to remain inactive, the rebels cannot. The days which do not win them positive advantages are all small defeats to the waning cause of treason. The rebellion is bleeding to death, and though we, too, suffer somewhat in the same way, and should hasten the catastrophe for our own sakes, we should not feel despondent because the battles are not continuous. The history of the war has been that, while the record of victories and defeats is nearly evenly balanced, and the drawn battles have been very many, we have, nevertheless, by a species of bloody attrition, and by numerous minor successes and wise movements, gradually driven the enemy from district after district, and State after State, until they now hold little more than half of the territory claimed by them in their first "Congress" at Montgomery. Moreover, whenever they have established themselves at any given point of great strategetical value for position or for strength, they have, in due time, been compelled to give it up to us. Witness Fort Donelson, Island No. 10, New-Orleans, Nashville, Corinth, Memphis, Roanoke Island, Manassas, and others. Some, it is true, for which we have striven, are yet under the "Stars and Bars," but in due time they, too, must fall.

THE PRESENT OUTLOOK

After a careful survey of the premises, with some facilities for so doing, I am deliberately convinced that without some great and now improbable disaster, sufficient to cripple us for the time, we must have Vicksburg and Port Hudson before the Fourth of July, and with them the control of the Mississippi from its sources to its mouth.[22] Texas and Arkansas will then be ripe apples, ready to fall whenever shaken vigorously.

Not quite so near or so sure is our success in Tennessee, but the probabilities, in a military point of view, are very decidedly in our favor. In Eastern Virginia, in spite of all said to the contrary, the enemy are far nearer to the yielding point than before the late battles. They are sensibly and visibly weakened, and cannot offer so strong a resistance to the next blow, while we can hit harder than before in many ways.

STONEWALL JACKSON

And this suggests another point: There is not a division of their army which the enemy hadn't better have lost than "Stonewall" Jackson.[23] Whether he was a *great* leader or not, his *name* was great on both sides. They adored and followed him, while his presence in our front was a continual terror to both our leaders and our soldiers. It is well, and a striking evidence of the magnanimity and Christian civilization of our people, that the press of the nation, with almost one accord, have joined to speak well of the dead soldier, and to recognize his many claims to our respect.

Many, however, have carried their magnanimity too far; for my own part, I am glad that he is dead, and died as he did, bravely and well; glad that God has decided that he shall do no more harm to a good cause; glad, too, that a man with so many shining qualities is not to share the cup of wormwood that remains for those of his associates who are to feel the bitterness of final failure, and see the cause for which they have committed so many crimes go down into oblivion and infamy. The fact is, the wide-spread notion that a man is sincere in his errors and retains no stain of guilt if he *believes* that his sin is a glory, is a most pernicious fallacy. It is true that we are strong enough to be generous and merciful, but to-day belongs to the sword.

BLACK SOLDIERS

It is surprising to see how rapidly men are losing their silly prejudices against the use of black soldiers. I mean in the army. Of course the demagogues of the North are almost as loud as ever, but among the men in the field, the prevailing sentiment is getting to be, in the rough language of the soldiers, "If the nigger will fight, why, let 'em fight—they're as good as rebels, any day." There is reason to believe, too, that the military feeling is on the increase among the blacks themselves. The resurrection of a manhood buried so long and so deeply must needs be slow, and too many of them have been unable even to hear the call of the trumpet, but the race will yet rise to a newness of life, such as God gives in time to all the nations that are oppressed and cast down.

Many foreign officers of distinction and experience have given it as their opinion that the world in modern times has rarely seen such stubborn fighting as some of that the other day at Chancellorsville. They say that no army in Europe can equal it to-day; and while we must proudly agree with them, it seems a sad pity that so many brave men must die to save their country from such an attack—or even in *making* such an assault upon that which should be sacred to them.

WASHINGTON, CA. 1 JUNE 1863 (PUBLISHED 4 JUNE 1863)

I was prevented from sending my usual contribution last week by an "experimental proof" that, under all this fine weather of ours, there still lurk those treacherous fevers which have been, from the beginning of the war, more fatal than sword or shot to the strength of our armies.

GOOD HEALTH OF THE ARMY

It may not be amiss, however, in this connection, to call attention to the current bills of health of the Army of the Potomac, as showing conclusively that our veterans now in the field are thoroughly seasoned and acclimated, and as fit, or more so, than the natives themselves, to endure the heats and miasmas of this latitude. Doubtless their experience in taking care of themselves, and the better organization and management of the army, has much to do with it, but custom, and the "use which hardens," make the greater difference. Moreover, and the thought is at best a sad one, the infirm and weakly constitutions have long since succumbed to the varied assaults to which they have been subjected, leaving only the stronger in body to carry on the work. Alas for the gallant fellows whose spirit indeed was willing, but whose flesh was weak!

THE MOMENTOUS CONTEST AT VICKSBURG

The intense excitement of the past week, while our eyes have been straining Southwestward, is not yet over, and we still look on in painful suspense at the intermittent light and shade of doubt and glory that seems to cover the daring movements of General Grant.[24] Not that there is much reason to fear the result, for we here are fixed in the belief that he must and will succeed, after having overcome obstacles that might well have daunted a less determined spirit. It can be but a few hours, comparatively, before we shall know the whole, and prophecy is out of place that treads so closely upon fulfillment, or the reverse. If, however, as there is every reason to hope, the result is in accordance with our wishes, it will be difficult to overestimate the importance of the result; it may be summed up, or nearly so, in a few words. The Mississippi is once more and forever free to the commerce of all the West; the rebellion is cut in sunder, never to reunite; and in all future operations, eastward towards the coast, or westward to the wilderness, we shall have the great river as a base of operations, and an unfailing channel of supply. Henceforth the armies in the West can act in swift cooperation.

RUMORS ABOUT GENERAL LEE

None see these things so clearly as the rebel chiefs themselves, and while they have striven with desperate energy to prevent this catastrophe, they are now undoubtedly planning grand movements and achievements which may in part, at least, counterbalance this terrible blow to their strength. The air itself seems to have teemed with rumors, for some days, as to proposed movements by Lee and his subordinates. That they will attempt *something* cannot be doubted, but just what it will be is another question. You may rest assured, however, that our own rulers are not asleep, but are watching every movement of the rebel army with lynx eyes, ready for defence or attack, and prepared to turn his least blunder into a disaster. Just what precautions they are taking, no man knoweth, or knowing, no man telleth. If Lee contemplates a rapid and prolonged rush at some point which he may imagine unguarded, how terribly he will miss the man who has so long been in all such matters the right hand of the rebellion. There is no Stonewall Jackson now, to be in our front to-day and in our rear to-morrow, equally dangerous in either position; and if the rebels do not feel the difference, *we do*. I say this in no spirit of mean exultation over a fallen enemy, but merely as pointing out a great falling off in the power of our foes to do us injury.

A FUNERAL IN WASHINGTON

The funeral of General Kirby was an imposing affair, worthy of the brave spirit to whose memory the tribute was paid.[25] It was simple—no show, no glitter, no pomp—but the cavalcade of infantry, cavalry, and artillery, that preceded the hearse, had a plain, serviceable, soldierly appearance, as if they had just come from the field to bury the dead chieftain, and were ready to march from his grave into battle again. We are getting only too well used to the roll of the muffled drums, and the draped flags, and the slow march of the "riderless steed" behind the coffin of his master.

CHARTER ELECTION OF THE CITY

This week the charter election of the city of Washington takes place. All the tickets are headed "Unconditional Union;" and in any event, the result will be noised abroad as a "Union triumph." It does not signify much, for here, at least, "copperheadism" is unpopular and dangerous. The traitors are many, but look on in mute bitterness to see all power in other hands than theirs.

WASHINGTON, CA. 8 JUNE 1863 (PUBLISHED 11 JUNE 1863)

All the week we have been adding to the already splendid record of the heroism of our brave troops in the Valley of the Mississippi. Such fighting has rarely been seen before on this or any other continent. Such patriotic self-devotion from so many plain men at this hour of the struggle, furnishes almost a guaranty of the happy result.

COURAGE OF THE WHOLE ARMY

It is to be regretted that some of your contemporaries of the press seem disposed to use these successes in the West for the purpose of disparaging the courage and soldierly qualities of the men of the East. A little more careful notice of the returns, and a little more knowledge of the composition of the armies under Grant and Banks, might save these gentlemen from a mistake as injurious as it is unjust. Not only are there very many regiments from the Eastern States in the Army of the West, who have fully kept pace with their comrades in all these bloody conflicts, but the Western armies themselves are to a large extent made up of men of Eastern birth.

How many, either of officers or privates, in the Kansas, Iowa, Wisconsin, or Minnesota regiments, now so distinguished for good conduct, were born in the States where they enlisted? Let us be reasonable, and proudly aver that State lines make no variation in the men they separate, but that the free blood of our American citizens almost invariably contains iron enough to brace it to deeds of daring. It is not *now*, at all events, that wise men should breathe one word to foster undue State pride, or to breed unnecessary sectional prejudices. It is true that there are too many unfortunate days in the record of our army in the East, but whatever may be the cause of this, the battle-thinned ranks of our regiments are an eternal and eloquent protest against charging our misfortunes upon our soldiers.

One more thing we have learned, those of us who had it yet to learn, from the late operations in the West, to wit, that our black regiments will *fight*, that they are firm under fire, that they stand killing, and our Copperhead neighbors may take the lesson to their hearts.

ADMIRAL FOOTE AT CHARLESTON

The sending Admiral Foote to relieve Dupont in the command of the fleet off Charleston, naturally leads the public mind to place some reliance on the complaints, which have been so freely made of the old-fogyism and dilatoriness of the latter.[26] Dupont certainly has done good service, and accomplished many important undertakings, but if he cannot keep step with the rapid march of improvement in naval warfare, he must needs give way to some man who can. His successor in the command of the fleet off Charleston is a man in whom the people have great faith, and from whom they will expect very much. There is little reason to fear that they will be disappointed.

THE RUMORS ABOUT LEE

It appears that all the rumors about Lee's grand movement, the evacuation of Fredericksburg, &c., come down to the reality that the camps of both armies have been moved somewhat, perhaps for sanitary purposes. Meanwhile, believing that Lee intends to strike a blow somewhere, and remembering the rapid movements of former days, our citizens listen eagerly to every rumor, and show a zeal in propagating and expounding every item of news unequalled since 1861—and *that* summer can never be surpassed in this respect.

SIEGE OF VICKSBURG

The siege of Vicksburg still drags on slowly, though not from any lack of energy or determination on the part of the brave men before it. The siege of Troy itself never was half so interesting, or offered so many points of stirring interest to the pen or tongue of the narrator. It is a little curious to watch in the rebel papers the rapid revival of the old blustering and self-confident tone, so lately turned to querulous complaints and dark forebodings, by what they indistinctly term "our disasters in the Southwest." They seem fully confident that Pemberton—so lately cursed by them as "a renegade Yankee, and necessarily a traitor"—will fully succeed in holding his own, and forcing his assailants to an inglorious retreat or a shameful surrender.[27] There is good reason to hope that this effervescence of theirs, like all former ones, will soon subside under the all-controlling cork of another heavy "disaster."

THE NATIONAL RESOURCES
Among the noticeable features of the country's prosperity at this time, worthy of special attention from all who take an interest in the increase of our national strength, is the general awakening in the minds of our business men to the development of our internal resources. Never before were schemes of internal improvement of such a gigantic character set on foot. The great highways of travel and of transportation are being enlarged, extended, improved, and new ones that but a little time ago were dreams in the minds of men who "woke too early," are giving fair promise of speedily becoming solid realities.

And in speaking of the development of our resources, I fancy that many of your readers are unaware of the vast increase in the value and productiveness of our *mines* for the past two or three years. This is not the time or place to go into statistics, but a few hours in the mineral room of the Land or Patent Offices, with a mere glance at the data there collected, will warrant the most skeptical in accepting as a fact the assertion of one of our Representatives in debate last winter—"The national debt, Mr. Speaker, the national debt? Why, sir, there are *square miles* in the Western mountains rich enough to pay the whole of it."

WASHINGTON, CA. 15 JUNE 1863 (PUBLISHED 18 JUNE 1863)
It is a task to write letters concerning current events, when every hour is so heavily laden with momentous possibilities. Not to speak of the West, where so much depends on the issue of two desperate struggles now going forward—struggles of life and death, from which one or the other of the contending forces must come in ruins—letting our eyes rest from that terrible spectacle, we find that here at home the clouds of war are rapidly thickening.

LEE'S MOVEMENTS
The gallant conduct of Pleasanton's cavalry at Beverly's Ford the other day, has, no doubt, driven the idea of a surprise, or a swift cavalry raid, from the mind of General Lee;[28] but he is slowly drawing his army up the banks

of the Rappahannock, and watching eagerly for an opportunity to strike a blow upon his wary opponent, or to elude him altogether, and cast his large army, with sudden force, upon some less thoroughly protected portion of our lines. I presume that it is not contraband to say that I have every reason to believe that the rebel leader will find us ready for him at every point, and that such a movement as he is now supposed to be making, may be very easily turned into a terrible disaster for his army and his cause. Nevertheless, we are anxious here in Washington, not knowing at what moment we may hear tidings of bloody doings "in the front."

It would be strange, indeed, if the war in Virginia should this summer drift back to its old battle-fields, and the roar of the conflict once more be brought to us from Warrenton, Manassas, and Centreville.

Some of the New-York papers, it seems, are disposed to think that things look black in this vicinity; there never was a greater error. Of course we cannot prophesy the event of battles which are by no means certain to take place; but we are by no means over-sanguine when we almost pray that Lee *may* move forward, and learn at some new Antietam that the gates of the North are securely closed against the armies of the Rebellion.

THE PRESIDENT'S LETTER

Perhaps *the* event of the week is the reply of the President to the Albany Democrats.[29] It is a grand document, strong, plain, simple, without one sparkle of tinsel ornament, yet dignified as becomes the ruler of a great people when the nation is listening to what he says. It should be printed in every Northern paper, and read by every citizen. It will go far to free the minds of many from unpleasant fears and doubts, and the angry thoughts so carefully instilled and cherished by the race of demagogues whose doom the President foretells. It is well that he has spoken, and all the nation should hear what he has said.

VALLANDIGHAMS'S NOMINATION

The name of Vallandigham, fast drifting to oblivion behind the dim barriers of the "lines," reminds us of the very funny position voluntarily assumed by the Ohio Democratic (falsely so called) Convention. It is in evidence that the managers were anxious to secure the name of Gen. M'Clellan to head their ticket, and received a not too courteous response from an officer who has led too many men to battle in *defence* of the Government and the Union, to consent to lead a lot of political hacks *against* them. Finding the soldier too patriotic and too wise, they try the "martyr"—the suffering and bleeding victim of an atrocious tyranny, the man who had come nearer than any of the rest of them to getting his just deserts. It is said that the "victim" was nominated unanimously, and so far all went well; but just then a sense of their condition seems to have come over them, and in a series of ferocious resolutions, they turn upon the President and demand their candidate. "We've gone and nominated him for Governor of Ohio, and now we want him. In fact, we *must* have him. If we can't have him, he can't go into the canvas, and the grand show of the 'victim' will be a failure; besides, if he should be elected, it will be of no use, if we can't have him *here*." Indeed, Mr. Editor, it seems very funny to me, especially as the President can so truly reply—"I haven't got your candidate; the last I heard of him, he was on a pleasant little visit to his Southern friends. I reckon he is safe among them—certainly, safer than I should be."

But perhaps all this levity is wrong. Indeed, I might well be reproved for it by some lonely widow or helpless child in Indiana, Illinois, or Ohio, whose husband or father has been shot down in his own door, or in the discharge of his duty, by the deluded followers of these same men, set on to cowardly crime by the "harmless criticisms" of the candidate for Governor of Ohio. It is to be feared that more of this unnatural mischief will yet be done in the darker districts of some of the States; but if *so*, I mean no cruelty or bitterness in saying that the woods in those parts are likely to bear a fruitful crop of the "strange acorns" which have been such common fruit in other and more barbarous civil wars.

WASHINGTON, 5 JULY 1863 (PUBLISHED 9 JULY 1863)
The dull and damp atmosphere, which seems always to follow on the heels of a great battle, has for two days past settled heavily over the valley of the Potomac. Not upon the spirits of the people or the army, however, for we are beginning to have a strong faith that at last the much-enduring and unfortunate Army of the Potomac has won a great and substantial success. We are waiting now, hoping to hear that the redoubtable Lee is once for all beaten, and his army destroyed. Coming, as this does, upon such cheering indications in the West, the effect is doubly enlivening. It enabled us to celebrate our Fourth of July with unexpected zest and earnestness.

THE FOURTH IN WASHINGTON
Speaking of that celebration, in outward appearance it was just an old-fashioned "commemoration," with an unusually large show of soldiers, flags, societies, citizens, and fireworks; but morally it marked a great revolution in the composition of the population of the national capital. The fact is, that they never *had* a Fourth of July here before, and the

ancient burghers looked on amazed to see what a fuss their new neighbors made over it. All passed off well, however, amid cheers for the President and Gen. Meade.[30]

CONFIDENCE IN GEN. MEADE

The present commander of this army seems to have the confidence of Government, people, and "army men," to an extent unequalled by any of his predecessors, unless it was McClellan in his palmiest days. Since his appointment, I have heard no one speak evil of him, while it is well known now that he was the unanimous choice of the corps commanders. This last point alone is of vast importance, when we remember the fearful things we have suffered in time past from the jealousies and differences among officers of high rank.

So that to-day, Mr. Editor, all things look well from this standpoint, and by the time this letter is before your readers, they will doubtless be able to study the facts at their leisure.

THE WEST

At the same time, however, we are looking westward with more than a little anxiety. The brave Banks appears, with his small but splendid army, to be surrounded by difficulties and dangers, though none the less persistently hammering away at the defences of Port Hudson, and providing as best he can against the different bands that threaten his rear and his communications. He is still supposed to be able to take care of himself, as he has done heretofore.[31]

The newspapers seem to think that Bragg has abandoned Tullahoma for the purpose of marching against Grant's rear at Vicksburg. I believe that it is to be hoped that this is true. The enemy seem to be losing their senses. Vicksburg is a doomed city, and the more trouble, expense and loss the rebels undergo in their desperate efforts to relieve it, the better all loyal men will be satisfied.

THE LAST GREAT BATTLE-FIELDS

The handwriting is on the wall. Even Belshazzar can see it now, and, alas for him! he needs no Daniel to tell him what it means. This month of July, with its long days and its brilliant nights, will see the last *great* battle-fields of the war. The Confederacy of rebellious slaveholders is fast crumbling before the terrible blows it has received and is still receiving. Not that the war is over, or nearly over. Do not let any of our readers lay *that* flattering unction to their souls. The war will not be ended even if we win all the battles now impending. This tiger is wounded unto death, but it will die hard, and fight to the last. Moreover, if we slacken in our efforts because of our successes, there is great danger that the hard-won fruit of them will be torn from us again, and, for a time at least, "the deadly wound be healed."

THE NEGRO REGIMENTS

The work of raising and drilling the negro regiments goes bravely on, and all prejudice is rapidly dying out. It is an old story, now, to see a black battalion on parade, and no one makes much fuss over it except the colored people themselves. It is sometimes very funny to see the darkies following or preceding the ranks of their armed brethren—men, women, and children. The little "nigs," with eyes and mouth open, indulging in wonderful gyrations on the pavement; the men grinning, or looking darkly thoughtful, according to their cast of mind; and the women, arms a-kimbo, heads up, proudly keeping step to the music, and in the fullest sense of the phrase, "glorying" in the new step towards freedom and manhood which their race is making.

This arming the negroes is a great thing in many ways. It is my deliberate opinion, that it will yet solve, in the right way, too, the oft-repeated question–"What shall we do with the South, and with the negroes, after the war is over?" We are educating a new race of freemen, who will take care of the South and of themselves too. Even if they labor under white employers, which is most probable, they will not, and they cannot return to their servile condition, for "the sword ennobles."

OFFICIAL MATTERS

I see that the "Cabinet-makers" have been again at work for the past few weeks, building up and tearing down. They may spare themselves the trouble, for good or bad, the Cabinet remains as it was, with its varied elements of weakness or of strength.

The militia of the District, including Government employees of all sorts, are being mustered for military duty, to enable as many as possible of the veterans in garrison here to be sent into the field. It is a good move, though it causes no little grumbling among salaried place-men of all grades.

WASHINGTON, CA. 13 JULY 1863 (PUBLISHED 16 JULY 1863)

Another glorious week has rolled away, full of good tidings, full of hope, full of cheer, yet not unladen with the heaviest anxieties. We are, in fact, not only a mercurial, but in one sense an *insatiable* people. We no sooner succeed in comprehending the reality of a great and important fact, a great good or a great evil, than we turn with feverish petulance to the future, and demand what may be next in store for us. The excitement about the battle of Gettysburg hardly outlasted two editions of the New-York dailies, and the crowning triumph at Vicksburg is already swallowed up by the coming events that cast their dim shadows upon the banks of the Potomac.[32]

DISCREDITING THE SURRENDER

By the way, I see by the papers that not a few men in New-York to the very last endeavored to throw doubt and discredit upon the announcement of the surrender of Vicksburg, and gravely labored to "prove their position" in various ways. Great souls! determined that, whoever else might be taken, *they* at least would not be made the dupes of the false statements and lying bulletins of an "abolition despotism." Or is it possible that the condition of the gold and cotton markets had anything to do with this superabounding incredulity? All that is settled now, however, and the most skeptical can reasonably doubt no longer. Vicksburg *has* fallen, and Port Hudson must in due time follow it, and then, after a brief war upon pirates and guerillas, the Father of Waters will be open from its sources to its mouth. It has been a long and a desperate struggle, fought out on both sides with a tenacity and courage truly American, but the great result is ours at last.

LEE AND HIS PERIL

The various misstatements and silly stories of all kinds from the field of Gettysburg are rapidly being corrected, and we find that we won a substantial victory, whose results will be of vast importance in almost any event, but whose most valuable fruits yet remain to be gathered on the banks of the Potomac. Would that the carnage were already over, and the victory ours! or rather, would that we could claim the grand reward without paying the fearful price of blood which our foes yet demand of us. A glance at a good map will show your readers that Gen. Lee has taken a position, partly by compulsion and partly by choice, which possesses great natural advantages for either crossing the Potomac if time is given him, or for making an effective resistance to any assault that may be made upon him. It is indeed an admirable position, but along with its advantages it seems to carry the one great danger, that *if* he is defeated in the approaching contest there is no apparent escape for him. He must win a decisive victory, or utter ruin stares him in the face. Should Meade succeed in concentrating in time—for time is here the great element of success or failure—the large forces at his disposal, it would seem impossible that the rebel "army of Virginia" can remain in existence *as* an army for three days longer. It is indeed not unlikely that at this very moment, while I am writing, the great event is being put to the bloody arbitrament of a pitched battle.

We know only too well what obstacles have been in the way of our gallant General and his army—what rivers of mud in the shape of roads, what rugged passes, what hindrance from the arms of the daring and untiring enemy—but still we hope and believe that he now hems in the best of the rebel generals and by far the best of the rebel armies, with a force from which there can be no escape, and to which all resistance will be futile. If so, a few hours may settle the matter, and once more carry to the eager multitudes of the North the glad news of a great victory.

NO COMPROMISING WITH TREASON

And then—*what then*? The rebellion is not crushed—the fighting is not over—the fearful disease of treason is not wholly cured: Johnston, and Beauregard, and Bragg, are still in the field at the head of powerful armies, and they will surely make one more grand stand before they give up as hopeless the unholy cause for which they have sacrificed so much, and on behalf of which they have not scrupled to commit the greatest crimes yet known to Christian civilization. If they fight for nothing else they will fight for "conditions," and will make a desperate struggle rather than permit themselves to be given over, bound hand and foot, to be tried by the power against which they have so grievously offended. It is my notion that the Administration expects this, and is so far convinced of it that they are straining every nerve to prepare for the battles yet to come. There will be no encouragement to the beaten chiefs of the falling Confederacy in the attitude or the action of the Federal Government. The conscription will be rigorously enforced, and every arsenal and manufactory will be used to its utmost to furnish the men and the means for speedily crushing the last shadow of resistance to the National authority. There will be no imperfect work—no partial pacification—no weak-minded coming to terms. Stephens and his friends may knock as loudly as they please at the gates of Fortress Monroe—and the rebel Congress may discuss terms of reconciliation to their hearts' content, and the crowned heads of Europe may offer "mediation" to any imaginable extent, but we fully believe that to one and all the stern reply of the President will be "The whole country; complete surrender; universal obedience to the Constitution and the Laws!"

I apprehend that during the next few weeks much will be said by the Copperhead organs at the North, and even by demagogue sheets of a somewhat different stripe, about the duty of Government under existing circumstances to "once more extend the olive branch to our misguided

Southern brethren;" and so they will—the same olive branch that has been extended from the beginning of the war—"The Union and the Laws." Let no man deceive himself or be deceived. No half-way work will do, nor any compromise be admitted for a moment. The hour of our final triumph draws nearer and nearer, and when it comes we shall all see, if so be that our rulers are wise, true to themselves, true to us, and true to the great future, that we have won that which was well worth all the blood and treasure which it will have cost us—a redeemed and regenerated country, fit to lead the world in every good word and work for all future time.

WASHINGTON, 31 AUGUST 1863 (PUBLISHED 3 SEPTEMBER 1863)
After a somewhat prolonged absence from my post, I take pleasure in again assuming my duties as your Washington correspondent. I find local matters but little changed, and with hardly a ripple to disturb their placid dullness. The White House is deserted, save by our faithful and untiring Chief Magistrate, who, alone of all our public men, is *always* at his post. He looks less careworn and emaciated than in the spring, as if, living only for his country, he found his own vigor keeping pace with the returning health of the nation. There are rumors that he is about to address to his fellow-citizens another of those homely but powerful appeals which have more than once been almost equal to battles won. The people are just now in a good frame of mind to listen kindly to anything which he may have to say, and I for one shall wait with some degree of impatience for the promised document. The newspaper stories about the President's going West, or North, are all untrue, for he himself denies them.

A LOOKED-FOR CARNIVAL
Socially, the Capital is asleep. The *beau monde* is all away at the North, adding its little quota to the unwonted swarm at the watering-places and other summer resorts. I am told, however, that they are to return prepared for a "grand season"—a sort of carnival of show, extravagance and dissipation. It may be, and in these feverish times it may be all unavoidable, but a different course would show better national temper and better individual taste.

THE POTOMAC WARRIORS
What will be the nature of the fall campaign in the front it is just now impossible to predict. The general opinion seems to be that Lee is still strong enough to assume the offensive, were he not warned therefrom by

past experience. Still the cool and pleasant weather which has now set in seems admirably adapted to military operations, and we are strongly of the opinion that they will not be allowed to go to waste. The weather is indeed beautiful; a trifle warm in the sun at midday, but with plenty of air stirring, and with cool, breezy nights, wherein the soundest sleep may be enjoyed. This, however, is the season when the Potomac mosquito attains his majority, and his greatest size and ferocity. This is the only known animal of his size which never sleeps, but continues his unparalleled exertions day and night without resting.

POLITICAL DOINGS

The political movements now going forward in several of the more important States awaken the keenest interest here. We turn for a moment from watching the campaign, to see if the people at the North are awake to the duties which fall upon them. It is earnestly hoped, however, and generally believed, that Copperheadism has had its day, and that the people at home will rally round the Government with unfaltering patriotism. There are but two parties now, and they who are not sustaining their President, are, in one form or another, bolstering the falling fortunes of Jeff. Davis and the Slaveholders' Rebellion.

THE EMANCIPATION POLICY

Even in my brief absence I can notice a great improvement of sentiment as regards the cause and the treatment of the rebellion. The Emancipation policy, and the arming of the black men—the two great measures of the Administration—are swiftly vindicating the wisdom of their author. In the opinion of several of our best and foremost generals—old Democrats, too—they have been the heaviest blows yet given to our enemies. Such measures, for which there could not possibly be found any adequate precedent, must ever be judged by their results, and the results are presenting themselves each day for our examination. How many troublesome questions will be settled at once and forever by that same Proclamation, can only be understood by the men who had command in rebel districts before it became the law of the land, and who honestly endeavored to carry out "the compromises of the Constitution," in the management of their commands.

Said one gentleman, weak in the faith, and with the egg-shell of State Rights (in rebel States) still upon his head, to another, "But if you conquer all these States, or if they now voluntarily return, what course will you take with the slaves? Say in North Carolina?" "My dear sir," was the reply, "I was not aware that there *were* any slaves in North Carolina. The black people of that and other rebellious States have been freemen in the eye of *our* law this long time."

Such is now the current tone of thought and speech among our leading men, and many who were slow to come to a knowledge of the truth, see it now very clearly. A most important point is that the *army* is with the Administration in all its policy. The men of many battle-fields, now more than ever the free *citizens* of the Republic, have forgotten all old party trammels, and come out for the great truths which they have learned through such terrible experience. When these men go home, laying down the musket to use thenceforward the ballot only, the face of our national politics will be changed forever, and many a demagogue, now loud and blatant, will shrink from facing the bronzed faces of those who have *seen* what he *talks about*. But I shall weary you. I only want to call attention to what seems to me to offer a key to many doors in the future.

WASHINGTON, 7 SEPTEMBER 1863 (PUBLISHED 10 SEPTEMBER 1863)
We are certainly enjoying the finest of fall weather—days sunny but not too warm, and nights cool and breezy. Everybody is cheery and hopeful, but in the absence of other news we are again becoming a "rumor-producing people." We weary of looking towards Charleston and Sumter, and wonder what Lee is doing all this while. No one now has many doubts as to the fate of the birthplace of treason. The process may be slow, but the end is sure. Charleston is doomed, and while the military importance of the fact is over-estimated by many, we can hardly say too much of its *moral* influence. The place that knew it must know it no more forever. I am not vindictive, but if I had my way, I would make Charleston as Tyre, "a place for fishermen to dry their nets," and from amid its ruins the horned-owls of that latitude should hoot a great moral and political lesson to traitors for all future time.

EAST TENNESSEE
Just as I am writing, we have a confirmation of the rumor that Knoxville, Tenn., is really in the hands of Burnside. East Tennessee, the long-persecuted, harried, stricken, the Abdiel of the States—faithful found among the faithless—is once more free. Her loyal children need no longer hide in dens and caves of the rocks, but may once more avow their fealty to the old flag undisturbed. They have had a bitter cup pressed to their unoffending lips, and we at the North little know their heroism and devotion. The "Tories" and weak-hearted were numerous, it is true, but there were enough of

witnesses who resisted unto death. The only fear is that they will turn now, with all their wrongs burning at their hearts, and say to their oppressors, "It is now *our* day!"

God grant that the speedy fall of Chattanooga may soon open to us all the vast region to which it is the door, and save us from a more prolonged contest for the permanent security of Tennessee and the West. The war is not by any means over in the West, and we have many a sharp fight before us, but verily we have done much.

OUR FOREIGN AFFAIRS

Our foreign affairs still seem in the same state of delightful uncertainty—an international tinderbox, only waiting for the spark and the breath to arouse a flame that will be hard to quench. We all are well enough satisfied that the President and his advisers will do all in their power to prevent any European complications at present; but it is not beyond the range of possibilities for the daring and able gambler who controls the destinies of France, to take such steps as will render a collision inevitable. All this fills the minds of the thoughtful with a sense of uneasiness and uncertainty which is to a high degree painful and embarrassing. We believe, however, that the condition of our own affairs, and the *position of our armies* will, ere long, relieve the Emperor and his agent, Marshal Forey, from any strong temptation to cross the Rio Grande, or to risk all his hard winnings in chasing the *ignis fatuus* of a Franco-Rebel alliance.[33] A few months later, and it may be that we shall feel beyond any alarm from causes such as these.

THE POLITICAL CONDITION

The political condition of the country, though uncertain and exceedingly feverish, is rapidly becoming more and more favorable to the Administration. The people are rallying around the President as the central figure of all this melee, and are ready to give him all the aid and support he will require. It is by no means an uncommon assertion that his letter to the Springfield Convention was worth as much as a victory.[34] I am informed that it is not improbable that he may, after all, make a brief trip to the North before fairly entering upon his winter's work.

LOCAL MATTERS

In the city all things go forward as usual; and not the least interesting feature is the amount of *building* going forward. It is mostly, however, for business purposes, and there is still [a] great lack of dwellings, hotel accommodations, boarding-houses, &c. This, indeed, is a terrible nuisance, and enables a few landlords to fleece the people, residents and sojourners, unmercifully.

Why do not intelligent capitalists at the North come on, and make a few excellent investments of their surplus cash? It seems to me that they could hardly do better. The improvements on the public buildings go forward steadily, and many of them begin to wear almost a finished look. Speaking of improvements, one of the bad failures of the day is the effort to have the engraving and printing for the Government done here, in the Treasury building. Much elaborate puffery has been wasted upon this undertaking, also much money; but the new Government bonds just being issued are a sad commentary on the taste and skill of the Government employees. They are emphatically a "botch"—a wilderness of bad engraving and poor ink, daubed around an emaciated "hen-hawk."

WASHINGTON, 14 SEPTEMBER 1863 (PUBLISHED 17 SEPTEMBER 1863)
I am sorry to see that my predictions, as to the duration of the siege of Charleston, are being fulfilled. And yet the pear may ripen any day, and the success of a few hours may place in the hands of our persevering army and navy the coveted result of months of labor and sacrifice. The best military authorities, while not sanguine as to a *speedy* triumph, seem to entertain no doubts whatever as to the final result, and *some* fine morning the welcome news will come that the Stars and Stripes once more, and for all time, are waving above their own.

THE GREAT EVENTS IN TENNESSEE
In Tennessee the course of the late campaign has been to the last degree puzzling, while thus far eminently satisfactory. If I may credit what I am accustomed to consider good authority, the surrender of Cumberland Gap, and the evacuation of Chattanooga, were unexpected and unaccountable events to our leaders.[35] We may in truth look upon them as in themselves not less important, and in their indications vastly more significant, than the fall of Vicksburg, or the retreat of Lee from Pennsylvania. The degree of weakness and demoralization in the rebel armies which compelled them to abandon East Tennessee, Northern Georgia, and the passes of the Alleghanies, without striking, or trying to strike, so much as one heavy blow in their defence, is something for which we were not prepared to look. They, themselves, in spite of overweening pride and self-conceit, seem to see how all the world will understand this new "strategy," and already we hear rumors of desperate efforts to be made in various directions to redeem the tremendous vantage ground which they have lost. Whether they will gather their legions to throw them upon Burnside or Rosecrans, or whether there will be one grand effort more to "carry the war into Africa," is more

than we can gather from the vague hints which reach us. It is only evident that they must and will try something, and that soon.

THE LAST GREAT TRIAL

If it is ever safe to attempt a sifting of truth from countless rumors, the most likely conclusion would be that, staking all that is left them for one last throw, they will gather the wrecks of their several armies, and trust them all to their best and favorite leader, Lee, for a last great trial of strength against the Army of the Potomac. There are reasons why this is really their wisest course, and, if successful, it would certainly give to their worn-out Confederacy a new lease of life. It is possible that for such an effort they could put two hundred thousand men in the field, most of them tried and veteran troops. Nor can it be many weeks before the veil will rise, and we shall see if they have indeed acquired that sort of wisdom which is born of desperation in the minds of brave and able men.

THE COMING REPRESENTATIVES

In the meantime, the ground which they have lost has only too evidently passed from them forever. There will be Union Representatives from half the territory claimed by the Confederacy in the coming United States Congress. East and West Virginia, Maryland, Kentucky, Missouri, Tennessee, Louisiana, and North Carolina, will all be there. In diminished numbers, some of them, but all represented.

The grand tragedy draws towards its "Fifth Act." The closing scenes cannot fail to be desperate and bloody ones, and if, in the course of events, the evil star of the rebellion sank forever on the field where it rose—the bloody plain of Manassas—as is not unlikely, would not even "poetic" justice be in part satisfied?

MR. SUMNER'S GREAT SPEECH

In the loyal States, the great event since the President's inimitable letter, is the oration of Mr. Sumner.[36] His utterances, as a great legal scholar, as the Chairman of the Senate Committee on Foreign Affairs, and as Charles Sumner, are entitled to all attention. Certainly, there is little to be asked for, at the conclusion of his masterly argument, adorned as it is by a peculiar and vigorous eloquence, and only disfigured by a few expressions which show that the deep scars in his memory had made him forget that invective is not necessarily coarse, that it may be bitter.

To the careful reader, this remarkable production is as much a prophecy of the future, as it is a record and a criticism of the past. We see clearly the position now occupied by our Government, and also a dim shadow of the different one which they must one day take. We see that under the most ungenerous treatment, under insults almost intolerable, they have *refused to take offence*, preferring tó bear all, rather than peril in any manner the speedy accomplishment of the great work before them. We know that they will continue thus until the end, but that the end is nearer now than when we set forth. And here comes in an unexpected something, that hints of what must be in the future. It is hardly worth while now to talk of it, but we cannot doubt that when the responsibilities of the present are removed, the responsibilities of the future will be assumed with an alacrity at least cheerful, both by Government and people.

Washington, 21 September 1863 (published 24 September 1863)
I almost grieve to say it, in face of so many gentlemen of the press, who appear to know just what has become of Lee and his army; but the truth is, that all the skillful maneuvering and gallant skirmishing of the past week has developed very little reliable information as to the force and intentions of the enemy in our front. Something more decisive may be at any hour accomplished, and the promise of a great battle stares our army daily in the face. No one seems to question that a large part of Lee's army has been drawn to some other field of operations; but the questions remain unsettled as to how many have gone, and how many have been left on the Rapidan.

THE RESULT AWAITED

One of these important points is no doubt to be answered by to-morrow or next day's dispatches from Rosecrans.[37] That brave and able general, as a natural consequence of the extent and bearing of his recent achievements, finds that the rebel leaders are concentrating a large force in his front, for the evident purpose of checking his further advance, or, if possible, of compelling him to some retrograde movement. For several days he has been briskly engaging his adversaries, and by the time this number of THE EXAMINER goes to press, the whole country will in all likelihood be fully advised of the result. If we could only look down on the hills and valleys around Chattanooga, to-day, what a load of suspense and anxiety might be taken from our minds. This is *one* of the last great efforts of the rebellion. Where the other, or others, will be, is a thing yet of the future.

THE RESIGNATION MALADY

At Charleston the slow processes of the siege go steadily forward, and in spite of rumors to the contrary, both Gillmore and Dahlgren seem to be doing their whole duty, nor have either of them yet "resigned."[38] There are some of our generals who seem to be in a chronic state of "resignation," but these two will hardly add their names to the unsavory list, with Charleston before them yet untaken.

THE STORM TO COME

It is evident that, whether we will or no, we are once for all admitted as a full member of the "European family of nations," with all the dangers and responsibilities of that eminence. The powers of the old world can no longer make their wars, their treaties, or their "entangling alliances," without gravely considering the course likely to be taken by the United States in the premises. If anything more were required to prove this, we could understand it by a brief perusal of the latest leaders of prominent English papers. Rarely has so great a change of tone been adopted in so short a time. Even our old enemy, the "*Times*," seems to be awaking to a sense of the real position held by this country and by Great Britain. Without writing a dissertation of foreign politics, it may be said that the Emperor of the French finds his position daily becoming more and more perplexing, and it is to be feared that like his august Uncle, he will ere long decide to cut the diplomatic knot with his ever ready sword. Where he will strike in that case is, unfortunately, only too far within the range of calculation.

The instincts of our people, which from the first have taught them to fear Europe far more than they fear the rebels, have been, as usual, true to the mark. In spite of all optimistical prophecies and denials of the danger, the bold truth stares us in the face, that any of the steamers which almost daily approach Cape Race may send ashore in the pilot-boat such news as shall stir the land like the Bull Run defeat.

Some day or other, sooner or later, that day and that steamer will surely come, and it is to the lasting praise of the able statesman at the head of the State Department that it has not come ere this. That he will still labor to postpone the day of our reckoning with Europe we may well believe. That he will succeed, for some time to come, is also probable; but that he can be permanently triumphant is almost beyond the range of probabilities. In the meantime, we are rapidly consolidating our power, reuniting with us, by indissoluble ties, those portions of our land which have been temporarily severed, and getting all things in readiness for such future as Providence may have in store for us.

PARTY PLANNING

Here in Washington, though the old feeling of suspense prevails, and we cannot believe that the era of our disasters has wholly passed from us, it is evident that men generally are beginning to think of something besides the war, and even to prepare plans and mould material for the things that are to come *after* the war. New parties, forming slowly throughout the country, are already represented here by committees and juntas, sitting in solemn conclave in hotel parlors, or gathered in the private apartments of great men. May they work well and wisely, for after the soldiers have had their day, the civilians have a vast and most important work before them.

THE WINTER'S WORK
The political business of the winter that is coming bids fair to be altogether without precedent, and already has commenced. Almost every day some active or prominent personage comes in on the cars to take a look at his field of operations, or even to settle, for a few weeks' hard labor, before the arrival of his colleagues or opponents. Very few of our migratory families have yet returned, and we hardly expect them before October. After the late heavy rains, the weather is cloudy and cold, almost rendering a small fire necessary, and we realize that summer is indeed gone, and that the autumn is upon us. We have, however, without doubt, many weeks of that clear and pleasant weather, which is the charm of this latitude, still before us, previous to the setting in of our winter rains, and the mingling of our winter's allowance of red mud. May the autumn be a long one, and the winter slow and late in his coming.

WASHINGTON, 28 SEPTEMBER 1863 (PUBLISHED 1 OCTOBER 1863)
When I went down town next morning after my last letter to you, I found the faces of all men clouded with an expression of sorrow and alarm. "Rosecrans is defeated at Chattanooga." The battle which we here knew must there come off, had gone against us. How completely, and with what fearful accessions of loss and disgrace, no one could yet tell—not even the War Department.[39]

Since then all has been cleared up. We now know how really near we were to a complete and terrible overthrow. We know that for long hours the fate of East Tennessee, so recently emancipated from rebel thraldom, and just beginning once more to taste the blessings of freedom from violence and oppression, hung trembling in the balances of doubtful battle. With great rapidity, secresy, and good judgment, the enemy had massed an immense army in front of the hero of Iuka and Murfreesboro', and hurled it upon him with their usual headlong courage and impetuosity.

It will yet be long before the complete accounts will inform the country with what desperate tenacity our gallant fellows held their own against great

odds, and with what admirable good generalship they were managed.—
Relying upon their superior numbers and the vehemence of their attack,
the enemy had looked for nothing less than a complete and speedy victory.
The whole Confederacy was looking on, and expected nothing less. In this
confident hope and expectation, army and people were disappointed. All
their grand preparations, draining their resources of every man and every
gun, succeeded only in checking temporarily the victorious advance of the
Union armies. It is true that Rosecrans was compelled to retreat to Chattanooga, to entrench himself, and to await the arrival of his reinforcements
before again assuming the offensive; but in their three days' hard fighting,
the rebel host was too badly battered to think of again assailing their terrible
adversary.

That Union army turned at bay upon the heights of Chattanooga, is
not a thing to be lightly considered by the most powerful opponent; and
to this has been added their forced uncertainty as to the number and
proximity of the additional forces which were well known to be within
call of our General. Now, every hour increases their perplexity, and adds to
the certainty of their overthrow, if they again try the chances of an attack;
while who can doubt that a few days will leave to the rebel leaders only the
choice between rapid, inglorious retreat, and almost certain destruction.

The dying Confederacy seems hard to galvanize into anything like
confidence in its own vitality. From a file of late rebel papers lying before
me, I can gather few cheering words for their readers, even among their
comments upon the supposed victory of Chickamauga. In the language of
their own slaves, they look upon their cherished creation as "done gone,
dead," or so near it that a few more blows must terminate its brief and
feverish existence. This prevailing tone, showing itself even in rejoicings
over a seeming victory, is the more remarkable from its strong contrast
with the tone of the same journals only a few months since.

From Charleston we have very little that is interesting. A siege conducted
as this of Charleston necessarily has been, must needs be of slow and
tedious progress. The sand islands are worse than Sumter! The peculiar
conformation of the coast places the attacking party greatly at disadvantage.
Nor would it be of any great use, in a military point of view, merely to tumble
down what is left of the traitor city itself. Beauregard's army, behind their
battlements, or their sand-hills, are the objects of the strenuous efforts of
Gillmore and Dahlgren. When these are beaten thoroughly, Charleston will
in truth be taken, and not before, though we should first wipe out every
trace of the town.

It was one of our grave errors, in the early part of the war, to put too much stress upon the capture of cities, and the gravest error of one of our generals [McClellan] was in refusing to see that the *real* garrison of Richmond lay before him in camp at Manassas.

There is little that is of interest in our local affairs, but if you, Mr. Editor, ever doubted my statement in a former letter, as to the moral condition of our city, I would refer you to the just published report of our Superintendent of Police, from which it appears that with less than a third of the resident population of Brooklyn, we have about *double* the number of arrests per annum. Figures are things that condense statements wonderfully, and I leave the above to tell its own story of vice, corruption and crime.

The various churches are beginning to recover their scattered congregations, and the educational institutions, so long closed by the presence of war at our doors, are beginning to re-open, and call once more for their inmates.

The gentle slope of the hillside on the south bank of the Potomac, shorn of its crowning woods, and for a long time bare and brown, trodden under foot by marching armies, and cut up by heavy wheels, has lately begun to look green and pleasant again, with a singular woody growth that is neither grass, brush nor thistles, but which, after all, does put us faintly in mind of the ancient beauty of this country, which has been so desolated by the crimes of its former possessors. A new race will be kinder to the "mother of the Presidents [i.e., Virginia]."

WASHINGTON, 5 OCTOBER 1863 (PUBLISHED 8 OCTOBER 1863)
After the usual amount of swashing equinoctial rain storms, the climates of Washington (and their name is Legion) have settled down into glorious autumnal weather, good for man and beast. There will be from eight to ten weeks yet for military operations in the field, and it is evident to every observing eye that the time will be "well put in."

A WEEK OF EXPECTATION
There has been some glorious marching done during the past ten days, and our armies generally finish off a grand march with a grander fight. From various knowing ones, connected with various branches of the public service, I hear so many hints of the probability of our hearing good news this week, that it seems as if there must really be something in it. If there is indeed a great battle coming off, for instance, in the Southwest, God grant that we may have something tangible to show for the inevitable expenditure of blood. East Tennessee was the hard-won fruit of Chickamauga, to us;

but to the rebels, in the mournful language of the Richmond papers, "only a ghastly array of dead bodies."

"DIDN'T WE TELL YOU SO?"
It is to be regretted that so many loyal papers are assailing the army before Charleston for their supposed inaction. By-and-by, we hope their tune will change, but even then they may attribute to one day's desperate exertion the real result of long weeks of patient labor. I have known such things, and then seen the complacent and self-approving editor turn proudly to his back files, and say to his readers "Don't you see? If he had only taken *our* advice, this would all have been done before. We presume he takes and profits by the daily ———."

GOING HOME WITH A FLEA IN THE EAR
The event of the week here has been the arrival and reception of the Delegation of Missouri Radicals.[40] Alas for them! Not content with getting one big reception, each petty clique must afterwards sneak singly or in squads to the Executive Mansion, each to tell some slightly *corrected* edition of the general tale. The general impression here is that the Delegation failed in their object, though treated with the utmost courtesy and kindness, and travelled home again with a somewhat large-sized flea in their collective ear.

General Schofield has at least followed one portion of the President's letter of instructions—he has got himself soundly abused by pretty nearly all parties, because he will side with no one.[41]

THE EFFECT OF WIFELY CARE
The return of Mrs. Lincoln, to resume her wifely care of the President's valuable health, seems to have already given a more cheerful look to his Excellency's care-worn face. The family are still at the Soldier's Home, and for some weeks will remain there. The other absentees will speedily follow the lady of the White House, and in a few weeks the forlorn looking *attaches* and officers, who now parade the Avenue of a sunny afternoon, will be ready to vote that Washington is once more inhabited.

GEN. MEADE AND HIS ARMY
From the Army of the Potomac we have very few rumors. No one seems to have any idea as to Gen. Meade's intentions, or even whether he has any, and anything like a battle on the Rapidan or the Rappahannock, would be an utter astonishment. Still, it won't do to count on continued quiescence in this region—something might happen almost any day.

A NEW AND GREAT AFFAIR

Among the new features in this vicinity is the new Cavalry camp, on the point of land east of the city, and below the Insane Asylum. A bend of the river on one side, and a gentle acclivity on the other, with enough of level ground for parade and exercise, make the site an admirable one. Any man who has kept a horse or a livery stable, may figure upon a few items that follow: There will be "quarters" for six thousand men, and twelve thousand horses. The horse hospital will accommodate four thousand debilitated equines. Six thousand, or perhaps ten thousand cavalry can be handled on the parade ground. There will be proper arrangements for storage of food, &c., and on the whole it will be a grand affair. It is under the personal supervision of Maj. Gen. Stoneman, Chief of the Bureau of Cavalry, now permanently stationed here.[42] It will be a camp of instruction and preparation, and cannot fail to be of vast value to this important arm of the service. I may at some future time, when the whole is complete, attempt a more accurate description of a thing hitherto unknown on this continent, but deemed essential to every army in Europe.

THINGS IN GENERAL

Of other matters of interest the Capital has for the past week been singularly destitute.—The crowds of visitors, business men or others, have come and gone, and left singularly little mark upon the current of events. All things have gone on smoothly. The gay crowds have assembled as usual to hear the Marine Band in Lafayette Square or the Capitol Grounds; the usual number of odd rumors have been started and run to earth; but after all, we have had a quiet week of it—far more so, I fear, than will be the one before us.

WASHINGTON, 12 OCTOBER 1863 (PUBLISHED 15 OCTOBER 1863)

In the language of the stage critics, "the plot thickens." The rebels have failed utterly in their several movements on the right flank of Rosecrans. They have lost over a thousand "picked men," and have accomplished literally *nothing*. Meanwhile our army at Chattanooga, strengthened by reinforcements, powerful enough to make an army by themselves, is only waiting the proper moment to dissipate into thin air the deceptive vision of a Confederate victory.

THEIR "WATERLOO"

I see by late Richmond papers that they count on nothing less than a speedy reoccupation of Tennessee and Kentucky. In this, I am happy to say that the future, as viewed from this side of the lines, gives them no hope.

The stake is an immense one. The party winning it wins *permanently*. Our people cannot too clearly understand that if the rebels fail here, and fail they will, they fail *utterly*. If they cannot drive Rosecrans from Chattanooga, their tremendous experiment, their new nationality, become things of the past. They must take Chattanooga, they must drive back Rosecrans and Burnside, or they are finally, completely, and forever *defeated*.

I do not think that this is fully recognized by the "good folk" at the North, and in explanation I need only appeal to any man's plain common sense and his map. There is no doubt that the last remaining strength of the Rebellion will be poured out like water to accomplish this object, and it is with a feeling of sobered but intense satisfaction that I express my decided conviction that all will be in vain; that Rosecrans cannot be driven; that Burnside will retain East Tennessee and the passes of the Alleghanies, and that in a few weeks Bragg must retreat upon Atlanta, or fight a superior force with almost a certainty before him of a defeat which must be a Waterloo to the Confederacy.

ANOTHER "GETTYSBURG"

Meantime there is some little activity in other quarters. The severe cavalry skirmishes on the banks of the Rapid Ann, continuing as they have for several days, might be interpreted in various ways, but if they mean that Lee is preparing for another advance, we may rest in the belief that another and a greater Gettysburg is in the immediate future.

Our army in Virginia is in admirable condition—never better—and all reports as to its depletion and weakness are unmitigated nonsense.

AN AUTHORITATIVE DENIAL

Speaking of our armies in the field, I wish to say one word about Charleston, and to deny, *authoritatively*, that there is or has been any difficulty between Gen. Gillmore and Admiral Dahlgren, or that any jealousy exists between the army and navy at that point, which can interfere with their harmonious cooperation for the accomplishment of the great end in view. The conduct of certain newspapers and their reporters, in this connection, has been criminally selfish and mean. I have seen, over their own hands, the strong expressions of the indignation felt by the two brave and patriotic commanders in question, at the use made of their names, and the injury so done to the cause. You will do them a favor by placing their view of the case in a strong light before your readers.

THE FAMILY OF REPUBLICS

We seem, in the midst of our own fearful embarrassments, to be drawing more and more closely the ties which bind us to the other Republics of this continent. Even in our distress they seem to look up to us as their appointed guardian and protector. Even the Central American States, so stormy and petulant in their previous career, come forward and concede almost everything to complete our alliance; and unhappy Mexico seems to be able to discern no ray of hope in the future, except when here and there she can see the "Star-Spangled Banner" between the clouds.

As to the proposed new alliance between *all* the Republican States of the New World, it presents yet too intangible and uncertain a shape to admit of serious consideration. Still, it is one of the "signs of the times" which we cannot look upon with indifference. This fellow-feeling among the Republics of the New World is a feature which European despotisms and oligarchies will do well to take into consideration, in making their calculations for future action.

ODDS AND ENDS

The weather here continues beautiful—cool, sunny, and bracing, and for once the denizens of the Capital go about without growling. The reign of dust is over; this is the interregnum, and before long King Mud will be here. Secretary Cass [Stanton] has gone West for a brief visit. When he returns our summer absenteeism will be over, and the winter's work will begin.

WASHINGTON, 19 OCTOBER 1863 (PUBLISHED 22 OCTOBER 1863)

Every few months, since the rebellion broke out, with a periodical regularity that is almost mysterious, the progress of the war has brought the excitement and the peril to the very doors of the Capital. In the course of events that crisis has come again. The army under Meade, after a forced retreat from the Rapidan to the Rappahannock, has fallen back from the Rappahannock line to the entrenchments on the Centerville heights; and in discussing the chances of the day we are compelled once more to use such old familiar names as Bull Run, Chantilly, Drainsville, Leesburg, and Fairfax Court House.[43]

Of course, Meade has not made this movement without adequate military reasons therefor, but, to the uninitiated, many points of his strategy are hard to comprehend. It is a singular thing, at this stage of the war, to be again in doubt as to whether Lee will risk another invasion of Maryland. Such, however, is now the case, nor dare I prophesy as to whether he will or will not. Rumors vary as to his exact force, from sixty to ninety thousand effective men, and the truth doubtless lies in some numerical word somewhere between these two extremes. That he considers himself stronger than Meade is proven by the boldness of his manoeuvres. That he may be mistaken in his estimate of the Union forces is not at all unlikely, and may be the key to another great overthrow of rebel hopes and anticipations.

We here are prepared at any moment to listen to the reverberations of the cannon of a third Bull Run battle. We heard the guns of the gallant fight of the Second Army Corps very distinctly. It is difficult to see how it is made out by the newspapers as a "victory," unless it is that we foiled the enemy in a desperate attempt to cut off our rear-guard. However, if the country will accept it as such, the Government has no reason to complain.

THE WALL STREET SHYLOCKS

Everything looks well, and promises *well*, but the whole week has shown no changes whatever that we can mark distinctly as for the better or the worse. The denizens of Wall street, however, have availed themselves of the uncertainties of the moment to depreciate the national currency twenty-five per cent., so that, while we are nearer the end of the war, while all things look better in every department, while our foreign affairs are vastly more satisfactory, "greenbacks" are twenty-five per cent. lower than they were a few weeks ago. I hope to see these fellows who have done this, fearfully bitten within the next twenty days, and our currency restored to its actual value.

Yours is not a financial journal, but no man can see with indifference the reckless rascality with which selfish men accomplish changes in the gold market, which immediately affect the price of almost every article of necessary use in the general market. Tales, rumors—reports of army operations studiously presented in their darkest and most unpromising forms—reports of foreign troubles, which have no foundation except in the fertile brain of the editor who is "long" on gold—these are the means, by the skillful use of which the hard-working farmer or mechanic is made to pay his diminished earnings in double ratio for all the comforts of life.

THE ELECTIONS

The late Elections have demonstrated that the masses of the people have full confidence in the honesty and wisdom of the Executive. No man of sense had any idea that Ohio would elect a known and boasted traitor as her chief magistrate, and *that* was hardly the question at issue.[44] The point really was, whether the people as a whole approved of the various great measures of the present Administration, and willed that it should be fully sustained by their State authorities. The verdict given is eminently satisfactory, and must have sent a thrill of pleasure to the heart of our good President. The people are evidently with him. It is not true, any longer, that all his friends "are in the army." In spite of reverses, in spite of unfulfilled hopes and anticipations, in spite of all political machinations, the people are with the President. And now he calls upon them for more substantial aid. How like a dream must this appear to European sovereigns:—in the third year of a great war, after unexampled sacrifices of men and money, the President can yet call upon the people with confidence for a fourth offering of three hundred thousand lives upon the altar of National unity. All this for an idea! And the new sacrifice will be freely and promptly made, and instead of the coming spring finding us, as our enemies fondly hoped, without an army, we shall have not only our new recruits and our conscripts of *to-day*, but a quarter of a million of fresh and well-drilled soldiers, ready for any great ends that may then remain to be accomplished.

I will close this letter with an expression of satisfaction at the good promise of the work before us, that all things will work together for the welfare of the Republic.

WASHINGTON, CA. 26 OCTOBER 1863 (PUBLISHED 29 OCTOBER 1863)
We have had a somewhat stormy week, atmospherically, but it has cleared up gloriously this morning, and the new one begins with the good omen of a bright October sun. The yellow leaves on the trees in the President's grounds look golden in the radiance, and even the sombre evergreens in Lafayette Square appear more cheerful than usual. The present is bright, but we cannot pass over the last few days without finding something worthy of remark.

GEN. GRANT AND CHATTANOOGA
The sweeping changes in the Western army seem to be acquiesced in by the people with great unanimity, and very few are found grumbling at seeing the hero of Vicksburg preparing for another and a grander campaign.[45] I say "grander," but I mean not only that, but "more important," bearing even more directly upon the fate of the rebellion and the termination of the war.

The enemy are concentrating their forces to meet us at or near Chattanooga. There is no doubt but they will do their uttermost to secure a success; and on our side, we, too, are not insensible to the peril or the hope. There will be much manoeuvering, perhaps, and the two commanders will have fine opportunities for "strategy," but at the last there must be another desperate struggle of great armies; one of those truly American fights which so puzzle the military men of the Old World, where the object of the combatants is actually to destroy each other, and upon which an epauletted Austrian decided that "it could not be dignified with the name of *war*; why sir, war is a *science*." Yes, sooner or later the great fight must come, and more than one of them.

MEADE AND LEE

We were very near to one here the other day, and there are those who say that the failure to bring it on has cost Gen. Meade all the glory that he won at Gettysburg.[46] He has not been removed, as yet, it is true, and there is no new tombstone in the "Graveyard of the Generals;" but the Army of the Potomac must not again retreat before little more than half its own numbers, without accomplishing some good end thereby.

Now that we think of it critically, we can but admire the daring generalship of Gen. Lee, even while we see clearly that he ran a tremendous risk by his bold movement. So far as we can now see, he has won nothing thereby, however, except to destroy a few miles of railroad, and lose the fight at Bristow Station.[47]

The Secretary of War is again at his post, and as busy as ever. The current opinion, until we saw him on his return, was that he went West to enjoy the professional skill of a celebrated *barber* at St. Louis, but it was an error.[48] Mr. Watson, his assistant, is also here again, in better health, and the two together ought to accomplish *something*.

ALL RIGHT AGAIN

Gratifying reports come back from Missouri and Kansas, and from Boston—which is little else than *Kansas sur mer*, in matters of opinion—approving the reply of the President in the case of Gen. Schofield, and showing that the people are generally satisfied with the wisdom of his action.[49] They will be still better satisfied before all is over.

THE WAR OF THE SUCCESSION

It is worthy of note, that in every portion of the country the "war of the succession" has fully begun, and the many men who have *the* great ambition are busily at work. A very prominent Western orator, in a speech a few days since, in his fear to commit himself, did a rather funny thing: he went over a long list of our most prominent names, saying something very neat and flattering of each one as he went along, and then went off into a sort of prayer for a new man to come up in the next few months, greater and better than any of them. Safe invocation! men do not grow that fast now-a-days, nor is there any deft and cunning machine, no mill of miraculous power, wherein such things are manufactured. Safe man! type of an over-numerous class—whoever shall be nominated, *his* record is clear—he supported him from the first.

FOREIGN ENTANGLEMENTS

Foreign affairs look oddly enough; there is no end to the tanglement of European politics. They look now as if they were fast getting into a knot which only the sword can open. I am neither a prophet nor the son of a prophet, but I predict that there will be many cannon cast in Europe this winter, in a vague fear that the spring will call them into active use. It is really a comfort to the lovers of peace, to reflect that in a few short weeks the Baltic will be sealed by iron frost, and the stormy Black Sea will soon be protection of itself for the kingdoms upon its shores, while certain memories of former wars will be ample security against a winter campaign of any magnitude in Central Europe. Nevertheless, when there are so many elements of strife at work as are now going in and out among the jealous sovereignties of the Old World, we cannot reasonably hope for a bloodless solution of all these difficult questions. Meanwhile, if fear of each other will induce them to let *us* alone, we may well be pleased spectators of this act in the great tragedy which men call the History of Europe.

THE GREAT RAILROAD

Among the interesting events of the coming week is the meeting in New York for the final organization of the Pacific Railroad. The subscription list contains the signatures of almost all the leading financial men of New-York and other commercial centres, and is a wonderful array of moneyed power. This mighty undertaking, really, in all its bearings, the grandest of its kind that the world ever saw, is at last taking tangible form, and promises to become a fact.

That it will require years of toil and vast expenditure, is nothing; that it will then be years more before it will even sustain itself and pay its own expenses, is nothing; that it will sink every dollar of its original capital, is nothing;—the people fully understand all this, and they will build the *Road*, as they carry on this *War*, because the safety of the nation demands it. Much will depend upon the wisdom of the stockholders in selecting competent managers; but from such men as are now interested, we have a right to expect prudence and good judgment.

WASHINGTON, 2 NOVEMBER 1863 (PUBLISHED 5 NOVEMBER 1863)

Doubt and waiting once more for another weary seven days. Skirmishing everywhere; everywhere mighty armies in motion. Lee's movements still an unrevealed mystery; Burnside's march a shadowy outline, fruitful of stirring rumors, and promising great things in aid of the greater blows threatening at the north and south of him, and yet impressing us all the while with a vague sense of a great risk run by his gallant and not over-numerous army.

THE ONE "GLORY-GILDED STAR"

Grant has assumed command, and will undoubtedly afford us all satisfaction, if we do not straightway press upon him an exorbitant demand for some military miracle. If he shall entirely succeed, as we hope and pray, there is no doubt that his will be the great military reputation durably erected by the war; and we may be thankful that it has so arisen and will so shine as not in any way to dazzle the most grateful and enthusiastic of the people whom he is serving. Indeed, one of the great dangers with which this revolution has threatened us, from first to last, has been that, among all these turnings and overturnings, some one man, some single man, the glory-gilded star of many battle-fields, might become too great, too strong for the future peace and welfare of the nation. We may now rest safe and sure that such will not and cannot be the case. We have developed no possible Napoleon, no imaginable Caesar, and there now remains no time or place for one to grow in; and among the great civilians of the day, the greatest and the strongest, our good Chief Magistrate, is great and strong chiefly because the people have perfect faith in him that he has no ambition, no selfish lust of power, nor any hope for the future unconnected with the welfare of his country. Destroy this faith, and the power of the President would disappear, or would at best sink to the level of his Cabinet officers, and the patriotic leaders, and Governors of States, who stand by him and sustain him.

ANOTHER YEAR'S WORK

Gradually and sadly the people are arriving at the conclusion, which they should never have failed to accept, that this fall campaign is not to close the war for the Union. In my humble opinion, it cannot be too distinctly asserted, nor too clearly understood by all, that the rebels are to have a long winter in which to recuperate their failing energies. Let us win what victories we may between this and the 1st of January, the winter months will come in too soon for us to reap the fruits of them, and the returning spring will find us still in the field, with armed masses of rebels in our front.

However, if we are to have no great and disheartening reverses—and the battle of Chickamauga was nothing of the kind—we may rest assured that another year of progress like the last, and the war will be virtually over. Two

[t]hings of vast moment have been done already. First, the Border States are secured beyond any doubt or peradventure, and we are fast making them ours politically, as well as in a military point of view; and this done, is a blow from which the rebellion can never by any possibility recover. Without them the Confederacy, even if established on the Gulf and the Atlantic coast, is a mere shell; weak, easily wounded, powerless for the future, without room to grow in, or power to protect its interminable frontier. Second, with the control of the Mississippi they have irretrievably lost the West and Southwest, and the control of the Gulf of Mexico. The campaign in Texas, owing to the peculiarities of the climate, can well be extended into January, if need be, and in that time Gen. Banks can wipe out the last vestige of Confederate authority between Sabine Pass and the Rio Grande.

THE NEXT REBEL CONCLAVE

It is, however, a pleasanter thing to look at what we have, than what we hope for. We wonder what the rebel Congress will do and say at its coming session. When these bold conspirators come once more to look each other in the face, and recall the grandiloquent promise and prophecies of one short year ago, with what heart and hope will they gaze into the future. We hope between this time and that to give them some other topics for wholesome cogitation. It may be that still further variations will be made in the magnificent map published by the Richmond *Examiner* in 1861, and that still greater numbers of their so-called representatives will be minus their constituencies. It may be that before that time we shall hear from Charleston and Mobile, and Galveston and Atlanta. In truth, they have little enough to encourage them in prosecuting their mad and criminal design. In vain will they strain their eager eyes across the wintry Atlantic. There are not too many places left where they may dare to venture within sound of his breakers, and in many of these even the thunder of the waves is mingled with the roar of National cannon and the bursting of National shells.

THE WEEK AND ITS HOPES

The week before us, one of the few now left before our troops must ensconce themselves in their snug winter quarters, has in its bosom many promises and many fears. Upon its events, or its lack of events, will depend the tone and feeling of both sides for the entire winter. It may control the action of Congress, the tone of public discussion and feeling, and it may have an important bearing upon the changes in the attitude of European powers, when they shall come to lay out their programmes for Eighteen Hundred and Sixty-four.

We at the National Capital are waiting with feverish interest for the returns from your New-York elections. It is impossible to regard otherwise than with the deepest anxiety the position assumed by the people of the most populous and powerful State in the Union. It is not enough that all the rest are right, if New-York is wrong. The triumphs of the Government supporters in the centre and West will have a hollow sound, if the commercial and financial heart of the nation does not beat full and true. Even a small majority against copperheadism will hardly answer. There must be a complete victory, or even good news from Chattanooga will hardly convince us that the time for rejoicing has fully come. We wait and hope for the best—the *very* best.

WASHINGTON, 9 NOVEMBER 1863 (PUBLISHED 12 NOVEMBER 1863)
After a few days' absence, I am once more a looker-on at the central point of news and rumors. In the first place the weather is magnificent—bright, sunny, cool but not cold, a trifle windy, but just the weather for marching and fighting. The roads are excellent, the armies in fine spirits and good condition, and everything would seem to be in favor of active operations in the field.

BALANCING THE PROBABILITIES
The general belief seems to be that we have a bloody week before us in more than one Department of the Army. Among other strong indications, we here have learned to notice, with all the great and knowing ones who guide these movements, a certain careful reticence, a sort of disinclination to communicate, whenever there was an immediate prospect of stirring news. Witness the newspapers of the past few days;—not even the reporters can find out anything of importance. The general public, however, will welcome all signs of activity as a joyful relief from their present suspense.

For my own part, I question if any great results, thus late in the season, can be attained north of Chattanooga. We could hardly follow up a victory in Virginia for any length of time, and a winter campaign would be a matter difficult of accomplishment. If, however, Bragg should be beaten, Grant would still be able to push on further towards the Gulf, or the Atlantic, as he pleased. Much might thus be prepared for spring work, and in that latitude spring comes very early. In Texas also, in spite of the rains and the "northers," a great deal can be done. By the way, if I am any judge of such matters, Banks has deceived both his friends and his foes, and will strike his blow on some point of which little if anything has been said, either in Northern newspapers or in Southern councils of war. The "little iron man of Waltham" is not going to throw away his gallant little army in the snaky swamps of the Louisiana coast.

The siege of Charleston drags slowly on, to all outward seeming, but the end is nearer than it was, and some say, when other events have drawn our attention briefly in other directions, the news will come that the hard task is over at last, and Charleston has fallen. There is another alternative, too gloomy for full mention, possible, but not probable, and we will not look for it or fear it.

THE NORTH SPEAKING

The result of the New-York election must be a cheering thing to the Administration, and as chilling on the other hand to the rebels.[50] The whole North has now spoken, State by State, and all with the same spirit. Those of which we had no doubt have fully equalled our expectations, and the rest have far exceeded them. So mote it be! The people are more and more fully grasping the great ideas of the day, and making them their own. Gradually but surely the faith and hope of this great strife for freedom and civilization are working *downwards* through the really lower orders of the people, reaching stratum after stratum of mental or moral obtuseness and obliquity, till by and by the whole national mass shall be alive with it. It may be that the electric patriotism may finally reach even your New-York mob, and send your very rioters into the field. It may be that it may find its way lower still, and reach the hearts of some of your semi-rebel political leaders. That, however, is a thing scarcely to be hoped.

LIVELY READING

It is good fun to read the comments of the English press over the very hospitable manner in which we are treating our Russian friends.[51] From the *Times* over to *Punch*, there comes one continued strain of acrid remark, mixed with elegant sneers about Tartars and Calmucks and Cossacks, &c., that are quite refreshing, considering their source. As if we were not always hospitable. If, as a nation, we *have* a weakness, it is for doing the kind thing by our visitors. Look back on the history of our many visitors, O John Bull, and see in what liberal style we have entertained them all. The fact is, that while European nations thought themselves a united family against us, we were of no manner of importance to any of them; but now that they find their mistake, it really becomes an affair of weight and consequence in what direction we are looking for our friends. We may make another tea party one of these days, and there is some curiosity as to who will be apt to receive an invitation.

As to our foreign affairs, generally, they seem to wear a very pleasant aspect. Napoleon is still too busy with his Mexican elephant to give much attention to his contemplated Texas purchase, and may by this time begin to apprehend that by the time Forey, or any other Frenchman, could reach the Rio Grande, that remarkable stream will have too much *banks* for him to occupy.

WASHINGTON, 16 NOVEMBER 1863 (PUBLISHED 19 NOVEMBER 1863)
After a swashing November rain-storm, which pelted down pitilessly on roof and tent all night long, the bright autumn sun has claimed his own again, and the dripping yellow leaves shine like gold in the unclouded light.

PICKET SPECULATIONS ON THE PROBABILITIES
The fellows on picket, who have stood guard in the rain, or bivouacked in the mud, can stretch their stiffened limbs in the welcome warmth, and prepare their coffee in comfort. I can see them now, "in my mind's eye," only a short distance over there, across that abominable muddy river, gathering in little chilly groups to enjoy the sun, and to discuss the probabilities of the military position. Having served an apprenticeship to this sort of weather in a Virginia camp, I can understand what they are saying and feeling, even at this distance. They do not believe, in the first place, that Meade will get another big fight out of Lee before spring, but that if he does, he will whip him thoroughly. Secondly, they do not believe the newspaper stories about starvation in Dixie, or at all events in the *camps* of Dixie, for the hundreds of prisoners they took at the fords of the Rappahannock the other day were about as well clad as usual—a little better, if anything—and so far as they can learn from communicative "rebs," the fare in Lee's camp is as good as it ever was. Moreover, when they moved forward the other day, they found that the huts prepared by Lee's men for their winter quarters, and abandoned on their approach, were of the most substantial and comfortable description, such as men can healthily and safely live in during a Virginia winter.

They believe that the rebellion will survive the winter, and will be in the field in the spring with an army of at least three hundred thousand ablebodied, effective men. They look forward to great battles yet to come, and long marches and sieges, and hardships, and they are entirely ready for all. They growl a little—these unreasonable soldiers—that the folks at home are at all divided about sustaining "Father Abraham" and the Government.

They use a few "army words"—the profane wretches—because the people do not do more towards filling up their thinned regiments, and supplying the places of their gallant comrades who have fallen. On the whole, however, they are a cheerful, hardy, patriotic set, anxious to serve their country, and contented with their rations, if they can only get them.

Of course these dirty and weather-beaten fellows do not understand the signs of the times so well as newspaper men at home, nor can they see the end of the war one half so clearly; but so long as they are determined that they *will* see the end of it, or die trying, for my part I am disposed to look at matters a good deal as they do.

A CHATTANOOGA BATTLE NOT FAR OFF

Things in the West look well, but move slowly. There will be a battle *there* before the season is over, or all signs are false. It seems to a looker-on from this distance, that Grant and Bragg, or whoever commands the rebel army, are manoeuvering for positions and advantages, and that some fine morning they cannot fail to swing their large and splendid armies full against one another. This strategy is a dangerous business, and I have known more than one hard fight to grow out of it. Besides, it is evident that Grant *wants* a great battle, and that the whole Southern Confederacy is behind their army pressing it on to the conflict. As usual, the Southern press expects a tremendous victory, and will be sure to claim one in any event, but there are two opinions as to the chances of the coming struggle.

THE STATE OF THINGS IN DIXIE

Taking all the accounts we can get from the South, affairs are in a frightful condition, and there will be much suffering there between this time and next harvest, but not an actual famine. History teaches us, if it teaches anything, which I sometimes seriously doubt, that a nation, any nation, will endure a vast amount of mere everyday hardships and privations. The South will do so, unquestionably, and the only thing for us is to go on breaking up their military organizations, and reclaiming steadily State after State, and at the same time see to it, so far as we can, that every month draws the cord of scarcity closer. The harvest, which was small in 1863, must be smaller in 1864. The ports which have been left open must be closed. The remaining depots of army stores must be destroyed. We did a great deal of this last summer, more than most men have taken note of.

So shall the end come. I don't want to be barbarous in my allusions, but there is a saying recorded of the old tormentors in "thumbscrew" and "boot" times, that, however hardy and obstinate the subject in hand might be, if they only "kept on turning, he'd either faint, die, or confess." That's just what this rebellion will do, with a few more turns of the screw.

THE WEDDING
The social event of the past week was the wedding of Senator Sprague and Miss Chase. Never did anything go off more neatly.[52] The "tableau," as they call it, at the marriage itself was charming; and the dress reception in the evening, and the informal one next day, were entirely pleasant. The presents were magnificent—silver, pearls, diamonds, &c., to the tune of a hundred thousand or so. The worthy young couple certainly have a very fair start in life, and hosts of friends to wish them joy and success.

WASHINGTON, 30 NOVEMBER 1863 (PUBLISHED 3 DECEMBER 1863)
I see that my last did not reach you in time. The fact is that the mails, railroad trains, &c., between here and the civilized portions of our beloved country, never any too accurate or regular, have just undergone an entire readjustment for the winter. We welcome eagerly every symptom of improvement, and every change which brings nearer to each other, in time or travel, the commercial and the political centres of the nation.

THE WEEK OF GREAT EVENTS
The past week has been a glorious one, and we indeed had a joyous Thanksgiving. Our great victory was won with less of bloodshed and misery than have been thrown away upon utterly useless combats by other Generals in the history of this war.[53] It seems indeed to be the peculiar genius of General Grant to accomplish more important results at a less expense, than any of his compeers. For there are great results to follow upon our late well-won triumph. The enemy have lost all that they gained at Chickamauga; all that Longstreet proposed to himself in his rapid and well-managed raid into East Tennessee; all of Tennessee, a large portion of Georgia, and all hope of regaining control of Alabama and Mississippi. Mobile is now a ripe apple—we can pluck it whenever we are ready, and think it worth the while. Savannah and Charleston may, from our new position, be threatened in the rear, for the mountain ranges are the military key to all the Atlantic States.

Unless the rebels can win back what they have just so utterly lost, they themselves can hardly fail to see that their attempt at a separate existence has failed, and that the war, so far as successful resistance is concerned, *is over*.

Strange as it may seem, our new positions once more bring out Richmond as a point of some military importance, apart from the political significance of its possession. As the head of navigation on the James River, and as a railroad centre, admirably located for communication with a wide region of country, it possesses a value, with reference to future operations, which make "On to Richmond," almost for the first time, a battle-cry with some sense in it.

The campaign promises to be continued all winter at various points, so far as I can see. There are no perceptible signs, on our part, of a disposition to go into winter quarters anywhere, and thus far there has been very little weather unsuitable for operations in the field. We had a premonitory storm on Friday, interfering somewhat with the Army of the Potomac on their march, but the roads were by no means ruined, and a few days of this November wind has dried them very well. The fact is that our soldiers would endure anything and attempt anything for the purpose of demolishing the rebellion. They would camp in the snow and mud all winter for this, and without a murmur.

BANKS IN TEXAS

You will perhaps remember my prediction that General Banks would effect a landing at some unexpected point in Texas, and that the rebel forces would be utterly nonplussed by his debarkation. Well, there he is on the banks of the Rio Grande—or north of there by this time—with the whole State at his mercy. And "mercy" it will be, indeed, after three years of misrule and plunder such as that fertile and beautiful region has been compelled to submit to.

We may now make up our minds deliberately that, whatever disasters and drawbacks we may have on this side of the Mississippi, beyond that river the rule of the rebellion is forever broken. It is hard to imagine a condition of things in which we should be compelled to give up the territory which we have made so thoroughly our own.

THE CLERICAL "BOURBONS"

Thanksgiving Day passed off very well, and was almost universally observed, the churches being very well filled. Among our ministers here, however, are some of those Bourbons "who have learned nothing and forgotten nothing" in these three years of National growth and glory, and who carefully abstained, in their sermons or prayers, from any thankful or patriotic allusion to the victories we have been blessed with, and who breathed no hope for others yet to come. Most of these contented themselves with briefly expressed wishes for "peace," but some almost ignored the great fact of the day—*the war*. This thing used to be apologized for on the plea of "not offending any who might be present of different political views." This would be almost funny now, if it were not almost criminal. I would not give a straw to listen to any American clergyman who could not and would not thank God, on such an occasion, for the wonderful things he has done for us—even for the very fire in which he is trying this his chosen people. I wonder if you have any clerical "Bourbons" as far North as New-York?

CONGRESSIONAL PREPARATIONS

This week will witness the arrival of most of the members of the two Houses of Congress. Some of them are here already, and are busy with the organization. Some men predict an exciting time over it, but the majority seem to think that Colfax, or some other good man, will be quietly chosen Speaker; a new Clerk will be made in place of Emerson Etheridge, and the business of the session will be industriously entered upon.[54] Perhaps the most important business will be the election of the next President, which they will attempt to do, forgetting that there is a something in the hearts of the people which has already done that thing for them, and which will make the mere matter of the *election* a formula fit to be observed, and only that.

The President's Message, and the various budgets of the Cabinet, all promise to be of unusual interest, and their respective authors are busy upon them. The President has been ill for several days, and one of our Washington *on dits* is that a great part of the Message has been written by him *in bed*.

WASHINGTON, 7 DECEMBER 1863 (PUBLISHED 10 DECEMBER 1863)

It is a glorious day this, with a sunlight as brilliant as June; the air clear, bracing, full of electricity and life, yet cold enough to make the blazing logs in the fireplace yonder decidedly agreeable. It is warm in the sunlight, to be sure, but in these old Washington houses it is almost impossible to "avoid the draft," except by emigration. In fact, to paraphrase a somewhat familiar saying, "we fight; we pray, *and thus* we emigrate."

The Army of the Potomac could move in such matter very handsomely, and there must be some very good reason why it does not. It is beyond my humble comprehension entirely. I would like to see here a few days of Grant, of Rosecrans, of Thomas, to see what they would do anyhow, and would rather have even rash, gallant, "fighting Joe Hooker," than this eternal do nothing.[55]

Are you aware that work is still going forward on the permanent fortifications of Washington, as if they were one day to be used? There are forts, left incomplete before [the] Gettysburg fight, now steadily extending their sodded ramparts, their curtains, rifle-pits, and other surroundings in a manner that would convey the idea to the mind of an unprejudiced observer, that it was not impossible they might one day be called into service. It is a comfort to think that when they are *done*, and before a great while, a comparatively small garrison will be able to hold the Capital, and the Army of the Potomac may move with very little reference to the great bone of contention over which it has for so long a time stood guard.

One of the events of the week was the establishment of the "Goddess of Freedom," on the apex of the dome of the Capitol. It was very neatly done in the presence of a respectable crowd of spectators, and the image was saluted on its dizzy height by cheers and salvos of cannon. I notice a contradiction between the effect of elevation upon men and statuary. The higher you lift the bronze or the marble, the smaller it appears, while human beings, especially politicians and generals, expand before our eyes as we ourselves from year to year hoist them higher. That the expansion is real and not apparent, is evidenced by the fact that so many of them burst like bubbles when we lift them beyond a certain point.

But the attention of the public here is at present entirely distracted from the army, the forts, or the public buildings. The exciting topic is the organization of the House. But by the time this reaches your readers all will be over, and probably *well* over, and they will probably never appreciate the fact that a battle as important, almost, as that of Chattanooga, is now being quietly fought out among the members of the Thirty-Eighth Congress.

This is by no means the first time when great interest has centered upon such events. Men are everywhere recalling old struggles, and searching the records for precedents, from the time when old John Quincy Adams put aside the Clerk and organized the House on his own responsibility, to the famous contest when it took weeks to put Nathaniel P. Banks in the Chair, and the Southern members so loudly and clearly threatened and prophesied the very war which is now raging as an inevitable consequence of the success of their opponents.[56]

There will be much history, and the vivid visions of many deeply interesting scenes, gathering around the opening of the Thirty-Eighth Congress. When we opened the Thirty-Seventh, we had serious doubts of its ever closing its sessions in the old halls. Lee was at our very gates, and the sound of rebel cannon more than once sent its dull reverberations in to fill the pauses in the anxious debates. Many of the old familiar faces will be there, and it will be pleasant to welcome them back. The very echoes of the huge chambers will deal kindlier with accustomed voices which have so long and so well spoken out for freedom and for Union.

I shall go up and take notes of the new body, not in the way of personalities, but just to see to what sort of a looking crowd of men this nation has committed its destinies for the remain[d]er of this Presidential term. They should be well selected, for an hour like this, and we may well pray that the people do not find themselves mistaken in their choice.

WASHINGTON, CA. 14 DECEMBER 1863 (PUBLISHED 17 DECEMBER 1863)
The President's Message, and the accompanying Proclamation, are universally applauded here, and I am sorry to see that some professedly loyal prints at the North extend to it so chilling and suspicious a greeting.[57] One would think, to read their viciously penned leaders, that the "old gentleman at the White House," as they civilly call him, had suddenly become metamorphosed into the deepest and most designing of intriguers for personal popularity. It is not necessary for me, or any other man, to step forward in defence of Abraham Lincoln from any such imputation; but permit me to point out to your readers one or two of the immediate effects which the President may have proposed to himself as among the reasons for issuing such a tremendous appendix to his Message.

If they, the said readers, will examine with due care the reports of the condition of affairs, political and military, in large portions of Louisiana and Arkansas, and in almost the whole of Tennessee, they will be apt to discover a very considerable degree of preparation for the efficient action of such a plan of reconstruction and pardon as the President has promulgated. The persons especially excepted from the proposed pardon, are almost to a man now absent from the States above mentioned, and no consideration for them in the minds of their fellow citizens can interfere with the success of the plan. Such will be very apt to be the case with other States before many months are past. It is almost a pity that the only men who are not pardoned are the only men who will never be caught, for when they really make their minds up that their improvised hulk of a ship of State is actually sinking, they will be the very first to take to the boats and make off.

WASHINGTON, 28 DECEMBER 1863 (PUBLISHED 31 DECEMBER 1863)
It is really winter to-day, if there was only a trifle of snow on the ground. The wind rudely flutters the capes and reddens the noses of the sentries on the ramparts of the forts, and in the shelter-tents the outlying pickets huddle together closely to keep warm, longing even for heat, and dust, and long marches.

The different reports of the Cabinet officers, &c., are all in, and it will perhaps be enough to say of all of them, that they have increased for their authors, in each case, the same kind of reputation and popularity which they had before. Towards all our feelings are likely to remain unchanged, "only more so."

CONGRESS—ITS WORK AND ITS MEN

Congress seems to find it difficult to get fairly into its work. Indeed, it is almost an established usage that each new Congress should spend the few days before the holidays in sparring and fillibustering. Rarely ever has any work of value been done before New Year's. Thus far we have had nothing but votes of thanks, lukewarm resolutions, speeches upon the Government reports, and criticisms of the Administration by the opposition. The latter threatens to be fractious and disagreeable—prone to waste time, and to use the petty arts of the parliamentary skirmisher to embarrass the action of their opponents. They will soon weary of this, for the majority against them is too strong, and the outside pressure of public opinion is imperative that this Congress *must work*. When the members come back from their Christmas dinners and New Year's calls, and the reports of the great Committees begin to tumble in, each with its huge budget of facts and theories, there will be a general girding up of loins, and a frowning down of all trivialities. I am convinced that there is a great deal of ability among the men who now represent the people here. There is more experienced *business capacity*, more practical knowledge of affairs, *if* less eloquence and less deep and far-seeing statesmanship, than we have been in the habit of seeing here.

There are not many men in either House who have what is called an "intellectual appearance," but there are a great many men of strongly marked, rugged faces, firm-looking, clear-eyed, with that in their deportment, dress and *tout ensemble*, which gives one confidence in their manliness and good sense. A few there are with "Compromise" written all over them—men who never stood up straight and fought anything out to the bitter end in all their lives. However, who knows but they may be made of some use before we get through.

The new Speaker is getting into his harness pretty well, though he sometimes gets people into the wrong State by the wrong name when he "recognizes" them.[58] He will soon get over that, as the faces become familiar, and if there was any such thing as keeping members in their seats, he would be materially aided by the geography of the Hall. Keeping still is a lost art to a busy Congressman. I thought I would follow one uneasy little fellow the other day, to see if I could really locate him on any one seat; but I got tired of it in the course of an hour or so, and I don't know where that Member's seat is yet.

THE PRESIDENT

The President is steadily recovering his health and strength, and his friends say that he will be rather improved than otherwise by his brief struggle with fever.[59] He received his guests at the Reception the other day with a good deal of his usual hearty cheerfulness, though compelled to avail himself of occasional opportunities for a brief resting-spell.

I wonder what deep plans his sagacious brain is meditating for the great year before him. This New Year's Day must come with solemn step to him. It cannot be any light matter to look forward to another year of war and bloodshed, and to imagine the possibilities of the coming struggle. To think, too, that for all blunders and errors of all men, with all their consequences, multitudes will with ungenerous and senseless bitterness hold him responsible. Now we are thinking of it, there must be a *personal* side to the musings of such a man at such a time: how many valued friends have gone out from his presence to the battle field to return no more! The list began with his gallant favorite Ellsworth, and no battle of any consequence since but has swelled the number. There must be many more missing by the end of the year, and the thought may well weigh heavily upon the kind yet strong heart to whom they will come for the orders or the commissions which send them forth.

This is a merry time, however, compared with one year ago, and we may well hope that God will send us a merrier one this day twelve months.

BEGINNING TO SEE IT

I am happy to see, by the English papers, that even our transatlantic cousins are beginning to see the matter in a different light. On the whole, it may be that we have expected too much of Europe, all things considered. They never understood American affairs, and don't understand them *now*, except as they get a glimpse or two in the light of National victories. They all know what it means to be well whipped, and they see that the Rebellion is "catching it." They don't exactly like the result, it is not just what they prophesied, but only wait and see how friendly they will all be when we are once more out of trouble.

CHAPTER FOUR

1864–1865

WASHINGTON, 4 JANUARY 1864 (PUBLISHED 7 JANUARY 1864)
If we had planned the weather of the past week ourselves, we could not have made it furnish better symbols of our National regrets and hopes. The last day of the old year was singularly gloomy, stormy, and disagreeable. Towards night dim masses of driving mist gathered around the Capitol, and almost hid it from view, and through the heavy rain of the later evening it loomed up like a great white ghost of the Past of the Republic. The storm went on until after midnight, and the morning of New Year's day was foggy and cloudy; but a cold, bracing wind came from the northwest, changing the air, freezing the mud, and letting the bright winter sunlight in on us again. At once every one seemed to become more cheerful, for none of us are independent of the weather—hospitable houses all over the city, in greater numbers than ever before, were thrown open to the merry crowd of "callers," and the day passed off in fine style. All men seemed full of hope, and not a few added to their usual "Happy New Year"—"and peace in the spring." "God grant that it may come—and come to stay, and so come as to be worth the having!"

THE LEVEE
The members of the Cabinet and other high functionaries kept open house, but as usual, the center of attraction was the President's House. Many of the readers of THE EXAMINER may not be aware that time-honored custom has prescribed that on each recurring New Year's day the President must hold a grand levee, to which all who choose to come are welcome. The White House is thrown open, the entrance is draped with flags, and the "first servant of the Republic" waits to receive his employers. From eleven o'clock A.M. untill twelve, he receives the representatives of foreign powers, who come in all the blaze of court dress, orders, &c., and make a truly brilliant appearance. The attendance of the diplomatic body this year was markedly large in comparison with some other similar occasions during this administration. Then in due order, mingling with the last arrivals of the *diplomats*, come the Cabinet, the Supreme Court, the officers of the

army and navy, Senators, Congressmen, if any are here; and then the gates are thrown open, and all the world without, who for an hour have been crowding against the patient police, come on in steady streams, orderly, respectful, full of curiosity, and, this time at least, of sincere good will, to shake hands with the President. Soldiers, ladies, children, citizens of every grade and color, all looking up to "father Abraham" as they pass him, to see how he is bearing it all, and audibly wondering how he can stand so much hand-shaking. There were about eight thousand of them the other day.

It is a strange sight to foreigners, as many of them have told me, and they like it or dislike it according to their own political tendencies. European democrats go into ecstasies over so palpable a sign of our universal equality, and join the crowd enthusiastically, to take their share in the great lesson of the hour. European aristocrats, attaches of legation, tourists, and the like, turn up their noses somewhat scornfully at so singularly American a custom, wondering how so and so (referring to the idol of their particular national or social worship) would look, chatting and laughing and hand-shaking with *such* a crowd. Perhaps they too may get a lesson while they are looking on—who knows!

A BREAK AGAIN, AND THE ABSENTEES

We Washingtonians are suffering again from a break in our communications with the North. That unlucky route seems never to be in a healthy state—there is always a bridge destroyed, or a train off the track, or something of the kind to try the patience of irritable travellers, and of all the multitude who send or receive letters by mail. We hope that Congress will do something for us in this respect, before the winter is over.

Generally speaking, the city is very dull during this holiday recess. There are few rumors, no excitements, and if you ask for any man, the chances are two to one that he is out of town for the holidays. To-morrow, however, the two Houses will reassemble, the absentees come back, bringing with them numerous family additions to our population, and then the pressure upon our hotels and boarding-houses will culminate, and the tyranny of their keepers will grow less and less oppressive until spring shall emancipate us.

BEING IN WINTER QUARTERS

The Army of the Potomac is in winter quarters, blowing its frozen fingers around its camp-fires, glad that there is no winter campaigning [in] this bitter cold weather, and counting the days until the return of spring. They are now about half through with the actual winter of this latitude, and February is very often a mild and pleasant month. Still, they cannot be kept altogether comfortable. Imagine a night tramp up and down the ramparts of a fort in one of these nor'westers, with the cold rifle-barrel getting colder, and the heat gathered at the fireside in quarters rapidly leaving a poor fellow's chilled and shivering limbs. Don't forget these brave men, you who snuggle around roaring grates or cosy "air-tights," these nights, when the mercury in the thermometer is trying to hide its head entirely. They are where they are, in order that you may be with safety where you are.

WASHINGTON, 11 JANUARY 1864 (PUBLISHED 14 JANUARY 1864)
The intense cold weather for this latitude, by interrupting travel, prevented Congress from reassembling very promptly, and individual stragglers are still missing. Several peculiarly pointed sets of resolutions have been passed, which have probed very deeply into the mental and moral composition of our National Legislature. The time will come, if I am not mistaken, when some of our Northern Senators and Representatives will be glad to hide the record of the votes they have lately given upon such subjects as peace, reorganization, &c. The debates, however, are conducted with a degree of decorum and dignity which would once have been impossible to preserve. The absence of the knights of the bowie knife and revolver has changed materially for the better, both the matter and the manner of our great debates.

THE LEARNED ONES
The meeting of the "Academicians," has been one of the interesting points of the week.[1] Much attention was shown them on all hands. Secretary Seward gave them an elegant entertainment, and, for all any one could see, the men of science enjoyed their stay in the capital hugely. Man is a singularly deceptive animal—no one, just by *looking* at these learned gentlemen, would imagine that they knew so much, though some of them were noble specimens of the *genus homo*.

THE NEW TAX LEVY
Speaking of the work in Congress, they are somewhat slowly and nervously approaching a business which touches us all in many ways: I refer to the adjustment of the taxes for the year to come. We have got to raise more money by taxation than we did last year, that is certain, but the point is how to do it. Here the taxing power is almost crushing the life out of some growing and promising enterprise, which petitions frantically for relief; and there it treads upon the gouty toes of overgrown corporations and giant monopolies, and after a growl of wrath, a "delegation" comes on to

Washington to "protect the rights of this great and important interest." The general opinion is that the mere luxuries of life will catch it pretty heavily all around. Gold mining may be made to yield something, and some new avenues of revenue may be opened up. Fellows with big incomes begin to draw long faces and talk of Democracy, and "jealousy of the rich," and all that sort of thing, for they have a shrewd suspicion that none too much mercy will be shown them. If Congress only *will* take the course here indicated, the great mass of the people will sustain them in it, and Europe will have learned another lesson of republican America. It is a comfort to think, now that for the first time in our national existence we are heavily taxed, that we ourselves control the amount and the manner, and that no privileged class can shun or shirk any portion of the burden.

A GOOD THING TO STUDY

The news from Louisiana and Arkansas is a good thing to study. The evidence is accumulating daily that there really exists in those States abundant and excellent material for a reorganization. Tennessee also is furnishing good proof of returning loyalty and good sense. No doubt our good President is anxiously watching every indication, and studying how far it is safe to entrust the management of so much power in the hands of the repentant citizens. It must be a bitter thing for the leaders of the conspiracy to look on, while the fairest and richest portions of their proposed slave empire once more array themselves around the old flag, and turn against the rebellion. I wonder if Mr. Davis sleeps soundly o'nights, or if grim visions of a future only too nearly upon him do not torment, or prevent his slumbers. Memories, too, of such things as Gettysburg, and Vicksburg, and New-Orleans, and Chattanooga, must be forever whispering in his ear, "It *might* have been."

TWO "GREAT" THINGS

There is a great National (means Washingtonian) Sanitary Fair coming off here in a few days, and it promises to be a great thing, or rather *two* great things, for, owing to some slight variances among the lady managers, the undertaking has divided itself into two. However, perhaps a little competition will be of good service in the end.

GETTING USED TO IT

Officers and men who have come in from the front since the cold weather set in, represent the army as being for the most part quite comfortable, but it is probable that the thorough hardening and seasoning process they have gone through helps amazingly towards the said "comfort." There was a cavalry man riding with me yesterday in his "shell jacket," who "did not think it a very cold day," while every one else was muffled to the eyes—"for use doth breed such changes in a man."

WASHINGTON, 18 JANUARY 1864 (PUBLISHED 21 JANUARY 1864)
The humiliating confession must be made at all hazards—Washington, at least to the dwellers therein, is *dull*, insufferably dull. True, Congress is in session, and is doing very well, but it is not doing anything exciting. Even the expulsion of Garrett Davis, if he is to be expelled, would not excite anybody.[2] The social parties are charming, and sufficiently numerous, but there is no excitement in *them*, except to a few unfledged young officers, in the glory of new uniforms. The weekly receptions at the President's House are charming, and call together long lists of our most distinguished citizens, both soldiers and civilians; but a brilliant crowd does not make a man's heart beat or his breath come quickly. No, everything is tame and dull.

The truth is, that we dwellers at the capital begin to realize, that for three years and more we have been living a life of intense excitement. The days have been crowded with great events, and the nights have had their own peculiar horrors to us all. We have seen the panic-stricken multitudes crowding over Long Bridge from the first Bull Run. We have seen the white-faced orderly who came in from opposite Ball's Bluff. We have seen, on many another day, the long lines of ambulances file slowly towards our hospitals, full of the victims of Stone Bridge, the second Bull Run, Chantilly, Fredericksburg, Chancellorsville, and other bloody fields. We have seen McClellan's mighty host embark on his countless flotilla, and we have seen them return again—poor fellows, transported from Chickahominy to Bull Run. The Carthagenians have been so long so near the gates of this Rome of ours, and the air has been so crowded thick with ghastly rumors, that the ordinary events of civil life are slow to arouse our cloyed and jaded minds.

AN INEVITABLE RESURRECTION
Wendell Phillips, Miss Dickinson, Fred Douglass, come here and speak, and a crowd of non-residents assembles to hear them;[3] but the chief point, to the *blasé* Washingtonian, is a sleepy comparison of the present, when such men and all others dare speak here, with the past, when for their lives they dare not; and we prophesy that thus it will yet be all over the South. From the Potomac to the Rio Grande the buried right to free speech will find its resurrection. It begins here, and that is almost an excitement, for it is a part of the war, and we have lived in the war altogether. People at the

North, far from camps and bloody fields, do not understand the feelings of men who are used to hearing frequently the sound of distant cannon, sometimes not so distant, either.

THE DANGER OVER
But there is another point in this relaxed and unstrung state of mind which I refer to. The instinct of all, rather than the reasoning, teaches us, as it has the rest of the country, that once and for all the danger is over. Lee will never again array his armies on the banks of the proud Potomac—loyal now forevermore—and we are never to listen in the streets to frightened rumors of the doings of another Stonewall Jackson. We know that the rebels are gathering all their remaining energies for another desperate effort in the spring; we believe that they will make one more daring rush upon the encircling armies of the Union, but we know that the rebel flag will go down in that wild charge, to rise no more. This, you may reflect, is the central rendezvous for refugees, "converted" secessionists, men who have fled from the wrath to come, or rather which has already come, upon the whole South. Every day we meet with and talk with such men. We compare their descriptions, all concurring with and sustaining one another, of Southern destitution, depletion and weakness, with what we know to be the undiminished strength which God has given and is still giving to the North, and we clearly see what the end will be. Yesterday I talked for a long time with a man who had been a clergyman of wealth and standing in Richmond, and who had just escaped. It was the same old story of suffering and wrong among the lower classes, of an iron military tyranny, and of a bitter determination among the upper and privileged ranks. The leaders of the conspiracy cling to their evil purpose with a stubborn tenacity which belongs to the Anglo-Saxon race, and as yet show no signs of yielding, but among their subordinates a different feeling is growing up.

The President's Proclamation of Amnesty was a heavy blow to the rebellion, and is eating into its strength like a potent poison—a trifle slowly at first, but surely and inevitably. Southerners of both sorts tell me that "*that* was a shrewd thing on the part of Old Abe, almost as shrewd as his Emancipation movement." They will hear from our President again before they get through with this business.

A FOREGONE CONCLUSION
Another cause of the sluggish feeling here is the absence of any great political movement. The Presidential year has begun, but we miss the usual pulling and hauling and intriguing. Every one seems to look upon the

affair as settled, and that Mr. Lincoln's reelection is a foregone conclusion. The necessary voting, as a matter of form, will have to be done, but the quadrennial occupation of our politicians is gone. However, a canvass, divested beforehand of all bitterness and excitement, would be a good thing for the country now, and it is to be hoped that nothing will occur to disturb the tide of feeling, which seems to set so steadily and so peacefully in one direction.

A SENSATION STORY

Exaggerated rumors of the prevalence of small-pox here have got into the sensation prints at the North. It is mostly confined to the colored population—among whom it has been singularly fatal—although it now and then strikes some victim in a far different walk in life. There are now but about twelve hundred cases in the District, and these, to a large extent, in the camps and outlying hospitals; and the city authorities and the War Department are doing their best to protect the public health.

WASHINGTON, 1 FEBRUARY 1864 (PUBLISHED 4 FEBRUARY 1864)

The passage of the bill for a Constitutional Convention by the Maryland Legislature, was only what we have all been looking for, this long time. In feeling, in its interests—to all present purposes and intentions—Maryland is already a free State. The small faction which now remains of the slave-owning oligarchy, so powerful three years ago, struggles in vain against the steady tide of public opinion.

WHAT WE MUST EXPECT

Here, as elsewhere, the constant attrition of the great thoughts belonging to such a cause as ours, is doing more with the hearts of men than our armies can do with their bodies. Grant and Meade are in winter quarters, but we are daily winning substantial victories. And yet, while all this is true, and while every word from the South tells of the failing strength of the rebellion; while our lines open every hour to receive troops of deserters and refugees; while North Carolina promises to cut loose from the ruinous mass which has dragged her along so far;—while, in short, all signs seem to promise well, we must not deceive ourselves as to the actual state of things.

The "speedy collapse," "bursting of the bubble," "grand crash," and all that sort of thing so freely predicted by Northern orators and editors, is not exactly at the doors. The winter is mostly over in some portions of our great battle-ground, and in a few short weeks armies will once more be in motion. The armies of the rebellion will be as numerous, as brave, as well commanded as they were at Chancellorsville, at Chantilly, or at Chickamauga, and they will be hurled upon our lines with all the energy of desperation.

Between this and July there will be fighting of more or less severity all along the bloody border marked by our encircling forces. Especially will the enemy strike for the repossession of East Tennessee. The mountain passes will run red with the blood of those who hold and of those who would win them. Reverses to our arms are no more impossible now, though far less probable, than a year ago. All I mean by all this is, that the time for exultation has not yet come, and much remains to be done.

A NOTED CORRESPONDENCE

The Seward-Adams diplomatic correspondence is attracting deserved attention here and abroad.[4] It certainly places our Government in a most dignified attitude before the world, and cannot fail to add largely to the reputation of the ripe and mature statesman, to whose courage, candor and moderation we owe so much.

A hot temper, a weak or prejudiced mind, in either our Envoy to England or our Secretary of State, might have wrought incalculable mischief to the Commonwealth. Mr. Lincoln has been unfortunate in some of his appointments, but the country was never so well represented at the courts of the Old World as it is now.

A SOCIAL PHENOMENON

Socially, the capital has been very gay for a number of days, but the season for entertainments of any considerable size is mostly at an end. Mr. Fernando Wood, of New-York, gave a grand party the other evening, which, to the surprise of some, was largely attended by Republicans and Abolitionists of the most ultra stripe. It would have been funny to have read out in the parlors the names of those guests who have, at sundry times and places, declared themselves in favor of hanging as a felon this somewhat remarkable host of the evening. The general principle is, however, not to carry political animosities into social life—which means that whatever bad things you may think or say of a man, still, so long as he can get himself elected to Congress or the Senate, you are to eat his dinners and dance to his music, and remember all sorts of maxims about Christian charity, et cetera. In short, one of the charming features of life in Washington is, that people say their ugly things about each other behind each other's backs, and are commendably cordial and friendly in all personal intercourse.

THE CONGRESSIONAL WORKSHOP

Congress still hammers away, but the real *work* of the session has thus far been in the committees. These little squads of men, in their separate rooms in the Capitol, examine documents, listen to arguments, receive and read communications, call for testimony, papers, &c., and digest a vast mass of crude matter bearing upon each subject, which could by no means be brought before the House. Many of those who do the least talking for effect on the floor of either Chamber, are the most valuable and efficient of men in the real workshop of the Committee-room.

There are a number of experienced men of business in this Congress, and they are manfully grappling with a vast and complicated accumulation of varied affairs, and in due time we may hope to see order coming out of more than one chaotic heap. The Committee of Ways and Means is suffering slow martyrdom from delegations of New-York speculators, who want this thing done and that thing undone, and no two of whom seem to pull in the same direction. They endure it manfully, however, and seem to be sincerely bent on getting the largest amount of revenue with the smallest degree of injustice.

THE LIEUTENANT-GENERAL QUESTION

Among the matters for discussion is the question of bestowing the rank of Lieutenant-General upon U.S. Grant. The general opinion is that it will be done, in spite of our traditional national jealousy of high military titles. Other nations, even some far inferior to us in military power, bestow upon their heroes or their favorites several grades of rank higher than any known to our military system. With the exceptional case of General Scott, we have never had a Lieutenant-General. England, for instance, recognizes that and the additional grades of General and Field-Marshal. Other nations have still other distinctions of rank. It is almost unnecessary to add that these high ranks are borne in Europe, for the most part, by men who have not seen a tithe of the active service, or won any glory to compare with that of the gallant officer whom Congress now proposes to elevate. There are some who say "*Wait*," and add that the war is not yet over, and talk of the old enthusiasm for McClellan and other officers, but no one seems to fear that Grant will ever lose the laurels he has so gallantly won.

WASHINGTON, 6 FEBRUARY 1864 (PUBLISHED 11 FEBRUARY 1864)

Society here, and elsewhere, I presume, is acquiring new features. The old secession or semi-secesh element, is steadily sinking in the scale of social position, and to be deemed unpatriotic is now to "lose caste." It has been my good fortune to witness several very pleasing exhibitions of this of late, as for instance: At a hop the other evening were several officers whose crutches or empty sleeve debarred them from the dance—the former even from the promenade; and it was refreshing to see the assiduous care which the young belles of the evening took for their entertainment. They were not left alone for a moment. Sympathy, attention, the brightest smiles, were considered their just due. Small things, does any one say? Yes, but these little things indicate the beating of the national heart, more truly than any more showy demonstration.

A TABLE HAVING A HISTORY

A very fine affair was the annual dinner to the *Corps Diplomatique* at the President's House. These dinners are official, strictly "regulation," to be sure, but sometimes they deserve attention for their success in a social point of view. By the way, it would be a grand thing if the long table in the old "Congressional Dining-room" at the White House had been a short-hand reporter, and had taken notes during the changing years of its official history. Over it have chatted and hob-nobbed the worthies and celebrities of successive political eras. Hardly any man of national reputation, politically, but has at one time or another put his feet under it. A host of foreigners of distinction have there met with *our* nobility. The room itself is plain and simple in its appointments, and hardly large enough for the demands of the present day, as it only admits three dozen or so to the table; but no other room in the country has more, or more pleasant historical associations. The council-table in the President's business office is equal in some things to its neighbor, but *its* memories are all too dry, and there comes a sense of oppression and exertion when one attempts to summon up its past.

THE TWO COLUMNS OF OPPOSITION

The debates in Congress have been tolerably spicy of late, and some of the speeches have been remarkable for power and point. The opposition seems gradually to divide into two columns;—the one composed of the irreclaimable Copperheads, who openly assail the Administration and invariably vote against its every measure, in a spirit of blind bitterness in no wise mitigated by a vivid consciousness of their want of power. The other division is growing more and more reasonable, and readily accepts as accomplished facts the great changes which are taking place in the political economy of the nation. These latter frequently vote on the Government side on questions of general utility, or, if they do not, will seek carefully for excuses full of wordy patriotism for their opposition.

THE BALLOT-BOX CAMPAIGN

The politicians are getting busier and busier as the spring draws nearer, and the preparations for "the campaign" begin to assume a definite form in more than one direction. I may be excused for noticing one indication of partisan sagacity—the friends of the various *new* candidates are all in favor of a Party and a Convention, and loud in expressions of their willingness to abide by its decisions; while those who argue for a continuation of Mr. Lincoln in his post for another term would be perfectly willing to let the campaign run itself, and dispense with formality and machinery.

I am not politician enough to point out the meaning of this, unless by the analogy, that when labor-saving machinery is most sought for, it is an indication that "hands" are scarce. The fact is, that several times in the history of the country the results of National Conventions have been singularly unlike what the popular heart expected.

All that sort of thing will work out its own solution in due time, and the masses will have more to do with the next Presidential election, in any event, than they have had for this long time. Still, it is interesting to a looker-on to watch the course of events, and see how men work, and *why* they work. The game is a great one, and great things may be depending upon the issue of it. It beats the chess champion, but reminds us of the well-known scene—a dozen eager players, with their eyes and fingers on their own games, against one, who will not touch a piece, and who turns his back upon the boards.

WASHINGTON, 15 FEBRUARY 1864 (PUBLISHED 18 FEBRUARY 1864)

The weather here is like spring, warm and bright, with an unlimited supply of dust. We have March before us yet, but in this latitude March is frequently entirely "available" for military purposes.

NEW MOVEMENTS

All along the lines the armies appear to be waking up from the inactivity of their winter quarters, and some of their movements have attracted far more attention than they deserved. No matter what the newspaper men may say—and they will say almost anything to make a sensation or spice a letter—no great movement will be undertaken so long as the chances remain that a storm will defeat it. Of course our generals will not neglect any opportunities to harass or damage the enemy, and they will send out expeditions in all directions to feel the strength of the enemy, ascertain their positions, and prevent them from doing anything of importance without our knowledge. By thus distracting the rebel generals, and compelling them perpetually to guard against our attacks, we force them into a defensive position far more difficult than that of an assailant, and which effectually masks our real plans for the spring campaign. Nor is it impossible that some reconnoitering party, like that of Butler on the Peninsula the other day, may find an unguarded spot where a telling blow may be rapidly and sharply dealt.

THE PEOPLE AT WORK

Meantime the evidence accumulates that the people are determined upon a vigorous and decisive campaign. All your readers have noted the state of feeling in their own neighborhoods; but among the indications more distinctly visible here are the numerous plans, devices, and inventions for the injury of the enemy, submitted to the Government. Our people are essentially a thinking and inventive people, and have dwelt upon the great subject of the day until each one imagines that he has worked out a solution of the great problem, and straightway brings his creation before the powers that be.

Earnest, enthusiastic men, wrapped up in their plans, sure of their success, blind to all obstacles or defects, throng the Patent-Office and the War Department, bitterly wroth with the "red tape" and official stupidity which will not see their darling offspring in the same golden light that they do. Guns, ships, balloons, shells, infernal machines, incendiary missiles, armor, indescribable nonpareils of unknown aim and origin—some involving principles which, unknown to the simple inventors, are in daily use, others that have been antiquated long ago, others that are useless, others whose only charm is the ingenious complexity of their bewildering machinery, and here and there grains of wheat among bushels of chaff, bright thoughts of true genius worked out by the patient hand of practical sense. The balloon business has tormented a large number of busy brains, but the funniest thing yet is the proposition lately made to the Government for the speedy dissemination of the President's various proclamations. Some patriotic genius has invented a balloon which is warranted to "get up his own steam and steer hisself," and proposes to freight a lot of such machines with copies of the documents in question, head them southward, and so arrange them that at fixed distances they will *burst*, and secure a wide circulation for their precious cargo. There is something original, not to say sublime, about this invention.

But while some of its manifestations partake of the absurd, far be it from me to make fun of the spirit which prompts all this. By this and by all other signs, we know that the mind as well as the heart of a great people has concentrated itself upon the one great object to such an extent that all but the coolest and most collected souls are getting feverish and impatient.

SIGNS FROM DIXIE

Significant signs of the times continually turn up in the dingy and moribund sheets which do service as newspapers in the dominions of Jefferson Davis. Growls of discontent and mutterings of mutiny against their horrible despotism; despairing views of the future; not less despairing expressions of desperate determination; harsh criticisms of military failures, from which even Lee and Longstreet do not now escape; and a thousand things to tell us of the fallen condition of our once mighty adversary.

One last grand effort they will make, no doubt, but their last army is in the field, and if they fail now to strike us a vital blow, Good bye, Confederacy and slave empire! So far as the *end* is concerned, we can have little or no doubt; but the malice of our foes has it yet, it may possibly be, in its power, to strike us one hard blow, and inflict one more deep wound upon the people already so deeply and fiendishly wronged and injured by this rebellion; to wit: if by dint of hard fighting and good generalship, or any folly or supineness on our part, they can manage to protract the war much beyond the limits now assigned it by our statesmen, so as to load us still further with debt, and still further derange our national finances, they may give us still further reason to hate forever the names of the authors of the conspiracy.

This it is, as much as anything else, which makes it necessary for us to have half a million men in the field in the spring, and which will sharpen the swords of our soldiers for the great battles towards which time is so rapidly bringing us.

DOINGS IN CONGRESS

The passage of the Enrollment Bill by the House, in spite of filibustering and opposition, assures us that the men will all be "on hand," while the rate at which volunteers are coming in promises that for many States the bill will be a warning only.

The bill for the establishment of a new Executive Department, under the supervision of a "Secretary of Industry," is yet in its infancy, but seems to meet with more than a little favor. Very much that should be done remains undone under the present arrangement, unavoidably.

THE FAIRS

Socially, the people of Washington are doing very little besides attending to our great Sanitary Fair, in behalf of which no little enthusiasm and energy is being enlisted. Working for the Fair is a good deal better than dancing until morning, looked at from every point of view, and though I do not believe in "Lent" to any very great extent, the young people here who do are thus turning the absence of dancing parties to very excellent account.

WASHINGTON, 22 FEBRUARY 1864 (PUBLISHED 25 FEBRUARY 1864)
We have had a quiet week of it here—no excitement of any kind among the general public, and not much beside routine work among officials. As to Congress, some of us will begin to lower our opinion of that august body if they do not soon get to work in better fashion. At this rate they are likely to be a trifle late with some of the most important measures on the tapis. The opposition is getting more and more into its old ways. Several times during the week, listening to the loud-voiced speeches of many Northern men, I could have shut my eyes and imagined that we were back in the "old times." They rehearsed all the old twaddle about "inferior and superior races," the necessity of keeping the black men in bondage for their own good, the patriarchal character of Southern slavery, and its benignant influence on the slaves, and were not even contented without lugging in a great deal of that dismal stuff about Puritans and Cavaliers, Southern chivalry, and all that. One fellow even had the temerity to assail New-England in general, and Massachusetts in particular, as criminally accessory to the death and downfall of the peculiar institution. He supported his indictment very well, and it must have been a proud moment for all the right-minded New-England men on the floor. Some of them shook hands over it in open exultation. It is too true, and pity 'tis 'tis true, that while so many of the inferior race are casting off their rusty fetters, far too many of their white superiors still take a lunatic's delight in considering them ornaments, and exhibiting them to the world. When *all* the old slave States shall be represented in Congress by emancipationists, as in due time they will, can any Northern State excuse itself for sending pro-slavery men to Washington?

HOW THE ARGUMENT RUNS
The men who manage the Ship of State are looking anxiously across the Atlantic to see the progress of the great European trouble. Deeply as all good men must regret a great war, and terrible as it is to think of all the horrors that seem not unlikely to come upon some of the world's most civilized nations, we can well believe that some good may result even to them, and there are not wanting men whose somewhat selfish patriotism argues after this manner:—A war in Europe means a general overturning, or at least the danger of it, and will send much European gold into American

government securities for safety, to the great relief of our exchange and gold markets, and the enhancement of the value of our national stocks. It will also create anew the "war demand" for American breadstuffs, and pour into the purses of the Great Republic, through every avenue, the "sinews of war." It can hardly fail to operate beneficially upon our shipping interest. It will force all the nations concerned to a stricter construction of those laws of neutrality which they have so loosely dealt with during the past three years. Last, but not least, it will shut out from the hearts of the rebel chiefs any lingering hope of a possible foreign intervention, and we shall be left permanently alone to grapple with our failing foe. Whether all these calculations are correct or not, your readers must judge, and, possibly, the future may determine. God grant, however, that no other nation may be called on to drink of the bitter cup which has so long been pressed to our unwilling lips.

THE FOURTHS OF MARCH

A few days more will bring us to the Fourth of March, and to the end of three years of a fearful struggle. Is it too much to say that we shall then be richer, stronger, more numerous, better able, by far, to carry on the war, than we were when Abraham Lincoln took the oath of office at the east front of the Capitol? I think not; our best men say all that and more. We have marched bravely on under the cloud and through the crimson sea, and our trial has been a bitter one; but somehow we have grown wiser and more powerful through it all. We are more united, more earnest, more sober—a greater and a worthier people. Can our enemies say the same?

I do not mean to "sermonize," but the Fourth of March *is* a great day to us, and thinking of it, I cannot help but recall with vivid distinctness the day of Mr. Lincoln's inauguration. (If I am saying too much about it you can clip off this part of my letter.) There was the long procession up to the west front of the Capitol, and the crowds on the sidewalk—some earnestly anxious lest evil might befall the nation's chosen servant; and some glaring at the plain man from Illinois, as he sat in his carriage, with eyes full of bitter hatred which the war has since found an expression for. Then followed the solemn ceremony in the shadow of the unfinished Capitol, the old Judge in his long robes administering the oath which has been so well kept. The vast crowd listening breathlessly to the clear, homely, brief, but eloquent address. The little band of citizen soldiers who looked like so insignificant a guard, the germ, they, of the mighty army who were to follow. Then the crowd broke up, the procession went back down the Avenue, and as the new

President stept slowly and thoughtfully over the threshold of the Executive Mansion, the nation began to grow dimly conscious of a great change, and timidly hopeful of a new and better life. That inauguration ceremony was the first grand tableau in a series of which the world has as yet seen only a few. The curtain will soon fall from before the next, however.

WASHINGTON, 29 FEBRUARY 1864 (PUBLISHED 3 MARCH 1864)
It is a warm and spring-like day, with a promise of rain in the murky and heavy sky, and the air which comes in at my open windows might be that of May. The crocusses are in full bloom in the public gardens, and here and there other early plants are beginning to be confident that winter is almost gone. The whole city, apart from the pacing guards, and an occasional army wagon, wears a most peaceful appearance. And yet there has been no time for months when there was so much anxiety and activity in military circles.

The movements of the enemy in Florida, and the strong force they have sent to check our advance, prove that they, at least, comprehend the importance and the effect of Gen. Gillmore's plan. It is too bad that we got beaten there the other day; a little more caution, and a little less reckless courage, would have prevented any such catastrophe.[5] It was only a temporary check, and we hope soon to hear of better results.

The greatest interest, however centres upon Sherman and his daring movement, which no one but Grant and his generals seem clearly to understand.[6] So much the better, in every way; let the rebels puzzle over it all they can until the blow has fallen—somewhere. Military men here seem to think that Sherman's position is anything but a safe one, and the croakers are by no means few who bid us prepare for an unfortunate ending. That, I suppose, is because they, like the rebels, do not understand it, for we may surely trust Grant and his advisers not to risk so large a body of men on a very doubtful errand. This is beginning the spring campaign sufficiently early, and promises great energy in the prosecution of it. If Sherman is successful, what may we not hope to accomplish before summer?

We hope to hear something from Texas before a great while. The work there and in Arkansas consists of "reorganization at the point of the bayonet," and may have very few brilliant battles in it, at the same time that it promises to be permanent after it is once done.

Our foreign relations seem to look all the better for the troubles in Europe, and these are by no means over, or nearly over. From almost every Court of the Old World, we are continually receiving assurances of good feeling, and a steadily increasing disposition to abide by their neutrality in good earnest and sincerity. So far so good; the year opens very well, but who shall prophesy its ending?

In the political circles of the Capital, an increase of activity is clearly discernible. The unfortunate "secret circular," issued by a more zealous than discreet friend of Secretary Chase, has turned all eyes upon him more than ever, as the most prominent opponent of the reelection of President Lincoln, and, as his wiser supporters seem to think, very unfortunately for him.[7] Our people, as a general thing, have a prejudice against "secret circulars." Other candidates are mentioned, and even the Vice-Presidency is seriously talked of among the class of men out of whom it has heretofore been our practice to select that very honorable but very powerless official.

There is as yet very little heat or acrimony, almost all discussions being carried on with a very fair degree of courtesy and good humor. This, of course, will hardly be the case by and bye, but at present it looks very well indeed. If I were a politician, I think it would be my opinion that all this pulling and hauling and pipe-laying was so much labor thrown away, and that by the time the National Convention meets, in June next, of the party which will beyond all doubt elect the next President, the *people* will have so clearly designated *their* candidate, that the said Convention will more resemble a ratification meeting than anything else. But I may be mistaken, and we shall see in due time.

Speaking of the current events in Washington, we are having lively times here just now with Spiritualism, several sets of travelling prestidigitateurs of that stamp having opened their shows here at once. Now I don't pretend to deny that I have seen phenomena produced at other times and places which were sufficiently wonderful, but as for the persons now raising an excitement here, (a declining one) they are by no means equal to Signor Blitz and his brethren. A "spirit" who has to get into a big box with two men to help him, and have the gas turned off, before he can be persuaded to keep bad time on a banjo, or throw things out of a hole in the box, should remember that Blitz's "bottle-imp" is worth a dozen of him, and isn't as noisy.

Among the important measures to be brought before Congress this week, is the Act authorizing another through route between here and New-York. It ought to be passed as soon as possible, and for one I shall look hard at the record of any man who votes against it. A monopoly is a mean thing, any way—and more so when it is a mean monopoly. The two most important "centres" on the continent ought to be brought as near to each other as possible, and this seems to be the only way to do it at present.

WASHINGTON, 7 MARCH 1864 (PUBLISHED 10 MARCH 1864)
Another week of the spring campaign has passed, and as yet no results seem to have been obtained beyond the destruction of rebel commissary stores, and cutting off important lines of communication for their armies. This is something, and we must needs suppose that these things are a preparation for further and more important movements.

KILPATRICK'S RAID
As to the dash to the gates of Richmond, if it had not been widely hoped that Kilpatrick would succeed in striking a blow at the city itself, his exploit would receive great praise for its boldness, celerity, and for the widespread consternation and dismay he caused through the most rebellious portion of Virginia.[8] It is not improbable that other results may yet flow from this rapid ride into the heart of the Old Dominion.

HOLDING NORTH CAROLINA
In further token of the manner in which this year's war is to be conducted, we have constant reports of a desperate attempt to drive us out of North Carolina. For many months now we have securely held our positions on the coast, and have been thereby a thorn in the side of the Confederacy of no mean size and offensiveness. That we shall now retain our hold with desperate tenacity is a matter of course, but the peculiar character of the country is such that none of these positions are remarkably strong by nature, and we must mainly rely on the conduct of their defenders. Perhaps the increased activity of our forces in other departments may render it difficult for the rebels to concentrate an overwhelming force on Newbern.

THE LOUISIANA ELECTION
The election of Mr. Hahn as Governor of Louisiana is a fact of deep significance to all who are watching the slow but steady process of State Reorganization.[9] Around the government now being created in that recovered commonwealth will gather all that is loyal, substantial, earnest, within its borders. The President may point to it and say, "To a very great extent this is the work of the three Proclamations," at the same time that he bids the brave Banks to preserve it with the strong hand of the army. The new political feeling in Louisiana is fast becoming "radical" enough. There is little fear of a relapse into slavery and barbarism. It is and will forever be a free State. The rebel leaders may give it up forever, and with it the mouths of the great river, and what they so vauntingly term the Trans-Mississippi Department of the Confederacy, "with which," as says Mr. Davis, in one

of his messages, "our communications are at present somewhat interrupted and uncertain."

THE LIEUTENANT-GENERALSHIP

We are a little puzzled here as to what the President will do with General Grant, now that he outranks all other generals in the field. It is pretty well known that Mr. Lincoln believes Grant to be in his proper place, and about the same of Halleck. If this is the case, he will no doubt find some means of keeping them both where they are, and the question is *how* he will do it. It seems as if it would be a great pity to stop Grant, now that he appears to be in such a fair way to drive Johns[t]on's army back into the interior of Georgia, leaving two large States almost at our mercy. Let him alone, and let him carry out the plans he has been working out during his three months of comparative inaction.

THE SPRING ELECTIONS

Much anxiety is felt here about the spring elections at the North. Now, if ever, is the time for those who intend to stand by the Administration next November, to see to it that no accidents happen to raise the drooping spirits of the Copperheads. The danger is that so many good and earnest men have lately gone into the army that the voting, too much of it, will be left to the hands of those who have so long preferred the political to the more dangerous "campaign." Nor are the politicians disposed to give up the "main point" without one more struggle, and we are likely to be deluged with circulars and manifestoes between this and June next. It is to be hoped that the President's friends will not drag *him* into the arena. His own good sense and steady unselfishness would keep him out of it, but all his supporters are not so wise, and some one may yet do for him what [Pomeroy] did for [Chase].

CONGRESSIONAL ORATORS

Congress has not done a great deal of work lately, and the amount of "spouting" has been something fearful to think of. Our orators must be kept in practice, however, and our new members must be taught parliamentary tactics by exercise, and so, if the people choose to foot the bills, there is no reason why the thing should not go on. The everlasting whisky business is nearly settled, and now we may hope for action upon other points. Among the measures for the week to come are several bearing upon the currency, and its fluctuations in apparent value as compared to gold. The Committee of Ways and Means of the House, and the Senate Finance Committee, are said to have a full understanding on this subject. High tariffs, heavy taxation, to diminish imports and insure large revenues, and at the same time such measures as shall check the demand for gold for foreign exchange, bring cotton to the seashore, foster the production of native gold, and make speculation in gold or exchange a dangerous or unprofitable affair—these are the weapons with which Congress proposes to come to the rescue of our slowly-sinking currency. Now, then, if Grant or Meade will "join in" with them, and wipe out a rebel army or so, and give us Mississippi and Alabama, with their hoarded bales of cotton, people will soon have a higher idea of "greenbacks" than they seem to have at present.

RUSHING FOR THE LOAN

The impression at the Treasury is that there will be a great rush for the new five per cent. ten-forty bonds, and that there will be little or no difficulty in placing the whole loan. If they are right (and who shall say that they are not?) it will be a new and powerful evidence of our people's confidence in their Government, and determination to sustain it at all hazards to purse as well as to person.

WASHINGTON, 14 MARCH 1864 (PUBLISHED 17 MARCH 1864)

Spring is really here at last. The air is bright with glorious sunshine, the wind is from the south, the roads are drying fast, and everything looks bright for the Republic.

LIEUTENANT-GENERAL GRANT

You see, by the papers, that Gen. Grant has returned to the field where he belongs. The hopes, fears and prayers of a whole nation go with him to his arduous work. Truly a vast responsibility is on his shoulders—greater by far than any one man would willingly *assume*. He has not taken the burden of his own wish or will, but his country has placed it upon him, believing him able and worthy to bear it. We shall soon see if we have done well and wisely, or the reverse. The whole resources of the people will be placed at his disposal—a grand army, unlimited supplies, unlimited power, unlimited confidence. Surely great results must follow.

There was very little fuss made over his visit here; every one was eager to see him, and to do him honor, and many expressed disappointment when they found what a plain, sober-looking, unassuming sort of person was the hero of so many battles and so many important triumphs. The scene in the President's room, where the new Lieutenant-General received his commission, was simple, manly, dignified—worthy of him, and of the other plain and earnest man at whose hands he received it. No pomp, no show, no vulgar ostentation—that would have done in other countries, as for instance if he had been the darling of some haughty and therefore vulgar aristocracy, but not *here*. Some day that scene will be made the subject of the painter's best skill—and be well worthy of it.

THE DEATH OF DAHLGREN

The campaign has but just opened, and already we have added another to the brilliant list of those who have died too early for their country, but not too early for lasting fame. We are all—all who knew him—full of bitter indignation at the manner in which these cowardly traitors have treated the remains of the brave Colonel Dahlgren, at the same time that they have done their best to blacken his memory.[10] I knew him well, and write about him with a feeling of deep sorrow for his loss, mingled with just anger at the baseness of the men who are unable to appreciate a brave and generous enemy. The truth is, he scared them too badly to be easily forgiven, even in death. Young, handsome [some words illegible], honorable, chivalrous, a true gentleman, full of the most sincere patriotism—I saw him last full of high spirits, and looking forward, as he had a right to, to a bright and honorable future—and it is very hard to-day to imagine him sleeping in an unknown grave, away down in the heart of the rebellion. We will win that grave yet, and find where he is laid, and his monument shall tell of him as he really was. Alas, how many such must yet be sacrificed before this long martyrdom is over.

THE "CORNERED WOLF" POSITION

In this connection, let me call attention to the sort of "cornered wolf" position in which the rebel chiefs are trying to place their people. "War to the knife," they say, and literally cut the throats of their prisoners whenever they can so hide the deed as to obviate the danger of retaliation. Their cup is almost full, if indeed it does not already run over somewhat. There will be fewer prisoners taken on either side hereafter, and fights will be more bloody and stubborn even than heretofore. Our armies are heaping up wrath against the day of wrath, and we may well fear that in some dark hour, when their blood is hot from some long battle, our soldiers may for a while forget their mercy, and remember only the deserts of their vanquished foemen.

A BUSY WEEK AT THE CAPITOL

Congress has had a somewhat busy week of it, and seems at last awakened to the necessity of coming to the rescue of the national currency. If they will only "keep it up," the good bulls of Wall and William streets may well take warning, and desist from their nefarious practices. The Committee of Ways and Means of the House are to get at the Revenue and Tariff Bills this week, and all taxation or duties we have hitherto seen imposed in this country will be as nothing to the "heavy weights" which will now be put on. Such at least is the current talk, in and out of Congress, and the Senate is more than ready to say "Amen" to the highest figures. This is all right; and if it shall seem at first a trifle hard, the people will soon become accustomed to it, will see the necessity of it, and will fully sustain their representatives in so doing.

THE CHASE WITHDRAWAL

The letter of Secretary Chase, withdrawing his name from the list of candidates for the Union nomination for President, was not altogether unexpected.[11] It would have come earlier with a better grace, but it has been well done now—with dignity, and without presumption or unnecessary words. The contest is greatly narrowed by this withdrawal, for there are not many men on our side of the House who will have the vanity to urge their personal claims, when Mr. Chase himself has seen and said that *he* cannot patriotically do so. I can think of a man who will not be so retarded; but I imagine him to be so determined to run, that he will "go it alone," with little reference to propriety or consequences. How far such a man can run remains to be seen, but his course may take what has politely been called "an agricultural turn."

ANOTHER FALSE ALARM

So far as has transpired here, there have been none of the portentous changes in our foreign relations indicated by some of the New-York papers. It may be that Europe has made up its mind that it has not enough to do at home, but thus far we are ignorant of the fact. Had not that report something to do with the operations of the proverbially honest men who get the time o' day by looking up to the clock in Trinity church steeple [on Wall Street]?

WASHINGTON, 11 APRIL 1864 (PUBLISHED 14 APRIL 1864)

The past two weeks have been for the most part stormy and inclement, to such a degree as to render extensive army movements next door to an impossibility. The rain has fallen in torrents, and the roads have been rivers of mud. So you see that at the very outset of his career in Virginia, General Grant has been met by our old enemy in full force, for the red mud of the Old Dominion has from the first been as good as another army corps added to the strength of Lee's army. Mud it was that scared McClellan away from Manassas, crippled him on the Peninsula, delayed Burnside's pontoons, drove back one of Meade's advances, and did more than anything else to facilitate Lee's escape at Falling Waters, after the Gettysburg fight.

Still, I fancy that we shall find, ere long, that even this obstacle has not prevented our Western hero from completing the organization of his army, and preparing for those active movements which he is planning for the return of good weather. Like our farmers at home, he is busy getting his tools in order, mending his harness and his ploughs, and as his experienced eye tells him that "the ground is ready," you will see him a-field, and the furrow he will make will be a long and a deep one.

There is no use in being impatient: brave and prompt as Grant is, he will not run any unnecessary risks, when he has a certainty in his hands. He will not attack to-day with fifty thousand when he can do so to-morrow with a hundred thousand. The time has come for crushing work. Never before have we been able to concentrate our forces, or those of the enemy, into so narrow a space. Never before have they had so small an area to draw upon for supplies. Never before has either side been able to bring so well appointed and efficient an army of veterans into the field. The time which is to elapse between this and our next great battle is hourly growing shorter, and the army as well as the people are getting feverish about it. Trust me, it is a greater thing to the men on whom the fate of it depends, than it can be to those who are only to look on from a distance.

CONGRESS AND ITS DOINGS

We have lately had some singular occurrences in the House of Representatives. Such an unwonted degree of frankness on the part of the rebel sympathizers in that body was somewhat unlooked for, though it could not occasion much surprise among those who have watched the previous course of the two members from Ohio and Maryland. It is a comfort that the number of such men is very small, and is steadily decreasing. It is to be hoped that the whole North does not now contain a constituency who will knowingly send back to Congress a man who is openly in favor of the recognition of the Southern Confederacy. If there is such a constituency, it ought to emigrate to South Carolina in a body.

I have never been an admirer of Charles Sumner, but cannot help adverting to his able and eloquent speech in the Senate on the 8th inst.[12] It contains nothing which one could wish had been left unsaid—no acrimony, no bitter assaults on individuals; but enunciates principles which we cannot deny and long retain our freedom, or our existence as a nation.

MARYLAND FARMS

One of the signs of the times, which he who runs may read, is the positive increase in the value and price of real estate in Maryland. Sales have lately been made of several farms between here and Baltimore, at decidedly better prices than they could have touched in 1859 or 1860. Real estate in Baltimore itself has for some time been looking up, and all over the State there seems to be a vague yet hopeful impression of a "better time coming." And truly there is every reason to hope for a new era of progress and improvement for that old, but worn-out commonwealth. No, not worn out, either; it is more like a badly mismanaged estate, which a few years of wise and skillful care will easily develop into new wealth and beauty. To any one who has been over any considerable portion of Maryland and Virginia, it is a wonder that anybody ever went West while all this beautiful and fertile region—so admirably situated with reference to markets of all kinds, so well adapted to every class of farming enterprise—lay undeveloped, and much of it almost unoccupied. The soldiers say the same thing, and when the war is over they will see to it that this, and not this only, but many another possible paradise, no longer spreads its smiling acres begging for the sinews and the brains which are to make it bud and blossom as the rose.

THE SANITARY-COMMISSION MONEY

I have noticed in many papers lately very reasonable and temperately expressed inquiries as to what becomes of all the money given to the Sanitary Commission. There have been, of course, many answers, no doubt satisfactory, but it will do no harm if I add a bit of testimony from my own observation, having been so long in a pretty good position for taking notes. I have no long story to tell, only to say that if these honest inquirers could have seen, as I have, after many battle-fields, in many permanent hospitals, in the everyday accidents and discomforts of the soldier's life, everywhere, the outstretched hand of the Sanitary Commission, full of help, hope, and all kindness, they would glory in an institution which is so preeminently *Christian.*

WASHINGTON, 18 APRIL 1864 (PUBLISHED 21 APRIL 1864)

More rains and another instal[l]ment of mud *may* have interfered with Grant's plans somewhat; but then again they may not, for it is more than likely that he was not ready to strike in any direction yet. The sky still looks threatening, and we are hoping and praying for fair weather.

Perhaps some fireside tactician will say: "What, is Grant going to be defeated by McClellan's old bugbear? I thought *he* was made of different stuff." But did it never occur to you, dear critic, that perhaps in that one point every one has not been entirely just to McClellan? We will admit, if you wish, any number of faults in that commander, and even whisper the heresy that his "more successful successor" may not be quite perfect; but let me ask you if ever you ever helped pull a field-piece or an ammunition wagon through a slough of red-clay mud? Or did you ever march fifteen or twenty miles in such clinging stuff, carrying a soldier's load? No, you never did? Then keep still on that question until you have tried it; for you don't know what you are talking about. The new Commander-in-Chief is getting no end of advice, which he never sees, in the Northern newspapers. Some worthies hereabouts even pretend to interpret his plans with a good deal of accuracy. All very well, so long as *they* enjoy it; but for once the whole thing is encouragingly dark and incomprehensible. Having read his Chattanooga Report, and seen how he got out *that* plan, which was by no means a bad one, it seems like walking in a fog to predict what he will do now. Perhaps he does not know it himself as yet, but some fine morning, as in that case, he will see a weak point in Lee's lines, or some new way of combining our often repulsed forces so as to give them double power; and then the country will be electrified with the news of a great battle. God send that it be a great victory as well.

There are two phases of military doctrine afloat here now-a-days—both of which may be set down as correct, but only one of which can be put into practice. The first, sound enough, with an "if," is that the rebellion is growing rapidly weaker with the very efforts, desperate, exhausting, which it is making to maintain its military establishment. So are we, but we can stand it twenty years longer than they can. So if we did not strike another heavy blow, but acted on the defensive and Fabian policy, merely consolidating and perfecting our occupation of the regions we now hold, and driving in the smaller armies of the rebels, they must soon go under. All very true, but our people have not faith enough to wait, they *must* go in and finish the business. The other creed, the faith of Lincoln and Grant, is that every great battle, even if it is a drawn one, is a defeat to the rebels in its necessary consequences. A battle in which thirty thousand men a side were put *hors du combat*, killed, wounded and missing, but in which neither party could claim a victory, would, nevertheless, drive Lee back to the Lynchburg line, and place Richmond almost at our mercy. Such a thing is horrible to contemplate, but great and desperate battles must and will come.

The black-flag business seems to have been fairly begun by the rebel savages to whom Fort Pillow surrendered.[13] That due revenge will be taken for that massacre, with or without orders, is a foregone conclusion. Man for man, blood for blood, the terrible reckoning will be taken. Revenge—retaliation—is unchristian to the last degree, that is very true; but war is not a Christian institution in any point of view, and many of its *necessities* are as heathenish as the Tartar conqueror's monument of skulls.

Congress, spurred and stung on every side, is beginning to get a little ashamed of itself, and to promise better things. There were too many new men in it, and each man had his special bag of wind to empty. Many of them are manifestly relieved, and it may be that a few are dimly conscious that they have not been doing all that they were sent here for.

A week or two more of gassy debate about abstractions, personal collisions, and the peculiar style of blackguardism which we may properly call "Congressional"—and all sorts of things going wrong. The Internal Revenue Bill will suit every class and trade in all its features but one, that one being the particular tax or duty which said class or trade must pay. The tendency in the House will be to increase rather than to diminish the items. The Tariff Bill will not be ready for some time, but I can assure the consumers of all things foreign that they must pay high for their tastes hereafter.

The social amusements of Washington are fast "drying up." One by one the receptions, the lions, &c. are going to the wall, and there will be nothing to fill their places. It is actually Spring once more—and Summer is coming.

WASHINGTON, 2 MAY 1864 (PUBLISHED 5 MAY 1864)
And we have had May Day—the day of traditional flowers and dances. It is true that the trees are full of buds and blossoms, and some are even putting out their small green leaves to make sure of the spring, and a few adventurous birds are singing, now and then, but it must be from a sense of duty, for the day had no spring sunshine in it, nor any temptations to make music. It is not altogether because it is cold and raw and chilly, after a heavy rain in the night, or that the clouds cover the sky grimly from horizon to horizon; but it is more than this, because somehow or other we have all made up our minds that the veil of secresy which covers Grant's plans and movements will soon be rent asunder, and all will be made plain to us by the red light of terrible battle-fields. This oppressive sense of something coming—this pause and hush before the coming of the hurricane, is really something dreadful. The excitement of waiting for slow-coming despatches from the battle is not more exhausting or depressing. And yet it may be

days and days before we hear that anything has stirred. It *may* be, however, that your readers will have heard of some great fight before this letter is laid before them.

OUR SILENT-WORKING GENERAL

A strangely unostentatious, silent-working man, is this same Lieutenant-General of ours, from whom we all expect so much. The troops have imbibed a singular degree of confidence in him already. There is a kind of mystery about him. He comes and goes silently, disturbing nothing, disquieting nobody. No long train of staff officers gallops and jangles at his heels. No one, not the knowingest of newspaper men, dare pretend to a knowledge of his plans; every one would laugh at the pretence; and yet all things move and change about with wonderful celerity, and his orders are obeyed with a sort of inward conviction that they *mean* something. Now this man Grant may be beaten in the coming struggle. Lee may be proved the better general, and our forces may be hurled back on the defences of Washington once more, and the personal reputation won at Vicksburg and Chattanooga may be lost among these terrible Virginian hills; but it will be a fearful surprise to the men who have seen this silent, shabby-looking genius take hold of this army. Perhaps we are too confident; we have been so once or twice before; but we cannot help it. The General has such confidence in himself, that all other men around him "do as he does." It is a grand thing, yet a terrible [one], to be the commander of all these magnificent armies, and to order so many gallant men to march to suffering and death. Do the ghosts from lost battle-fields ever come back to trouble the souls of unsuccessful or incompetent commanders? If so, how can such, and such, and such an one ever sleep?

THE PEOPLE'S REPRESENTATIVES

Congress seems determined to mix up useless and even disgraceful matters with its more important duties. Will they never learn to rise above such things, these Representatives of the People? I fear not. The assault on the Treasury the other day may end in good, after all. Some minor corruptions may be exposed, and sundry petty scandals brought to light; all the better, for if they are concealed they cannot be corrected. But if the Committee do their work well, it cannot fail to be seen that, on the whole, there has been great, though unrewarded honesty, under signal temptations, and that honesty alone, and not our boasted system of "checks and balances," has preserved the public money during the enormous disbursements of the past three years. Among other things not to be despised, Congress is at last bestowing some little attention upon the cleanliness and convenience of this most uncleanly, unhealthy, and ill-conditioned "metropolis."

THE TIMES' HEAVY NOTHINGS

By the way, have you noticed the London *Times* of late on the Danish war, spreading its heavy nothings over six and seven mortal columns of report and comment upon what would, in *our* war, be an almost unnoticed skirmish?[14] This, it is to be presumed, is *sci-* [some words illegible] do the thing in Europe, where they know all about it; but how long would they have been in getting to the top of Lookout Mountain or Missionary Ridge, at this rate? Can it be possible that the school of the great Frederick, and the super-disciplined hosts of Austria, and it may be of *other* trans-Atlantic powers, have anything to learn from "half-trained irregulars" like ours? Forbid it, Pipeclay! Forbid it, ye "numismatic" bosoms of generals who never saw a battle!

THAT MEXICAN "EMPIRE"

It takes a long time to get that new Mexican Empire in running order. If greater haste is not made, we may be out of our own troubles first, and have a large army and navy on our hands, anxiously inquiring among themselves as to the nature of the Monroe Doctrine. Perhaps that is what Louis Napoleon and the little new Emperor are waiting for. If we are badly beaten, Maximilian's crown will put on a brighter lustre;[15] but if by any chance the rebellion gets the worst of it in the grand tug, the new Mexican Loan will be slow of sale—unless it be in exchange for Confederate Cotton Bonds.

WASHINGTON, 16 MAY 1864 (PUBLISHED 19 MAY 1864)

Heavy rains have for several days seriously interfered with military movements. They could not prevent fighting in the front, but have rendered the roads from Fredericksburg to the front, bad enough at any time, almost impassable for heavy trains or artillery. Even the ambulances have had a slow time of it in getting through, adding to the fatigue and suffering of our thousands of wounded. Now, as so often before, we are thankful for our control of the river, as it saves us fifty miles of land transportation. The boats run to Belle Plaine, and from there the road is good to the crossing at Fredericksburg. It is now not too early to make comments and answer criticisms on the management of this wonderful campaign.

THE CRITICS OF THE CAMPAIGN

The most frequent query that I have heard, is, "Why did not Grant, if he had two hundred thousand men, or more, in Virginia, concentrate them, and crush Lee's army at once?" At a superficial examination this does seem a sound criticism, but on a closer look at the map and the record, we find that the nature of the ground, and the character of the enemy's position is such that at no time has Grant been able to employ at once nearly all the troops he had with him, and was able constantly to bring supports and reinforcements from the large reserves he actually had; and the fact that Lee was similarly circumstanced is one reason for the prolonged and bloody character of this struggle. Now, at the last, when he really desires fresh troops, he has only to draw on the troops who held his lines of communications from the Rapidan to Washington, and the heavy reserves of infantry and artillery here and in Maryland; and in a sufficiently brief time his battered antagonist will be dismayed by the approach of unbroken, unwearied columns of veterans, eager to emulate their comrades, and whose full ranks have not as yet been weakened by battle. The result is by this management placed beyond the region of doubt, so far as human eyes can foresee.

It is also to be borne carefully in mind that the destruction of Lee's army is only a portion of the spring campaign in the East. I do not wish, even by implication, to accuse our great Captain of arrogance, but I am well assured that from the first Grant has had no serious doubts that he should defeat his opponent. Therefore, while holding his collateral columns well in hand, until the result was reasonably sure, he has so disposed of them that they will be in positions to best assist him in reaping the full results of his central success. It will yet be seen, as a consequence of this, that no considerable portion of the rebel army will get away; that with Richmond will fall Lynchburg; and that with the Old Dominion we shall recover North Carolina, and *promptly occupy* it, with an army that by that fact instantly threatens the South Carolina border.

Am I prophesying too much? I think not. It may take some time yet to complete the victory over Lee; but the longer the delay the more complete the achievement.

THE ENEMY DESPERATE

A queer saying is attributed to the Lieutenant-General; it is said that in the third day's fight he turned to Gen. Meade, standing by him, thus: "Well, Meade, if they are going to make a Kilkenny cat affair of this, our cat has got the longest tail." Whether he said it or not, it is not a bad illustration of the present position, or of the whole war itself. Accustomed as Lee has been to see our troops fall back after a great battle, or to be allowed to retreat in safety, it must have been a bewildering thing to be thus clung to with deadly and desperate pertinacity, day after day, and to find columns that had fought him all day, charging "home" again *after sunset*. His various attempts to retreat have all been thus baffled, and he has at last turned desperately at bay. We know very well how dangerous is the despair of such men under such a leader. We know that a stern contest is yet before us, but under the circumstances we think the end secure. Any ordinary man in Lee's position would feel like giving the matter up; but not so the indomitable Virginian. No man can avoid a feeling of admiration for him and his rebel battalions. Beaten for ten days, and ready to fight again on the eleventh! There are no other troops on earth that could have stood up to the work of death as both sides have during the past fortnight. It is more than ever evident that we are in the last death-struggle. That army of veteran soldiers cannot be replaced by the Confederacy. In disabling so many as we already have done, we have rendered Virginia almost untenable. If they could retreat and get away, they would, and trust to the future for a better chance to redeem their fortunes; but they cannot.

BUTLER AND HIS WORK

You see that I say little about Butler and his movements. His part is a subordinate one, and he never was expected to strike a great blow. The rebels at Richmond will be in a trap when Lee is beaten, and whether they stand a siege or not, they are doomed to capture or destruction.

SHERMAN AND HIS CAMPAIGN

Reports come more slowly from the West. Sherman has a most difficult and dangerous country to operate in, and his opponent can easily retire before him, and draw him into the open country. But this will matter little. There can surely be little gained by the enemy in surrendering half of Georgia into our hands, as they must do if they are driven back on Atlanta. The campaign in the West will be drawn out into the summer, unless our Eastern successes are sufficiently great to precipitate the end of the war. That is not impossible, but it is not probable. Be our victories what they may, it will require all the remainder of this year to gather in their harvest.

HOPE AND ANXIETY

With faith, with hope, but nevertheless with deep and heartfelt anxiety, we now look forward to the end. "It is not now so distant as it was." Every minute, marked sadly by the death of a hero, brings us nearer to the goal. But if any man is inclined to intemperate or unseemly rejoicing, he should come with me to the wharf and see the wounded disembark, or walk to the hospitals with the hundreds of tearful people who are hunting for their own among the suffering and dying. It is a glorious time, true, but a very sad one.

THE SCAVENGERS DISAPPOINTED

Much evil talk and scandal has been caused of late by supposed developments of crime and corruption in the Treasury Department; but an investigation does not seem to gratify the prurient appetites of those who looked for and prophesied so much that was evil. In fact, there is a general feeling of relief, among decent people, as they discover how very little can really be proved. A portion of the public press, never devoted to public morals, except as scavengers, is busily publishing all that is bad, and suppressing all refutation; but all that must and will have a reaction. Indeed, I should not mention this here, if they had not striven to fasten the sins of individuals upon the Administration, and to make of private scandal a national disgrace.

AN OLD BUILDING COMING DOWN

Preparations are being made for the demolition of the old State Department building, and for the completion of the north wing of the Treasury building, whose magnificent proportions will thus include rather more ground, in addition to the present structure, than is now occupied by the old "grey brick." There are many associations connected with that (for America) ancient and modest-looking affair on the corner by the President's house. Webster, and Marcy, and a long list of our distinguished names, have by turns ruled in its shabby halls and offices, and from there have sent out documents to determine peace or war, and influence the destiny of nations and races.[16] No doubt, future history will unearth strange things from the musty piles of documents stored away in those dusty archives.

HOW RETALIATE?

Now that Messrs. Wade and Gooch have made their terrible report about the Fort Pillow tragedy, the question is, "How shall we retaliate?" and few believe that our merciful and kindly Chief Magistrate can so far harden his heart as to do justice to these offenders against all laws, human and divine.[17] The retaliation will come, however, and it is a relief to be certain at the same time that nothing will be done in cruel and heathenish revenge, and that what is done will be in such a manner that the whole civilized world will be compelled to approve the sentence and its execution.

WASHINGTON, 23 MAY 1864 (PUBLISHED 26 MAY 1864)

We have had another week of suspense, anxiety and doubt, varied by bloody but indecisive engagements at various points. To-day, on a careful review of all, I am satisfied that the results have been largely in our favor. The only drawback worth noticing is on the Peninsula, where Butler is fast losing whatever of reputation as a General he may have heretofore acquired.[18] If we may credit what we hear from unofficial sources, he has at last found himself in a position where self-will does not supply the place of knowledge, experience, and military ability. He has, however, thanks to the services of his corps-commanders, accomplished all that will for the present be asked of him, and need now only wait patiently for the completion of Grant's other plans.

NORTHERN GEORGIA OURS

In the West, the operations sketched in my last have gone forward satisfactorily, and Northern Georgia, including all the mountain country, and the important positions lately held by the enemy, are in our possession. Evidently the campaign in the West will be prolonged and tedious, but Gen. Sherman has only to go on as he has begun, and the end is secure.

RUMORS OF DISASTER SCATTERED

From Arkansas and Louisiana the latest returns scatter to the winds the hideous rumors of disaster set on foot by Wall street stockjobbers. The day must come when these latter gentry must be brought to a terrible pecuniary judgment. One grand success will break down the wall of incredulity and fear which they have so studiously built up, and in its fall it will crush many of those who now make fancied fortunes under its shadow.

THE GREAT CENTRAL CONTEST

But to return to the centre of military operations and of national interest. If any spectator can form a fair idea of the plans and purposes of a General so wonderfully reticent, so closely secret in all his ways, we may conclude that Grant has very far from thrown away these few days of sunshine and good roads. This is evident, if from nothing else, from the continual dashes made by Gen. Lee—always at large expense of men whom he can ill spare at this time—with the manifest purpose of unmasking the position and movements of our forces. He sees, as clearly as his great adversary, that a death grapple is steadily approaching, and well will it be for him if he can discern the where and the when of our attack. I firmly believe that he will not be able to do this—that night, and darkness, and storms, and skillful maneuvers, will be made to cover from all eyes the direction of our heaviest columns, and the thunderbolt will fall in an unexpected quarter.

No doubt but that the good generalship of Lee has thus far done much to retard and disconcert our movements, but not enough to more than delay the final catastrophe. As firmly as ever do I believe that only a broken and beaten fragment of the rebel host will ever be allowed to leave Virginia, unless we are unexpectedly overcome in the trial of strength itself, and that can hardly be.

It is a significant fact that the Richmond papers, preeminent for rhodomontade and simulated self-confidence, are beginning to assume an anxious tone, to admit heavy losses, and to make unwonted admissions as to the bearing and consequences of the battles now being fought. They do not yet see the handwriting on the wall, but through the delirium of their dreams of empire, something like a hand beginning its work is becoming visible to them. When the writing is finished, they will need no Daniel to interpret the terrible vision of defeat and ruin.

But there are good reasons for their refusal to believe as yet that the great defeat is before them. Lee still stands behind his well-drawn lines of earthworks, stubborn, determined—a lion at bay—surrounded by veterans of many fields, who have rarely known defeat, and who have by no means lost any portion of heart or hope. They know that he will fight with more than his usual ability and courage; they know that General after General, whom we have sent against him, has, after a more or less prolonged struggle, withdrawn battered and broken columns to the safe shelter of the Washington defences. They believe that the present will be like the past, and their faith will not waver until they actually know that all is over.

And, after all, there is a possibility of our repulse; there may come a contingency that will render victory incomplete or worthless. We must not school ourselves to an overweening confidence, nor pin our faith to any gasconading bulletin, sent by excited officers in the heat and hurry of temporary success; but when, if ever, the silent man at the head of the army turns from his absorbing duties, and tells the nation that all is safe, we may believe *that*. Delays may come, but they cannot now be greatly prolonged.

In the political world matters move slowly. The Baltimore Convention is getting closer at hand; but all excitement connected with it is disappearing, now that we know that it can have but one result.[19] Some interesting scenes there will be; some eloquent speeches; some "side shows;" and then Mr. Lincoln will be unanimously nominated, and the nation will breathe a trifle freer.

The new delegation from Arkansas has arrived, and are of about the average Congressional stamp of men.[20] They were elected by a large vote, and it is generally thought that there will be no great amount of opposition to their reception as representatives from that State. Whatever opposition they do meet with, will come from men who have allowed "State suicide" or "territorializing" theories to run away with their common sense. There will be one State more permanently restored to the Union, to freedom, and to civilization, by the action of its own people.

THE SOLID RESULTS

We should not, in our hours of despondency, overlook the *solid* results of our three years of war and sacrifice. If, in the providence of God, we are yet compelled to recognize the independence of a portion of the Confederacy, as a punishment for our sins, or a consequence of our want of faith and endurance, we may now be sure that the Gulf States alone, not including Louisiana, will ever be so surrendered. The mere statement of this proposition would seem to indicate the impossibility of any such termination of this struggle. The South will never consent to that, and we will never give up what we now hold; and so the war must go on until a more favorable result for one or the other is obtained, even if a brief interval of cessation from fighting should be dignified with the name of a "peace."

There is good reason to hope that the week upon which we are entering may be rendered memorable by achievements that will relieve us forever from the imagination of any such disastrous future.

WASHINGTON, 30 MAY 1864 (PUBLISHED 2 JUNE 1864)

The past week has been a variable one, but on the whole not unfavorable to military operations. Both armies have been straining every nerve, and watching each other's every movement with the sleepless eyes of men who know that blunders now on either side might bring the most fatal consequences. In the war of strategy, Gen. Grant has undoubtedly beaten his antagonist, and has apparently forced him into a most dangerous and uncomfortable position. When Lee was at Spottsylvania he had all Virginia behind him, but the case is different now. It seems that he has but three courses open to him. Either to gather all the spare troops in Richmond, and give Grant a battle, hoping to defeat him, which is the likelier step for the rebel chief to take; or in the second place to retreat on Lynchburg, if Grant will let him, with as much of his army as he can get away; or in the third place, if he should turn ever so little insane and retreat into Richmond, to be surrounded and starved out *a la Vicksburg*. It cannot now be long before we receive decisive news one way or the other, for Gen. Grant is a man who dislikes pauses, and who will give his enemy less rest than Noah's dove had, so long as he has the power to assail him. His power in that respect, I may add, is little diminished from what it was when he crossed the Rapid Ann. The flow of reinforcements has been steady, and has had a valuable effect in keeping up the high spirits of the army. Nor should we overlook the character of the reinforcements sent. A large proportion are veteran *regiments*, and the so-called *new* regiments are anything but raw militia. A good deal has been said in the papers about our "raw troops" beating Ewell's veterans in one of the Wilderness fights; all nonsense—those raw troops had nearly all served before as one year, two years' and three years' volunteers, and were in glorious condition after their self-terminated furloughs. It is worthy of remark, also, that there are a good many such men among the "hundred days" militia from Ohio, and other States, who have been coming in here for several days. Any man who sees them march can pick out those who have served before, and thankful enough we should be that we find so many. They are a seasoning which makes all the rest of the regiment they are in of greater value in a battle.

THE GEORGIA CAMPAIGN

Sherman seems to be doing a great work in the West. All that terrible mountain country which has cost us so much toil and blood is now in our possession, we believe permanently. Still, a long campaign is no doubt before us ere we can call ourselves masters of Georgia. Our people should not deceive themselves; the day of sacrifice and trouble has not yet gone by, though the end is evidently fast approaching.

OUR WOUNDED HEROES

Here in Washington we are busy with the sick and the wounded. The hospitals are full, and even with all the preparation so wisely made, we are not always able to do as much as we wish for the brave sufferers. And they are brave—worthy of as high a praise, as sincere an admiration, for their conduct in the hospital as in the field. They are almost universally patient, with few complaints, unselfish, bearing pain with heroic fortitude, and rarely, if ever, expressing any regret for the sacrifices they have made. Glorious fellows! and what a confidence, almost amounting to fanaticism, many of them are acquiring in their successful leader! They do not believe that Lee will be able at any time, or in any place, to prove himself a match for General Grant. They will follow him anywhere, and attempt any undertaking, however seemingly difficult, to which he may order them.

A REBEL PRISONER'S QUANDARY

Very different is the state of feeling among the rebel prisoners. Numbers of them want to be released under the amnesty proclamation, and join our troops. These may be conscripted Union men, for the most part; but a good many are original secessionists, who are now weary of the war, and who no longer believe in the success of the Confederacy. Even among those who will betray no symptom of a desire or intention of abandoning their ill-starred flag, there are many who have no longer any hope that it will not soon go down. One of these latter, a war-battered veteran of Longstreet's Corps, made a funny remark to a friend of mine, a prominent politician, who conversed with him while coming in from the front. Said he, "I do not understand all this: Lee won a big victory over Grant on the Rapid Ann, and told us so, and that night we retreated. Then he won another in the Wilderness, and told us so, and we retreated to Spottsylvania. Then he won another tre-*men*-jus victory, and I got tuk prisoner; but I reckon he has retreated agin. Now, when we *used* to lick them, the Yanks fell back and claimed a victory, and we understood it. Now Lee claims victories and keeps a fallin' back, and I *can't understand it.*"

The fact is, that it is very hard for any commander long to deceive his own soldiers as to the real nature of their operations. The veterans of both these armies have seen too many victories and defeats not to know pretty accurately "which is which;" and an army which *feels* whipped, is twice beaten.

Our rebel prisoners, despite the frequent insufficiencies in their toilets, are a fine-looking set of men for fighting purposes—the very men to make an army out of; and the rebel chiefs did make a splendid army out of them; and it goes to one's heart to think how many of these deceived and misguided men we have got to destroy before we can hope for a permanent peace.

THE TARIFF-BILL

Congress has at last got to the discussion of a tariff-bill, and again the delegations are beginning to come on, each to get some one of the many interests off as easily as possible. It is of no use, however—"heavy is the word;" and the only question is, whether Congress will not raise the figures reported by the committees. They certainly ought to do so, and that with an unsparing hand.

WASHINGTON, 6 JUNE 1864 (PUBLISHED 9 JUNE 1864)

The campaign has, as I prophesied in a former letter, dragged its inevitable length into the summer. I do not believe that General Grant ever expected any other result, or that he shared at all in the delusion about "cleaning out Virginia in sixty days." He is too sober, too cool, too farsighted to be deceived or unduly elated by partial success. It is possible, but not at all probable, that by some error, some gross military blunder, such as he has rarely committed hitherto, General Lee may lay himself open to a sudden and crushing blow. If he would do so, no doubt that Grant will promptly take advantage of it. In default of any such golden opportunity, I can see no reason why Lee may not retain his Richmond position until he is slowly hammered out of it by days and days, it may be *weeks* of hard fighting. That hard pounding is now going on all the time, with a steadily increasing advantage to us. The steady courage of the enemy is wonderful, but they well know that they must win this fight or go under. Still, they must begin to lose somewhat of their confidence. They know very well that our reinforcements are constantly coming up, and that we are as strong as ever. They are no doubt well informed as to our strength, and the condition of their own diminished columns must be such as to fill them with the most gloomy forebodings. Still, they are well supplied, their defences are strong and well built, and they know very well that they can hold their own for some time to come, and in the meantime they may hope for some grand changes in the position of affairs—a vague something which may make us weak and them strong.

Perhaps there could not be a more exact parallel to the campaign in the East than the campaign in the West. Sherman also has beaten the enemy out of his strongest military defences, after hard fighting, and is now pressing him home, and bringing up his reinforcements for the last prolonged and bloody struggle. What is true of Grant and *his* campaign is to a remarkable extent true of Sherman and his. The same difficulties are still before them, and they will both move steadily forward with the same fixed determination to win.

The statements of the rebel press concerning the daily occurrences of the war, as we obtain them from time to time, confirm me in an old theory, that there are men born into this world with a "genius for lying"—men mighty in untruth, and strong in an evil ability to produce plausible falsehood. Such men now control the rebel press and pulpit. If untruth is a power in the world, what a tremendous reinforcement they are bringing to the aid of the sinking Confederacy!

Here, in Congress, a good deal of work is being done, and questions of the last importance are beginning to loom up. The tariff and the revenue bills still linger in the hands of our Representatives, and progress only too slow towards completion. At the same time, the question as to the future management of States which have been or now are in a state of rebellion, is becoming immediate and practical. If the Arkansas delegation is admitted into the Senate and House, the President's moderate and liberal policy is endorsed, and the way is clear; if they are rejected, it will look very much as if Congress condemned the Amnesty Proclamation, and the future treatment of those States becomes food for debate, and a wide field full of doubt and danger is opened in our future. I do not mean to say that there are not better plans than the one proposed by the President; he may have other ideas of his own yet to present. Moreover, the present condition of our trans-Mississippi Department is anything but satisfactory, and Gen. Canby may find that he is as yet unable to restore that degree of peace and order which should belong to a regenerated State.[21]

The Baltimore Convention has less attention here and is creating less excitement than one would imagine because its most important action is considered a foregone conclusion. There is some question as to who shall be Vice-President, but there will hardly be a dissenting voice to Mr. Lincoln's nomination. Other bodies, and some "dis-embodieds," will meet in the same city at the same time; and it remains to be seen whether they will be able to create any considerable amount of excitement or disturbance. It is a very singular manifestation of the confidence of the people, this renomination under such singular circumstances. The many inevitable errors in the conduct of the war are all apparently understood, and attributed to the proper persons. The people will not cast upon the head of their favorite the corruptions of subordinates whom he never saw, or contractors whose affairs he never heard of. They seem to have made up their minds deliberately to elect the President this time themselves, and we shall hear their voice on the subject in the Convention this week.

WASHINGTON, 20 JUNE 1864 (PUBLISHED 23 JUNE 1864)
The weather for the past week has been singular—mostly cool, favorable to military operations, with one or two sultry days, and no rain. It is to be noted, however, that, by some mysterious operation of natural causes, these cool days have been most unfavorable to health; and that the number of sick on the army returns, and of deaths in the hospitals, was materially and markedly increased by them, while among civilians "everybody is complaining."

GRANT'S GREAT MOVEMENT
Grant's new flank movement has thus far been a great military success, in the secresy, rapidity, and admirable order with which it has been executed. Future students of the art of war will eagerly examine the manner in which so large an army was transferred to a new scene of operations, in face of a

brave, powerful, and skillful enemy, in so short a time, and without loss or hindrance. When our great Captain has fully attained his new lines, I do not hesitate to say that his very position will be a disaster to the enemy. It may lead to the most desperate efforts by Lee to extricate himself; it may bring on the most sanguinary battles of the war; but at one stroke of daring and genius we have the rebels at a disadvantage. Now truly comes the tug of war, and the whole campaign, with all its already terrible cost, and all its tremendous possibilities, hang suspended upon the operations of the next thirty days.

There is no necessity for Lee to strike at once, for he undoubtedly has large supplies of all kinds laid up in Richmond, and he will be likely to watch and wait for a favorable opportunity, rather than risk all upon one or two battles. In either case the chances are against him. I hope he reads the Richmond *Examiner*, and the different rebel papers published in New-York, for it must be such a comfort to him to know from *reliable* sources that we have lost a hundred thousand men since we crossed the Rapid Ann; that our soldiers are discontented, and deserting; that they have lost confidence in Grant; that all the veterans are going home; that he will have little to fight besides militia, foreigners, and negroes; all of which triumphant facts are fully set forth, beyond all shadow of a doubt, in these various prints. I say I hope he *reads*; because if he will only believe, and *act* on his belief, it would be such a good thing for us.

A LOOK INTO OTHER FIELDS

In other fields our armies, all reports to the contrary notwithstanding, have steadily progressed. Johnston seems still to be slowly "drawing Sherman on to destruction," leaving in his hands occasionally, "as a bait," a few guns, a few hundred prisoners, some fortified positions, and about one-third of the State of Georgia. A friend complained to me once that he had wasted a whole lobster to catch one blackfish with, and *didn't get him after all.* The rebel General must look out for *his* lobster, or he may share the same sort of disappointment.

Nor should we overlook the improving condition of the trans-Mississippi country. The guerillas are bad enough, to be sure; but the large force which met Banks has either melted away, or split up into small fragments to procure its own supplies. Banks's defeat was, superficially viewed, a military accident.[22] The enemy could not have kept so large a force before him many weeks, and a General who has *time* on his side need never be entirely defeated. As to the guerillas, I have good reason to believe that Gen. Canby has very correct notions as to the proper method of dealing with them, and is determined to apply his sovereign specific as speedily as possible. The admission of the Tennessee, Louisiana and Arkansas delegations to the National Convention was in part a vote of confidence in Canby—the expression of a belief in the speedy pacification of that department.

WHAT BLACK MEN THINK AND DO

Speaking of the black troops, however, it is found not to be such good fun to fight them as was originally supposed. These "spiritless brutes"—"crushed by long servitude and plantation toil"—"peaceful by nature, and destitute of all the elements of the soldier"—have somehow been waked up to a terribly aggressive military manhood. Can it be possible that the mere idea of liberty for themselves and their children makes these follows so good at the bayonet? Can it be that *they*, the degraded, the downtrodden, the mere "cattle" of so much legislation and of so much commerce—that *they* can feel any generous enthusiasm for a Government and a people who are doing so much for them? Of course not! The white man monopolizes all these finer and better feelings, and the negro I was talking with the other day was only a parrot. I will tell you a part of what he said. It was at Barnum's Hotel, Baltimore. Noticing that I was wonderfully well waited on by several darkie friends, I began a chat with one of them. "Oh, yes, massa, we knows you: we *heerd* you at de contraband camp; we knows who *you* is." In this he was referring to some humble efforts of mine a year or so ago. "Oh, yes, we is all here *now*, but we is going out to help Grant pretty soon. Most all de rest of us has gone. We knows very well what it all means, and *you see if de black man can't fight for dose men as be fighting for him.*" The good fellow's face had been all smiles till this last, which closed the conversation, and then it darkened into an expression of the sternest resolution, and the black face wore an expression that would have added a dignity to the purest Caucasian lineaments.

The fact is, then, that the men who have all their lives carried napkins are not thereby unfitted to carry the bayonet. And herein is a great political secret. Herein lies the ability of the United States to carry on this war indefinitely, and should we *not* succeed in breaking the strength of the rebellion before January next, there is that vitality, that force, in the President's policy of employing the black men, that will at the worst go far to make up all losses, and that must eventually set the seal of success upon his efforts to save the nation. It must be a bitter pill to the proud aristocrats of Virginia and the Carolinas to weigh their lives in the fearful balances of war against those of men who were once their property. There will be a great deal of that weighing done before this year is over.

THE NOMINATIONS

The past few days have been truly important ones. In the first place, the supporters of the Government—call them a "party," if you will—who met in Convention at Baltimore, have declared the will and determination of the people, in terms honorable to themselves and to the nation. The future historian, writing of the third year of the great civil war, will find few parallels to the moral grandeur of the position assumed by this Convention. It is evident that the people are firm—firmer than ever before, better grounded in the right, and as ready as ever to sacrifice and suffer. We have a right to be proud of all this, even if the worst should yet come. That the candidates thus nominated will be elected there can be very little doubt, but the nature and degree of opposition to them will be greatly influenced by the events of the next four months.

THE CONGRESSIONAL WORK

Congress is busily at work, with very little genius, a good deal of confusion of ideas, an immense amount of want of information, but a very general patriotic desire to do its best for itself and the country. The tendency is to increase rather than diminish every tax or duty, a tendency zealously fostered by Secretary Chase, who is justly alarmed at the slow motion of that very heavy body towards the end of securing a sufficient revenue. The tax bills "will come, however, and come to stay, and so come as to be worth the having." Indeed, it is evident that one of the points upon which party lines will hereafter be drawn will be the permanence or speedy extinguishment of the public debt, and our best economists are of opinion that we might pay very nearly all our current expenses, if we really made the effort. It is a pity we did not sooner discover and act upon this very important truth. Well would it be for us if our legislators had the nerve to act upon it *now*.

WASHINGTON, CA. 3 JULY 1864 (PUBLISHED 7 JULY 1864)

After some days of great heat, a thunderstorm has left us a deliciously cool and cloudy morning. It is a good day for a retrospect—quiet, undisturbed by even a rumor. This day one year ago and we were, as now, waiting for news from Grant, and Vicksburg was within twenty-four hours of a surrender. One year ago, at the hour that I am writing, the armies of Meade and Lee were closing, under dense clouds of dust and smoke, in the final struggle for the great victory at Gettysburg. We can all recall the intense anxiety, the torturing suspense, with which we waited. Our very hearts seemed to be stilled to listen. Rumors of every sort and size seemed to fill the air. On that day the tide of victory turned against the rebellion, never more to ebb northward.

Then, however, as now, many hearts, even of the bravest and most patriotic, were full of doubt and trouble. The prospects of the country were dark indeed, for Chancellorsville had followed in the track of Fredericksburg, gold had gone up to an immense premium, there were constant rumors of foreign interference, the opponents of the Administration were in power in the North, and it seemed as if the very existence of the Republic was in danger. Well, that cloud lifted in flashes of glorious sunshine, and the Fourth of July was decorated with hundreds of captured flags and cannon, and many thousand rebels passed the anniversary under the old flag, as prisoners.

Now again, to-day, matters look a little dark. Again there are faint rumors of foreign trouble. We fear that our friends in England are going out of power; Sherman has been temporarily checked; Marmaduke has overrun Arkansas, and threatens Missouri; Grant lingers, without as yet a decisive success, before the stubborn defences of the rebel capital; again gold is at an enormous premium, and again the people murmur under their heavy burden of loss and sorrow.[23] This time we may not hope for tidings of great victories on the ever-glorious Fourth; but thinking deeply the thoughts that belong to the day, the people will pray to the God who made us a free people, and, as in times past, He will answer us with bright successes.

GRANT'S PLANS AT WORK

In the meantime, according to the best information that I can procure, the siege of Richmond progresses *well*. It must be a work of time, but, as on previous occasions which you may remember, I think I see what Grant is a[i]ming at, and the plan seems to involve a grand and complete success. I do not believe, as I said three months ago, that Lee will ever carry more than a battered remnant of his once terrible army over the North Carolina border. If he does he must start soon, for time is an element now and forever against him. The desperate fights of the past ten days on the lines of the various railroads which supply Richmond, show how thoroughly Lee comprehends his danger, and how desperately he will "fend off." By the results of those fights we can also see how impossible it is for him, or any general, to protect such long lines of railroad against a numerous and well appointed cavalry, led by experienced and enterprising generals. If repaired, by painful labor and much sacrifice, in one place, they will be cut in another, and all the while the supplies of Lee's army will grow "small by degrees, and beautifully less."

He loses *men*, too, whom he cannot replace. Taking the reports and rumors most entirely favorable to him, he must by this time have lost a third of the army he commanded on the first of May. Taking, probably, a more correct estimate, we may say that all the reinforcements he has received leave him one-third short of his original strength. We, on the other hand, are very nearly as strong as ever, and can continually take the offensive, and fully protect any movements which Grant may inaugurate. In all soberness and moderation, we may say that unless something now unforeseen occurs—something on which we have no reason to count—there is no doubt of Grant's success in his present campaign.

CONGRESS, AND THE SECRETARY OF THE TREASURY

Congress is on the eve of an adjournment. Last night they remained in session until three o'clock in the morning. They have managed to put off so much important work, that now the cool weather is all wasted, they are compelled to sit up all night, in rooms whose stifling heat is momentarily increased by the blaze of their gas-lights and the presence of their crowds. It will always be so, for it is an established thing that Congressmen will and must do a given amount of mere talking.

Perhaps *the* event of the past week was the generally unexpected resignation of Mr. Secretary Chase.[24] The financial world do not seem to regard his retirement as a national calamity, and in a political point of view the general opinion here is that he has injured himself far more than any one else. The people are not in a temper to regard with favor any officer, civil or military, who "resigns in presence of the enemy without sufficient cause." Every one who knows anything at all about it, knows that Mr. Chase did not resign for any principle, or because any great measure of his had been defeated, or because the Government or Mr. Lincoln did not sustain him; but because *for once*, among so many thousand appointments, he could not have his own way. The people will in this matter approve of the course of Mr. Lincoln.

The first nomination for a successor was a deserved tribute to Mr. Chase's own State and to the War Democracy of the Union; the second is universally recognized as a selection eminently fit and proper to be made.[25] No man, however, can envy Mr. Fessenden his new position, taking it as he does at such a time, and burdened as it must be with such tremendous difficulties and responsibilities. If his somewhat feeble health, however, will only hold out, we all hope, here, for the very best results from his management of the national finances.

WASHINGTON, 11 JULY 1864 (PUBLISHED 14 JULY 1864)

I see by a little item in the last EXAMINER, that you are already aware that this is the last of my somewhat prolonged series of Washington letters. You will next hear from me from some point nearer the setting sun, for I should be sorry to sever entirely my long acquaintance with your readers. I began three years ago last May, and looking back to that time now, I can but think how strangely this day of rumor and panic and peril in which I am writing resembles the time of my beginning; for then, as now, the capital and its communications were threatened by armed masses of rebels. My own opinion is that it was then in far more real danger than at present, though even now it is difficult to be positive about anything but current facts, and the future is beyond the reach of prophecy.

This invasion of Maryland, well planned and admirably executed as it has been by the rebels, is obviously a desperate effort to create a diversion in Lee's favor, and force Grant to let go his hold, now tightening hourly upon the rebel capital.[26] The Virginia campaigns repeat themselves strangely in many particulars; and the same dangers, buried as we thought them under the red turf of old battlegrounds, arise again to mock us with the apparent barrenness of our hard-won victories. We have not yet forgotten the times when Stonewall Jackson and his men used to come down the Valley whenever McClellan moved southward; and if, as some rumors state, Lee himself has escaped from Richmond to join this movement, the great battle of the closing scenes of the war may give Maryland another name of terrible memory to add to South Mountain, Antietam, and Gettysburg. I do not, for my own part, at all believe that this desperate maneuver will succeed, and if it fails at all, it will be for the rebels a *great* failure. Its success now depends entirely on the events of the next, comparatively, few hours. Here, as at Richmond, *time* is against the rebels. The changing light on the dial of each succeeding day is in alliance with Freedom and the Union. Time, then, we are now gaining, and the opportunities for them to strike us a disastrous blow are passing rapidly away from them. Time will bring our reinforcements from the rising North. Time will reveal the whereabouts of Hunter, and complete other arrangements of offence and defence, of which, perhaps, the less said the better. Having the firmest faith in our success, not believing that Grant has made a great blunder, or Lee achieved a great advantage, I may add, *then* will come a retreat, and with it the last hope Lee may have of long continuing to retain his position at Richmond or in Virginia.

We shall see. The despatches are following each other thick and fast, and the leaves of this fearful history are being rapidly written out. I cannot yet, however, even in this hour of clouds and darkness, feel as I felt when, a private in the army, I paced the southern "draw" of Long Bridge, with a secesh picket in full view, at pistol shot distance, at the end of the bridge, and the rebel banner floating defiantly from the north gable of Arlington House. So it was when I began to write for THE EXAMINER. For many months after that the Potomac was closed against us, and Washington was almost as much a besieged city as Richmond is now. Since then how much has changed for the better, even if things are now "at their worst!" I will not recapitulate the changes; any war-map has them all shown upon its face. But, as I sit and write, I recall many strange things. The long lines of regiments pour in from "the uprising of a great people." The disgraced and panic-stricken multitudes, dripping in the rain, return from Bull Run. The white-faced messenger rides in to tell of Ball's Bluff. The many months go by while McClellan is preparing his grand army, while his brilliant but "invulnerable" staff gallop madly in all directions. Then came the embarkation of his troops for the Peninsula, and the long horrors of that campaign; the defeat of Pope, and the swarms of straggling runaways. Then, in endless train, the events that have brought us where we are.

Pardon me if I add here—for we all now have such memories—that with the changing pictures of this panorama come a host of brave and friendly faces of a long list of my highest prized and best, who will never come to any other muster until at that last, when God shall summon them. From Ellsworth to Dahlgren, all brave, all true, all noble—and all gone; and as I remember them, my blood quickens and my heart grows stronger; for I know, by the presence of so great a crowd of "witnesses," that our cause shall not now be brought to an evil end. Others have stepped into their places as they fell, and others will follow these in turn, if need be; and the glorious procession—so glorious, but so sad—will move on, until the world is certified that the soil they have sanctified shall never be given over to the slave and his driver.

The sinking of the *Alabama* has again stirred up the naval ideas of the Old World, and in mute amazement Europe looks on to see how helpless are its vaunted armaments.[27] We will teach them many another wholesome lesson before we are done with them. Has not somebody who thinks Secretary Welles an idiot, something to say against the *Kearsarge*? I think it would be safer to run down the *Alabama*, as slow, unarmed, and with nobody on board. All that story about her having guns was a mere trick of this Abolition despotism to deceive the people and reelect Mr. Lincoln; but it won't do, you know.

Now that Chase is gone out of power, it is astonishing how few there are who "ever thought him anything of a financier!" Let us be generous, if not just; he had much to contend with, and he strove nobly, earnestly, patriotically to do well for his country. He labored early and late, during all fortunes, careless, seemingly, of praise or blame. Admitting that he may have done some things unwisely, that he had some prominent faults as a financier, let us add that he now well deserves respect and affection from every man who ever really wished him to succeed in caring for the national finances.

The week before us will be a stirring and unsettled one, and the events must come upon us rapidly now. Perhaps by the end of it we shall have more light than now upon the pathway of the nation. If not, we must continue to "walk by faith," not doubting of the end. I am sorry that I shall not be here to act as chronicler, but in leaving this post of duty I do not mean that you shall have heard the last of ["]Illinois["].

WASHINGTON, CA. 2 OCTOBER 1864 (PUBLISHED 6 OCTOBER 1864)
After a long silence, enforced by illness and absence, I am glad to find myself writing to you again, being for a day or so at my old quarters. And yet I feel little of the glib satisfaction of the summer tourist, in recalling what I have taken note of in a long and somewhat eventful journey— down the Mississippi, up the White River, into the heart of the Southwest, and through the borders of pleasant Tennessee. All that could be seen, in passing through the peaceful States, was to a great extent "hum-drum" and "customary." The farmers were at work, the fields brightened with harvests, the cities echoed to the footsteps of busy, happy, and thriving multitudes. Peace was everywhere; and if the hand of war was in any way *felt*, it was at least *unseen*. Once on the Mississippi below Cairo, however, and new realities, such as I had seen before elsewhere, but none the less terrible, forced themselves upon me. I dislike exceedingly that muddy ditch called the "Father of Waters," with its serpentine channel and its endless scenery of sandbanks and cottonwood groves; but the romance of war-like history has now settled upon its banks, to ennoble it henceforth during all time. All the way down, the traveller sees the ruined villages; the chimneys standing like monuments above the cold hearthstones; the deserted plantations growing up again with cane and cottonwood; here and there battered earthworks, mournfully reminding him of a vain defence and a broken cause; places that were once young cities busy with traffic, with no boats waiting at the levee; a land stripped and peeled—its occupants, of all kinds, fearful, watchful, and with minds intent on the war alone and its belongings; the churches, the schoolhouses, always few, now deserted, and all their noble agencies no longer at work for good; "society," with its amenities and its civilizing influences, for the present destroyed or inactive.

But it is to little purpose to attempt a faint and inadequate picture of a region over which the feet of civil war have trodden. I would rather look forward to what seems the inevitable future of a country far richer in all resources, in all capacities for development and greatness, than I had ever before imagined.

My new home is to be at Little Rock, a pleasant town on a high bluff of the Arkansas river. It was the centre of that small and arrogant clique of rich aristocrats who so long misruled, and at last ruined this beautiful State; and their fine residences, with their surroundings, attest their wealth, now departed, and their refinement, whose intense selfishness destroyed itself.

The State of Arkansas presents every variety of topographical surface, from the swampy but rich lowlands by the Mississippi and the lower waters of its tributaries, to the somewhat mountainous country in the far interior. Most of the country is high, rolling, and well wooded—very fertile, and with an equable, healthful and delightful climate. The best lands exceed all others in the world in their capacity for producing cotton, and all the fruits and cereals of the temperate zone, while most of its roots and vegetables thrive well and give excellent returns to the agriculturist. There is plenty of coal, lead, iron, and other metals and minerals, while the waters of the Ouachita (Wachitaw), Arkansas, White, and St. Francis rivers offer easy transportation for the products of the fields they fertilize.

Of the larger portion of the former population, the less said the better, for there is little in them to attract any one but the very devoted missionary. There is, however, a large and powerful element that is better worthy of notice:—the farmers and others of moderate wealth, men whose habits of daily labor made them naturally Union men, and the steady enemies of the old aristocracy and their rebellion. I have been frequently asked, "Are these sufficiently numerous, brave, earnest and intelligent to form a safe basis or nucleus for a new and free commonwealth?" Undoubtedly they are, and they are now looking Northward and Eastward for the coming tide of free labor and free thought, which they believe will develop the grand capacities of their hills and valleys, and redeem Arkansas to civilization and progress forever. That such an immigration is to come I cannot doubt. Thousands of soldiers, at the end of the war, and other thousands who will hear from them of the new opportunity to acquire easy wealth, will soon settle in this State; and every man of them all, old settlers and new comers, will be imbued with a bitter hatred of slavery, of aristocracy, and of all who brought upon the country the manifold sorrows of the Great Rebellion. This is not anything in the way of a "prophecy;" it is rather a calculation, founded upon known social laws, aided a good deal by common arithmetic and actual knowledge of the place and the men. The same may be true, and probably is, of other Southern States, but I can only speak for the one I know most of.

I remember reading once, with a disposition to mark the passage thus (?), that during the desolations of the Thirty Years' War in Europe, in many districts wolves and other wild animals multiplied exceedingly, to a far greater number, indeed, than they ever attained before civilization had partially destroyed them; but I believe it now, for it is a fact that bears, deer, all feathered game, and the minor animals classed as "varmints," never were so numerous in the country between the White and Arkansas rivers as they now are. Indeed, sundry bears and deer did our steamer the honor to come down to the "water margin" and quiz her in a sort of half-inquiring, half-skeptical manner, that would have made the fortune of a cockney tourist. The fact is, a genuine black bear only needs an eye-glass and a little less retiring (into the canebrake) politeness.

At present, whether owing to military errors and indolence or not, the whole Southwest is overrun with guerrillas, in bands of from five men upwards; they say Kirby Smith has nearly twenty thousand, who wage an aimless and useless war, full of all war's cruelties and sins, and without any of its customary excuses.[28] This species of warfare is self-defeating, and in due time burns itself out, after destroying much and accomplishing nothing. This is the season for it, just as for certain kinds of game:—the grass is fair, the corn is ripe, the rivers are low and fordable, the season of labor is over, and all things are favorable to rapid movements and the easy support of small and moving armies. It is a pretty good time, too, to thrash them well, if our generals will be as wise as their half-armed and half-despised opponents. This great evil once fairly put down, as it must soon be, and a large portion of the Southwest will be quiet. It is a current belief there, that the more restless and ungovernable spirits will go West, or cross over into Mexico, to fight for one side or the other, or to betray both, as circumstances may indicate. I have little doubt that many dangerous men will relieve the quiet folk from the plague of their presence in this manner. They will seek the sheltering wilderness or the congenial anarchy, and the new civilization will have no need to charge itself with their restraint or extermination. It will not be difficult to deal with the less dangerous and more respectable quadruped "wild beasts."

I cannot now dwell upon the horrors suffered by the Unionists of Arkansas. You have heard from East Tennessee; paint that picture several shades darker, and say: "And this is the history of Arkansas during the war."

MEMPHIS, CA. 15 NOVEMBER 1864 (PUBLISHED 24 NOVEMBER 1864)
We have the news that the reelection of ABRAHAM LINCOLN is a *finality*, if that word will express my meaning; and the staunchest rebels are slowly beginning to comprehend that by this the door of hope is forever closed upon them. The doom of the Confederacy is thereby sealed, and the great stone of Lincoln's known policy is rolled across the mouth of the grave where it is buried, nor will any angels ever come to roll it away. Now that the future promises no compromise, and the whole North has again declared its intention to fight this fight out to the bitter end, the dullest and the bitterest are able to see clearly what that end must and will be.

And to a large and important class, especially in these intermediate, half-conquered States of Kentucky, Tennessee, Arkansas and others, this great stern fact comes home with convincing and controlling power. Useless now are any further sacrifices of property—worse than useless any further offerings of blood on the altar of the Southern Moloch. This is the beginning of the end, and in this the result can be more clearly seen than in Sherman's movements, Sheridan's victories, or even Grant's terrible grip on Richmond. The best of it will shortly appear, when, by a thousand indications, we shall be made aware that the people of the whole South see and understand that their last hope has faded with the setting star of the Peace Democracy.

As to matters here, there is little excitement except from rumors of a probable advance by Hood into this region of country, though no one seems able to say *why* that eminently unsuccessful General should so far oblige Sherman as to advance into West Tennessee.[29]

The general business of Memphis has been for a week in an excited state of activity, produced by the promulgation of the new "Treasury Regulations for the Cotton trade"—but the excitement is fast dying out, as all prudent and sensible men are beginning to see that the grand scheme so carefully prepared in Washington is a crude, useless, contradictory, inoperative humbug. Congress will have to tinker that business again. I am sorry for Secretary Fessenden, that he has made in this so signal a failure, the more as the fault lies rather in the law itself than in any measures he has taken in pursuance thereof. The host of cotton speculators, allured by the seeming promise of opening trade, will return home with empty pockets, and really they are to be pitied, for they have acted in good faith, relying on Government representations. If any man is making a fair living at home he had better stay and make it, for it is more than he can do in trying to manipulate cotton *here*.

The Mississippi and its tributaries are all very low, and numbers of steamboat accidents occur in consequence, but the rains are beginning earlier than usual, and we hope for a better state of things before long. A few weeks, and the guerrillas may give it up, for there will be no more boats aground for them to plunder and burn.

The city of Memphis, from which I write, has singular natural advantages, and the dullest man must see that it is destined to become a great commercial centre. It must eventually drain as large an area of rich country, almost, as that which has built up St. Louis. The location is healthy, and there are even some advantages in the way of beauty. The bluff is high, and though only partially sloped and paved for a *levee*, when that work is completed, the river-front of the city will present a most attractive spectacle. Nature has made her preparations here for a great city, nor do I doubt that in the resurrection of this shattered and ruined cotton world, the expectations of the most sanguine will be fully realized. Already capital and "business men" are beginning to come in from the North, of a different character from the camp followers of the "sutler" kind who are the curse of all garrison towns. In a few days I shall start for White River, and you will hear from me next from among the cane-brakes.

AT THE MOUTH OF THE WHITE RIVER, ARKANSAS, CA. 25 NOVEMBER 1864
(PUBLISHED 8 DECEMBER 1864)

If there is anything in this work-a-day world lazier than steamboating at low water, it must be flat-boating. We left Memphis yesterday morning, and after the rather badly acted farce of pretending to search our baggage had been gone through with by the "Treasury Aid," we pursued our slow way down the river, with a coal barge in tow.

Cargo, crew and passengers are of a sufficiently miscellaneous character, the living freight embracing specimens of about *all* the various classes of human beings who have made the great West the queer conglomerate it is—not to speak of a hundred and fifty horses, and a few mules, and a dozen boxes of live poultry, which cackle and fight on the hurricane deck. Two of the more ambitious chickens got out to-day and tried to fly ashore. They did not succeed, but were swimming well when last seen. To-night we are tied up, with a dozen other boats, at the mouth of White River, where we are likely to remain for several days. The other boats are crowded to overflowing with soldiers belonging to Gen. Canby's Arkansas expedition, and the general opinion is that there is to be a lively campaign in this region before winter sets in. Whenever we *do* move, we shall do so with the comfortable consciousness that every mile of our way is tracked by guerrillas along shore, and that at any moment a stray bullet may come on board. That was the way Gen. Canby was hit. Some skulking would-be-murderer lurked in the bushes, and could not withstand the temptation of the tall form of the General commanding.

The cabin of the boat presents a curious spectacle, with its scattered novel-readers, yawning over their books, and its groups of noisy cardplayers working hard to kill time. Here and there a table is surrounded with busy writers. The bar is closed, for we are at a military post, and I am more than usually glad of it, for the barkeeper is nearly gone with consumption, and it was a ghastly thing to see his waxen and deathlike face, looking out upon his half-tipsy customers from behind his tinkling glasses. The river is shrinking from all its fair proportions, and seems lost in the vast basin that forms its bed at high water. It is hard to believe that the high bluff above us will, before spring, in all probability, be hidden by the muddy waters which now ripple humbly at its base.

We had a high wind yesterday, and I was struck by a new evidence of the exceedingly slight construction of these river boats; for the whole frame of the boat yielded readily to the motion of the waves, bows and stern rising and falling with a quiet independence of each other that was something new to a man accustomed to the stronger structures of the Atlantic coast. It is not true, however, that the White River boats are so loosely built that they bend to follow the crooks in the river, though it is evident that such a craft would be a great desideratum. We will have to lighten our boat to-morrow, as we draw a trifle more than six inches too much. Think of that, for a close calculation of water power. They are now beginning to rig up extra sleeping apparatus, and in half an hour the whole cabin will be a dormitory.

There is a good excuse for a new city at this point, though it had never been anything but a bare bluff until the war found how convenient a depot it was for quartermasters' and commissaries' stores. I, for one, cannot understand why it has been so neglected. Both the White and Arkansas rivers find their way into the Mississippi hard by, a levee could be made to protect the bluff against the highest floods at a small expense, and railroads would come, as a matter of course, in time; but I am forgetting that all this country has been hidden under the deep shadow of the slave power, ever since white men first found their way through its canebrakes and forests. Thanks to Him who has sent upon us our great tribulation, I believe a better day is dawning, and that an era of free labor will yet discover and develop much that would also have remained in the future as useless as in the past.

It is almost amusing to hear our young officers and soldiers, especially the Western men, gravely discussing these questions, many of them, no doubt, proposing to take an active part in working out the fulfillment of their own prophecies. To the men of the Northwest the building up of new States, the founding of cities, the turning of the wilderness into farm land and gardens, present no unfamiliar ideas, but they rather feel at home in planning and calculating undertakings, from the magnitude of which any other race would shrink appalled. When once the return of peace leaves them at liberty to abandon the camp and the duties of the soldier, you will see with what a steady enthusiasm, with what a breadth of view, with what an unquestioning faith in themselves, their institutions, and their final success, they will undertake the regeneration of this rich and beautiful Southwest.

LITTLE ROCK, ARKANSAS, 10 JANUARY 1865 (PUBLISHED 26 JANUARY 1865)
We are now passing through the season that comes to the Southwest instead of winter. We have had some cold days when ice would form, some heavy rain-storms, and once or twice a flurry of snow and sleet, brought by strong north winds; but on the whole, the winter, though more severe than usual, seems wonderfully mild and beautiful to a Northern man, and from this time forward, so we are told by the old settlers, we may expect still milder weather. Everybody seems to be in good health, as good as in any average town in New-York, and thus far I am well pleased with all the indications of the climate. Whether the summer will find me as well satisfied remains to be seen.

I cannot help, sitting *here* and writing to a Northern journal, painting two pictures to my mind's eye, and drawing a comparison. I can clearly see Broadway, with its surging tides of people, its blue-coated police, its endless evidences of wealth, civilization, law, order, the varied developments of a State completed, of results long labored for, and to a great extent attained. Here, around me, is a different condition of things—a vast extent of territory, rich in all natural resources, full of all great capacities for future development, but only partially peopled, scoured from end to end by armed forces of all kinds, to a great extent ungoverned—no law, no order, except within range of the cannon of the several armies; society a chaos, and all progress temporarily paralyzed.

A dark picture, you will say; truly so, but with the utmost reverence, let it be added, that over this chaos, as over the primal one, the Spirit of God is brooding, and that without this temporary anarchy we might have waited centuries for the new era which is now within the reach of two generations, and much of which will be seen by the men who are now working to bring it about. To be more precise and practical—if your readers will look at the map—this is our condition: the order for the evacuation of the posts on the upper Arkansas has been countermanded, so that we are still to hold the lines of that river to the Indian Territory. We are also, probably, soon to resume the occupation of the White River as far up as Batesville. Our forces at present are mainly concentrated at Little Rock, Duvall's Bluff, the mouth of White River, Helena, Pine Bluff, Fort Smith, and Van Buren. South of the Arkansas River we have no military *post* of consequence, but there is no rebel force *north* of that river, nor any known to be north of the line of the Ouachita. Then there is a moderate-sized army of traitors, but no great number believed to be now this side of Shreveport, on the Red River. Our scouting parties go where they please, almost unmolested, except by straggling banditti.

The greater portion of the vast region described, always thinly peopled except in a few locations, is now one great desolation. All who could leave it have gone, and many counties no longer offer sustenance even to the robbers. Still, a score of predatory bands, hated and feared by all parties alike, composed of the offscourings of both armies, ride hither and thither, plundering, burning, and committing deeds of brutal and cowardly violence. Of late they are being fast depleted by the judicious orders of both Union and rebel generals to "shoot them as fast as they can be caught." Was there ever a country so desolated and so cursed? It will be a work of time to restore order over so large a space, but it can and will be done.

Within our lines, reaching for several miles in every direction out from Little Rock, we can see a far different picture. Here is order, safety, and industry. Here everybody is busy, and every one is rapidly making money. Every foot of available land will be in cultivation during the year to come, at higher rents than anywhere else in the Union away from our great cities. A good cotton farm brings ten dollars per acre rent. The entire population is being reinspired with energy and hope. New men and new capital are coming in from the North. Labor is in great and constant demand—labor of every kind—and eagerly employed at high prices. A somewhat similar state of things prevails at all our larger posts. The circle of this improvement will steadily and rapidly expand. It will be multiplied more than tenfold during the year to come, and carry with it the elements of its own protection and further expansion. The conditions of its growth will compel closer settlement, more thorough organization, and the best class of immigrants—men of courage, enterprise, and experience. The rewards of labor and agricultural enterprise must for a long time be enormous. A hundred acres, yielding a bale of cotton to the acre, at current prices nets the producer over fifty thousand dollars, if he manages well, and meets with no great losses. Men will come to such inducements in swarms.

If we could only get labor enough, there would be a hundred more plantations opened around Little Rock this season, even in localities not considered altogether safe from guerrillas.

The labor question will for a long time be our greatest difficulty. The destruction of the old order of things leaves a vast preponderance of the real estate of the country waiting for new owners. Fine plantations, valuable forests, rich mineral lands, and an immense quantity of first-class unimproved land, will be sold by Government for little or nothing. A wise provision in the law gives a decided advantage to discharged soldiers in making purchases at the Government sales. It would be still wiser if the amount (three hundred and twenty acres) which each such man is now allowed to purchase, should be made his by free gift, on actual settlement. The people do not want any money from their defenders, and their defenders do want these cotton lands. This is as true of every rebel State as it is of Arkansas; but as the proper authorities have commenced work here, I wish some patriotic Congressman would take the matter in hand, so that justice may be done before it is too late. The real citizens of Arkansas—those who, in my opinion, have the soundest views of what is best for our new State—do not wish to see a return of the old curse of a landed aristocracy, holding in single families immense tracts of territory, which they cannot cultivate and will not sell. Still less do we care to see our rich bottom lands and fertile uplands held by non-resident speculators. We need *men*—not "*proprietaires.*"

The sentiment of the Union men of this State is intensely radical. Those who are not for us are against us, and the fight is to the bitter end. Middle ground there is none, and "conservatism" is an abomination, for life and all are at stake. We hope for the recognition of our State government, and the reception of our Congressional delegation, but failure in both cannot crush us, for the "State" is *here*, and is a living entity, destined in the future to a strong and prosperous life.

Notes

Editor's Introduction

1. Reminiscences of William O. Stoddard Jr., quoted in Edgar DeWitt Jones, "Lincoln's Other Secretary and His Son," typescript, p. 5, Edgar DeWitt Jones Papers, Detroit Public Library. The Detroit Public Library owns the manuscript version of Stoddard's autobiography, referred to here as "Memoirs." The material in this introduction is taken in part from the introduction to William O. Stoddard's *Inside the White House in War Times: Memoirs and Reports of Lincoln's Secretary*, ed. Michael Burlingame (Lincoln: University of Nebraska Press, 2000), vii–xxi.

2. William O. Stoddard, *Abraham Lincoln: The True Story of a Great Life* (New York: Fords, Howard, & Hulbert, 1884). John G. Nicolay and John Hay, *Abraham Lincoln: A History*, 10 vols. (New York: Century, 1890). Stoddard wrote other books about Lincoln, including *Abraham Lincoln and Andrew Johnson* (New York: F. A. Stokes, 1888); *The Boy Lincoln* (New York: D. Appleton, 1905); *The Table Talk of Abraham Lincoln* (New York: F. A. Stokes, 1894); and *Lincoln at Work: Sketches from Life* (Boston: United Society of Christian Endeavor, 1900). On Nicolay and Hay's journalism, see Michael Burlingame, ed., *Lincoln's Journalist: John Hay's Anonymous Writings for the Press* (Carbondale: Southern Illinois University Press, 1998), and Michael Burlingame, ed., *With Lincoln in the White House: Letters, Memoranda, and Other Writings of John G. Nicolay, 1860–1865* (Carbondale: Southern Illinois University Press, 2000).

3. Washington correspondence, 8 July 1861, *New York Examiner*, 11 July 1861.

4. Washington correspondence, 7 October 1861, *New York Examiner*, 10 October 1861.

5. Washington correspondence, 24 March 1862, *New York Examiner*, 27 March 1862.

6. In the summer of 1863 Hay reported to Nicolay that Lincoln "is managing this war, the draft, foreign relations, and planning a reconstruction of the Union, all at once.... I am growing more and more firmly convinced that the good of

the country absolutely demands that he should be kept where he is till this thing is over.... I believe the hand of God placed him where he is." Hay to John G. Nicolay, Washington, 7 August 1863, in Michael Burlingame, ed., *At Lincoln's Side: John Hay's Civil War Correspondence and Selected Writings* (Carbondale: Southern Illinois University Press, 2000), 49.

7. Washington correspondence, 17 November 1862, *New York Examiner*, 20 November 1862.

8. Washington correspondence, 21 July 1862, *New York Examiner*, 24 July 1862.

9. Washington correspondence, 2 November 1863, *New York Examiner*, 5 November 1863.

10. John Eaton, *Grant, Lincoln and the Freedmen* (New York: Longmans, Green, 1907), 184.

11. Washington correspondence, 18 August 1862, *New York Examiner*, 21 August 1862.

12. Washington correspondence, ca. 14 September 1862, *New York Examiner*, 18 September 1862.

13. Washington correspondence, 6 April 1863, *New York Examiner*, 9 April 1863.

14. Henry B. Van Hoesen, "Lincoln and Hay," *Books at Brown* 18 (1960): 155–56.

15. Stoddard, *Inside the White House*, 101.

16. As the editors put it, "One could wish that this remarkable quotation came from a more reliable source." Don E. Fehrenbacher and Virginia Fehrenbacher, eds., *Recollected Words of Abraham Lincoln* (Stanford CA: Stanford University Press, 1996), 426.

17. Lending further support to Stoddard's reminiscence is John Hay's recollection that on the gloomy morning following the first battle of Bull Run, "when many thought seriously of the end," Lincoln "said, with some impatience, 'There is nothing in this except the lives lost and the lives which must be lost to make it good.' There was probably no one who regretted bloodshed and disaster more than he, and no one who estimated the consequences of defeat more lightly." John Hay, "The Heroic Age in Washington," in Burlingame, *At Lincoln's Side*, 126.

18. Washington correspondence, 12 May 1861, *New York Examiner*, 16 May 1861.

19. Washington correspondence, 16 September 1861, *New York Examiner*, 19 September 1861.

20. Washington correspondence, 20 October 1862, *New York Examiner*, 23 October 1862.

21. Washington correspondence, n.d., *New York Examiner*, 8 May 1862.

22. Washington correspondence, 1 December 1862, *New York Examiner*, 4 December 1862.

23. Washington correspondence, n.d., *New York Examiner*, 18 May 1863.

24. Washington correspondence, 5 July 1863, *New York Examiner*, 9 July 1863.

25. Washington correspondence, 20 June 1864, *New York Examiner*, 23 June 1864.

26. See, for example, Lincoln's editorial dated 12 December 1860, in Roy P. Basler, et al., ed., *Collected Works of Abraham Lincoln* 9 vols. (New Brunswick NJ: Rutgers University Press, 1953–55), 4:150. See also Glenn H. Seymour, "'Conservative'— Another Lincoln Pseudonym?" in *Journal of the Illinois State Historical Society* 29 (July 1936): 135–50; "Lincoln—Author of Letters by a Conservative," *Bulletin of the Abraham Lincoln Association* 50 (December 1937): 8–9. J. G. Randall thought that Seymour's thesis "is ingeniously presented, and the reasoning seems pretty sound.... The main arguments for Lincoln's authorship seem to be his connection with the Journal and the test of literary style. The letters do seem to have a kind of Lincoln tang." See Randall to Arthur C. Cole, n.p., 20 March 1936, copy, J. G. Randall Papers, Manuscript Division, Library of Congress. William E. Barton contended that during the secession crisis, "It is practically certain that the *Illinois State Journal* gave forth editorial utterances which had Lincoln's approval, and some of them may have come from his own pen." William E. Barton, *The Life of Abraham Lincoln* 2 vols. (Indianapolis: Bobbs–Merrill, 1925), 2:2. See also James H. Matheny's interview with William Herndon of November 1866, in Douglas L. Wilson and Rodney O. Davis, eds., *Herndon's Informants: Letters, Interviews, and Statements about Abraham Lincoln* (Urbana: University of Illinois Press, 1998), 431; Simeon Francis to Anson G. Henry, n.p., 14 July 1855, in Anson G. Henry Papers, Illinois State Historical Library, Springfield; Andy Van Meter, *Always My Friend: A History of the State Journal–Register* (Springfield IL: Copley Press, 1981), 48–49, 67–68; Audus Waton Shipton, "Lincoln's Association with the Journal: An Address, delivered by A. W. Shipton, publisher of the Illinois State Journal, Springfield, Illinois, at a conference of newspaper publishers and executives, at Coronado, California, 27 September 1939;" *Herndon's Lincoln*, Paul M. Angle, ed. (Cleveland OH: World, 1942), 184, 197, 296–97; Robert S. Harper, *Lincoln and the Press* (New York: McGraw Hill, 1951), 2, 14–15; memo by William Henry Bailhache, San Diego, 14 January 1898, in Ida M. Tarbell Papers, Allegheny College, Meadeville PA; statement of Col. J. D. Roper, 22 October 1897, enclosed in J. McCan Davis to Ida M. Tarbell, ibid.; Albert J. Beveridge, *Abraham Lincoln, 1809–1858* 2 vols. (Boston: Houghton Mifflin, 1928), 1:171n, 183, 205n; and William E. Barton, "Abraham Lincoln, Newspaper Man," typescript, and "Lincoln Editorials," handwritten memo, both Springfield IL, 28 December 1928, William E. Barton Papers, Regenstein Library, University of Chicago.

27. Agreement dated 3 June 1857, in Basler, *Collected Works of Lincoln*, 2:410.

28. Basler, *Collected Works of Lincoln*, 3:383.

29. See Harper, *Lincoln and the Press*, 76; and Harry J. Carman and Reinhold H.

Luthin, *Lincoln and the Patronage* (New York: Columbia University Press, 1943), 121–29.

30. Carman and Luthin, *Lincoln and the Patronage*, 121.

31. Stoddard, "Memoirs," 1:312.

32. A Washington correspondent told the managing editor of the *Tribune* that "Stoddard wants his papers if you do not publish: has no other copy." Adams S. Hill to Sydney Howard Gay, [Washington], n.d., Gay Papers, Columbia University, New York.

33. William O. Stoddard Jr., ed., *Lincoln's Third Secretary: The Memoirs of William O. Stoddard* (New York: Exposition Press, 1955), 45; William O. Stoddard Jr., ed., "A Journalist Sees Lincoln," *Atlantic Monthly* 135 (February 1925): 171. In the late 1860s Scroggs (1817–74) served in the Illinois state legislature and as a trustee of the University of Illinois. Wilson and Davis, *Herndon's Informants*, 770.

34. Stoddard, *Lincoln's Third Secretary*, 46, 193.

35. Stoddard, *Lincoln's Third Secretary*, 47. Stoddard's name appears as co-editor for the first time on the issue dated 18 August 1858.

36. Stoddard to James R. B. Van Cleave, Madison NJ, 7 April 1909, William O. Stoddard Papers, McKee Library, Southern Adventist University, Collegedale TN.

37. John W. Scroggs to William H. Herndon, Champaign IL, 3 October 1866, Wilson and Davis, *Herndon's Informants*, 365.

38. *Central Illinois Gazette*, 4 May 1859.

39. Stoddard, "A Journalist Sees Lincoln," 172.

40. Stoddard to James R. B. Van Cleave, Madison NJ, 7 April 1909, Stoddard Papers, McKee Library. Cf. Stoddard to Mrs. J. B. Van Cleave, Madison NJ, 10 March 1909, enclosed in Oliver R. Barrett to Albert J. Beveridge, Chicago, 7 July 1926, Albert J. Beveridge Papers, Manuscript Divison, Library of Congress.

41. *Central Illinois Gazette*, 7 December 1859.

42. Stoddard, *Lincoln's Third Secretary*, 55–63; William E. Baringer, *Lincoln's Rise to Power* (Boston: Little, Brown, 1937), 48–89.

43. Stoddard, *Lincoln's Third Secretary*, 62–63.

44. Stoddard, *Lincoln's Third Secretary*, 64–65.

45. Stoddard to Herndon, Champaign IL, 27 December 1860, Lincoln Papers, Library of Congress. Stoddard erred in his memoirs when he contended that Lincoln wrote to him in early December, saying, "Close up your affairs and go to Washington and wait for me." Stoddard, *Lincoln's Third Secretary*, 65–66.

46. Stoddard to Lyman Trumbull, Champaign IL, 27 December 1860, Lyman Trumbull Papers, Manuscript Division, Library of Congress.

47. Stoddard, "Memoirs," 2:332.

48. Donald W. Riddle, *Lincoln Runs for Congress* (New Brunswick NJ: Rutgers University Press, 1948), 81–90.

49. Benjamin F. James to Lincoln, Chicago, 27 September 1860, Lincoln Papers, Library of Congress.

50. Henry C. Whitney to William H. Herndon, 23 July 1887, in Wilson and Davis, *Herndon's Informants*, 619.

51. Stoddard, "Memoirs," 2:429.

52. Stoddard, *Lincoln's Third Secretary*, 66–71. A photographic reproduction of his commission, dated 17 July 1861, also can be found opposite p. 74. His appointment was announced in the *Central Illinois Gazette* on 10 April.

53. Washington correspondence by W. O. S., 25 February 1861, *Central Illinois Gazette*, 6 March 1861. In that dispatch Stoddard was especially critical of Norman B. Judd. See also Stoddard to Martin B. Anderson, Washington, 28 February 1861, in *Catherine Barnes: Autographs & Signed Books, Catalogue 14* (1994), 15–16. Martin Brewer Anderson (1815–90) served as president of Stoddard's alma mater, the University of Rochester (1853–88).

54. William O. Stoddard Jr., ed., "Face to Face with Lincoln," *Atlantic Monthly* 135 (March 1925): 332.

55. Stoddard, *Lincoln's Third Secretary*, 76–77.

56. Nicolay to Paul Selby, Washington, 11 March 1895, draft, John G. Nicolay Papers, Manuscript Division, Library of Congress.

57. William O. Stoddard Jr. to William E. Barton, Detroit, 15 February 1930, Barton Papers.

58. Stoddard to George P. Hambrecht, Madison NJ, 5 August 1921, copy, Lincoln Collection, Chicago Historical Society. Cf. Stoddard, *Lincoln's Third Secretary*, 196–97, and Stoddard, *Inside the White House*, 124–25.

59. Stoddard, "Memoirs," 1:307. In August 1861 Nicolay reported to his fiancée that "John Hay met me in New York. He himself has also been sick and was compelled to leave. He is going to Illinois to stay three or four weeks." Nicolay to Therena Bates, Washington, 31 August 1861, Burlingame, *With Lincoln in the White House*, 54.

60. Stoddard, "Memoirs," 1:313.

61. Stoddard to James R. B. Van Cleave, Madison NJ, 7 April 1909, Stoddard Papers, McKee Library.

62. Hay to Nicolay, Washington, 25 September 1863, Burlingame, *At Lincoln's Side*, 56.

63. Hay to Nicolay, Washington, 7 August 1863, Burlingame, *At Lincoln's Side*, 49.

64. Hay to Nicolay, Washington, 11 September 1863, Burlingame, *At Lincoln's Side*, 53.

65. Hay to Nicolay, Warsaw IL, 26 August 1864, Burlingame, *At Lincoln's Side*, 93.

66. Stoddard, "Memoirs," 2:364.
67. Stoddard, "Memoirs," 1:307.
68. Nicolay to Paul Selby Washington, 11 March 1895, draft, Nicolay Papers.
69. Stoddard to Hay, New York, 12 February 1885, John Hay Papers, John Hay Library, Brown University, Providence RI.
70. Stoddard to Hay, New York, 25 March 1885, Hay Papers.
71. An undated Washington dispatch by "Illinois" in the *New York Examiner* dated 4 June 1863 read: "I was prevented from sending my usual contribution last week by an 'experimental proof' that, under all this fine weather of ours, there still lurk those treacherous fevers which have been from the beginning of the war, more fatal than sword or shot to the strength of our armies."
72. Stoddard, "Memoirs," 2:440. In the published version of the memoirs Stoddard said: "Once again Lincoln employed me as a reporter. He directed that I make an inspection of the armies of the West and South." Stoddard, *Lincoln's Third Secretary*, 200.
73. Stoddard to Manton Marble, [New York], 8 July 1864, Manton Marble Papers, Manuscript Division, Library of Congress.
74. Washington correspondence by "Illinois," 11 July 1864, *New York Examiner*, 14 July 1864.
75. Lincoln Papers, Library of Congress.
76. Washington correspondence by "Illinois," n.d., *New York Examiner*, 6 October 1864.
77. Stoddard, *Lincoln's Third Secretary*, 215.
78. On 26 January 1865 Stoddard's nomination was submitted to the Senate for confirmation. Basler, *Collected Works of Lincoln*, 8:242n. On 14 February 1865 he was officially confirmed as marshal. Stoddard, *Lincoln's Third Secretary*. A photographic reproduction of Stoddard's commission is located opposite p. 216.
79. Jones, "Lincoln's Other Secretary," 5. When he went to Arkansas he intended "to be returned in due course as United States Senator." Biographical sketch of Stoddard, William O. Stoddard Papers, Detroit Public Library.
80. Stoddard, *Lincoln's Third Secretary*, 217.
81. Stoddard to Lincoln, Little Rock, 13 and 14 December 1864 and 16 January 1865, Lincoln Papers, Library of Congress.
82. Stoddard to Elihu B. Washburne, Little Rock, 11 February 1865, Elihu B. Washburne Papers, Manuscript Division, Library of Congress.
83. Stoddard to Hay, Little Rock, 22 April 1865, Hay Papers.
84. "Having lost my health in the discharge of my duty," he told the president, he was forced to resign. Stoddard to Andrew Johnson, New York, 28 May 1866, Andrew Johnson Papers, Manuscript Division, Library of Congress.

85. Jones, "Lincoln's Other Secretary," 6.
86. This volume was subtitled *Dedicated by the Author to the Sachems of Tammany, and to the Other Grand Magnorums of Manhattan* (New York: Russell's American Steam Printing House, 1869).
87. Jones, "Lincoln's Other Secretary," 6.
88. Stoddard to Nicolay, Madison NJ, 3 November 1898, Nicolay Papers.
89. Stoddard to Nicolay, Madison NJ, 17 December 1898, Nicolay Papers.

CHAPTER ONE. 1861

1. The Sixth and Eighth Massachusetts and the Seventh New York regiments occupied the Capitol. William Sprague (1830–1915) was governor of Rhode Island (1860–63) and U.S. senator from that state (1863–75). Henry Villard thought Sprague, commander of the Second Rhode Island regiment, a man with "very limited mental capacity" who "had reached political distinction at an early age . . . through the influence of real or reputed great wealth." Henry Villard, *Memoirs of Henry Villard, Journalist and Financier, 1835–1900*, 2 vols. (Boston: Houghton, Mifflin, 1904), 1:175. The First Rhode Island regiment, commanded by Ambrose E. Burnside, occupied the Patent and Post Offices. The Fifth Massachusetts regiment occupied the Treasury.

2. Congress was to meet on 4 July.

3. Elmer Ephraim Ellsworth (1837–61), a kind of surrogate son to Lincoln, had upon the outbreak of war abandoned his post as adjutant and inspector general of militia to recruit a regiment from the fire departments of New York. Col. William Wilson's Sixth New York Infantry, known as "Wilson's Zouaves," was sent to Santa Rosa Island, Florida, where Confederates under Gen. Richard Heron Anderson routed them on the night of 8–9 October 1861.

4. Fortress Monroe was located at the tip of the peninsula formed by the York and James Rivers in Virginia.

5. Gen. Ben McCulloch (1811–62) was a Texan who in February of that year had received the surrender of Union forces at San Antonio. At this time McCulloch was stationed west of the Mississippi River. Rumor had it that McCulloch planned to dash from Richmond to Washington with five hundred men and abduct the president, the cabinet, and Gen. Winfield Scott. Charles Winslow Elliott, *Winfield Scott: The Soldier and the Man* (New York: Macmillan, 1937), 710.

6. Winfield Scott (1786–1866) was commander of the Union army.

7. John Savage had edited the *Washington States and Union* from 30 January 1861 until its demise on 20 April 1861. The paper, founded in 1857, had been previously edited by James S. Holland, and before that by John P. Heiss.

8. In 1847 Edwin D. and Henry A. Willard took over Fuller's City Hotel,

which stood two blocks from the White House at Fourteenth Street and Pennsylvania Avenue. They remodeled it and renamed it the Willard Hotel. Nathaniel Hawthorne said that it "may much more justly [be] called the centre of Washington and the Union than . . . the Capitol, the White House, or the State Department." Hawthorne, "Chiefly about War Matters," *Atlantic Monthly* 10 (July 1862): 59.

9. Ellsworth was killed in Alexandria, Virginia, on 24 May 1861, shortly after tearing down the Confederate flag from atop a hotel.

10. When Ellsworth died Lincoln was devastated and "mourned him as a son." John Hay, "A Young Hero," *New York World*, 16 February 1890. Upon receipt of the news the president burst into tears, telling his official callers, "Excuse me, but I cannot talk." After he had collected himself, he explained, "I will take [make] no apology, gentlemen, for my weakness; but I knew poor Ellsworth well, and held him in great regard." Lincoln's Washington correspondence of 24 May 1861, *New York Herald*, 25 May 1861. When a congressman expressed satisfaction that the Stars and Stripes now flew in Alexandria, Lincoln replied, "'Yes, but it was at a terrible cost!' and the tears rushed into his eyes as he said it." Recollections of John A. Kasson in Allen Thorndike Rice, ed., *Reminiscences of Abraham Lincoln by Distinguished Men of His Time* (New York: North American Review, 1888), 36. At Ellsworth's funeral, which was conducted in the White House, the president cried out as he viewed the corpse, "My boy! my boy! was it necessary this sacrifice should be made!" Ruth Painter Randall, *Colonel Elmer Ellsworth: A Biography of Lincoln's Friend and First Hero of the Civil War* (Boston: Little, Brown, 1960), 263.

11. Ira Harris (1802–75) was a senator from New York (1861–69).

12. The *Pensacola* was a three thousand–ton steam sloop launched in 1859.

13. Illinois senator Stephen A. Douglas (b. 1813) died on 3 June.

14. Invented by John A. Dahlgren (1809–70), the Dahlgren gun was a rifled cannon called the "soda-water bottle" because of its peculiar shape. The largest version fired twenty-inch shells, the smallest, nine-inch shells.

15. In May 1861 Isaac F. Quinby (1821–91), who taught mathematics and science at the University of Rochester, raised the "Rochester Regiment," officially known as the Thirteenth New York Volunteers. In 1862 he became a general and the following year participated in the Vicksburg campaign.

16. F.F.V. was an acronym for "First Families of Virginia."

17. Gen. Ambrose E. Burnside (1824–81) of Rhode Island commanded the Army of the Potomac briefly (1862–63).

18. In the 1850s Ambrose Burnside invented a light, breechloading carbine for use by the cavalry.

19. The *Washington National Republican* began publication on 26 November 1860 and ceased publication in 1888.

20. The message is in Basler, *Collected Works of Lincoln*, 4:421–41.

21. John C. Breckinridge (1821–75) of Kentucky served in the U.S. House (1851–55), the U.S. Senate (1861), and also served as vice president of the United States (1857–61).

22. John J. Crittenden (1786–1863) was a Unionist member of the U.S. House of Representatives from Kentucky (1861–63). Crittenden previously had served as a U.S. senator from Kentucky (1817–19, 1835–41, 1842–48, and 1855–61).

23. Andrew Johnson (1808–75), a leading Tennessee Unionist, represented his state in the U.S. Senate (1857–62); Conservative Unionist Emerson Etheridge (1819–1902), a slaveholder from west Tennessee, represented his district in the U.S. House (1853–57, 1859–61), and served as clerk of that body (1861–63).

24. Gen. George B. McClellan (1826–85), who replaced Irvin McDowell (1818–85), the hapless commander of Union forces at the battle of Bull Run, quickly restored morale among the discouraged troops.

25. Prince Napoleon Joseph (1822–91) was a cousin of the French emperor Napoleon III.

26. George Harrington (1815–92) had long been a clerk in the Treasury and in 1861 became assistant secretary of the department. From 1865 to 1869 he served as U.S. minister to Switzerland.

27. Long Branch was a fashionable beach resort in New Jersey.

28. When the Seventy-ninth New York Highlanders mutinied, McClellan sternly ordered regulars to confront them and demand that they obey orders. The mutineers complied. The organizers of the mutiny were jailed and their regimental colors removed.

29. Confederate general Pierre Gustave Toutant Beauregard (1818–93) commanded the Confederate forces in northern Virginia.

30. In 1861 John F. Potter (1817–99), a U.S. representative from Wisconsin (1857–63), chaired a committee to investigate the loyalty of government employees.

31. On 27 August Union forces under Gen. Benjamin F. Butler and Com. Silas H. Stringham attacked the forts guarding Hatteras Inlet on North Carolina's Outer Banks. The Confederates abandoned Fort Clark without a fight on 27 August; Fort Hatteras, after a heavy pounding by Stringham's ships, surrendered the next day.

32. The *New York Herald* covered Mrs. Lincoln's doings at Long Branch in elaborate detail.

33. On 4 and 5 September the New York Democratic state convention met in Syracuse and adopted resolutions condemning both southern secessionists and northern antislavery leaders.

34. On 2 September Lincoln wrote to John Charles Frémont (1813–90), commander of Union forces in Missouri, ordering the general to modify his proclamation of 30 August that had freed the slaves of disloyal masters in Missouri and had

called for the execution of captured guerillas. Basler, *Collected Works of Lincoln*, 4:506.

35. William Henry Seward (1801–72) of New York was Lincoln's secretary of state (1861–65).

36. Simon Cameron (1799–1889), a prominent Republican leader in Pennsylvania, was Lincoln's secretary of war (1861–62).

37. Gideon Welles (1802–78) of Connecticut was Lincoln's secretary of the navy (1861–65).

38. Salmon P. Chase of Ohio (1808–73) served as Lincoln's secretary of the treasury (1861–64).

39. German-born Ludwig Blenker (1812–63) commanded a division of the Army of the Potomac.

40. Frémont protested against Lincoln's instruction of 2 September, and his supporters, who were among the more militant opponents of slavery, rallied to his cause. Basler, *Collected Works of Lincoln*, 4:507.

41. On 20 September Col. James Mulligan surrendered his 3,600 Union troops to Confederate general Sterling Price at Lexington, Missouri, after withstanding a siege of nine days.

42. Responding to charges of corruption and inefficiency in Frémont's department, Lincoln dispatched Postmaster Gen. Montgomery Blair, Quartermaster Gen. Montgomery Meigs, and Gen. David Hunter to investigate. In November Frémont was replaced by Gen. Samuel R. Curtis.

43. James Buchanan, president of the United States (1857–61), lived on an estate in Pennsylvania called Wheatland.

44. Munson's Hill, near Alexandria, Virginia, was abandoned by Confederate forces on 28 September.

45. On 29 October a federal expedition under the command of Samuel Du Pont sailed for Port Royal, South Carolina, which it captured on 7 November.

46. The *New York Tribune*, edited by Horace Greeley, had supported Frémont in his controversy with Lincoln.

47. On 21 October Union forces suffered a defeat at the battle of Ball's Bluff near Leesburg, Virginia.

48. Col. Edward D. Baker (1811–61), a close friend of Lincoln's, was killed at the battle of Ball's Bluff.

49. Stephen W. Stryker was colonel of the Forty-fourth New York Infantry. John Hay described that unit, known as "Ellsworth's Avengers," thus: "It is the People's Ellsworth Regiment of New York, selected from every town in the State with the exception of the cities of New York and Troy. Magnificent in physique and morale, well dressed, well equipped, well armed, officered by the perfectly trained Chicago boys and commanded by Ellsworth's friend and companion, Col.

Stryker, lacking the effeminacy of the Seventh and the brutality of the Fire Boys, it unites the refinement of the one with the muscle of the other, and goes into the field animated by the loftiest motives of patriotism and the highest incentives to daring." Washington correspondence, 26 October 1861, *Missouri Republican* (St. Louis), 31 October 1861 in Burlingame, *Lincoln's Journalist*, 127.

50. On 31 October Gen. Winfield Scott resigned his post as commander of Union forces. The following day his duties were assumed by Gen. George B. McClellan.

51. German-born Gen. Franz Sigel (1824–1902) commanded a brigade in the Army of Southwest Missouri. In 1849 he had led revolutionary forces in Baden in their battle against Prussia.

52. Sometimes called the first battle of the Civil War, the skirmish at Fairfax Court House, Virginia, on 1 June saw seventy-five Union cavalry enter Fairfax and then retreat; on 25 October Maj. Charles Zagonyi led Union cavalry against Springfield, Missouri, where they routed a handful of Confederates; on 9 October federal forces repulsed one thousand Confederates on Santa Rosa Island off Fort Pickens in Pensacola Bay, Florida.

53. On 10 August Nathaniel Lyon (1818–61) died leading Union forces at the battle of Wilson's Creek, Missouri.

54. Taking exception to certain arrangements made when the army was reorganized into separate corps, Blenker complained to McClellan, who in turn rebuked him. Blenker thereupon threatened to resign his command. Fellow officers intervened and smoothed matters over. Washington correspondence, 26 November 1861, *New York Tribune*, 27 November 1861. It was alleged that Blenker had imposed an illegal tax of one hundred dollars per month on sutlers. *New York Tribune*, 26 November 1861.

55. James M. Mason (1798–1871) of Virginia was Confederate diplomatic commissioner to Great Britain.

56. In 1860 U.S. senator Joseph Lane (1801–81) of Oregon had been the vice presidential running mate of Democrat John C. Breckinridge.

57. On 5 December, at the camp of the Harris Light Cavalry (Second New York Cavalry regiment) near Arlington House, Senator Ira Harris presented a stand of colors to that unit as President Lincoln and his wife, along with Secretary of War Cameron, observed the ceremony. Lt. Col. Henry Eugene Davies (1836–94) was breveted a brigadier general in 1863 and commanded a brigade of cavalry in the Army of the Potomac for the rest of the war.

58. Judge Henry Ebenezer Davies (1805–81) served on the New York Supreme Court in the 1850s, and from 1859 to 1867 was a member of the New York Court of Appeals. He was the father of Lt. Col. Henry Eugene Davies.

CHAPTER TWO. 1862

1. On 20 December Union and Confederate forces clashed at Dranesville, Virginia.

2. Ohio senator John Sherman (1823–1900) was the brother of Gen. William T. Sherman.

3. McClellan had been appointed general in chief of all Union armies in November 1861; Lincoln reduced his command to the Army of the Potomac, effective 11 March 1862.

4. The "Lady President's ball," which took place on 5 February, was widely criticized as inappropriate merrymaking in wartime.

5. Jesse D. Bright (1812–75) of Indiana was a U.S. senator from 1845 until his expulsion (on 5 February 1862) for pro-Confederate utterances and activities.

6. A Pennsylvania attorney, Edwin M. Stanton (1814–69), served as secretary of war (1862–68).

7. From December 1861 to April 1862 Ambrose E. Burnside (1824–81) of Rhode Island commanded the North Carolina Expedition Corps, which captured Roanoke Island on 8 February and New Berne on 14 March.

8. Confederate general Sterling Price (1809–67), after capturing Lexington, Missouri, in September 1861, had been driven out of that state by Union general Samuel R. Curtis, who defeated him badly at the battle of Pea Ridge, Arkansas, on 7 and 8 March.

9. Federal troops occupied Bowling Green, Kentucky, on 14 February; captured Fort Donelson, Tennessee, on 16 February; and occupied Columbus, Kentucky, on 3 March.

10. Union general Don Carlos Buell (1818–98) captured Nashville, Tennessee, on 25 February.

11. Gen. Nathaniel P. Banks (1816–94) was in command of the Potomac Valley area; Gen. Daniel E. Sickles (1819–1914) commanded the New York Excelsior Brigade.

12. Lincoln's eleven-year-old son Willie died on 20 February.

13. David Hunter (1802–86) commanded Union forces in Kansas from November 1861 to March 1862.

14. The panic was caused by the Confederate ironclad *Merrimack*, a Union ship that had been scuttled in 1861, then raised by the Confederates and converted into an ironclad ram, which they christened the C.S.S. *Virginia*. On 8 March she sank the U.S.S. *Cumberland* (a thirty-gun ship), forced the surrender of the U.S.S. *Congress* (a fifty-gun ship), and drove the U.S.S. *Minnesota* aground.

15. The *Ericsson* was the U.S.S. *Monitor*, commanded by John L. Worden (1818–97) and designed by Swedish-born John Ericsson (1803–89).

16. On 7 and 8 March Union forces under Samuel R. Curtis defeated Confed-

erates led by Earl Van Dorn at the battle of Pea Ridge, Arkansas. On 11 March Union forces occupied Manassas, Virginia, which the Confederates had evacuated. On 14 March federal troops captured New Madrid, Missouri, on the Mississippi River.

17. Union forces under Gen. Ulysses S. Grant captured Fort Donelson on 16 February. On 6 February Confederate forces had surrendered Fort Henry on the Tennessee River. The French military engineer Sebastien Le Prestre de Vauban (1633–1707) made significant innovations in siege warfare and defensive fortifications. Count E. I. Todleben was the Russian military engineer who organized the defenses of Sebastapol during the Crimean War.

18. Thomas "Tad" Lincoln (1853–71) was the youngest of the president's four sons.

19. On 7 April Gen. John Pope captured Island No. 10 in the Mississippi River.

20. Federal troops occupied Winchester on 12 March 1862.

21. On 25 February Congress passed the Legal Tender Act, which authorized the issuance of $150 million worth of Treasury notes that became known as "greenbacks."

22. General McClellan's advance on Richmond up the Virginia peninsula was delayed by Confederate general John B. Magruder (1807–71), whose troops at Yorktown intimidated the Union commander. McClellan resorted to a month-long siege instead of attacking the vastly inferior Confederate forces.

23. William Howard Russell (1820–1907), a special correspondent for the *London Times* whose dispatches describing the Union rout at Bull Run angered many Northerners, wanted to accompany McClellan to the peninsula, but Secretary of War Stanton refused the necessary permission. When the exasperated journalist appealed to Lincoln, the president declined, hinting that the pro-Confederate stance of the *Times* was the main obstacle in Russell's way. In despair Russell returned to England.

24. Confederate general Albert Sidney Johnston (1803–62) commanded the western theater of operations.

25. The battle of Pittsburg Landing, Tennessee (also known as Shiloh), was fought on 6–7 April.

26. Also known as Fort Wright, Fort Pillow on the Mississippi River was abandoned by the Confederates on 3–4 June. Memphis fell to Union forces on 6 June.

27. Frémont took command of the Mountain Department on 29 March.

28. On 16 April Congress abolished slavery in Washington.

29. The Second Confiscation Act, enacted on 17 July, stipulated that all slaves who reached Union lines "shall be deemed captives of war and shall be forever free."

30. Andrew Hull Foote (1806–63), known as the "Gunboat Commodore," had captured Fort Henry on 6 February. In April he was sent to command the fleet at Charleston but died en route to his new assignment.

31. Gen. Irvin McDowell (1818–85), who had led the Union army to defeat at first Bull Run, commanded a corps in the Army of the Potomac.

32. Accompanied by Secretary of the Treasury Chase and Secretary of War Stanton, Lincoln left Washington on 19 April to confer with General McDowell at Acquia Creek, Virginia. They returned to Washington the next day.

33. New York congressman Charles Henry Van Wyck (1824–95) chaired a House committee investigating government contractors.

34. An Indiana attorney, Schuyler Colfax (1823–85) served in the U.S. House (1855–69) over which he presided as Speaker (1863–69); Thaddeus Stevens (1792–1868) of Pennsylvania chaired the House Ways and Means Committee (1861–65).

35. Because she was mourning the loss of her son Willie, Mary Todd Lincoln refused to grant permission for the band concerts to continue as usual. When John Hay asked her if she would consent to have the concerts moved from the White House grounds to Lafayette Square, she replied in writing: "It is hard that in this time of our sorrow, we should be thus harassed. The music in Lafayette square, would sound quite as plainly as here. For this summer, at least, our feelings should be respected. Mrs. Lincoln." Michael Burlingame, *At Lincoln's Side*, 221 n.122. In 1863 Mrs. Lincoln continued to refuse permission, much to the irritation of Secretary of the Navy Gideon Welles, who recorded in his diary on 8 June 1863: "Spoke to the President regarding weekly performances of the Marine Band. It has been customary for them to play in the public grounds south of the Mansion once a week in the summer, for many years. Last year it was intermitted, because Mrs. Lincoln objected in consequence of the death of her son. There was grumbling and discontent, and there will be more this year if the public are denied the privilege for private reasons. The public will not sympathize in sorrows, which are obtrusive and assigned as a reason for depriving them of enjoyments to which they have been accustomed and it is a mistake to persist in it. When I introduced the subject to-day, the President said Mrs. L. would not consent, certainly not until after the 4th of July. I stated the case pretty frankly, although the subject is delicate, and suggested that the band could play in Lafayette Square. Seward and Usher who were present advised that course. The President told me to do what I thought best." Howard K. Beale, ed., *Diary of Gideon Welles, Secretary of the Navy under Lincoln and Johnson* 3 vols. (New York: Norton, 1960), 1:325.

36. Reverdy Johnson (1796–1876), an eminent attorney and a U.S. senator from Maryland (1863–68), played a key role in keeping his state in the Union.

37. On 25 April Union admiral David Farragut entered New Orleans, which surrendered officially two days later.

38. Norfolk was taken by Union forces under Gen. John E. Wool on 10 May. The Confederates had abandoned Yorktown on 3 May, just as McClellan was about to attack it after a month-long siege.

39. On 5 May Lincoln left Washington to visit Fortress Monroe, Virginia. He returned on 11 May.

40. Clement L. Vallandigham (1820–71) of Ohio, leader of the northern Peace Democrats, was a member of the U.S. House of Representatives (1858–63) and unsuccessful candidate for governor of Ohio (1863). Samuel Sullivan "Sunset" Cox (1824–89) was a militant Democrat from Ohio who served in the U.S. House (1857–65, 1869–85).

41. "Contrabands" was a term used to describe slaves who had escaped to Union lines and thereby gained their freedom.

42. In 1862 the newly appointed military governor of North Carolina, Edward Stanly, forbade schools to be opened to blacks.

43. The "Soldiers' Home" was Lincoln's summer retreat, three miles outside the District of Columbia. Located on a hilltop, this facility for disabled troops was far cooler than the White House. In 1862, 1863, and 1864 the president and his family spent the summers in a stone cottage there.

44. On 16 June Gen. John Pope (1822–92) was appointed to head the Army of Virginia, consisting of all Union forces in the east except those serving under McClellan. Because Frémont refused to serve under Pope, whom he outranked, Frémont was removed from his command. Frémont resigned from the army in June 1864.

45. George Francis Train (1829–1904), a Boston-born merchant, author, and railroad promoter, made stirring pro-Union speeches in England while there on business.

46. Thomas Corwin (1794–1865) of Ohio served as Lincoln's minister to Mexico (1861–64).

47. In the Seven Days' Campaign near Richmond (25 June–1 July), McClellan was driven from the outskirts of the Confederate capital back to Harrison's Landing on the James River.

48. Count Adam Gurowski (1805–66), who had been a Polish revolutionary, worked in the State Department as a translator.

49. On 1 July Lincoln signed into law a revenue act imposing a federal income tax of 3 percent on incomes between six hundred and ten thousand dollars. All income above the latter amount was taxed at 5 percent. That same day the president also signed the bill that created the Union Pacific–Central Pacific Railroad, providing government aid for the construction of the transcontinental line.

50. Robert Y. Hayne (1791–1839) represented South Carolina in the U.S. Senate (1823–32). Daniel Webster (1782–1852) represented Massachusetts in the U.S.

Senate (1827–41). In a memorable speech he gave in January 1830, Webster rebutted Hayne's arguments in favor of state nullification.

51. On 11 July Gen. Henry W. Halleck (1815–72), who had commanded the Department of the Mississippi, was appointed commander in chief of all Union forces.

52. In February 1862 Malcolm Ives, who had just been named head of the Washington bureau of the *New York Herald*, was arrested at the order of Secretary of War Stanton, who resented the journalist's threats to have his newspaper oppose the Lincoln administration if it did not receive exclusive scoops from the War Department.

53. With two Confederate regiments, John Hunt Morgan (1825–64) launched a successful raid into Kentucky that caused panic in some Northern cities (July 4–August 1). On 13 July Stonewall Jackson moved against Gordonsville, Virginia.

54. On 5 August Gen. Robert McCook (1827–62) of Ohio, who was ill and being conveyed in an ambulance, was fatally shot while fleeing a band of Confederate guerillas. His killer, the captain of a group of partisan rangers, was tried for murder before a military court. Seventeen members of the McCook family fought in the Union army.

55. A leading Massachusetts abolitionist, Wendell Phillips (1811–84) spoke in Abington, Massachusetts, on 1 August, criticizing Lincoln for "intentionally waging a political war" and for being "more afraid of Kentucky than he is of the whole Northern portion of the nation." He declared his belief that "Mr. Lincoln is conducting this war, at present, with the purpose of saving slavery." He called the president "a first-rate second-rate man," and claimed that Illinois lawyers said of Lincoln, "He has no backbone. Had the American people asked for the man of all others least fitted to *lead*, they could not have got a man better suited than Abraham Lincoln. No man ever heard him say 'No.'" *New York Times*, 6 and 16 August 1862.

56. Martin Van Buren, who served as president (1837–41), died on 24 July 1862.

57. This campaign culminated in the second battle of Bull Run (29–30 August).

58. On 18 August Pope's Army of Virginia retreated to the north bank of the Rappahannock.

59. On 22 August Lincoln wrote a letter replying to an editorial written by Horace Greeley of the *New York Tribune*, in which he appealed to the president to emancipate the slaves. Lincoln told the editor, "What I do about slavery, and the colored race, I do because I believe it helps to save the Union; and what I forbear, I forbear because I do *not* believe it would help save the Union." Basler, *Collected Works of Lincoln*, 5:388–89.

60. On 2 September Pope ordered his troops to retreat to the entrenchments around Washington.

61. On 2 September McClellan was restored to full command of Union forces in Virginia and the Washington area.

62. Samuel Peter Heintzelman (1805–94) commanded the Third Corps of the Army of the Potomac; Fitz John Porter (1822–1901) commanded the Fifth Corps of that army.

63. Confederate general Joseph E. Johnston (1807–91) had commanded the forces defending Richmond until he was wounded at the battle of Fair Oaks (31 May) and was replaced by Robert E. Lee.

64. Gen. David E. Twiggs (1790–1862) commanded the Department of Texas at the time of the secession crisis (1860–61), when he committed treason by surrendering his command to Texas forces under Ben McCulloch (18 February 1861).

65. Stoddard here alludes to the battle of Antietam, which took place on 17 September.

66. Alfred Pleasonton (1824–97) commanded the cavalry of the Army of the Potomac.

67. Hannibal Hamlin (1809–91) was vice president during Lincoln's first term (1861–65).

68. At the battle of Antietam the Army of the Potomac lost 2,010 killed, 9,416 wounded, and 1,043 missing; the Confederates lost approximately 2,700 killed, 9,024 wounded, and about 2,000 missing. On 15 September Confederate forces captured the Union garrison at Harper's Ferry, Virginia, taking about 12,000 prisoners.

69. On 22 September Lincoln issued the preliminary Emancipation Proclamation, freeing all slaves held by disloyal owners; it was to go into effect on 1 January 1863.

70. On 24 September twelve Northern governors gathered at Altoona, Pennsylvania, to consider war policy.

71. On 26 September Lincoln met with the governors who had attended the conference in Altoona, Pennsylvania. He listened to the address drafted by Gov. John A. Andrew of Massachusetts.

72. On 14 September Union forces drove the Confederates from the field at South Mountain, Maryland.

73. On 1 October Lincoln left Washington to visit McClellan at his Maryland headquarters and to tour the battlefield of Antietam. He returned to the capital on 4 October.

74. Union general William S. Rosecrans (1819–98) won a victory over Confederate forces under Earl Van Dorn at Corinth, Mississippi (3–4 October).

75. Between 9 and 12 October Confederate cavalry under James Ewell Brown

"Jeb" Stuart (1833–64) rode completely around the Army of the Potomac, sacking Chambersburg, Pennsylvania, in the process.

76. On 8 October at Perryville, Kentucky, Union general Don Carlos Buell won a partial victory over Confederate forces under Braxton Bragg.

77. On 1 September Union general Philip Kearny (1815–62) was killed at the battle of Chantilly. Two months before his death Kearny told his wife: "McClellan's treason or mismanagement has thrown on us a great many partial Battles, of much severity, which he should have spared us. But all of which he invited by his bad arrangements. . . . I am fearfully tired out with the mismanagement, and incapacity of this man. . . . But what annoys me most, is that Congress has not passed on this Army one word of thanks. And yet I deserve it for Williamsburgh, which I made a complete victory. Thus McClellan despicably cheated me, there, and elsewhere." Letter dated Harrison's Landing, 1 July 1862, in William B. Styple, ed., *Letters from the Peninsula: The Civil War Letters of General Philip Kearny* (Kearny NJ: Belle Grove, 1988), 116. See also Kearny to Courtland Parker, Harrison's Landing, 10, 24, and 31 July 1862, ibid., 128–31, 137–38, 141–47.

78. On 14 October Democrats made gains in congressional elections in Ohio, Indiana, and Pennsylvania.

79. On 4 November Democrats achieved victories in state and congressional elections, especially in New York, New Jersey, Illinois, and Wisconsin.

80. On 5 November Lincoln removed McClellan from command of the Army of the Potomac. Don Carlos Buell wrote to Halleck on 22 October 1862, saying: "The spirit of the rebellion enforces a subordination and patient submission to privation and want, which public sentiment renders absolutely impossible among our troops." The day after this letter arrived, Lincoln removed Buell from command.

81. On 9 November Ambrose E. Burnside reluctantly assumed command of the Army of the Potomac.

82. Samuel C. Pomeroy (1816–91) represented Kansas in the U.S. Senate (1861–73).

83. Fort Warren in Boston was used as a military prison camp.

84. Fitz John Porter was court-martialed for disloyalty, disobedience, and misconduct during the second battle of Bull Run. He was found guilty and dismissed from the army on 21 January 1863. Irvin McDowell requested a court of inquiry to investigate his own conduct at second Bull Run. The court found him innocent of any misconduct.

85. British admiral John Byng (1704–57) was court-martialed and executed for his failure to relieve Minorca, which was besieged by the French during the Seven Years' War.

86. John Snyder Carlisle (1817–78) represented Virginia in the U.S. Senate (1861–65).

87. On 13 December the Army of the Potomac was badly defeated at the battle of Fredericksburg, Virginia.

88. Orville H. Browning (1806–81) of Quincy, Illinois, a long-time friend of Lincoln's, represented his state in the U.S. Senate (1861–63). Joseph Holt of Kentucky (1807–94) was judge advocate general of the army (1862–75). Indiana politician John Palmer Usher (1816–89), who had served as assistant secretary of the interior, became secretary of the interior on 3 January 1863.

89. Caleb B. Smith (1808–64) of Indiana, who served as secretary of the interior (1861–63), sat as a judge on the U.S. District Court of Indiana (1863–64).

90. On 31 December Lincoln signed the congressional statute creating the new state of West Virginia.

91. Lazare-Nicolas-Margurite Carnot (1753–1823), known as "the organizer of victory," was in charge of organizing and directing the armies of France in the 1790s and served as minister of war under Napoleon.

92. On 19 December a delegation of senators urged Lincoln to fire his secretary of state, William Henry Seward. Skillfully finessing this challenge to his authority, the president on 20 December met again with the senators and his cabinet and defused the crisis.

93. U.S. Rep. William D. "Pig Iron" Kelley (1814–90), a leading Radical Republican from Philadelphia, served in Congress from 1861 to 1890.

94. The commander of French forces in Germany, Marshal Henri de La Tour d'Auvergne, vicomte de Turenne (1611–75) was one of Louis XIV's more effective generals.

95. Horatio Seymour (1810–86) was governor of New York (1853–55 and 1863–65).

Chapter Three. 1863

1. The battle of Murfreesboro ("Stone's River"), part of the struggle for control of central Tennessee, began on 31 December and ended on 2 January. After much carnage that resulted more or less in a draw, the Confederates fell back thirty-five miles and went into winter quarters.

2. In December 1862 Union general Benjamin F. Butler (1818–93) was removed from his post as military governor of Louisiana. At the time this was written he was in Washington seeking a new command.

3. On 1 January Confederate forces captured Galveston, Texas, which had been occupied by Union troops a week earlier.

4. John B. Magruder (1810–71) had been commander of the U.S. Artillery in Washington. When he deserted to the Confederacy in April, he was entrusted with

the defense of the Virginia peninsula. He led the Confederate forces that captured Galveston.

5. William T. Otto became the assistant secretary of the interior. Walton J. Smith, son of Interior Secretary Caleb B. Smith, was the chief clerk of the office of the secretary of the interior.

6. New York–born James M. Edmunds (1809–79) served as commissioner of the General Land Office (1861–66), president of the Union League of America (1862–69), and postmaster of New York City (1869–79).

7. Peter H. Watson, the shrewd and energetic assistant secretary of war, was one of the nation's foremost patent lawyers.

8. Charles Sherwood Stratton (1838–83), a dwarf known as "Gen. Tom Thumb," married Lavinia Warren (1841–1919) on 10 February; the wedding received much press attention.

9. William Cornell Jewett, the descendant of an old Maine family, had settled in Colorado, where he was involved in gold mining interests. He began his career as a peacemaker as early as 1861, when he tried to win appointment as a delegate to the Peace Convention from Colorado. With former president Millard Fillmore he then attempted to arrange a compromise peace between North and South. Failing in that, he sought to enlist the aid of European powers to mediate the dispute between the sections. Attorney General Bates dismissed him as "a crack-brained simpleton, who aspires to be a knave." One historian called him an "imbecile optimist." Edward Chase Kirkland, *The Peacemakers of 1864* (New York: Macmillan, 1927), 70.

10. In January 1863 Napoleon III urged that the North and South negotiate a peace. On 5 February Seward wrote to the U.S. minister to France, William L. Dayton, that there were "no northern and southern states" but only "an insurrectionary party, which is located upon and adjacent to the shore of the Gulf of Mexico," and that the Union's resources were sufficient to win the war.

11. Democrat Daniel W. Voorhees (1827–97) of Terre Haute represented his district in the U.S. House (1861–66, 1869–73). He also represented Indiana in the U.S. Senate (1877–91).

12. Charles Mackay (1814–89), a poet, songwriter, and journalist, covered American events from New York for the *London Times* (1862–65).

13. Joseph Hooker (1814–79) commanded the Army of the Potomac (January–June 1863).

14. Thomas Wentworth Higginson (1823–1911), a Massachusetts abolitionist, commanded the First South Carolina Colored Infantry.

15. On 3 March Congress passed the Enrollment Act making all able-bodied men between the ages of twenty and forty-five eligible to be drafted.

16. On 1 April 1 the Rhode Island Republican ticket, headed by guberna-

torial candidate James Y. Smith, won an overwhelming victory, electing both congressmen and capturing a large majority of the state legislature. In Connecticut, Republican gubernatorial candidate William A. Buckingham defeated his Democratic opponent, Thomas H. Seymour, by a narrow margin. The Republicans also captured three of the state's four congressional seats and both houses of the state legislature.

17. Thomas B. Florence (1812–75), who had served as a member of the U.S. House of Representatives from Pennsylvania (1851–61), edited the *Washington Constitutional Union* (1863–68). Willard Saulsbury (1815–92) was a Democratic senator from Delaware (1859–71). William A. Richardson (1811–75) was a Democratic senator from Illinois (1863–65). Fernando Wood (1812–81), a leading Democrat, served as mayor of New York (1855–58, 1861–62) and as a member of the U.S. House (1863–65, 1867–81). His brother, Benjamin Wood (1820–1900), editor of the *New York Daily News*, served in the U.S. House (1861–65, 1881–83). James A. Bayard (1799–1880) was a Democratic senator from Delaware (1851–64).

18. A national fast was held on 29 April.

19. On 7 April a Union fleet under Adm. Samuel Du Pont made an unsuccessful attack on Fort Sumter in Charleston Harbor.

20. Lincoln visited the Army of the Potomac at Falmouth from 5 to 10 April.

21. Hooker's Army of the Potomac was soundly defeated by Lee's Army of Northern Virginia at the battle of Chancellorsville, Virginia (1–4 May).

22. General Grant was moving on Vicksburg MS, which he captured on 4 July. Gen. N. P. Banks was besieging Port Hudson LA, which fell on 8 July.

23. On 2 May Thomas J. "Stonewall" Jackson was wounded by his own troops. He died eight days later.

24. On 30 April Grant boldly crossed the Mississippi River below Vicksburg, cutting himself off from his supply base, and launched a campaign against Vicksburg, which he besieged in mid-May after winning battles at Port Gibson, Champion's Hill, and other sites in Mississippi.

25. On 28 May artillery captain Edmund Kirby (b. 1840) of New York died of wounds he sustained in the battle of Chancellorsville. On his deathbed he was promoted to general.

26. Andrew Hull Foote (b. 1806) died en route to his new post at Charleston. In July John A. Dahlgren replaced Samuel Du Pont as commander of the South Atlantic Blockading Squadron.

27. Pennsylvania-born John C. Pemberton (1814–81) commanded Confederate forces in the Department of Mississippi and Eastern Louisiana.

28. On 9 June Alfred Pleasonton, commander of the cavalry of the Army of the Potomac, fought the Confederate cavalry under Jeb Stuart at Beverly's Ford (also called Brandy Station) in the biggest cavalry battle of the war.

29. In a long public letter the president defended his administration against attacks made by an assemblage of Democrats in Albany, New York, on 16 May. Lincoln to Erastus Corning and Others, Washington, 12 June 1863, Basler, *Collected Works of Lincoln*, 6:260–69.

30. George Gordon Meade (1815–72) of Pennsylvania commanded the Army of the Potomac (1863–65).

31. In May, Gen. N. P. Banks had laid siege to Port Hudson, which surrendered on 8 July.

32. The Confederates surrendered Vicksburg to Grant on 4 July.

33. Achille Bazaine, Marshal Forey (1811–88), commanded French troops supporting the Emperor Maximilian in Mexico.

34. On 26 August Lincoln wrote a long letter addressed to his friend, James C. Conkling, to be read aloud at a mass meeting of unconditional pro-Union men at Springfield on 3 September. Basler, *Collected Works of Lincoln*, 6:406–10.

35. On 9 September federal forces captured the Cumberland Gap and Confederate general Braxton Bragg evacuated Chattanooga.

36. On 10 September Massachusetts senator Charles Sumner (1811–74) delivered a speech entitled "Our Foreign Relations" at New York's Cooper Union.

37. Union general William S. Rosecrans (1819–98) commanded the Army of the Cumberland.

38. Union general Quincy A. Gillmore (1825–88) commanded the Tenth Corps, Department of the South; John A. Dahlgren (1809–70) commanded the South Atlantic Blockading Fleet.

39. Union forces under William S. Rosecrans were defeated at the battle of Chickamauga, Georgia, 19–21 September 1863.

40. Radical delegations from Missouri and Kansas came to Washington in the wake of the Lawrence massacre on 21–22 August, perpetrated by William C. Quantrill and his bushwackers. Lincoln met with the Missouri delegation for two hours on 30 September.

41. John M. Schofield (1831–1906) commanded the Department of Missouri.

42. Gen. George Stoneman (1822–94) had commanded the cavalry of the Army of the Potomac under Hooker.

43. On 9 October Lee began to march northward. As Meade fell back, he was attacked on 14 October at Bristoe Station, Virginia. Meade repelled the attack and deployed his forces in a strong position at Centerville, near Manassas. Three days later Lee withdrew southward to his old position on the Rappahannock.

44. On 13 October Democrat Clement L. Vallandigham lost the Ohio gubernatorial race by a wide margin.

45. On 16 October Grant replaced Rosecrans as the commander of the Department of the Cumberland (later renamed the Department of the Mississippi).

46. During the Bristoe, Virginia, campaign (9–22 October), Meade passed up opportunities to attack Lee.

47. Lee attacked Meade at Bristoe Station, Virginia, on 14 October.

48. In mid-October Stanton had hurried west to confer with Grant and give him orders placing him in command of the new Department of the Mississippi.

49. Lincoln to Charles D. Drake et al., Washington, 5 October 1863, Basler, *Collected Works of Lincoln*, 6:499–504.

50. The Republicans won control of the legislature and captured the post of secretary of state by a wide margin, reversing the trend of the previous year when the Democratic gubernatorial candidate, Horatio Seymour, won by over ten thousand votes.

51. On 24 September elements of the Russian fleet arrived in New York, where their commander, Admiral Lisovski, and his men were received warmly. They enjoyed a similar reception in Washington and elsewhere.

52. Kate Chase (1840–99), daughter of Salmon P. Chase, married Rhode Island senator William Sprague on 12 November.

53. Grant's forces won the battle of Chattanooga on 23–25 November.

54. Schuyler Colfax of Indiana (1823–85) was elected Speaker of the House in December. At the same time, conservative Unionist Emerson Etheridge (1819–1902), a slaveholder from west Tennessee, was replaced as clerk of the House.

55. George H. Thomas of Virginia (1816–70) commanded the Fourteenth Corps of the Army of the Cumberland. In September 1863 he earned the sobriquet "The Rock of Chickamauga" when he prevented a complete Union rout at the battle of Chickamauga.

56. Etheridge hoped to disqualify many Republican representatives on a technicality. Lincoln sent a letter to senators James W. Grimes, Zachariah Chandler, and Jacob Collamer, as well as to Vice President Hannibal Hamlin, urging them to prepare for this parliamentary maneuver. Basler, *Collected Works of Lincoln*, 6:546–50. In December 1839, when the clerk of the House refused to call the names of five representatives from New Jersey (all of whose credentials were under challenge), Adams appealed to the members from the decision of the clerk and single-handedly organized the body, in effect becoming temporarily the Speaker of the House. In the winter of 1855–56 the House spent weeks wrangling over the selection of a Speaker. On the 133rd ballot Nathaniel P. Banks of Massachusetts, a Republican who had been a Know-Nothing, won the contest.

57. In his annual message to Congress, Lincoln spelled out a plan of reconstruction. At the same time he issued a proclamation of amnesty and reconstruction. Basler, *Collected Works of Lincoln*, 7:36–56.

58. On 7 December Schuyler Colfax was elected Speaker of the House.

59. Lincoln came down with a mild form of smallpox known as varioloid fever. He was quarantined in the White House for almost three weeks.

CHAPTER FOUR. 1864–1865

1. In January the National Academy of Science met in Washington. Lincoln was introduced to its members on the Eighth.

2. Garrett Davis (1801–72) was a Democratic senator from Kentucky (1861–72).

3. Anna E. Dickinson (1842–1932) of Philadelphia was a mesmerizing antislavery lecturer and an outspoken Radical. Frederick Douglass (1817?–95) was the leading black abolitionist.

4. Charles Francis Adams (1807–86) of Massachusetts served as American minister to Great Britian (1861–68).

5. On 20 February Union forces decisively lost the battle of Olustee, Florida.

6. On 3 February William T. Sherman launched a campaign against Meridian, Mississippi. He spent the month of February destroying Confederate railroads and supply depots in Mississippi.

7. Kansas senator Samuel C. Pomeroy (1816–91) was the author of the "Pomeroy Circular," which denounced Lincoln and called for Chase's nomination. It was distributed to scores of political leaders and published in the press. The full text can be found in Nicolay and Hay, *Lincoln*, 8:319–20.

8. From 28 February to 3 March Union general Judson Kilpatrick (1836–81) led a cavalry raid against Richmond.

9. On 22 February German-born Michael Hahn (1830–86) was elected the first Unionist governor of Louisiana.

10. Ulric Dahlgren (b. 1842), son of Adm. John A. Dahlgren, commanded a five hundred–man force in Kilpatrick's raid, during which he was killed.

11. On 5 March Chase wrote a public letter to James C. Hall announcing his withdrawal from the presidential race.

12. On 8 April Sumner gave a speech titled "No Property in Man," in which he endorsed the Thirteenth Amendment to the Constitution abolishing slavery throughout theUnited States.

13. On 12 April the Confederates captured Fort Pillow on the Mississippi. When Union troops threw down their arms and surrendered, their captors killed some of them in cold blood, including many blacks.

14. Denmark and Germany had long contended for dominance in the two "Elbe duchies" of Schleswig and Holstein. The crisis reached a head on 15 November 1863 with the death of King Frederick IV of Denmark, who had no male heir. The complex dispute threatened to provoke a general European war.

15. In 1863 Archduke Ferdinand Maximilian of Austria was installed as emperor of Mexico largely through the intrigues of Napoleon III of France.

16. Daniel Webster (1782–1852) served as secretary of state under William Henry Harrison, John Tyler, and Millard Filmore (1841–43 and 1850–52). William L. Marcy (1786–1857) of New York served as secretary of state under Franklin Pierce (1853–57).

17. Ohio senator Benjamin Franklin Wade (1800–1878), a leading Radical Republican, was born in Massachusetts and settled in the Western Reserve section of Ohio. A militant opponent of slavery, his frank manner and hot temper won him the sobriquet "Bluff Ben." During the war he was a fierce opponent of both the Confederacy and conservative Union generals. Daniel W. Gooch (1820–91) of Boston represented his district in the U.S. House (1858–65, 1873–75). On 12 April the Confederate cavalry under Nathaniel Bedford Forrest captured Fort Pillow, Tennessee, garrisoned by 557 Union troops, 262 of them black. The Committee on the Conduct of the War issued a report alleging that at least 300 of those men, mostly blacks, were murdered in cold blood after surrendering.

18. On 16 May Union general Benjamin F. Butler lost the battle of Drewry's Bluff and was subsequently bottled up on Bermuda Hundred, where his forces were rendered ineffective as part of Grant's campaign against Richmond.

19. The Republican Party, renamed the Union Party, was to hold its presidential nominating convention in Baltimore in early June.

20. James M. Johnson, T. M. Jacks, and Anthony A. C. Rogers formed the Arkansas congressional delegation. Their credentials were rejected by Congress, however, and they never took their seats.

21. General E. R. S. Canby (1817–73) was commander of the Military Department of West Mississippi.

22. In February Nathaniel P. Banks launched a campaign up the Red River in Louisiana which he was forced to abandon in May.

23. Confederate general John S. Marmaduke (1833–87), operating under the command of Gen. Sterling Price, won a minor battle against Union forces at Poison Springs, Arkansas, on 18 April. He captured 198 wagons.

24. On 30 June Lincoln accepted Chase's resignation. The secretary submitted it when the president would not honor his demand in a patronage dispute in the New York custom house.

25. Lincoln first appointed David Tod (1805–68), who served as governor of Ohio (1862–64), to replace Chase. When Tod declined the appointment, the president named Maine senator William Pitt Fessenden (1806–69), who served as secretary of the treasury from 1864 to 1865.

26. In July Confederate forces under Jubal Early drove up the Shennandoah Valley and menaced Washington.

27. On 19 June the U.S.S. *Kearsarge* sank the Confederate commerce raider *Alabama* near Cherbourg, France.

28. Confederate general Edmund Kirby Smith (1824–93) commanded the Trans-Mississippi Department.

29. Confederate general John Bell Hood invaded Tennessee, and at Nashville on 15–16 December George H. Thomas's Army of the Cumberland demolished his army.

Index

abolitionists, 83
Adams, Charles Francis, 205
Adams, John Quincy, 194
css *Alabama*, 242
Albany NY, Democrats in, 160
Alexandria VA, 2, 6; conduct of Union troops in, 16; *Gazette*, 2
Altoona Conference, 108
American character, 92
Amnesty Proclamation, 203, 235
Antietam campaign, 103–7
Arkansas: conditions in, 244, 249–50; Congressional delegation from, 230–31, 234–35; ignorance in, xxv; land policy in, xxv, 251; Stoddard in, xxiv, 243–51; struggle for, 59; Unionists in, 245, 251
Arkansas River, 248
Arlington Heights, 2, 10
Arlington House, 8, 242
Army of the Mississippi, 51
Army of the Potomac, 98, 150; conditions in, 36–37, 51, 129; epistolary habits of soldiers in, 46; foreign officers in, 43; at Gettysburg, 161; health of, 54, 56, 155; inaction of, 51–52, 193; morale of, 127; readiness of, 40; rumors about, 177; second corps of, 181; winter quarters of, 199
Army of Virginia, 83

artillery, 38–39
atrocities, 70. *See also* Fort Pillow

Baker, Edward D., 43, 46; death of, 39–40
Ball's Bluff, battle of, 39–40, 202, 242
Banks, Nathaniel P., 61, 83, 101, 187–88, 236; and Louisiana politics, 215; Port Hudson campaign of, 157, 162; as Speaker of the House, 194; Texas campaign of, 186, 192
Beauregard, P. G. T., 29, 175
Beverly's Ford, battle of, 159
black troops: discrimination against, xvii; effect of army service on, 237; importance of, xix; mistreatment of, by Confederates, 135; policy of recruiting, 167; prejudice against, 142, 155; psychological effect on, of army service, 163; qualities of, 135, 158; record of, xviii
blacks: assertiveness of, xvii–xviii; enthusiasm of, for military service, xvii; manhood of, xvii–xviii; morale of, xvi–xvii; nationalism of, xvi–xvii; reaction of, to freedom, xvii, 77–78; self-respect of, xvii–xviii. *See also* black troops
Blenker, Ludwig, 40, 42, 45; clash of, with McClellan, 45
Blitz, Signor, 214
blockade, 105, 119

Bragg, Braxton, 162
Brandy Station. *See* Beverly's Ford, battle of
Breckenridge, John, 14, 45
brigadierships, 44, 74–75
Bright, Edward, Jr., xix
Bright, Jesse D., 58
Bristoe [Bristow] Station VA, 183
Browning, Orville H., 126
Buchanan, James, 36
Buell, Don Carlos, 59, 61; removal of, 119; and Shiloh, 71
Bull Run, first battle of, 15–16, 18, 52, 202, 242
Burnside, Ambrose E., 13, 121, 126; failure of, 149; and Fredericksburg, 128; in North Carolina, 59, 80–81; in Tennessee, 168
Butler, Benjamin F., 132; on Peninsula, 209, 227, 229
Byng, John, 125

cabinet: activity of, 129; on brigadierships, 44; industry of, 93; reports of, 195–96; rumored changes in, 18, 77, 91–92, 108, 110, 128, 163. *See also individual cabinet members*
Cameron, Simon, 47, 62; criticism of, 28
Canby, E. R. S., 235, 236, 237; Arkansas expedition of, 247; wounding of, 248
Capitol, U.S., 75, 143, 194
Carlisle, John S., 125
cavalry camp, 178
censorship, of press, xiii
Central Illinois Gazette, xx
Champaign County IL, xxi
Champaign IL, xx
Chancellorsville, 151–52, 155
Charleston SC, siege of, 147, 158, 168, 170, 172–73, 175, 177, 179, 188
Chase, Kate, 191
Chase, Salmon P., 19, 216; banking plans of, 135; criticism of, 28; financial policy

of, 141, 242–43; presidential candidacy of (1864), 214, 219; resignation of, 240; visit of, to Union army, 74
Chattanooga, 169; evacuation of, 170; Grant and, 182, 190, 191
Chickamauga, 174–76, 185
churches, use of, as hospitals, 123
claim agents, 116
Colfax, Schuyler, 76, 193, 196
colonization, xvii, 123, 128
Committee of Ways and Means, 206
compromise proposals, 165–66
Confederacy: cavalry of, 118; Congress of, 111; morale in army of, 170; resources of, 11, 121; soldiers of, 100; strategy of, 93; war weariness in, 89; weaknesses of, 92
confiscation: debates on, 72–73; legislation enacting, 91
Congress, U.S., 16–17, 19; achievements of, 87; adjournment of, 86, 240; caucuses of, 43; committee work in, 206; Confederate sympathizers in, 220; conscientiousness of, 87; convening of, 193; debates in, 49, 76, 207, 223; divisions in, 47–48; and government finances, 52, 61, 130, 135, 136, 218–19, 223, 234, 238; inaction of, 136; industriousness of, 136; legislation passed by, 138–39; and Lincoln, 48, 123; orators in, 216; partisanship in, 53; personnel of, 87, 124, 196; reassembling of, 200
Conkling, James C., Lincoln's letter to, 169
Connecticut, elections in, 146
Conscription law [Conscription bill, Conscript law], 139, 144, 146, 150
Constitutional Union, 146
Cooper, Susan E., xxv
Copperheads, 125, 136, 139, 207
Corinth, battle of, 114
corruption, 20, 98–99; accusation of, 55–56; in U.S. government, 53–54
cotton trade, 246

Cox, S. S., 79
Crittenden, John J., 15, 45–46
Cumberland Gap, 170

Dahlgren gun, 10
Dahlgren, John, 172, 175, 179
Dahlgren, Ulric, 218
Davies, Henry Ebenezer, 47
Davies, Henry Eugene, 47
Davis, Garrett, 202
Davis, Jefferson, messages of, 98, 215–16
DeKalb Regiment, 37
Dickinson, Anna E., 202
disloyalty, among U.S. civil servants, 17, 22, 24, 30
Douglas, Stephen A., 45; death of, 10
Douglass, Frederick, 202
draft. *See* conscription law
Dranesville VA, battle of, 51
Dupont, Samuel, 158

Edmunds, James M., 133
elections: (1862): 110, 114–15, 117, 119; (1863): 181; (1864): 208, 216
Ellsworth Avengers, 40
Ellsworth, Elmer E., 4, 8, 197; death of, 7; Zouaves of, 1
emancipation, 90–91, 125; Act of (Washington DC), 77
Emancipation Proclamation, 107, 128, 134, 203; effect of, 112–13, 131, 167
emigration. *See* colonization
England: neutrality of, 109; press in, 188, 197; and privateers, 143; public opinion in, 11; relations with U.S., 51; and U.S. Civil War, 114
Enrollment Bill, 210
Ericsson, John, 64
Ericsson (Monitor), 63, 64
Etheridge, Emerson, 15, 193
Europe: and Civil War, 42, 52, 57, 59, 97–98, 109, 111; opinion in, 23–24, 87, 197; and relations with U.S., 120–21

Fairfax Court House, 43
fast days, 147
Fessenden, William P., 240, 246
finances: of Confederacy, 14; of Union, 14, 25–26, 31, 86, 127, 135, 153, 159, 216–17
Fire Zouaves, 1, 4, 6
Florence, Thomas B., 146
Foote, Andrew Hull, 73, 158
Fort Donelson, prisoners taken at, 62–63
Fort Monroe, 63
Fort Pillow, 71; massacre at, 222–23, 228
Fort Scott, 62
foreign relations, of U.S., 48–49, 51, 114, 118, 132, 143–44, 169, 173, 184, 189, 213–14, 219
Forey, Marshal, 169, 189
Forney, John W., xix
France, and U.S. Civil War, 114, 137
franking privilege, abolition of, 54–55
frauds, 98–99
Fredericksburg, battle of, xv, 123, 126, 127, 128, 129
USS *Freeborn*, 10
freedmen, 123; and Mexico, 79
Fremont, John C.: and Lincoln, 27; in Missouri, 31, 32, 33, 35, 38; resignation of, 83; in Shenandoah Valley, 71

Galveston TX, 132, 133
Georgetown Heights, 2
Georgetown, streets of, 27
Germans, in Union army, 28–29
Gillmore, Quincy A., 172, 175; in Florida, 213; and J. Dahlgren, 179
Goddess of Freedom, 194
gold market, 181
Gooch, Daniel W., 228
government employees: salaries of, 54. *See also* disloyalty, among U.S. civil servants
Governors' Conference. *See* Altoona Conference
Grant, U.S.: appearance of, 224; assumption of command by, of the Military

Grant, U.S. (*continued*)
  Division of the Mississippi, 185; character of, 224; Chattanooga campaign of, 182, 190, 191; Chattanooga report of, 222; comparison of, to Lee, 224; and lieutenant generalship, 206, 216–18; military strategy of, xv, 222; preparations of, for 1864 campaign, 219–20; on relative strength of North and South, 226; reputation of, 185; and Shiloh, 71; and Vicksburg campaign, 156, 157, 162; and Virginia campaign (1864), 225, 226, 227, 229, 231, 233, 235, 236, 239, 241, 246
greenbacks, 181
guerrillas, 12, 91, 94, 118, 236, 248
gunboat fleet, 10, 59
Gurowski, Adam, 85

habeas corpus, xiii
Hahn, Michael, 215
Halleck, Henry, 93, 99
Harper's Ferry, Union defeat at, 107
Harrington, George, 19, 25
Harris, Ira, xxii, 8, 47, 58, 72
Harris Light Cavalry, 47
Hatteras NC, expedition to, 23
Hay, John, xi, xii, xiv, xv, xxv; health of, xxiii
Heintzelman, Samuel P., 101
Herndon, William H., xxi
Higginson, Thomas Wentworth, 142
Holt, Joseph, 126
Hood, John Bell, 246
Hooker, Joseph, 138, 140, 149, 193; at Chancellorsville, 151–52
hospitals, 74, 82–83, 86, 123–24
House of Representatives: committee of ways and means of, 130; organization of, 194
Hugo, Victor, 104
Hunter, David, 62

Illinois Staatszeitung, xix

Illinois State Journal, xix
internal improvements, 87, 159
inventions, 9, 22–23, 149, 209
Island No. Ten, 67–68
Ives, Malcolm, 92

Jackson, Andrew, 96–97
Jackson, Thomas J. ("Stonewall"), 93, 99, 156; death of, 154
James, Benjamin F., xxii
Jewett, William C., 137
Johnson, Andrew, 15, 46
Johnson, Reverdy, 77
Johnston, Albert Sidney, 71
Johnston, Joseph E., 236

Kanawha. *See* West Virginia
Kearney, Philip, 116
USS *Kearsarge*, 242
Kelly, William D., 128
Kentucky, civil war in, 32
Kilpatrick, Judson, 215
Kirby, Edmund, 157
Knights of the Golden Circle, 146
Knoxville, 168

lancers, 68
land policy, xxv
Lane, Joseph, 46
Lee, Robert E.: comparison of, to Grant, 224; defeat of, 161; generalship of, 230; after Gettysburg, 164; and Meade, 180–81; rumors about, 156, 158, 171; in Virginia campaign (1864), 225–27, 236, 239, 241; as traitor, 4
Leesburg, battle of. *See* Ball's Bluff
letters of marque, 118–19
Lexington MO, 31
Lincoln, Abraham: amiability of, xx; appearance of, xi, xii, 14, 32, 38, 62, 88, 166, 177; appointments by, 205; approval of, 90; assassination of, xxv; character of, xi, xii, xx, 14, 122; common

sense of, 88; conscientiousness of, xii, 20, 55, 101, 166; coolness of, 88; cordiality of, xi; criticism of, xiii–xiv, 106; demands upon, xiv, 145; emancipation plans of, 90–91 (*see also* Emancipation Proclamation); endorsement of for president, by Stoddard, xxi; ; faith of people in, 103; fame of, xii, 122; and government departments, 94; and H. Greeley, 98; grief of, 62; health of, 55, 193, 197; honesty of, 90–91; horse of, 103; inauguration of (first), 212–13; indispensability of, xii, xiv, 74, 103; industriousness of, xii; journalism by, xix; kindness of, xi; leadership qualities of, xiii; levees of, 8, 14, 198–99; limits on power of, xi–xii; messages of, to Congress, 13, 110, 124, 195; military strategy of, xv, 7–8, 60, 222; modesty of, xx; mood of, xii, 38, 55, 62, 66, 85, 197; near accident of, xiv, 103; optimism of, 85; and patronage, xiv, xix; policy of, regarding black troops, xix; political savvy of, xxi; political standing of, xx; popularity of, xii, xiii, 28, 48, 88, 181–82, 185; powers of, 36; and press, xix; public expectations of, xi–xii; public faith in, xii–xiii; public letters of, 160, 169; as punster, xvi; on rebellion, 59; reelection of, 204, 246; on relative strength of North and South, xv; renomination of, 208, 230; as representative American, xii–xiii, 88; schedule of, xii; selflessness of, xiii; on slavery, 98; spirits of, xii; statesmanship of, xii; and W. O. Stoddard, xxiv, xx–xxi; and stress, xi, 32, 145; trustworthiness of, xiii, 88; vacation plans of, 169; visits of, to army, 73–74, 79, 112, 148
Lincoln, Mary Todd: criticism of, 139; and Lincoln, 177; receptions of, 49, vacations of, 20
Lincoln, Thomas ("Tad"), 66, 82

Lincoln, William W. ("Willie"), xii
liquor, punishment for selling of, to soldiers, 56
Little Rock AR, 244, 250
London Times, 70, 139, 173, 225
Long Branch NJ, 20
Long Bridge, 6, 10, 26, 241
Longstreet, James, 191
Louisiana, Reconstruction in, 215
Lyon, Nathaniel, 43

Mackay, Charles, 139
Madison NJ, xxvi
Magruder, John B., 132, 133
Manassas. *See* Bull Run
Marble, Manton, xxiv
Marine band, 77, 96, 178
Marmaduke, John S., 239
Marshal of Arkansas, duties of, xxv
Maryland: Confederate invasions of, 101, 241; constitutional convention in, 204; election in, 146; real estate in, 221; and slavery, 72
Mason, James M., 45
Massachusetts Eighth Regiment, 1
Matamoras, Mexico, 113
McCall, George A., 74
McClellan, George B.: appointment of, as general in chief, 41; assumption of command of eastern army of, 16; and L. Blenker, 45; career of, 120; caution of, 83; criticism of, 65–66, 116; defenders of, 121; and defenses of Washington, 100, 101; as disciplinarian, 43; enemies of, 85, 90; failure of, 149; friends of, 90; health of, 24; impatience with, of North, 50; mood of, 36; organizational skills of, 17, 103; peninsular campaign of, 37, 69; plans of, 49–50; and politics, 136, 160; popularity of, 21–22, 27, 148; popular opinion of, 73, 75, 82; removal of, from command, 119; responsibilities of, 57, 60; solicitude of, for troops, 27; staff of,

McClellan, George B. (*continued*) 242; strategy of, 176; and Yorktown, 71–72, 79
McCook, Robert, 94
McCulloch, Ben, 2
McDowell, Irvin, 101
Meade, George G., 162; and Grant, 226; and Lee, 164, 180–81; reputation of, 183
Memphis TN, 247
CSS *Merrimack*, 64, 67; destruction of, 79
Mexico, 180, 235; as site for freedmen to settle in, 79. *See also* Matamoras
Michigan Fist Regiment, 6
military trials, 125
Mississippi River, 156, 243, 247
Missouri: Radicals in, 177; struggle for, 59
Missouri Democrat, xix
USS *Monitor*, 145. *See also Ericsson*
Monroe Doctrine, 225
Morgan, John Hunt, 93
mud, 219–20, 221–22
Munson's Hill, 24, 37

Napoleon, Louis, 169, 173, 189, 225
Napoleon, Prince, 17
National Academy of Sciences, 200
National Rifles, xxii
Navy, Union, 51, 67
Navy Yard (Washington), 9
Newbern NC, 81
New York: elections in, 187; politics in, 24, 26; press in, 90, 151, 236; regiments from, 1, 6, 10, 21, 40, 47
New York Examiner, xix
New York Herald, xiii, 88; criticism of, 102; and Shiloh, 71
New York Tribune, xii, xix, 88
Nicolay, John G., xi, xiv, xv, xxii, xxvii
Norfolk VA, capture of, 79
North Carolina, 167–68, 204; military operations in, 80–81, 215

North: mood of, 100; public opinion in, 137

office seekers, xxii, 15, 30, 93, 96
Ohio: elections in, 161, 181; militia, 232
Olustee FL, battle of, 213
Otto, William T., 133

Pacific railroad, 80, 86, 184
pass system, 69–70
patronage, 93. *See also* office seekers
Pemberton, John C., 159
USS *Pensacola*, 9
Pensacola FL, 43
Perryville KY, battle of, 114
Phillips, Wendell, xiii, 95, 202
Pittsburg Landing. *See* Shiloh, battle of
Pleasonton, Alfred, 104, 159
political factions, in North, 33–34
polygamy, 86
Pomeroy, Samuel C., xvii, 123, 214, 216
Pope, John, 88, 99, 101; appointment of, to head Army of Virginia, 83; defeat of, 242; as a leader, 119; retreat of, 98
Porter, Fitz John, 101
Port Hudson LA, 154, 162, 164
Port Royal expedition, 37–38
Potomac River, 11; closing of, 37; condition of, 117
Potter, John F., 22, 24, 133
Price, Sterling, 59
prisoners of war: Confederate, 62–63, 232–33; Union, 97
pro-slavery argument, 211

Quinby, Isaac, 10

racism, 211
receptions, at White House, 202
Reconstruction, 195, 235
recruiting, suspension of, 70
religious sentiment, in North, 31

INDEX

Republican national convention (1864), 208, 230, 235, 237, 238
Rhode Island: elections in, 146; First Regiment, 1
Richmond *Examiner*, 236
Richmond, strategic importance of, 191–92
Rosecrans, William S.: and Chattanooga, 172, 178–79; and Chickamauga, 175; and Corinth, 113
Royal Decrees of Scanderoon, The, xxv
Russell, William H., 70
Russia, fleet of, 188

Sabbath observance, in Union army, 25
Sanitary Commission, 221
Sanitary Fairs, 201, 210–11
Schofield, John M., 177; letter to, from Lincoln, 183
Scott, Winfield, 3, 12, 13; retirement of, 41; strategy of, 8
Scroggs, John W., xx
Seward, William H., 48, 173; and C. F. Adams, 205; criticism of, 28; and France, 137; and National Academy of Sciences, 200
Seymour, Horatio, 130
Sheridan, Philip, 246
Sherman, John, 55
Sherman, William T., and Atlanta campaign, 227, 229, 232, 236, 239, 246
Shiloh, battle of, 71
Sickles, Daniel, 61
Sigel, Franz, 42, 101
slaves: insurrection of, 123; reaction of, to freedom, 77–78
Smead, Capt., 6
Smith, Caleb B., 126, 133
Smith, Edmund Kirby, 245
Smith, Walton, 133
snobs, in North, 33
Soldiers' Home, 82, 177
South Carolina, 29

South Mountain, 109
spies, 12, 24
spiritualism, 214
Spotsylvania, 231
Sprague, William, 6, 14; wedding of, 191
Springfield MO, 43
Stanly, Edward, 81
Stanton, Edwin M.: critics of, 85; and H. W. Halleck, 93; health of, 62; industriousness of, 66, 183; personality of, 140; public confidence in, 61; on rebellion, 55; reputation of, 122; and W. H. Russell, 70; travels of, 180
State Department Building, 228
Stevens, Thaddeus, 76–77
Stoddard, William O.: adventuresomeness of, xxv; ambition of, xxiv; appearance of, xi, xxv; application of, for presidential secretaryship, xxi–xxii; as author, xi, xxv; biographical sketch of, xx–xxvi; biography of Lincoln by, xi; ; in campaign of 1860, xxi; character of, xxvi; criticism of, xxiii; death of, xxvi; duties of, as presidential secretary, xxii–xxiii; health of, xxiii, xxiv, xxv; industriousness of, xxiii; and Lincoln, xxiv, xxv; and mail in White House, xxiii; marksmanship of, xxv; marriage of, xxv; military service of, xxii–xxiii, 6, 11, 241–42; as raconteur, xxvi; relationship of, with blacks, xviii; relations with Nicolay and Hay, xxiii–xxiv; reticence of, xxii; self-assessment of, xxvi; youth of, xx
Stoddard, William O., Jr., xxiv–xxvi
Stoddard, Mrs. William O. *See* Susan E. Cooper
Stoneman, George, 178
Stratton, Charles S. *See* Tom Thumb
Stuart, J. E. B., 114
Sumner, Charles, speeches of, 171–72, 220
Supreme Court, vacancies in, 62

Talleyrand, 125

Tammany Hall, xxv
Taney, Roger B., 212
tariff bill, 233
taxes, 86, 93, 99, 200–201, 238
Tennessee: antislavery sentiment in, 150; East, 168, 205; Union control of, 59; Unionism in, 168; Union success in, 154
Thumb, Tom, 137
Tolono IL, xx
Treasury Building, 25, 75, 142
Treasury Department, 19, 31; criticism of, 224, 228; difficulties in, 116; rules in, 68
Treasury notes, 35
Trumbull, Lyman, xxii
Tullahoma, 162
Twiggs, David, 103

Union army: conditions in, 85, 138; corrals of, 26; ethnic make-up of, 41–42; foreign-born officers in, 39; Germans in, 28–29; morale of, 9–10, 13, 86, 141; political attitudes in, 189–90; soldiers of, 100
Unionism, in South, 89, 168, 195, 245
Union, resources of, 12
Usher, John Palmer, 126, 133

Vallandigham, Clement, 79; and Lincoln, 161; nomination of, for Ohio governorship, 160–61
Valley campaign, 73
Van Buren, Martin, 96
Van Wyck, Charles, committee of, 76
Vicksburg MS, 113, 147, 154, 156; fall of, 164; siege of, 158–59
Virginia: landscape of, 47, 64–65, 176; roads in, 58
volunteering, for Union army, 91
Voorhees, Daniel, 139

Wade, Benjamin F., 228

Wall street, 86, 181
War Department: alleged corruption in, 20; plans of, 60; unpopularity of, 122
Washburne, E. B., xxv
Washington DC: abolition of slavery in, 72; anxiety in, 7; as armed camp, 1; churches in, 82; clergymen in, 192–93; communications of, with North, 191, 199; conditions in, 1, 4, 8, 17–18, 19, 33, 35, 39, 45, 54, 66–67, 70, 76, 93, 115–16, 134, 169–70, 176, 178, 195, 213, 225; defenses of, 2, 4, 8, 11, 16, 26, 193–94; elections in, 151; entertainment in, 96; gambling in, 53, 73, 116, 151; health of, 54, 77, 85, 204; hospitals in, 74, 82–83; militia of, 163; mood in, xvi, 3–4, 11–12, 22, 202; moral climate of, xvi; music in, 96; office seekers in, xxii; panic in, 63; police in, 73; post office in, 46; prices in, 132; roads in, 26–27, 134, 139–40; social life in, 55, 66, 78–79, 128, 137, 139, 140, 166, 205, 206–7, 210–11, 223; Southern element in, 66; theaters in, 76; threats to, 5; vice in, 151; visitors to, 56, 66; volunteers (3rd Battalion), 6; vulnerability of, 2, 17; women of, 86
Washington *Republican*, 13
Washington *States and Union*, xvi, 3
Watson, Peter, 133, 183
weaponry, 22–23, 30. *See also* inventions
Webster, Daniel, 88
Welles, Gideon, criticism of, 28
West Urbana. *See* Champaign IL
West Virginia, admission of, 125, 126
White House, 8, 18, 166; dinners at, 207; levees at, 14, 198–99; party at, 58; receptions at, 134, 202; refurbishing of, 23, 38, 45
White River, 243, 244, 247, 248, 250
Whitney, Henry C., xxii
Wilderness, battle of, 232

Willard's Hotel, 4, 44, 99
Wilson, William, Zouaves of, 1
Winchester, battle of, 68
Wood, Fernando, 205

Yorktown, 69, 70

Zangonyi, Charles, 43
Zouaves, 1, 7

www.ingramcontent.com/pod-product-compliance
Lightning Source LLC
Chambersburg PA
CBHW030107010526
44116CB00005B/133